# ADOBE DREAMWEAVER CS4 REVEALED

SHERRY BISHOP

# ADOBE DREAMWEAVER CS4 REVEALED

SHERRY BISHOP

DELMAR
CENGAGE Learning™

Australia • Brazil • Japan • Korea • Mexico • Singapore • Spain • United Kingdom • United States

**Adobe Dreamweaver CS4 Revealed**
**Sherry Bishop**

Vice President, Career and Professional Editorial:
Dave Garza

Director of Learning Solutions: Sandy Clark

Senior Acquisitions Editor: Jim Gish

Managing Editor: Larry Main

Product Managers: Jane Hosie-Bounar,
Nicole Calisi

Editorial Assistant: Sarah Timm

Vice President Marketing, Career and
Professional: Jennifer McAvey

Executive Marketing Manager:
Deborah S. Yarnell

Marketing Manager: Erin Brennan

Marketing Coordinator: Jonathan Sheehan

Production Director: Wendy Troeger

Senior Content Project Manager:
Kathryn B. Kucharek

Developmental Editor: Barbara Clemens

Technical Editors: John Shanley, Susan Whalen

Art Directors: Bruce Bond, Joy Kocsis

Cover Design: Lisa Kuhn, Curio Press, LLC

Cover Art: Lisa Kuhn, Curio Press, LLC

Text Designer: Ann Small

Proofreader: Harold Johnson

Indexer: Alexandra Nickerson

Technology Project Manager:
Christopher Catalina

Production Technology Analyst:
Tom Stover

For product information and technology assistance, contact us at
**Cengage Learning Customer & Sales Support,**
**1-800-354-9706**

For permission to use material from this text or product, submit all requests online at
**www.cengage.com/permissions**
Further permissions questions can be e-mailed to
**permissionrequest@cengage.com**

The Trademark BlackBerry® is owned by Research In Motion Limited and is registered in the United States and may be pending or registered in other countries. Delmar Cengage Learning is not endorsed, sponsored, affiliated with or otherwise authorized by Research In Motion Limited. Coca-Cola® is a registered trademark of The Coca-Cola Company. RealPlayer® and RealNetworks® are registered trademarks of RealNetworks, Inc.

Adobe® Photoshop®, Adobe® InDesign®, Adobe® Illustrator®, Adobe® Flash®, Adobe® Dreamweaver®, Adobe® Fireworks®, Adobe® Creative Suite® Flash® Player, PostScript®, and Shockwave® are trademarks or registered trademarks of Adobe Systems, Inc. in the United States and/or other countries. Third party products, services, company names, logos, design, titles, words, or phrases within these materials may be trademarks of their respective owners.

The Adobe Approved Certification Courseware logo is a proprietary trademark of Adobe. All rights reserved. Cengage Learning and Adobe Dreamweaver CS4—Revealed are independent from ProCert Labs, LLC and Adobe Systems Incorporated, and are not affiliated with ProCert Labs and Adobe in any manner. This publication may asssist students to prepare for an Adobe Certified Expert exam, however, neither ProCert Labs nor Adobe warrant that use of this material will ensure success in connection with any exam.

Library of Congress Control Number: 2008935168

Hardcover edition:
ISBN-13: 978-1-4354-8260-9
ISBN-10: 1-4354-8260-3

Soft cover edition:
ISBN-13: 978-1-4354-4192-7
ISBN-10: 1-4354-4192-3

**Delmar**
5 Maxwell Drive
Clifton Park, NY 12065-2919
USA

Cengage Learning is a leading provider of customized learning solutions with office locations around the globe, including Singapore, the United Kingdom, Australia, Mexico, Brazil, and Japan. Locate your local office at: **international.cengage.com/region**

Cengage Learning products are represented in Canada by Nelson Education, Ltd.

To learn more about Delmar, visit
**www.cengage.com/delmar**

Purchase any of our products at your local college store or at our preferred online store
**www.ichapters.com**

**Notice to the Reader**

Publisher does not warrant or guarantee any of the products described herein or perform any independent analysis in connection with any of the product information contained herein. Publisher does not assume, and expressly disclaims, any obligation to obtain and include information other than that provided to it by the manufacturer. The reader is expressly warned to consider and adopt all safety precautions that might be indicated by the activities described herein and to avoid all potential hazards. By following the instructions contained herein, the reader willingly assumes all risks in connection with such instructions. The publisher makes no representations or warranties of any kind, including but not limited to, the warranties of fitness for particular purpose or merchantability, nor are any such representations implied with respect to the material set forth herein, and the publisher takes no responsibility with respect to such material. The publisher shall not be liable for any special, consequential, or exemplary damages resulting, in whole or part, from the readers' use of, or reliance upon, this material.

Printed in the United States of America
1 2 3 4 5 6 7 13 12 11 10 09

## Revealed Series Vision

The Revealed Series is your guide to today's hottest multimedia applications. These comprehensive books teach the skills behind the application, showing you how to apply smart design principles to multimedia products such as dynamic graphics, animation web sites, software authoring tools, and digital video.

A team of design professionals including multimedia instructors, students, authors, and editors worked together to create this series. We recognized the unique learning environment of the multimedia classroom and created a series that:

- Gives you comprehensive step-by-step instructions
- Offers in-depth explanation of the "Why" behind a skill
- Includes creative projects for additional practice
- Explains concepts clearly using full-color visuals

It was our goal to create a book that speaks directly to the multimedia and design community—one of the most rapidly growing computer fields today. We think we've done just that, with a sophisticated and instructive book design.

—The Revealed Series

## Author's Vision

Through the work of many talented and creative individuals, this text was created for you. The Product Manager, Jane Hosie-Bounar, guided and directed the team from start to finish. Working with Barbara Clemens, the Development Editor, is always a joy. It is a bit bittersweet when a project with her is completed.

The copyright content was generously provided by my dear friend Barbara Waxer. Additional information on locating media on the Internet and determining its legal use is available in her Revealed Series book *Internet Surf and Turf Revealed: The Essential Guide to Copyright, Fair Use, and Finding Media.*

John Shanley and Susan Whalen, the Technical Editors, carefully tested each step to make sure that the end product was error-free. This part of the publishing process is what truly sets Delmar Cengage Learning apart from other publishers.

Tintu Thomas and Kathy Kucharek, our Content Product Managers, kept the schedule on track. We thank them for keeping up with the many details and deadlines. The work is beautiful.

Janice Jutras patiently contacted the websites we used as examples to obtain permission for their inclusion. They add much to the flavor of the book, and I am grateful both for each of the sites and for Janice making it possible to use them.

Harold Johnson quietly worked behind the scenes to ensure that my grammatical and punctuation errors were corrected. Thank you, Harold! Paula Melton authored the test banks. Thank you, Paula!

Special thanks go to Jim Gish, Senior Acquisitions Editor, and Sandy Clark, the Director of Learning Solutions. They have embraced the Revealed books with enthusiasm and grace.

The Beach Club (www.beachclubal. com) in Gulf Shores, Alabama, generously allowed us to use several photographs of their beautiful property for The Striped Umbrella web site. Florence Pruitt, the club director, was extremely helpful and gracious.

Typically, your family is the last to be thanked. My husband, Don, continues to support and encourage me every day, as he has for the last thirty-eight years. Our travels with our children and grandchildren provide happy memories for me and content for the websites. You will see the faces of my precious grandchildren Jacob, Emma, Thomas, and Caroline peeking out from some of the pages.

I would like to dedicate this book to the angel of our family, Angie Bishop. Angie struggled with cancer for several years with faith, courage, and dignity.

—Sherry Bishop

## Introduction to Adobe Dreamweaver CS4

Welcome to *Adobe Dreamweaver CS4—Revealed*. This book offers creative projects, concise instructions, and complete coverage of basic to intermediate Dreamweaver skills, helping you to create polished, professional-looking websites. Use this book both in the classroom and as your own reference guide.

This text is organized into 12 chapters. In these chapters, you will explore the many options Dreamweaver provides for creating dynamic Dreamweaver websites.

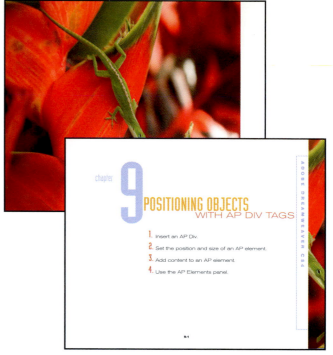

## What You'll Do

A What You'll Do figure begins every lesson. This figure gives you an at-a-glance look at what you'll do in the chapter, either by showing you a page or pages from the current project or a tool you'll be using.

## Comprehensive Conceptual Lessons

Before jumping into instructions, in-depth conceptual information tells you "why" skills are applied. This book provides the "how" and "why" through the use of professional examples. Also included in the text are tips, design tips, and sidebars to help you work more efficiently and creatively, or to teach you a bit about the history or design philosophy behind the skill you are using.

## Step-by-Step Instructions

This book combines in-depth conceptual information with concise steps to help you learn Dreamweaver CS4. Each set of steps guides you through a lesson where you will create, modify, or enhance a Dreamweaver CS4 website. Step references to large colorful images and quick step summaries round out the lessons. The Data Files for the steps are provided on the CD at the back of this book.

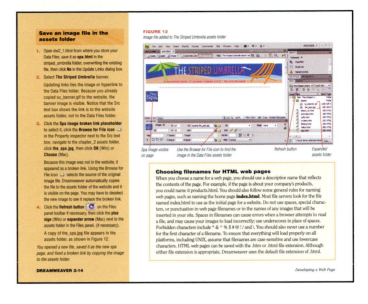

## Projects

This book contains a variety of end-of-chapter materials for additional practice and reinforcement. The Skills Review contains hands-on practice exercises that mirror the progressive nature of the lesson material. The chapter concludes with four projects; two Project Builders, one Design Project, and one Portfolio Project. The Project Builders and the Design Project require you to apply the skills you've learned in the chapter. Portfolio Projects encourage students to use their creativity to create a website of their own design.

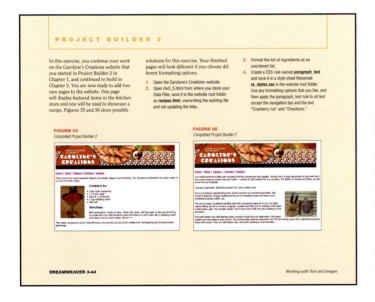

## What Instructor Resources Are Available with This Book?

The Instructor Resources CD-ROM is Delmar's way of putting the resources and information needed to teach and learn effectively into your hands. All the resources are available for both Macintosh and Windows operating systems.

## Instructor's Manual

Available as an electronic file, the Instructor's Manual includes chapter overviews and detailed lecture topics for each chapter, with teaching tips. The Instructor's Manual is available on the Instructor Resources CD-ROM.

## PowerPoint Presentations

Each chapter has a corresponding PowerPoint presentation that you can use in lectures, distribute to your students, or customize to suit your course.

## Data Files for Students

To complete most of the chapters in this book, your students will need Data Files. The Data Files are available on the CD at the back of this text book. Instruct students to use the Data Files List at the end of this book. This list gives instructions on organizing files.

## Solutions to Exercises

Solution Files are Data Files completed with comprehensive sample answers. Use these files to evaluate your students' work. Or distribute them electronically so students can verify their work. Sample solutions to all lessons and end-of-chapter material are provided.

## Test Bank and Test Engine

ExamView is a powerful testing software package that allows instructors to create and administer printed and computer (LAN-based) exams. ExamView includes hundreds of questions that correspond to the topics covered in this text, enabling students to generate detailed study guides that include page references for further review. The computer-based and LAN-based/online testing component allows students to take exams using the EV Player, and also save the instructor time by grading each exam automatically.

## CHAPTER 1 — GETTING STARTED WITH DREAMWEAVER

## CHAPTER 3    WORKING WITH TEXT AND IMAGES

## CHAPTER 4    WORKING WITH LINKS

## CHAPTER 5  POSITIONING OBJECTS WITH CSS AND TABLES

CONTENTS

CONTENTS

**CHAPTER 9**    **POSITIONING OBJECTS WITH AP DIV TAGS**

# CHAPTER 10    ADDING MEDIA OBJECTS

CONTENTS

# CHAPTER 11    CREATING AND USING TEMPLATES

# CHAPTER 12 · WORKING WITH LIBRARY ITEMS AND SNIPPETS

CONTENTS

## Intended Audience

This text is designed for the beginner or intermediate user who wants to learn how to use Dreamweaver CS4. The book is designed to provide basic and in-depth material that not only educates, but also encourages you to explore the nuances of this exciting program.

## Approach

The text allows you to work at your own pace through step-by-step tutorials. A concept is presented and the process is explained, followed by the actual steps. To learn the most from the use of the text, you should adopt the following habits:

- Proceed slowly: Accuracy and comprehension are more important than speed.

- Understand what is happening with each step before you continue to the next step.

- After finishing a skill, ask yourself if you could do it on your own, without referring to the steps. If the answer is no, review the steps.

## Icons, Buttons, and Pointers

Symbols for icons, buttons, and pointers are shown in the step each time they are used. Icons may look different in the files panel depending on the file association settings on your computer.

## Fonts

The Data Files contain a variety of commonly used fonts, but there is no guarantee that these fonts will be available on your computer. In a few cases, fonts other than those common to a PC or a Macintosh are used. If any of the fonts in use is not available on your computer, you can make a substitution, realizing that the results may vary from those in the book.

## Windows and Macintosh

Adobe Dreamweaver CS4 works virtually the same on Windows and Macintosh operating systems. In those cases where there is a significant difference, the abbreviations (Win) and (Mac) are used.

## System Requirements

**For a Windows operating system:**
-2 GHz or faster processor
-Microsoft Windows® XP with Service Pack 2 (Service Pack 3 recommended) or Windows Vista Home Premium, Business, Ultimate, or Enterprise with Service Pack 1 (certified for 32-bit Windows XP and Windows Vista)

-1 GB of RAM or more recommended

-9.3 GB of available hard-disk space for installation; additional free space required during installation (cannot install on flash-based storage devices)

-1,024×768 display (1,280×800 recommended) with 16-bit video card

-Some GPU-accelerated features require graphics support for Shader Model 3.0 and OpenGL 2.0

-Some features in Adobe®Bridge rely on a DirectX 9-capable graphics card with at least 64MB of VRAM

-DVD-ROM drive

-Quicktime 7.4.5 software required for multimedia features

-Broadband Internet connection required for online services

**For a Macintosh operating system:**
-PowerPC® G5 or multicore Intel® processor

-Mac OS X v10.4.11–10.5.4

-Java™ Runtime Environment 1.5 required for Adobe Version Cue® Server

-1GB of RAM or more recommended

-10.3 GB of available hard-disk space for installation; additional hard-disk space required during installation (cannot install on a volume that uses a case-sensitive file system or on flash-based storage devices)

-1,024×768 display (1,280×800 recommended) with 16-bit video card

-Some GPU-accelerated features require graphics support for Shader Model 3.0 and OpenGL 2.0

-DVD-ROM drive

-QuickTime 7.4.5 software required for multimedia features

-Broadband Internet connection required for online services

## Memory Challenges

If, instead of seeing an image on an open page, you see an image placeholder with a large X across it, your RAM is running low. Try closing any other applications that are running to free up memory.

## Building a Website

You will create and develop a website called The Striped Umbrella in the lesson material in this book. Because each chapter builds off of the previous chapter, it is recommended that you work through the chapters in consecutive order.

## Websites Used in Figures

Each time a website is used for illustration purposes in a lesson, where necessary, a statement acknowledging that we obtained permission to use the website is included, along with the URL of the website. Sites whose content is in the public domain, such as federal government websites, are acknowledged as a courtesy.

## Data Files

To complete the lessons in this book, you need the Data Files on the CD in the back of this book. Your instructor will tell you where to store the files as you work, such as the hard drive, a network server, or a USB storage device. The instructions in the lessons will refer to "where you store your Data Files" when referring to the Data Files for the book. When you copy the Data Files to your computer, you may see lock icons that indicate that the files are read-only when you view them in the Dreamweaver Files panel. To unlock the files, right-click on the locked file name in the Files panel, and then click Turn off Read Only.

## Images vs. Graphics

Many times these terms seem to be used interchangeably. For the purposes of this text, the term images is used when referring to pictures on a web page. The term graphics is used as a more encompassing term that refers to non-text items on a web page such as photographs, logos, navigation bars, Flash animations, graphs, background images, and drawings. You may define these terms in a slightly different way, depending on your professional background or business environment.

## Preference Settings

The learning process will be much easier if you can see the file extensions for the files you will use in the lessons. To do this in Windows, open Windows Explorer, click Organize, Folder and Search Options, click the View tab, then uncheck the box Hide Extensions for Known File Types. To do this for a Mac, go to the Finder, click the Finder menu, and then click Preferences. Click the Advanced tab, then select the Show all file extensions check box.

To view the Flash content that you will be creating, you must set a preference in your browser to allow active content to run. Otherwise, you will not be able to view objects such as Flash buttons.

To set this preference in Internet Explorer, click Tools, Internet Options, Advanced, then check the box Allow active content to run in files on My Computer. Your browser settings may be slightly different, but look for similar wording. When using Windows Internet Explorer 7, you can also click the information bar when prompted to allow blocked content.

## Creating a Portfolio

The Portfolio Project and Project Builders allow students to use their creativity to come up with original Dreamweaver designs. You might suggest that students create a portfolio in which they can store their original work.

# GETTING STARTED WITH
## DREAMWEAVER

# GETTING STARTED WITH
## DREAMWEAVER

## Introduction

Adobe Dreamweaver CS4 is a web development tool that lets you create dynamic, interactive web pages containing text, images, hyperlinks, animation, sounds, video, and other elements. You can use Dreamweaver to create individual web pages or complex websites consisting of many web pages. A **website** is a group of related web pages that are linked together and share a common interface and design. You can use Dreamweaver to create design elements such as text, tables, and interactive buttons, or you can import elements from other software programs. You can save Dreamweaver files in many different file formats, including XHTML, HTML, JavaScript, CSS, or XML, to name a few. **XHTML** is the acronym for eXtensible HyperText Markup Language, the current standard language used to create web pages. You can still use **HTML** (HyperText Markup Language) in Dreamweaver; however, it is no longer considered the standard language. In Dreamweaver, you can easily convert exist-

ing HTML code to XHTML-compliant code. You use a web browser to view your web pages on the Internet. A **web browser** is a program, such as Microsoft Internet Explorer or Mozilla Firefox, that lets you display HTML-developed web pages.

## Using Dreamweaver Tools

Creating an excellent website is a complex task. Fortunately, Dreamweaver has an impressive number of tools that can help. Using Dreamweaver's design tools, you can create dynamic and interactive web pages without writing a word of code. However, if you prefer to write code, Dreamweaver makes it easy to type and edit the code directly and see the visual results of the code instantly. Dreamweaver also contains organizational tools that help you work with a team of people to create a website. You can also use Dreamweaver's management tools to help you manage a website. For instance, you can use the **Files panel** to create folders to organize and store the various files for your website, and add pages to your website.

# Tools You'll Use

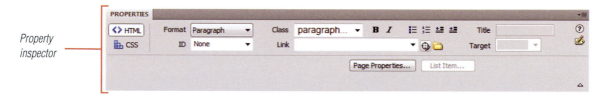

*Property inspector*

*Collapse to Icons button*

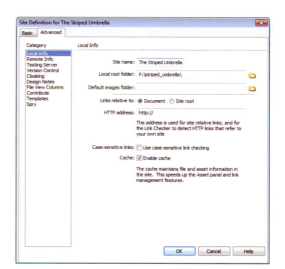

*Show Code and Design views button*    *Switch Design View to Live View button*

*Show Code view button*    *Show Design view button*

# EXPLORE THE
## DREAMWEAVER WORKSPACE

### What You'll Do

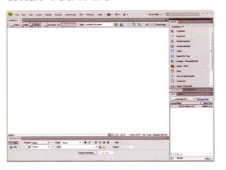

*In this lesson, you will start Dreamweaver, examine the components that make up the Dreamweaver workspace, and change views.*

### Examining the Dreamweaver Workspace

The **Dreamweaver workspace** is designed to provide you with easy access to all the tools you need to create web pages. Refer to Figure 1 as you locate the components described below.

The **Document window** is the large white area in the Dreamweaver program window where you create and edit web pages. The **Application bar**, located above the Document window, includes menu names (Windows only), a Workspace switcher, and other application commands. To choose a menu command, click the menu name to open the menu, then click the menu command. The Insert panel is displayed at the top of the Dreamweaver workspace on the right side of the screen. The **Insert panel** includes eight categories of buttons displayed through a drop-down menu: Common, Layout, Forms, Data, Spry, InContext Editing, Text, and Favorites. Clicking a category in the Insert panel displays the buttons and menus associated with that category. For example, if you click

the Layout category, you will find buttons for using div tags, used for creating blocks of content on pages; Table buttons, used for inserting and editing tables; and the Frames button, used for selecting one of 13 different frame layouts.

**QUICK**TIP

Two additional options are also available through the Insert panel drop-down menu. To display the icons in color, click Color Icons, or right-click the Insert panel, then click Color Icons. To hide the button labels, click Hide Labels.

The **Document toolbar** contains buttons and drop-down menus you can use to change the current work mode, preview web pages, debug web pages, choose visual aids, and view file-management options. There are two toolbars that are not displayed by default. They are the Style Rendering toolbar and the Standard toolbar. The **Standard toolbar** contains buttons you can use to execute frequently used commands also available on the File and Edit menus. The **Style Rendering toolbar** contains buttons that can be used to render different media types, but is available only if your document uses media-dependent style sheets. An example of a media-dependent style sheet would be one used to create and format pages for a cell phone. The Style Rendering toolbar also includes a button that allows you to enable or disable CSS styles while you are working. To display or hide the Document, Standard, and Style Rendering toolbars, right-click an empty area of an open tool-bar, then click the toolbar name you wish to display or hide or use the View, Toolbars menu. The **Related Files toolbar** is located below an open document's file-name tab and displays the names of any related files. **Related files** are files that are linked to a document and are necessary for the document to display and function correctly. An external CSS style sheet is a good example of a related file. The **Coding toolbar** contains buttons that are used when working directly in the code and is not visible unless you are in Code view.

When visible, it appears on the left side of the Document window.

The **Property inspector**, located at the bottom of the Dreamweaver window, lets you view and change the properties of a selected object. The Property inspector is context sensitive, which means it changes according to what is selected in the Document window. The **status bar** is located below the Document window. The left side of the status bar displays the **tag selector**, which shows

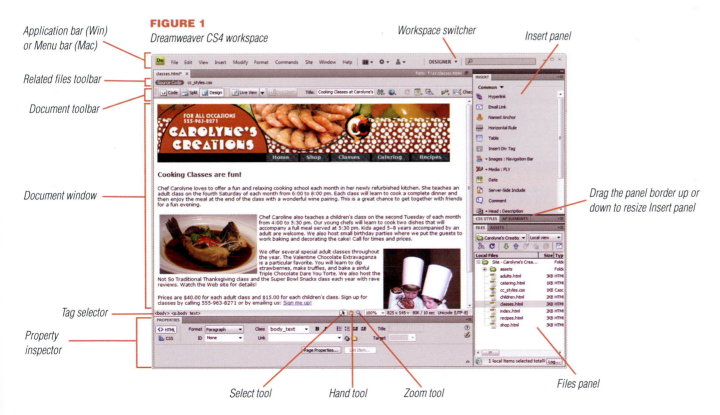

**FIGURE 1**
*Dreamweaver CS4 workspace*

Application bar (Win) or Menu bar (Mac)

Related files toolbar

Document toolbar

Document window

Tag selector

Property inspector

Workspace switcher

Insert panel

Drag the panel border up or down to resize Insert panel

Files panel

Select tool    Hand tool    Zoom tool

the HTML tags used at the insertion point location. The right side displays the window size and estimated download time for the current page, as well as the Select tool, used for page editing; the Hand tool, used for panning; and the Zoom tool, used for magnifying.

A **panel** is a window that displays information on a particular topic or contains related commands. **Panel groups** are sets of related panels that are grouped together. A collection of panels or panel groups is called a **dock**. To view the contents of a panel in a panel group, click the panel tab. Panels are docked by default on the right side of the screen. They can be undocked or "floated" by dragging the panel tab. To collapse or expand a panel group, double-click the panel tab or click the blank area in the panel title bar, as shown in Figure 2. When you first start Dreamweaver, the Insert, CSS Styles, AP Elements, Files, and Assets panels appear by default. Panels can be opened using the Window menu commands or the corresponding shortcut keys.

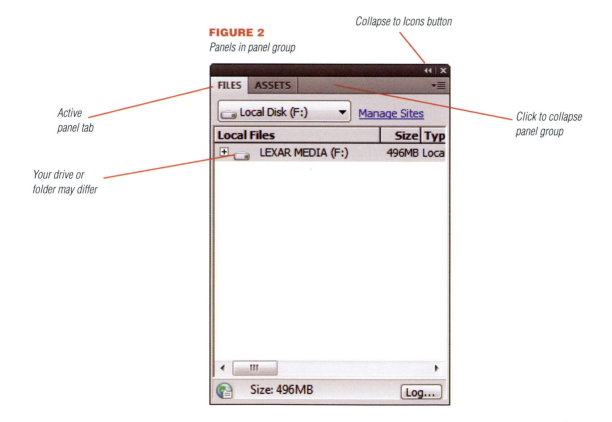

**FIGURE 2**
*Panels in panel group*

*Collapse to Icons button*

*Active panel tab*

*Click to collapse panel group*

*Your drive or folder may differ*

**QUICK**TIP

The Collapse to Icons button above the top panel will collapse all open panels to icons to allow for a larger workspace.

## Working with Dreamweaver Views

A **view** is a particular way of displaying page content. Dreamweaver has three working views. **Design view** shows the page as it would appear in a browser and is primarily used for designing and creating a web page. **Code view** shows the underlying HTML code for the page; use this view to read or edit the underlying code.

**QUICK**TIP

You can also split Code view to enable you to work on two different sections of code at once. To change to Split Code view, click View on the Application bar (Win) or Menu bar (Mac), then click Split Code.

**Show Code and Design views** is a combination of Code view and Design view. Show Code and Design views is the best view for **debugging** or correcting errors because you can immediately see how code modifications change the appearance of the page. The view buttons are located on the Document toolbar.

## Start Dreamweaver (Windows)

1. Click the **Start button**  on the taskbar.

2. Point to **All Programs**, click **Adobe Web Premium CS4** (if necessary), then click **Adobe Dreamweaver CS4**, as shown in Figure 3.

   TIP The name of your Adobe suite may differ from the figure.

3. If the Default Editor dialog box opens, click **OK**.

*You started Dreamweaver CS4 for Windows.*

**FIGURE 3**
*Starting Dreamweaver CS4 (Windows)*

Click Adobe
Dreamweaver
CS4

### Choosing a workspace layout

The Dreamweaver interface is an integrated workspace, which means that all of the document windows and panels are arranged in a single application window. However, individual panels can be "floated" or undocked from their set position and moved to any position on the screen. (The Mac OS interface is slightly different, in that documents can either be tabbed together in a single window or displayed in separate windows.) To view a tabbed document, click the tab with the document's file name. The **Workspace switcher** is a drop-down menu located in the top right corner on the Application bar. The Workspace switcher allows you to change the workspace layout. The default layout is the Designer workspace layout, where the panels are docked on the right side of the screen and Design view is the default view. In the Coder workspace layout, the panels are docked on the left side of the screen and Code view is the default view. However, the panels may be docked on either side of the screen in both Coder and Designer layouts. Other views include App Developer, App Developer Plus, Classic, Coder Plus, Designer Compact, and Dual Screen. To change the workspace layout, click the Workspace switcher, then click the desired layout; or click Window in the Application bar, point to Workspace Layout, then click the desired layout. You can also rearrange the workspace using your own choices for panel placement and save the workspace with a unique name using the "New Workspace" and "Manage Workspaces" commands on the Workspace switcher. The Reset' current view' option will reset the workspace layout to return to the default positions on the screen.

**FIGURE 4**
*Starting Dreamweaver CS4 (Macintosh)*

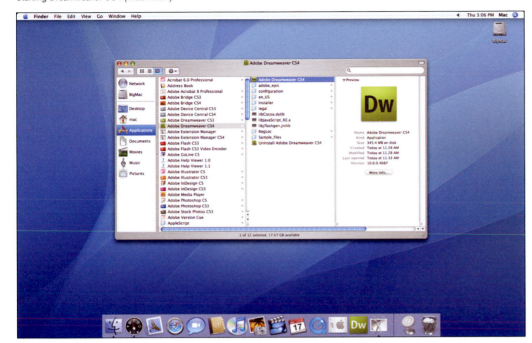

1. Click **Finder** in the Dock, then click **Applications**.

2. Click the **Adobe Dreamweaver CS4 folder**, then double-click the **Dreamweaver CS4 application,** as shown in Figure 4.

   TIP   Once Dreamweaver is running, you can add it to the Dock permanently by [control]-clicking the Dreamweaver icon, then clicking Keep In Dock.

*You started Dreamweaver CS4 for Macintosh.*

### Using two monitors for optimum workspace layout

One option you have for workspace layout is Dual Screen layout. **Dual Screen layout** is the layout you would choose when you are using two monitors while working with Dreamweaver. The Document window and Property inspector are displayed on the first monitor and the panels are displayed on the second monitor. It is quite seamless to work between the two monitors and provides optimum workspace by allowing you to have multiple panels open without compromising your Document window space.

## Change views and view panels

1. Click **HTML** in the Create New category on the Dreamweaver Welcome Screen.

   The Dreamweaver Welcome Screen provides shortcuts for opening files and for creating new files or websites.

   > TIP If you do not want the Dreamweaver Welcome Screen to appear each time you start Dreamweaver, click the Don't show again check box on the Welcome Screen or remove the check mark next to Show Welcome Screen in the General category in the Preferences dialog box.

2. Click the **Show Code view button** 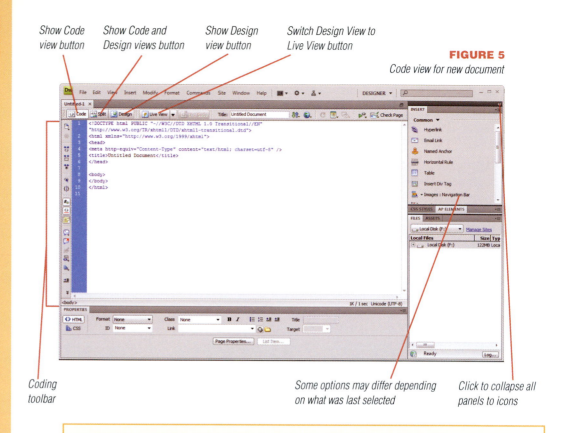 Code on the Document toolbar.

   The default code for a new document appears in the Document window, as shown in Figure 5.

   > TIP The Coding toolbar is available only in Code view and the Code window in Split view.

3. Click the **Show Code and Design views button** Split on the Document toolbar.

4. Click the **Show Design view button** Design on the Document toolbar.

   > TIP If your icons are not displayed in color and you would like to display them in color, click the Insert panel drop-down menu, then click Color Icons.

   *(continued)*

Show Code view button

Show Code and Design views button

Show Design view button

Switch Design View to Live View button

FIGURE 5
*Code view for new document*

Coding toolbar

Some options may differ depending on what was last selected

Click to collapse all panels to icons

### Using the Switch Design View to Live View button

The Switch Design View to Live View button is a new feature in Dreamweaver CS4. When you click this button, the open document will appear as if it were being viewed in a browser, with interactive elements active and functioning. The Switch Design View to Live View button is similar to using the Preview in Browser button. Next to the Live View button is the Shows the Live View source in code view button. When the Switch Design View to Live View button is active, the Shows the Live View source in code view button can be toggled on or off. When you click the Live View button the first time, you may see a message that you need to install the Flash plug-in from HYPERLINK "http://www.adobe.com" www.adobe.com. Download the plug-in and your page can then be viewed using Live View.

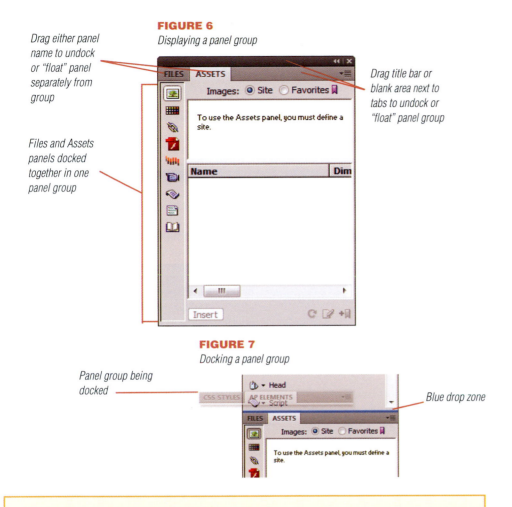

**FIGURE 6**
*Displaying a panel group*

Drag either panel name to undock or "float" panel separately from group

Drag title bar or blank area next to tabs to undock or "float" panel group

Files and Assets panels docked together in one panel group

**FIGURE 7**
*Docking a panel group*

Panel group being docked

Blue drop zone

## Hiding and Displaying Toolbars

To hide or display the Style Rendering, Document, or Standard toolbars, click View on the Application bar (Win) or Menu bar (Mac), point to Toolbars, then click Style Rendering, Document, or Standard. The Coding toolbar is available only in Code view and the Code window in Split view, and appears vertically in the Document window. By default, the Document toolbar appears in the workspace.

5. Click the **Assets panel tab**, then compare your screen to Figure 6.

   TIP  If the Assets panel is not visible on the screen, click Window on the Application bar (Win) or Menu bar (Mac), then click Assets.

6. Click each panel name tab to display the contents of each panel.

7. Double-click **Assets** to collapse the panel group.

8. View the contents of the CSS Styles and AP Elements panels.

9. Click and drag the **blank area** next to the AP Elements tab to the middle of the document window.

   The panel group is now in a floating window.

10. Click and drag the **panel title bar** back to its original position, then drop it to dock the panel group.

    Release the mouse only when you see the blue drop zone. **The blue drop zone** is a heavy blue line that appears when the panel is in the correct position to be docked. See Figure 7.

    TIP  If you have rearranged the panels from their original positions and want to reset them back to their default positions, click the Workspace switcher drop-down menu, then click "Reset 'Designer'." You will also have to reset the Color Icons, as color icons are not part of the default Designer workspace.

11. Click File on the Application bar (Win) or Menu bar (Mac), then click **Close** to close the open document.

*You viewed a new web page using three views, opened panel groups, viewed their contents, then closed panel groups.*

# VIEW A WEB PAGE
## AND USE HELP

## What You'll Do

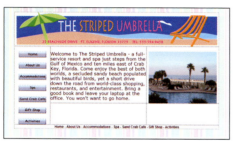

In this lesson, you will open a web page, view several page elements, and access the Help system.

### Opening a Web Page

After starting Dreamweaver, you can create a new website, create a new web page, or open an existing website or web page. The first web page that appears when viewers go to a website is called the **home page**. The home page sets the look and feel of the website and directs viewers to the rest of the pages in the website.

### Viewing Basic Web Page Elements

There are many elements that make up web pages. Web pages can be very simple and designed primarily with text, or they can be media-rich with text, images sound, and movies, creating an enhanced interactive web experience. Figure 8 is an example of a web page with several different page elements that work together to create a simple and attractive page.

Most information on a web page is presented in the form of **text**. You can type text directly onto a web page in Dreamweaver or import text created in other programs. You can then use the Property inspector to format text so that it is attractive and easy to read. Text should be short and to the point to prevent viewers from losing interest and leaving your site.

**Hyperlinks**, also known as **links**, are image or text elements on a web page that users click to display another location on the page, another web page on the same website, or a web page on a different website.

**Images** add visual interest to a web page. The saying that "less is more" is certainly true with images, though. Too many images cause the page to load slowly and discourage viewers from waiting for the page to download. Many pages have **banners**, which are images displayed across the top of the screen that can incorporate a company's logo, contact information, and links to the other pages in the site.

**Navigation bars** are bars that contain multiple links that are usually organized in rows or columns. Sometimes navigation bars are used with an image map. An **image map** is an image that has been divided into sections, each of which contains a link.

The way that navigation bars and other internal links are used on your pages is referred to as the **navigation structure** of the site.

**Rich media content** is a comprehensive term that refers to attractive and engaging images, interactive elements, video, or animations. Some of this content can be created in Dreamweaver, but much of it is created with other programs such

as Adobe Flash, Fireworks, Photoshop, or Illustrator.

### Getting Help

Dreamweaver has an excellent Help feature that is both comprehensive and easy to use. When questions or problems arise, you can use the commands on the Help menu to find the answers you need. Clicking the

Dreamweaver Help command opens the Dreamweaver Help page that contains a list of topics and subtopics by category.

The Search text box at the top of the window lets you enter a keyword to search for a specific topic. Context-specific help can be accessed by clicking the Help button on the Property inspector.

**FIGURE 8**

*Common web page elements*

*National Endowment for the Arts website – www.arts.endow.gov*

## Open a web page and view basic page elements

1. Click **File** on the Application bar (Win) or Menu bar (Mac), then click **Open**.

2. Click the **Look in list arrow** (Win), or **navigation list arrow** (Mac), locate the drive and folder where you store your Data Files, then double-click the **chapter_1 folder** (Win), or click the **chapter_1 folder** (Mac).

3. Click **dw1_1.html**, then click **Open**.

   You may not see the .html file extension if the option for hiding file extensions for known file types is selected on your operating system.

   TIP  If you want your screen to match the figures in this book, make sure the Document window is maximized.

4. Locate each of the web page elements shown in Figure 9.

   TIP  Because you are opening a single page that is not in a website with access to the other pages, the links will not work.

   *(continued)*

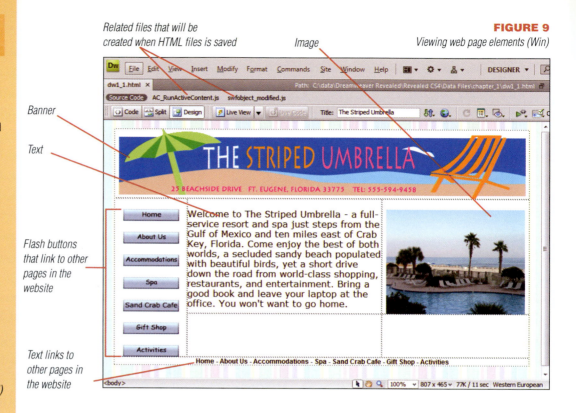

Related files that will be created when HTML files is saved

Image

**FIGURE 9**
*Viewing web page elements (Win)*

Banner

Text

Flash buttons that link to other pages in the website

Text links to other pages in the website

## Understanding Related Page Files

When an HTML file is opened that is linked to other files necessary to display the page content, these files are called **related files.** If the dw1_1.html file you just opened was saved to your computer, two supporting files would be created to enable the page content to work.  Although you can see file tabs for them, these files will not be created until the page is saved. These files are AC_RunActiveContent.js and swfobject_modified.js. See Figure 9. Related files are automatically opened when the page they support is opened. These two files will support the Flash buttons on the page and are required to make the buttons work in a browser. **Adobe Flash** is a program that is used to create animations and video content for the web. You will learn about Flash content in the media chapter.

*Getting Started with Dreamweaver*

FIGURE 9

*Viewing web page elements (Mac)*

Menu bar —

Related files toolbar —

Your Flash buttons may appear as placeholders —

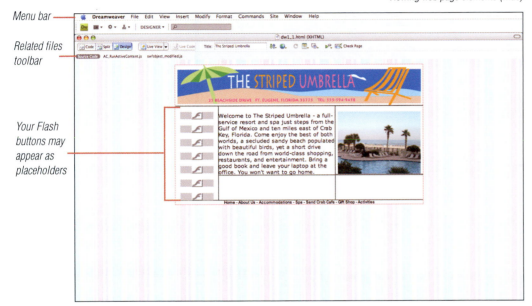

5. Click the **Show Code view button** `<> Code` to view the code for the page.

6. Scroll down to view all the code, then click the **Show Design view button** `Design` to return to Design view.

   TIP To view the code for a particular page element, select the page element in Design view, then click the Show Code view button.

7. Click **File** on the Application bar (Win) or Menu bar (Mac), then click **Close** to close the open page without saving it.

   TIP You can also click the X in the filename tab to close the page.

*You opened a web page, located several page elements, viewed the code for the page, then closed the page without saving it.*

## Use Dreamweaver Help

1. Click **Help** on the Application bar (Win) or Menu bar (Mac), then click **Dreamweaver Help.**

   The Dreamweaver Help and Support window opens.

   | TIP   You can also open the Help feature by pressing [F1].

2. Click the **Dreamweaver help (web)** link in the top right corner of the Dreamweaver Help and Support window, as shown in Figure 10.

   | TIP   If you don't see the link, enlarge or maximize the window.

3. Click the **plus sign** next to Workspace in the left column, click the **plus sign** next to Working in the Document window, then click **Switch between views in the Document window**.

   The topic opens on the right side of the Help window, as shown in Figure 11, and the plus signs change to minus signs, indicating that the topics are expanded.

4. Read the text in the content side of the Help window, then close the Adobe Dreamweaver CS4 window.

*(continued)*

### FIGURE 10
*Dreamweaver Help and Support web page*

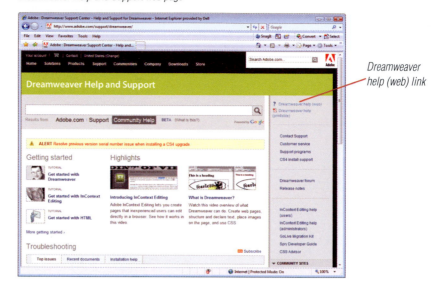

*Dreamweaver help (web) link*

### FIGURE 11
*Displaying Help content*

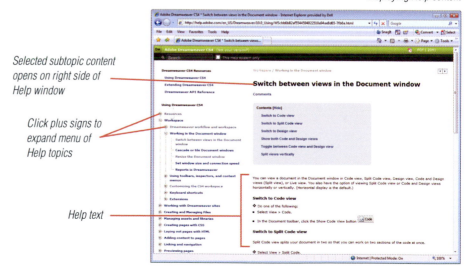

*Selected subtopic content opens on right side of Help window*

*Click plus signs to expand menu of Help topics*

*Help text*

*Getting Started with Dreamweaver*

**FIGURE 12**
*Searching for a topic in Help*

Type the search terms
in the search text box

Relevant topics
are listed

Click the list arrow
to change Adobe
applications

5. In the Dreamweaver Help and Support window, type **CSS Property inspector** in the search text box, notice that the Community Help button is selected, then press [Enter] (Win) or [Return] (Mac).

   A list of topics related to the search terms opens in the bottom of the window as shown in Figure 12.

6. Click one of the links to read information about one of the topics of your choice.

   You can either search the Adobe website, the Support Center, or the Community Help by clicking each link under the Search text box.

7. Close the Search Community Help window.

*You used Dreamweaver Help to read information in the Adobe Dreamweaver CS4 documentation and in the Community Help files.*

## Using Adobe Community Help

When you access the Help feature in Dreamweaver, you have a choice of using offline help (which is similar to searching in a Dreamweaver manual) or using online help. The online help feature is called Adobe Community Help. **Adobe Community Help** is a collection of materials such as tutorials, published articles, or blogs, in addition to the regular help content. All content is monitored and approved by the Adobe Community Expert program.

# PLAN AND DEFINE A WEBSITE

## What You'll Do

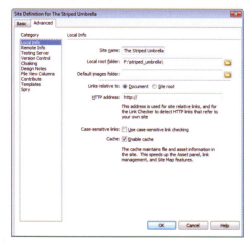

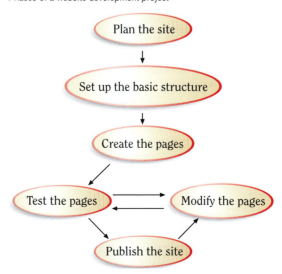

In this lesson, you will review a website plan for The Striped Umbrella, a beach resort and spa. You will also create a root folder for The Striped Umbrella website, and then define the website.

### Understanding the Total Process

Creating a website is a complex process. It can often involve a large team of people working in various roles to ensure that the website contains accurate information, looks good, and works smoothly.

Figure 13 illustrates the phases in a website development project.

### Planning a Website

Planning is probably the most important part of any successful project. Planning is an *essential* part of creating a website, and

**FIGURE 13**
*Phases of a website development project*

Plan the site

↓

Set up the basic structure

↓

Create the pages

↓

Test the pages ⇄ Modify the pages

Publish the site

is a continuous process that overlaps the subsequent phases. To start planning your website, you need to create a checklist of questions and answers about the site. For example, what are your goals for the site? Who is the audience you want to target? Teenagers? Children? Sports enthusiasts? Senior citizens? How can you design the site to appeal to the target audience? The more questions you can answer about the site, the more prepared you will be when you begin the developmental phase. Because

of the public demand for "instant" information, your plan should include not just how to get the site up and running, but how to keep it current. Table 1 lists some of the basic questions you need to answer during the planning phase for almost any type of website. From your checklist, you should create a statement of purpose and scope, a timeline for all due dates, a budget, a task list with work assignments, and a list of resources needed. You should also include a list of deliverables, such as a preliminary

storyboard, page drafts, and art for approval. The due dates for each deliverable should be included in the timeline.

## Setting Up the Basic Structure

Once you complete the planning phase, you need to set up the structure of the site by creating a storyboard. A **storyboard** is a small sketch that represents every page in a website. Like a flowchart, a storyboard shows the relationship of each page in the site to all the other pages. Storyboards are very

### TABLE 1: Website Planning Checklist

| question | examples |
|---|---|
| 1. Who is the target audience? | Seniors, teens, children |
| 2. How can I tailor the site to reach that audience? | Specify an appropriate reading level, decide the optimal amount of media content, use formal or casual language |
| 3. What are the goals for the site? | Sell a product, provide information |
| 4. How will I gather the information? | Recruit other employees, write it myself, use content from in-house documents |
| 5. What are my sources for media content? | Internal production department, outside production company, my own photographs |
| 6. What is my budget? | Very limited, well financed |
| 7. What is the timeline? | Two weeks, one month, six months |
| 8. Who is on my project team? | Just me, a complete staff of designers |
| 9. How often should the site be updated? | Every 10 minutes, once a month |
| 10. Who will update the site? | Me, other team members |

helpful when planning a website, because they allow you to visualize how each page in the site is linked to others. You can sketch a storyboard by using a pencil and paper or by using a graphics program on a computer. The storyboard shown in Figure 14 shows all the pages that will be contained in The Striped Umbrella website that you will create in this book. Notice that the home page appears at the top of the storyboard, and that it has four pages linked to it. The home page is called the **parent page**, because it is at a higher level in the web hierarchy and has pages linked to it. The pages linked below it are called **child pages**. The Activities page, which is a child page to the home page, is also a parent page to the Cruises and Fishing pages. You can refer to this storyboard as you create the actual links in Dreamweaver. More detailed storyboards will also include all document names, images, text files, and link information.

QUICK**TIP**

You can create a storyboard on a computer using a software program such as Microsoft Word, PowerPoint, or Paint; Corel Paintshop Pro; or Adobe Illustrator. You might find it easier to make changes to a computer-generated storyboard than to one created on paper.

In addition to creating a storyboard for your site, you should also create a folder hierarchy for all of the files that will be used in the site. Start by creating a folder for the site with a descriptive name, such as the name of the company. This folder, known as the **root folder** or **local root folder**, will store all the pages or HTML files for the site. Then create a subfolder called **assets** in which you store all of the files that are not pages, such as images and sound files.

QUICK**TIP**

You should avoid using spaces, special characters, or upper-case characters in your folder names to ensure that all your files can be read and linked successfully on all web servers, whether they are Windows- or UNIX-based.

After you create the root folder, you need to define your site. When you **define** a site, the root folder and any folders and files it contains appear in the **Files panel**, the panel you use to manage your website's files and folders. Using the Files panel to manage your files ensures that the site links work correctly when the website is published. You also use the Files panel to add or delete pages.

## Creating the Web Pages and Collecting the Page Content

This is the fun part! After you create your storyboard, you need to gather the files that will be used to create the pages, including text, images, buttons, video, and animation. Some of these files will

**FIGURE 14**
*The Striped Umbrella website storyboard*

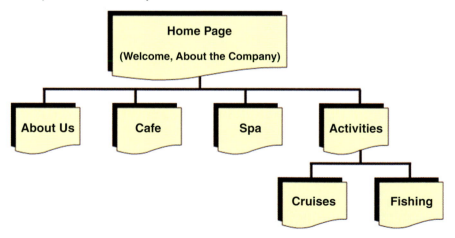

come from other software programs, and some you will create in Dreamweaver. For example, you can create text in a word-processing program and insert it into Dreamweaver, or you can create and format text in Dreamweaver.

Images, tables, colors, and horizontal rules all contribute to making a page attractive and interesting. In choosing your elements, however, you should always carefully consider the file size of each page. A page with too many graphical elements might take a long time to load, which could cause visitors to leave your site.

## Testing the Pages

Once all your pages are completed, you need to test the site to make sure all the links work and that everything looks good. It is important to test your web pages using different browser software. The two most common browsers are Microsoft Internet Explorer and Mozilla Firefox. You should also test your site using different versions of each browser. Older versions of Internet Explorer do not support the latest web technology. You should also test your site using a variety of screen sizes. Some viewers may have small monitors, while others may have large, high-resolution monitors. You should also consider connection download time. Although more people use cable modems or DSL (digital subscriber line), some still use slower dial-up modems. Testing is a continuous process, for which you should allocate plenty of time.

## Modifying the Pages

After you create a website, you'll probably find that you need to keep making changes to it, especially when information on the site needs to be updated. Each time you make a change, such as adding a new button or image to a page, you should test the site again. Modifying and testing pages in a website is an ongoing process.

## Publishing the Site

**Publishing** a website means that you transfer all the files for the site to a **web server**, a computer that is connected to the Internet with an IP (Internet Protocol) address, so that it is available for viewing on the Internet. A website must be published or users of the Internet cannot view it. There are several options for publishing a website. For instance, many **Internet Service Providers (ISPs)** provide space on their servers for customers to publish websites, and some commercial websites provide limited free space for their viewers. Although publishing happens at the end of the process, it's a good idea to set up web server access in the planning phase. Use the Files panel to transfer your files using Dreamweaver's FTP capability. **FTP (File Transfer Protocol)** is the process of uploading and downloading files to and from a remote site.

Dreamweaver also gives you the ability to transfer files using the FTP process without creating a site first. You simply enter login information to an FTP site to establish a connection by clicking New in the Manage Sites dialog box, and then clicking the FTP option. You would then use the Files panel to transfer the files, just as if you were transferring files in a website.

## Select the location for your website

1. Open or expand the Files panel if necessary to view the contents.

2. Click the **drive or folder** that is currently displayed in the pop-up menu in the Files panel. See Figure 15.

3. Click to select the **drive or folder** (or subfolder) in the list where you will store your folders and files for your websites.

   Dreamweaver will store all of the folders and files you create inside this drive or folder.

*You selected the drive or folder where you will create your website.*

Click to display the pop-up menu

**FIGURE 15**
*Selecting a drive in the Files panel*

Click to select the drive that you will use to store your files (your drive or folder may differ)

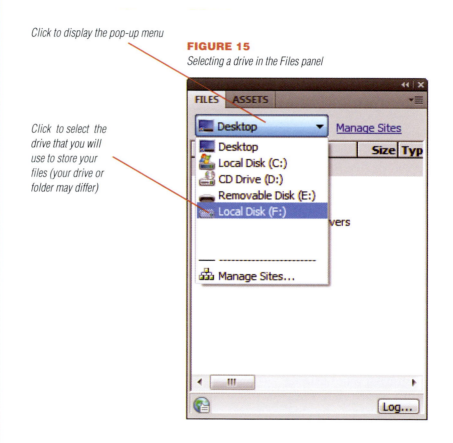

**FIGURE 16**

Creating a root folder using the Files panel

*Your drive or folder may differ*

*striped_umbrella root folder*

*If you just see a drive or folder name here, you do not currently have a website open*

**FIGURE 17**

Viewing an open website in the files panel

*striped_umbrella root folder*

*If you see the word "Site" here, you do have a website open and the toolbar appears.*

## Create a root folder

1. Select the drive or folder in the Files panel, **right-click** (Windows) or **control-click** (Macintosh), then click **New Folder.**

2. Type **striped_umbrella** to rename the folder, then press **[Enter].**

   The folder is renamed striped_umbrella, as shown in Figure 16.

   When you see a drive or folder in the pop-up menu, you do not have a website open. Notice the difference between Figure 16 and Figure 17. In Figure 16, you have only created the root folder, not the website. In Figure 17, The Striped Umbrella website has been created and is open. You have not created a website yet. You have just created the folder that will serve as the root folder after the site is created.

*You created a new folder to serve as the root folder for The Striped Umbrella website.*

## Define a website

1. Click **Site** on the Application bar (Win) or Menu bar (Mac), then click **New Site.**

2. Click the **Advanced tab** (if necessary), then type **The Striped Umbrella** in the Site name text box.

   The Basic tab can be used instead of the Advanced tab if you prefer to use a wizard.

   > TIP  It is acceptable to use uppercase letters in the site name because it is not the name of a folder or a file.

3. Click the **Browse for File icon** 📁 next to the Local root folder text box, click the **Select list arrow** (Win) or the **navigation list arrow** (Mac) in the **Choose local root folder for site The Striped Umbrella dialog box,** click the **drive and folder** where your website files will be stored, then click the **striped_umbrella folder**.

4. Click **Open** (Win) or **Choose** (Mac), then click **Select** (Win).

5. Verify that the Links relative to option button is set to Document.

6. Verify that the Enable cache check box is checked, as shown in Figure 18.

   This setting is very important to make sure your links work correctly.

*You created a website and defined it with the name The Striped Umbrella. You then verified that the correct options were selected in the Site Definition dialog box.*

**FIGURE 18**
*Site Definition for The Striped Umbrella dialog box*

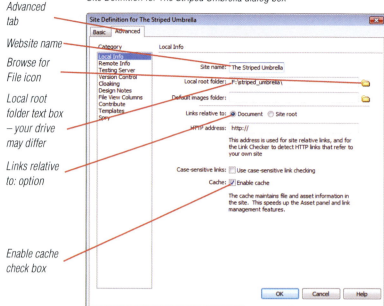

*Advanced tab*

*Website name*

*Browse for File icon*

*Local root folder text box – your drive may differ*

*Links relative to: option*

*Enable cache check box*

## Understanding IP addresses and domain names

To be accessible over the Internet, a website must be published to a web server with a permanent IP address. An **IP address** is an assigned series of numbers, separated by periods, that designates an address on the Internet. To access a web page, you can enter either an IP address or a domain name in the address text box of your browser window. A **domain name** is a web address that is expressed in letters instead of numbers and usually reflects the name of the business represented by the website. For example, the domain name of the Adobe website is *www.adobe.com,* but the IP address is 192.150.20.61. Because domain names use descriptive text instead of numbers, they are much easier to remember. Compare an IP address to your Social Security number and a domain name to your name. Both your Social Security number and your name are used to refer to you as a person, but your name is much easier for your friends and family to use than your Social Security number. You can type the IP address or the domain name in the address text box of the browser window to access a website. The domain name is also referred to as a URL, or Uniform Resource Locator.

**FIGURE 19**

*Setting the Remote Access for The Striped Umbrella website*

Remote
Info
category

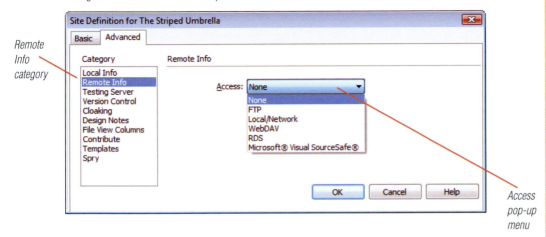

Access
pop-up
menu

1. Click **Remote Info** in the Category list, click the **Access pop-up menu** then choose the method you will use to publish your website, as shown in Figure 19.

   TIP  If you do not have the information to publish your website, choose None. You can specify this information later.

2. Enter any necessary information in the Site Definition dialog box based on the setting you chose in Step 1, then click **OK**.

   TIP  Your network administrator or web hosting service will give you the necessary information to publish your website.

*You set up the remote access information to prepare you for publishing your website.*

### Understanding the process of publishing a website

Before publishing a website so that viewers of the web can access it, you should first create a local root folder, called the **local site**, to house all the files for your website, as you did on page 1-23. This folder usually resides on your hard drive. Next, you need to gain access to a remote server. A **remote server** is a web server that hosts websites and is not directly connected to the computer housing the local site. Many Internet Service Providers, or ISPs, provide space for publishing websites on their servers. Once you have access to a remote server, you can then use the Remote Info category in the Site Definition dialog box to enter information such as the FTP host, host directory, login, and password. After entering this information, you can then use the Put File(s) button in the Files panel to transfer the files to the designated remote server. Once the site is published to a remote server, it is called a **remote site**.

# ADD A FOLDER AND PAGES

## What You'll Do

 *In this lesson, you will use the Files panel to create a new folder and new pages for the website.*

### Adding a Folder to a Website

After defining a website, you need to create folders to organize the files that will make up the site. Creating a folder called **assets** is a good beginning. There is nothing magic about the word "assets," though. You can name your folder anything that makes sense to you as long as you follow proper folder naming conventions such as avoiding the use of spaces. You can use the assets folder to store all non-HTML files, such as images or sound files. After you create the assets folder, it is a good idea to set it as the default location to store the website images. This saves a step when you import new images into the website.

> **DESIGN**TIP  **Creating an effective navigation structure**
>
> When you create a website, it's important to consider how your viewers will navigate from page to page within the site. A navigation bar is a critical tool for moving around a website, so it's important that all text, buttons, and icons used in a navigation bar have a consistent look across all pages. If a complex navigation bar is used, such as one that incorporates JavaScript or Flash, it's a good idea to include plain text links in another location on the page for accessibility. Otherwise, viewers might become confused or lost within the site. A navigation structure can include more links than those included in a navigation bar, however. For instance, it can contain other sets of links that relate to the content of a specific page and which are placed at the bottom or sides of a page in a different format. No matter which navigation structure you use, make sure that every page includes a link back to the home page. Don't make viewers rely on the Back button on the browser toolbar to find their way back to the home page. It's possible that the viewer's current page might have opened as a result of a search and clicking the Back button will take the viewer out of the website.

## Creating the Home Page

The **home page** of a website is the first page that viewers see when they visit your site. Most websites contain many other pages that all connect back to the home page. The home page filename usually has the name index.html (.htm), or default.html (.htm).

## Adding Pages to a Website

Websites might be as simple as one page or might contain hundreds of pages. When you create a website, you can add all the pages and specify where they should be placed in the website folder structure in the root folder. Once you add and name all the pages in the website, you can then add the content, such as text and graphics, to each page. It is better to add as many blank pages as you think you will need in the beginning, rather than adding them one at a time with all the content in place. This will enable you to set up the navigation structure of the website at the beginning of the development process and view how each page is linked to others. When you are satisfied with the overall structure, you can then add the content to each page. This is strictly a personal preference, however. You can also choose to add and link pages as they are created, and that will work just fine, too.

You have a choice of several default document types you can generate when you create new HTML pages. The default document type is designated in the Preferences dialog box. XHTML 1.0 Transitional is the default document type when you install Dreamweaver and will be used throughout this book. It's important to understand the terminology—the pages are still called HTML pages and the file extension is still HTML, but the document type will be XHTML 1.0 Transitional.

### Using the Files panel for file management

You should definitely use the Files panel to add, delete, move, or rename files and folders in a website. It is very important that you perform these file-maintenance tasks in the Files panel rather than in Windows Explorer (Win) or in the Finder (Mac). Working outside of Dreamweaver, such as in Windows Explorer, can cause linking errors. You cannot take advantage of Dreamweaver's simple yet powerful site-management features unless you use the Files panel for all file-management activities. You may choose to use Windows Explorer (Win) or the Finder (Mac) only to create the root folder or to move or copy the root folder of a website to another location. If you move or copy the root folder to a new location, you will have to define the site again in the Files panel, as you did in Lesson 3 of this chapter. Defining a site is not difficult and will become routine for you after you practice a bit. If you are using Dreamweaver on multiple computers, such as in labs or at home, you will have to define your sites the first time you change to a different computer.

## Add a folder to a website (Windows)

1. Right-click **Site - The Striped Umbrella** in the Files panel, then click **New Folder**.

2. Type **assets** in the folder text box, then press **[Enter]**.

   TIP  To rename a folder, click the folder name once, pause, click again, then type the new name.

3. Compare your screen to Figure 20.

*You used the Files panel to create a new folder in the striped_umbrella folder and named it 'assets'.*

## Add a folder to a website (Macintosh)

1. Press and hold **[control]**, click the **striped_umbrella folder**, then click **New Folder**.

2. Type **assets** in the new folder name text box, then press **[return]**.

   TIP  To rename a folder, click the folder name text box, type the new name, then press **[return]**.

3. Compare your screen to Figure 21.

*You used the Files panel to create a new folder in the striped_umbrella folder and named it 'assets'.*

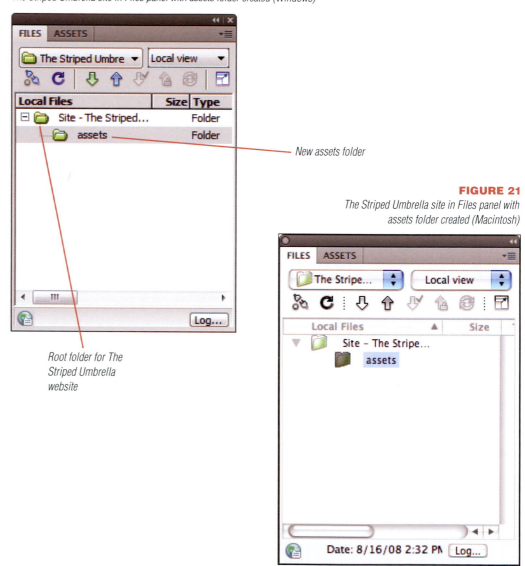

**FIGURE 20**

*The Striped Umbrella site in Files panel with assets folder created (Windows)*

New assets folder

Root folder for The Striped Umbrella website

**FIGURE 21**

*The Striped Umbrella site in Files panel with assets folder created (Macintosh)*

*Getting Started with Dreamweaver*

**FIGURE 22**

Site Definition for The Striped Umbrella dialog box with assets folder set as the default images folder

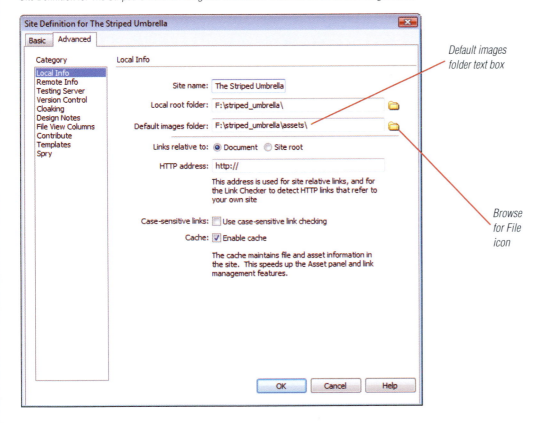

Default images folder text box

Browse for File icon

1. Click **The Striped Umbrella** in the Site list box in the Files panel, click **Manage Sites**, then click **Edit**.

2. Click the **Browse for File icon** 📁 next to the Default images folder text box.

3. If necessary, navigate to your striped_umbrella folder, double-click the **assets folder** (Win) or click the **assets folder** (Mac) in the Choose local images folder for site The Striped Umbrella: dialog box, then click **Select** (Win) or **Choose** (Mac).

   Compare your screen to Figure 22.

4. Click **OK**, then click **Done**.

*You set the assets folder as the default images folder so that imported images will be automatically saved in it.*

## Create the home page

1. Open **dw1_2.html** from where you store your Data Files.

   The file has several elements in it, including a banner image.

2. Click **File** on the Application bar (Win) or Menu bar (Mac), click **Save As**, click the **Save in list arrow** (Win) or the **Where list arrow** (Mac), navigate to the striped_umbrella folder, select **dw1_2.html** in the File name text box (Win) or select **dw1_2** in the Save As text box (Mac), then type **index.html.**

   Windows users do not have to type the file extension. It will be added automatically.

3. Click **Save**, then click **No** when asked to update links.

   TIP  As shown in Figure 23, the drive where the root folder is stored, the root folder name, and the filename of the page are displayed to the right of the document tab if the page is not open in a separate window. If open in a separate window, they are displayed on the document title bar. This information is called the **path**, or location of the open file in relation to other folders in the website.

   The banner image is no longer visible and the page contains a broken link to the image. This is because although you saved the .html file under a new name in the website's root folder, you have not yet copied the image file into the website's assets folder. The link to the banner image is still linked to the Data Files folder. You will fix this in the next set of steps.

   *You opened a file, then saved it with the filename index.*

**FIGURE 23**

*index.html placed in the striped_umbrella root folder*

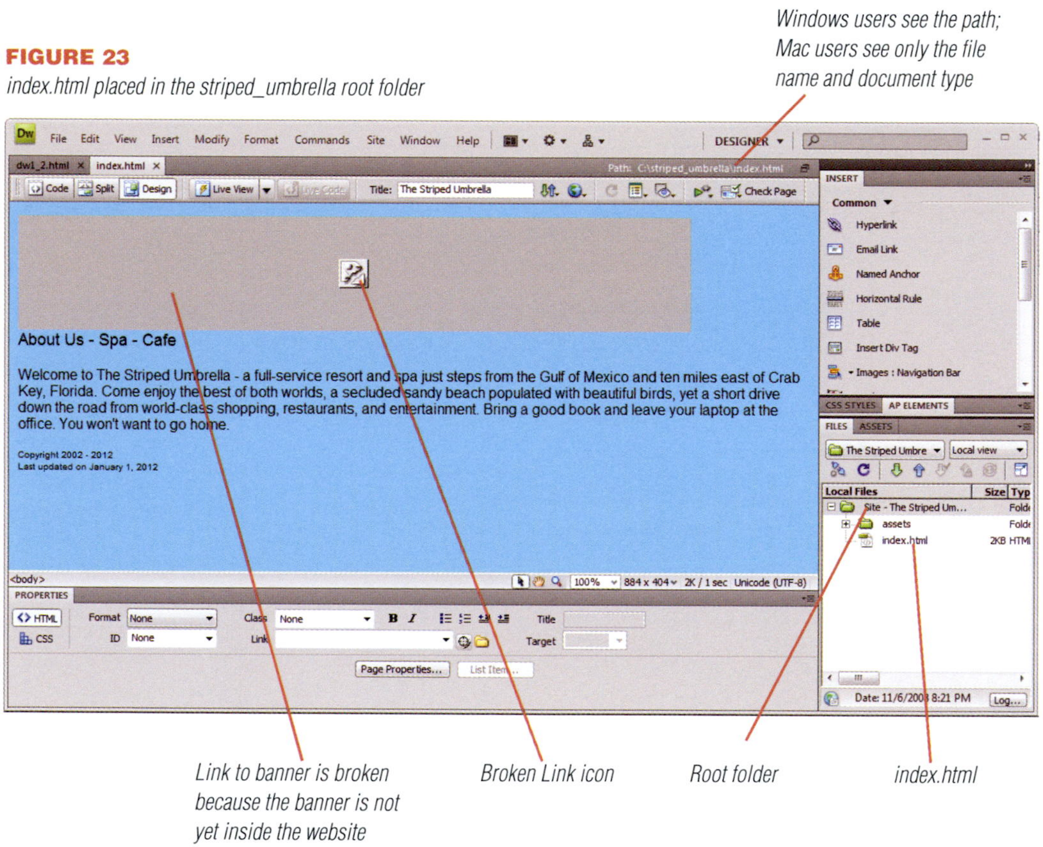

*Windows users see the path; Mac users see only the file name and document type*

*Link to banner is broken because the banner is not yet inside the website*

*Broken Link icon*

*Root folder*

*index.html*

The Striped
Umbrella banner

## FIGURE 24
*Property inspector showing properties of The Striped Umbrella banner*

Selection
handles

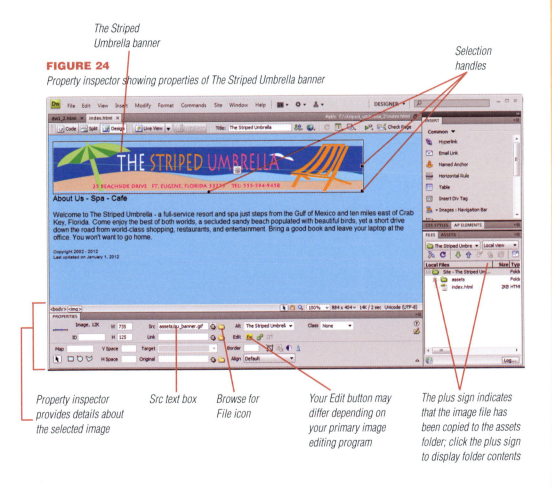

Property inspector
provides details about
the selected image

Src text box

Browse for
File icon

Your Edit button may
differ depending on
your primary image
editing program

The plus sign indicates
that the image file has
been copied to the assets
folder; click the plus sign
to display folder contents

## Save an image file in the assets folder

**1.** Click **The Striped Umbrella banner broken link placeholder** to select it.

Selection handles appear around the broken link. To correct the broken link, you must copy the image file from the Data Files folder into the assets folder of your website.

**2.** Click the **Browse for File icon** 📁 next to the Src text box in the Property inspector, click the **Look in list arrow** (Win) or **navigation list arrow** (Mac), navigate to the assets folder in your Data Files folder for this chapter, click **su_banner.gif**, click **OK** (Win) or **Choose** (Mac), then click in a blank part of the page. (Click the banner placeholder image again if the banner still doesn't appear.)

The file for The Striped Umbrella banner, su_banner.gif, is automatically copied to the assets folder of The Striped Umbrella website, the folder that you designated as the default images folder. The Src text box shows the path of the banner to the assets folder in the website, and the banner image is visible on the page.

TIP  If you do not see the su-banner.gif file listed in the Files panel, click the Refresh button 🔁 on the Files panel toolbar.

**3.** Select the banner to view the banner properties in the Property inspector, then compare your screen to Figure 24.

TIP  Until you copy a graphic from an outside folder to your website, the graphic is not part of the website and the image will appear as a broken link.

*You saved The Striped Umbrella banner in the assets folder.*

## Add pages to a website (Windows)

1. Click the **plus sign** to the left of the assets folder (if necessary) to open the folder and view its contents, su_banner.gif.

   TIP  If you do not see a file listed in the assets folder, click the Refresh button 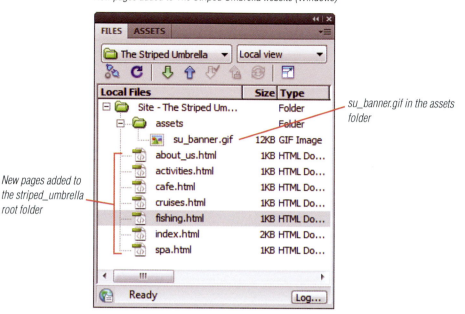 on the Files panel toolbar.

2. Right-click the **striped_umbrella root folder**, click **New File**, type **about_us.html** to replace untitled.html, then press **[Enter]**.

   Each new file is a page in the website. These pages do not have page content or page titles yet.

   TIP  If you create a new file in the Files panel, you must type the filename extension (.html) manually. However, if you create a new file using the File menu or the Welcome Screen the filename extension will be added automatically.

3. Repeat Step 2 to add five more blank pages to The Striped Umbrella website, naming the new files **spa.html**, **cafe.html**, **activities.html**, **cruises.html**, and **fishing.html**.

   TIP  Make sure to add the new files to the root folder, not the assets folder. If you accidentally add them to the assets folder, just drag them to the root folder.

4. Click the **Refresh button** on the Files panel to list the files alphabetically, then compare your screen to Figure 25.

5. Click **File** on the Application bar then click **Exit**.

   TIP  If you are prompted to save changes, click No.

*You added the following six pages to The Striped Umbrella website: about_us, activities, cafe, cruises, fishing, and spa.*

**FIGURE 25**
*New pages added to The Striped Umbrella website (Windows)*

su_banner.gif in the assets folder

New pages added to the striped_umbrella root folder

### DESIGNTIP  Adding page titles

When you view a web page in a browser, its page title appears in the browser window title bar. The page title should reflect the page content and set the tone for the page. It is especially important to use words in your page title that are likely to match keywords viewers might enter when using a search engine. Search engines compare the text in page titles to the keywords typed into the search engine. When a title bar displays "Untitled Document," the designer has neglected to give the page a title. This is like giving up free "billboard space" and looks unprofessional.

**FIGURE 26**

*New pages added to The Striped Umbrella website (Macintosh)*

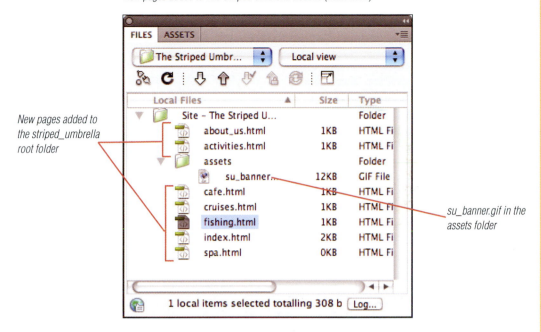

*New pages added to the striped_umbrella root folder*

*su_banner.gif in the assets folder*

**POWER USER SHORTCUTS**

| to do this: | use this shortcut: |
|---|---|
| Open a file | [Ctrl][O] (Win) or ⌘ [O] (Mac) |
| Close a file | [Ctrl][W] (Win) or ⌘ [W] (Mac) |
| Create a new file | [Ctrl][N] (Win) or ⌘ [N] (Mac) |
| Save a file | [Ctrl][S] (Win) or ⌘ [S] (Mac) |
| Dreamweaver Help | F1 |
| Show/Hide panels | F4 |
| Switch between Code view and Design view | [Ctrl][`] (Win) or [Ctrl][`] (Mac) |

## Add pages to a website (Macintosh)

1. Click the **triangle** to the left of the assets folder to open the folder and view its contents.

   TIP  If you do not see a file listed in the assets folder, click the Refresh button [C] on the Files panel.

2. [control]-click the **striped_umbrella root folder**, click **New File**, type **about_us.html** to replace untitled.html, then press **[return]**.

   TIP  If you create a new file in the Files panel, you must type the filename extension (.html) manually.

3. Repeat Step 3 to add five more blank pages to The Striped Umbrella website, naming the new files **spa.html**, **cafe.html**, **activities.html**, **cruises.html,** and **fishing.html**.

4. Click the **Refresh button** [C] to list the files alphabetically, then compare your screen to Figure 26.

5. Click **Dreamweaver** on the Menu bar, and then click **Quit Dreamweaver**.

   TIP  If you are prompted to save changes, click No.

*You added six pages to The Striped Umbrella website: about_us, activities, cafe, cruises, fishing, spa.*

**Explore the Dreamweaver workspace.**

1. Start Dreamweaver.
2. Create a new document.
3. Change the view to Code view.
4. Change the view to Code and Design views.
5. Change the view to Design view.
6. Collapse the panels to icons.
7. Expand the panels.
8. Undock the Files panel and float it to the middle of the document window. Dock the Files panel back to its original position.
9. View the Assets panel.
10. Close the page without saving it.

**View a web page and use Help.**

1. Open the file dw1_3.html from where you store your Data Files.
2. Locate the following page elements: a table, a banner, an image, and some formatted text.
3. Change the view to Code view.
4. Change the view to Design view.
5. Use the Dreamweaver Help command to search for information on docking panels.
6. Display and read one of the topics you find.
7. Close the Dreamweaver Help window.
8. Close the page without saving it.

**Plan and define a website.**

1. Use the Files panel to select the drive and folder where you store your website files.
2. Create a new root folder in this folder or drive called **blooms**.
3. Create a new site called **blooms & bulbs**.
4. Specify the blooms folder as the Local root folder.
5. Verify that the Links Relative to is set to Document and the Enable cache check box is selected.
6. Use the Remote Info category in the Site Definition for blooms & bulbs dialog box to set up web server access. (*Hint*: Specify None if you do not have the necessary information to set up web server access.)
7. Click OK, then click Done to close the Manage Sites dialog box.

**Add a folder and pages and set the home page.**

1. Create a new folder in the blooms root folder called **assets**.
2. Edit the site to set the assets folder as the default location for the website images.
3. Open the file dw1_4.html from where you store your Data Files, save this file in the blooms root folder as **index.html**, then click No to updating the links.
4. Select the broken image for the blooms & bulbs banner on the page.
5. Use the Property inspector to browse for blooms_banner.jpg, then select it to automatically save it in the assets folder of the blooms & bulbs website. (Remember to click off of the banner anywhere else on the page to show the banner as it replaces the broken image if necessary.)
6. Create seven new pages in the Files panel, and name them: **plants.html**, **classes.html**, **newsletter.html**, **annuals.html**, **perennials.html**, **water_plants.html**, and **tips.html**.
7. Refresh the view to list the new files alphabetically, then compare your screen to Figure 27.
8. Close all open pages.

**FIGURE 27**
*Completed Skills Review*

You have been hired to create a website for a travel outfitter called TripSmart. TripSmart specializes in travel products and services. In addition to selling travel products, such as luggage and accessories, they sponsor trips and offer travel advice. Their clients range from college students to families to vacationing professionals. The owner, Thomas Howard, has requested a dynamic website that conveys the excitement of traveling.

1. Using the information in the preceding paragraph, create a storyboard for this website, using either a pencil and paper or a software program such as Microsoft Word. Include the home page with links to four child pages named **catalog.html**, **newsletter.html**, **services.html**, and **destinations.html**. Include two child pages under the destinations page named **amazon.html** and **kenya.html**.

2. Create a new root folder named **tripsmart** in the drive and folder where you store your website files.

3. Start Dreamweaver, then create a site with the name **TripSmart**. Set the tripsmart folder as the local root folder for the site.

4. Create an assets folder and set it as the default location for images.

5. Open the file dw1_5.html from where you store your Data Files, then save it in the tripsmart root folder as **index.html**. (Remember not to update links.)

6. Correct the path for the banner by selecting the banner on the page, browsing to the original source in the Data Files folder, then selecting the file to copy it automatically to your TripSmart assets folder.

7. Create six additional pages for the site, and name them as follows: **catalog.html**, **newsletter.html**, **services.html**, **destinations.html**, **amazon.html**, and **kenya.html**. Use your storyboard and Figure 28 as a guide.

8. Refresh the Files panel.

9. Close all open pages.

**FIGURE 28**

*Completed Project Builder 1*

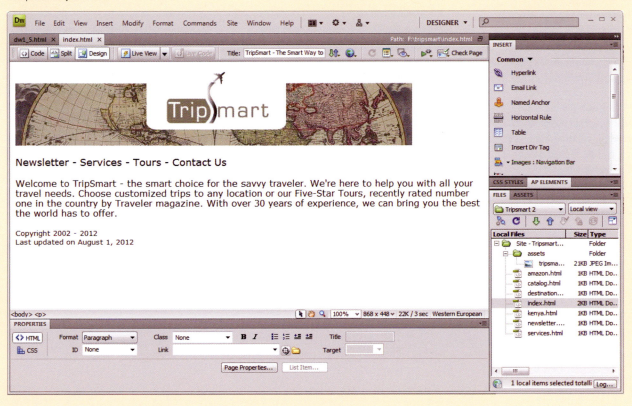

Your company has been selected to design a website for a catering business called Carolyne's Creations. In addition to catering, Carolyne's services include cooking classes and daily specials available as take-out meals. She also has a retail shop that stocks gourmet treats and kitchen items.

1. Create a storyboard for this website that includes a home page and child pages named **shop.html, classes.html, catering.html,** and **recipes.html.** Create two more child pages under the classes.html page called **children.html** and **adults.html**.

2. Create a new root folder for the site in the drive and folder where you save your website files, then name it **cc**.

3. Create a website with the name **Carolyne's Creations**, using the cc folder for the root folder.

4. Create an assets folder for the site and set the assets folder as the default location for images.

5. Open dw1_6.html from the where you store your Data Files then save it as **index.html** in the cc folder.

6. Reset the source for the banner to automatically save the cc_banner.jpg file in the assets folder.

7. Using Figure 29 and your storyboard as guides, create the additional pages shown for the website.

8. Refresh the Files panel to sort the files alphabetically.

9. Close all open pages.

**FIGURE 29**

*Completed Project Builder 2*

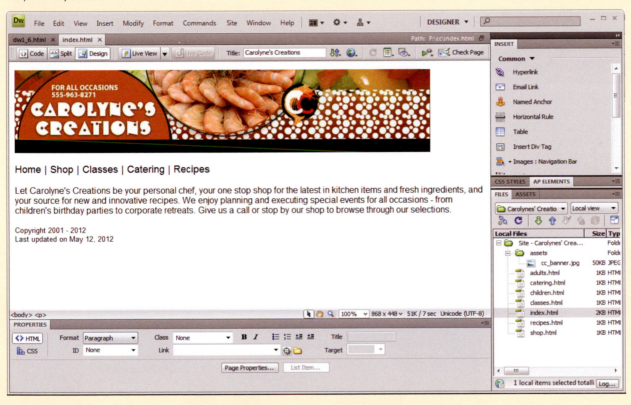

Figure 30 shows the Audi website, a past selection for the Adobe Site of the Day. To visit the current Audi website, connect to the Internet, then go to www.audi.com. The current page might differ from the figure because dynamic websites are updated frequently to reflect current information. Also, your page may default to the Audi of America site. The main navigation structure is accessed through the links along the right side of the page. The page title is Audi Worldwide > Home.

Go to the Adobe website at www.adobe.com, click the Showcase link under the Company menu, then click the current Site of the Day. Explore the site and answer the following questions:

1. Do you see page titles for each page you visit?
2. Do the page titles accurately reflect the page content?
3. View the pages using more than one screen resolution, if possible. For which resolution does the site appear to be designed?
4. Is the navigation structure clear?
5. How is the navigation structure organized?
6. Why do you think this site was chosen as a Site of the Day?

**FIGURE 30**
*Design Project*

*Audi website used with permission from Audi AG – www.audi.com*

# PORTFOLIO PROJECT

The Portfolio Project will be an ongoing project throughout the book, in which you will plan and create an original website without any Data Files supplied. The focus of the site can be on any topic, organization, sports team, club, or company that you would like. You will build on this site from chapter to chapter, so you must do each Portfolio Project assignment in each chapter to complete your website. When you finish this book, you should have a completed site that would be an excellent addition to a professional portfolio.

1. Decide what type of site you would like to create. It can be a personal site about you, a business site that promotes a fictitious or real company, or an informational site that provides information about a topic, cause, or organization.

2. Write a list of questions and answers about the site you have decided to create.

3. Create a storyboard for your site to include at least four pages. The storyboard should include the home page with at least three child pages under it.

4. Create a root folder and an assets folder to house the assets, then define your site using the root folder as the website local root folder and the assets folder as the default images folder.

5. Create a blank page named **index.html** as a placeholder for the home page.

6. Begin collecting content, such as pictures or text to use in your website. You can use a digital camera to take photos, use a scanner to scan pictures, or create your own graphics using a program such as Adobe Fireworks or Adobe Illustrator. Gather the content in a central location that will be accessible to you as you develop your site.

# 2

# DEVELOPING A
## WEB PAGE

1. Create head content and set page properties

2. Create, import, and format text

3. Add links to web pages

4. Use the History panel and edit code

5. Modify and test web pages

## Introduction

The process of developing a web page requires several steps. If the page is a home page, you need to spend some time crafting the head content. The head content contains information used by search engines to help viewers find your website. You also need to choose the colors for the page background and text. You then need to add the page content, format it attractively, and add links to other pages in the site or to other websites. Finally, to ensure that all links work correctly and are current, you need to test them regularly.

## Understanding Page Layout

Before you add content to a page, consider the following guidelines for laying out pages:

**Use White Space Effectively**. A living room crammed with too much furniture makes it difficult to appreciate the individual pieces. The same is true of a web page. Too many text blocks, links, animations, and images can be distracting. Consider leaving some white space on each page. **White space**, which is not necessarily white, is the area on a page that contains no text or graphics.

**Limit Media Elements**. Too many media elements, such as images, video clips, or sounds, may result in a page that takes too much time to load. Viewers may leave your site before the entire page finishes loading. Use media elements only if you have a good reason.

**Keep It Simple**. Often the simplest websites are the most appealing and are also the easiest to create and maintain. A simple, well-designed site that works well is far superior to a complex one that contains errors.

**Use an Intuitive Navigation Structure**. Make sure the navigation structure is easy to use. Viewers should always know where they are in the site and be able to easily find their way back to the home page. If viewers get lost, they may leave the site rather than struggle to find their way around.

**Apply a Consistent Theme**. To help give pages in your website a consistent appearance, consider designing your pages using elements that relate to a common theme. Consistency in the use of color and fonts, the placement of the navigation links, and the overall page design gives a website a unified look and promotes greater ease-of-use and accessibility. Template-based pages and style sheets make this task much easier.

# Tools You'll Use

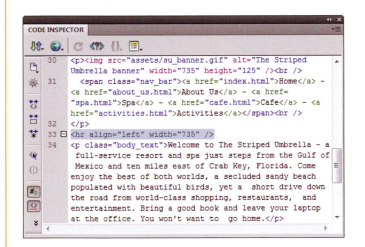

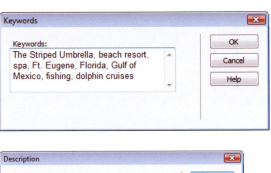

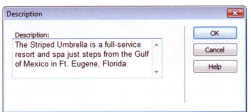

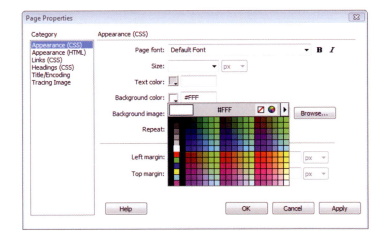

# CREATE HEAD CONTENT AND
## SET PAGE PROPERTIES

## What You'll Do

 *In this lesson, you will learn how to enter titles, keywords, and descriptions in the head content section of a web page. You will also change the background color for a web page.*

### Creating the Head Content

A web page is composed of two distinct sections: the head content and the body. The **head content** includes the page title that appears in the title bar of the browser and some important page elements, called meta tags, that are not visible in the browser. **Meta tags** are HTML codes that include information about the page, such as the page title, keywords and descriptions. Meta tags are read by screen readers (for viewers who have visual impairments) and are also used to provide the server information such as the PICS rating for the page. PICS is the acronym for **Platform for Internet Content Selection**. This is a rating system for web pages that is similar to rating systems used for movies. **Keywords** are words that relate to the content of the website.

**QUICK**TIP

Page titles are not to be confused with filenames, the name used to store each file on the server.

**DESIGN**TIP  **Using web-safe colors**

Prior to 1994, colors appeared differently on different types of computers. In 1994, Netscape developed the first **web-safe color palette**, a set of colors that appears consistently in all browsers and on Macintosh, Windows, and UNIX platforms. The evolution of video cards has made this less relevant today, although understanding web-safe colors may still prove important given the limitations of other online devices, such as cell phones and PDAs. If you want your web pages to be viewed across a wide variety of computer platforms, choose web-safe colors for all your page elements. Dreamweaver has two web-safe color palettes, Color Cubes and Continuous Tone, each of which contains 216 web-safe colors. Color Cubes is the default color palette. To choose a different color palette, click Modify on the Application bar (Win) or Menu bar (Mac) click Page Properties, click the Appearance (CSS) or Appearance (HTML) category, click the Background, Text, or Links color box to open the color picker, click the color picker list arrow, and then click the color palette you want.

A **description** is a short paragraph that describes the content and features of the website. For instance, the words "beach" and "resort" would be appropriate keywords for The Striped Umbrella website. Search engines find web pages by matching the title, description, and keywords in the head content of web pages with keywords that viewers enter in search engine text boxes. Therefore, it is important to include concise, useful information in the head content. The **body** is the part of the page that appears in a browser window. It contains all the page content that is visible to viewers, such as text, images, and links.

## Setting Web Page Properties
When you create a web page, one of the first design decisions that you should make is choosing the **background color**, or the color that fills the entire page. The background color should complement the colors used for text, links, and images that are placed on the page. Many times, images are used for backgrounds for either the entire page or a part of the page, such as a table background or Cascading Style Sheet (CSS) block.

**QUICK**TIP

A **CSS block** is a section of a web page defined and formatted using a Cascading Style Sheet.
A **Cascading Style Sheet** is a file used to assign sets of common formatting characteristics to page elements such as text, objects, tags, and tables. We will initially use the Page Properties dialog box to set page properties such as the background color. Later we will learn to do this using Cascading Style Sheets.

A strong contrast between the text color and the background color makes it easier for viewers to read the text on your web page.

You can choose a light background color with a dark text color, or a dark background color with a light text color. A white background with dark text, though not terribly exciting, provides good contrast and is the easiest to read for most viewers. Another design decision you need to make is whether to change the **default font** and **default link colors**, which are the colors used by the browser to display text, links, and visited links. The default color for **unvisited links**, or links that the viewer has not clicked yet, is blue. In Dreamweaver, unvisited links are simply called **links**. The default color for **visited links**, or links that have been previously clicked, is purple. You change the background color, text, and link colors using the color picker in the Page Properties dialog box. You can choose colors from one of the five Dreamweaver color palettes, as shown in Figure 1.

**FIGURE 1**
*Color picker showing color palettes*

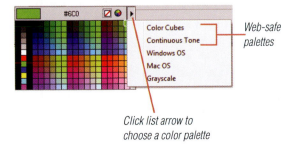

Web-safe palettes

Click list arrow to choose a color palette

**DESIGN**TIP   **Making pages accessible to viewers of all abilities**
Not all of your viewers will have perfect vision and hearing or full use of both hands. There are several techniques you can use to ensure that your website is accessible to individuals with disabilities. These techniques include using alternate text with images, avoiding certain colors on web pages, and supplying text as an alternate source for information that is presented in an audio file. Adobe provides much information about website compliance with Section 508 accessibility guidelines. For more information, visit the Adobe website at www.adobe.com/accessibility/. Here you will find suggestions for creating accessible websites, an explanation of Section 508, and information on how people with disabilities use assistive devices to navigate the Internet.

## Edit a page title

1. Start Dreamweaver, click the **Site list arrow** on the Files panel, then click **The Striped Umbrella** (if necessary).

2. Double-click **index.html** in the Files panel to open The Striped Umbrella home page, click **View** on the Application bar (Win) or Menu bar (Mac), then click **Head Content**.

   The Meta icon ▦, Title icon ▦, and CSS icon ▦ are now visible in the head content section.

3. Click the **Title icon** ▦ in the head content section.

   The page title The Striped Umbrella appears in the Title text box in the Property inspector, and the selected Title icon in the head content section changes to a blue color, as shown in Figure 2.

4. Click after the end of The Striped Umbrella text in the Title text box in the Property inspector, press **[Spacebar]**, type **beach resort and spa, Ft. Eugene, Florida**, then press **[Enter]** (Win) or **[return]** (Mac).

   Compare your screen with Figure 3. The new title is better, because it incorporates the words "beach resort" and "spa" and the location of the resort—words that potential customers might use as keywords when using a search engine.

   TIP  You can also change the page title using the Title text box on the Document toolbar.

   *You opened The Striped Umbrella website, opened the home page in Design view, viewed the head content section, and changed the page title.*

**FIGURE 2**
*Viewing the head content*

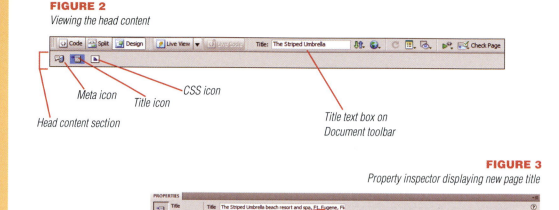

Meta icon

Title icon

CSS icon

Head content section

Title text box on Document toolbar

**FIGURE 3**
*Property inspector displaying new page title*

Scroll with arrow key to see the rest of the title

PROPERTIES
Title    Title  The Striped Umbrella beach resort and spa, Ft. Eugene, Fl

### DESIGN TIP  Using appropriate content for your target audience

When you begin developing the content for your website, you need to decide what content to include and how to arrange each element on each page. You must design the content with the audience in mind. What is the age group of your audience? What reading level is appropriate? Should you use a formal or informal tone? Should the pages be simple, consisting mostly of text, or rich with images and media files? Your content should fit your target audience. Look at the font sizes used, the number and size of images and animations used, the reading level, and the amount of technical expertise needed to navigate your site, and then evaluate them to see if they fit your audience. If they do not, you will be defeating your purpose. Usually, the first page that your audience will see when they visit your site is the home page. The home page should be designed so that viewers will understand your site's purpose and feel comfortable finding their way around the pages in your site. To ensure that viewers do not get lost in your site, make sure you design all the pages with a consistent look and feel. You can use templates and Cascading Style Sheets to maintain a common look for each page. **Templates** are web pages that contain the basic layout for each page in the site, including the location of a company logo or a menu of buttons. **Cascading Style Sheets** are sets of formatting attributes that are used to format web pages to provide a consistent presentation for content across the site.  Cascading Style Sheets make it easy to separate your site content from the site design. The content is stored on web pages, and the formatting styles are stored in a separate style sheet file.

FIGURE 4

Insert bar displaying the
Common category

Common
category

Head list
arrow

Your icon may
differ depending
on what was last
selected

Keywords
command

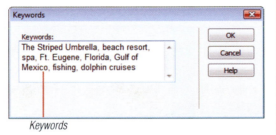

FIGURE 5

Keywords dialog box

Keywords

## Enter keywords

1. Click the **Common category** on the Insert panel (if necessary).

2. Click the **Head list arrow**, as shown in Figure 4, then click **Keywords**.

   TIP   Some buttons on the Insert panel include a list arrow indicating that there is a menu of choices beneath the current button. The button that you select last will appear on the Insert panel until you select another.

3. Type **The Striped Umbrella, beach resort, spa, Ft. Eugene, Florida, Gulf of Mexico, fishing, dolphin cruises** in the Keywords text box, as shown in Figure 5, then click **OK**

   The Keywords icon appears in the head content section; click it and the keywords will appear in the Keywords text box in the Property inspector.

*You added keywords relating to the beach to the head content of The Striped Umbrella home page.*

## DESIGNTIP   Entering keywords and descriptions

Search engines use keywords, descriptions, and titles to find pages after a user enters search terms. Therefore, it is very important to anticipate the search terms your potential customers would use and include these words in the keywords, description, and title. Many search engines display page titles and descriptions in their search results. Some search engines limit the number of keywords that they will index, so make sure you list the most important keywords first. Keep your keywords and descriptions short and concise to ensure that all search engines will include your site. To choose effective keywords, many designers incorporate the use of focus groups to have a more representative sample of words that potential customers or clients might use. A **focus group** is a marketing tool that asks a group of people for feedback about a product, such as its impact in a television ad or the effectiveness of a website design.

## Enter a description

1. Click the **Head list arrow** on the Insert panel, then click **Description**.

2. In the Description text box, type **The Striped Umbrella is a full-service resort and spa just steps from the Gulf of Mexico in Ft. Eugene, Florida**.

   Your screen should resemble Figure 6.

3. Click **OK**, then click the **Description icon** in the Head Content.

   The Description icon appears in the Head Content section and the description appears in the Description text box in the Property inspector.

4. Click the **Show Code view button** on the Document toolbar.

   Notice that the title, keywords, and description appear in the HTML code in the document window, as shown in Figure 7.

   | TIP   You can also enter and edit the meta tags directly in the code in Code view.

5. Click the **Show Design view button** to return to Design view.

6. Click **View** on the Application bar (Win) or Menu bar (Mac), then click **Head Content** to close the head content section.

*You added a description of The Striped Umbrella resort to the head content of the home page. You then viewed the page in Code view and examined the HTML code for the head content.*

**FIGURE 6**
*Description dialog box*

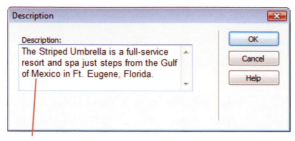

*Description*

**FIGURE 7**
*Head Content displayed in Code view*

*Opening Head tag*

*Title tag*

*Your head content line numbers may differ*

*Keywords tag*

*Description tag*

*Closing Head tag*

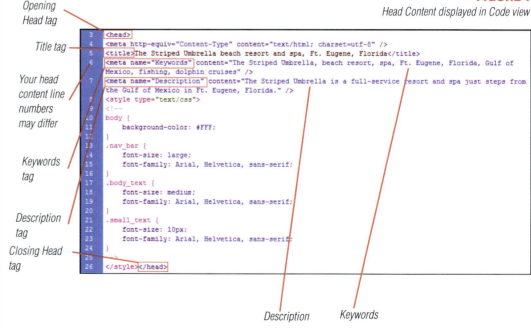

```
3  <head>
4  <meta http-equiv="Content-Type" content="text/html; charset=utf-8" />
5  <title>The Striped Umbrella beach resort and spa, Ft. Eugene, Florida</title>
6  <meta name="Keywords" content="The Striped Umbrella, beach resort, spa, Ft. Eugene, Florida, Gulf of
   Mexico, fishing, dolphin cruises" />
7  <meta name="Description" content="The Striped Umbrella is a full-service resort and spa just steps from
   the Gulf of Mexico in Ft. Eugene, Florida." />
8  <style type="text/css">
9  <!--
10 body {
11      background-color: #FFF;
12 }
13 .nav_bar {
14      font-size: large;
15      font-family: Arial, Helvetica, sans-serif;
16 }
17 .body_text {
18      font-size: medium;
19      font-family: Arial, Helvetica, sans-serif;
20 }
21 .small_text {
22      font-size: 10px;
23      font-family: Arial, Helvetica, sans-serif;
24 }
25 -->
26 </style></head>
```

*Description*          *Keywords*

**FIGURE 8**
*Page Properties dialog box*

*Background color box*

*Hexadecimal shorthand for white (number code is preceded with a # sign)*

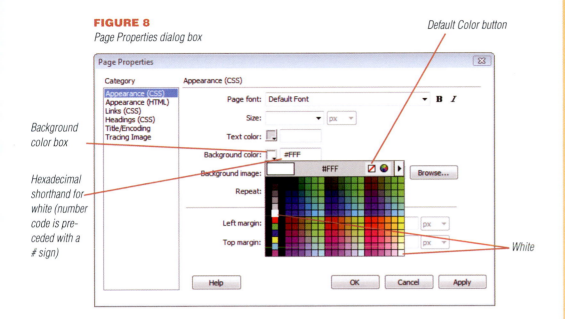

*White*

1. Click **Modify** on the Application bar (Win) or Menu bar (Mac), then click **Page Properties** to open the Page Properties dialog box.

2. Click the **Background color box** to open the color picker, as shown in Figure 8.

3. Click the rightmost color in the bottom row (white).

4. Click **Apply**, then click **OK**.

   Clicking Apply lets you see the changes you made to the web page without closing the Page Properties dialog box.

   TIP  If you don't like the color you chose, click the Default Color button ⬚ in the color picker to switch to the default color.

   The background color of the web page is now white. The black text against the white background provides a nice contrast and makes the text easy to read.

5. Save your work.

*You used the Page Properties dialog box to change the background color to white.*

## Understanding hexadecimal values

Each color is assigned a **hexadecimal RGB value**, a value that represents the amount of red, green, and blue present in the color. For example, white, which is made of equal parts of red, green, and blue, has a hexadecimal value of FFFFFF. This is also referred to as an RGB triplet in hexadecimal format (**hex triplet**). Each pair of characters in the hexadecimal value represents the red, green, and blue values. The hexadecimal number system is based on 16, rather than 10 in the decimal number system. Because the hexadecimal number system includes only numbers up to 9, values after 9 use the letters of the alphabet. "A" represents the number 10 in the hexadecimal number system. "F" represents the number 15. The hexadecimal values are entered in the code using a form of shorthand that shortens the six characters to three characters. For instance: FFFFFF become FFF; 0066CC becomes 06C. The number value for a color is preceded by a pound sign (#) in HTML code.

# CREATE, IMPORT, AND
## FORMAT TEXT

## What You'll Do

*In this lesson, you will apply HTML heading styles and HTML text styles to text on The Striped Umbrella home page. You will also import a file and set text properties for the text on the new page.*

### Creating and Importing Text

Most information in web pages is presented in the form of text. You can type text directly in Dreamweaver, import, or copy and paste it from another software program. (Macintosh users do not have the option to import text. They must open a text file, copy the text, then paste it into an HTML document.) When using a Windows computer to import text from a Microsoft Word file, you use the Import Word Document command. Not only will the formatting be preserved, but Dreamweaver will generate clean HTML code. Clean HTML code is code that does what it is supposed to do without using unnecessary instructions, which take up memory. When you format text, it is important to keep in mind that visitors to your site must have the same fonts installed on their computers as the fonts you use. Otherwise, the text may appear incorrectly. Some software programs can convert text into graphics so that the text retains the same appearance no matter which fonts are installed. However, text converted into graphics is no longer editable. If text does not have a font specified, the default font will apply. This means that the default font on

### Using keyboard shortcuts

When working with text, the standard Windows keyboard shortcuts for Cut, Copy, and Paste are very useful. These are [Ctrl][X] (Win) or ⌘[X] (Mac) for Cut, [Ctrl][C] (Win) or ⌘[C] (Mac) for Copy, and [Ctrl][V] (Win) or ⌘[V] (Mac) for Paste. You can view all Dreamweaver keyboard shortcuts using the Keyboard Shortcuts dialog box, which lets you view existing shortcuts for menu commands, tools, or miscellaneous functions, such as copying HTML or inserting an image. You can also create your own shortcuts or assign shortcuts that you are familiar with from using them in other software programs. To view or modify keyboard shortcuts, click the Keyboard Shortcuts command on the Edit menu (Win) or Dreamweaver menu (Mac), then select the shortcut key set you want. The Keyboard Shortcuts feature is also available in Adobe Fireworks and Flash. Each chapter in this book includes a list of keyboard shortcuts relevant to that chapter.

the user's computer will be used to display the text. Keep in mind that some fonts may not appear the same on both a Windows and a Macintosh computer. The way fonts are rendered (drawn) on the screen differs because Windows and Macintosh computers use different technologies to render them. It is wise to stick to the standard fonts that work well with both systems. Test your pages using both operating systems.

## Formatting Text Using the Property Inspector

Because text is more difficult and tiring to read on a computer screen than on a printed page, you should make the text in your website attractive and easy to read. You can format text in Dreamweaver by changing its font, size, and color, just as you would in other software programs. To apply formatting to text, you first select the text you want to enhance, and then use the Property inspector to apply formatting attributes, such as font type, size, color, alignment, and indents.

## Using HTML Tags Compared to Using CSS

The standard practice today is to use Cascading Style Sheets (CSS) to handle the formatting and placement of web page elements. In fact, the default preference in Dreamweaver is to use CSS rather than HTML tags.

However, this is a lot to learn when you are just beginning, so we are going to begin by using HTML tags for formatting until we study CSS in depth in the next chapter. At that point, we will use CSS instead of HTML tags. To change from CSS to HTML and vice versa, you select the CSS or HTML Property inspector. The Property inspector options will change according to which button is selected. Even if you have the HTML Property inspector selected, styles will be created automatically when you apply most formatting attributes.

## Changing Fonts

You can format your text with different fonts by choosing a font combination from the Font list in the CSS Property inspector. A **font combination** is a set of three font choices that specify which fonts a browser should use to display the text on your web page. Font combinations are used so that if one font is not available, the browser will use the next one specified in the font combination. For example, if text is formatted with the font combination Arial, Helvetica, sans serif; the browser will first look on the viewer's system for Arial. If Arial is not available, then it will look for Helvetica. If Helvetica is not available, then it will look for a sans-serif font to apply to the text. Using fonts within the default settings is wise, because fonts set outside the default settings may not be available on all viewers' computers.

## Changing Font Sizes

There are two ways to change the size of text using the Property inspector. When the CSS option is selected, you can select a numerical value for the size from 9 to 36 pixels or you can use a size expressed in words from xx-small to larger. On the HTML Property inspector, you do not have font sizes available.

## Formatting Paragraphs

The HTML Property inspector displays options to format blocks of text as paragraphs or as different sizes of headings. To format a paragraph as a heading, click anywhere in the paragraph, and then select the heading size you want from the Format list in the Property inspector. The Format list contains six different heading formats. Heading 1 is the largest size, and Heading 6 is the smallest size. Browsers display text formatted as headings in bold, setting them off from paragraphs of text. You can also align paragraphs with the alignment buttons on the CSS Property inspector and indent paragraphs using the Text Indent and Text Outdent buttons on the HTML Property inspector.

## Enter text

1. Position the insertion point directly after "want to go home." at the end of the paragraph, press **[Enter]** (Win) or **[return]** (Mac), then type **The Striped Umbrella**.

   Pressing [Enter] (Win) or [return] (Mac) creates a new paragraph. The HTML code for a paragraph break is <p>. The tag is closed with </p>.

   > TIP   If the new text does not assume the formatting attributes as the paragraph above it, click the Show Code and Design views button 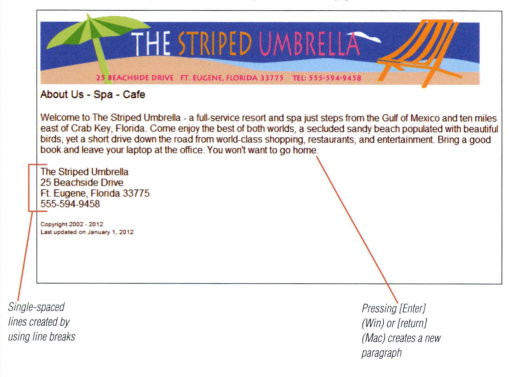 position the cursor right after the period after "home", then go back to the page in Design view and insert a new paragraph.

2. Press and hold **[Shift]**, press **[Enter]** (Win) or **[return]** (Mac), then type **25 Beachside Drive**.

   Pressing and holding [Shift] while you press [Enter] (Win) or [return] (Mac) creates a line break. A **line break** places a new line of text on the next line down without creating a new paragraph. Line breaks are useful when you want to add a new line of text directly below the current line of text and keep the same formatting. The HTML code for a line break is <br />.

3. Add the following text below the 25 Beachside Drive text, using line breaks after each line:

   **Ft. Eugene, Florida 33775
   555-594-9458**

4. Compare your screen with Figure 9.

   *You entered text for the address and telephone number on the home page.*

### FIGURE 9

*Entering the address and telephone number on The Striped Umbrella home page*

**THE STRIPED UMBRELLA**
25 BEACHSIDE DRIVE  FT. EUGENE, FLORIDA 33775   TEL: 555-594-9458

**About Us - Spa - Cafe**

Welcome to The Striped Umbrella - a full-service resort and spa just steps from the Gulf of Mexico and ten miles east of Crab Key, Florida. Come enjoy the best of both worlds, a secluded sandy beach populated with beautiful birds, yet a short drive down the road from world-class shopping, restaurants, and entertainment. Bring a good book and leave your laptop at the office. You won't want to go home.

The Striped Umbrella
25 Beachside Drive
Ft. Eugene, Florida 33775
555-594-9458

Copyright 2002 - 2012
Last updated on January 1, 2012

*Single-spaced lines created by using line breaks*

*Pressing [Enter] (Win) or [return] (Mac) creates a new paragraph*

### Preventing data loss

When you are ready to stop working with a file in Dreamweaver, it is a good idea to save your changes, close the page or pages on which you are working, and exit Dreamweaver. Doing this will prevent the loss of data if power is interrupted. In some cases, loss of power can corrupt an open file and render it unusable.

## FIGURE 10

Formatting the address on The Striped Umbrella home page

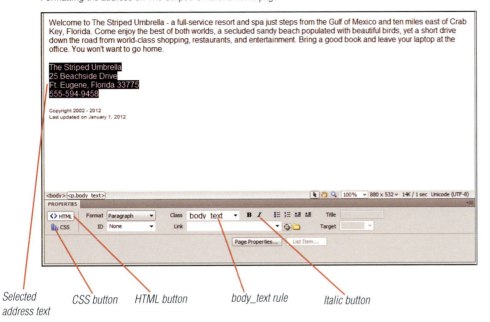

Selected address text   CSS button   HTML button   body_text rule   Italic button

## FIGURE 11

Viewing the HTML code for the address and phone number

"body_text" tag defines the CSS style in the original data file

Beginning <em> tag begins italic text

<p> tag begins a new paragraph

<br /> tags show line breaks from pressing [Shift] [Enter] at the end of each line

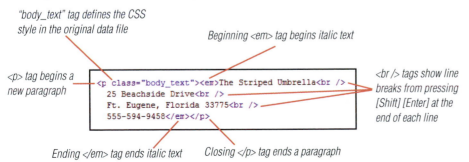

Ending </em> tag ends italic text

Closing </p> tag ends a paragraph

1. Select the entire address and telephone number, as shown in Figure 10, then click the **HTML button** `<> HTML` in the Property inspector (if it is not already selected) to change to the HTML Property inspector, as shown in Figure 10.

2. Click the **Italic button** `I` in the Property inspector to italicize the text, then click after the text to deselect it.

   The HTML tag for italic text is <em>.

   > TIP   The HTML tag for bold text is <strong></strong>. The HTML tag for underlined text is <u></u>.

3. Click the **Show Code view button** `<> Code` to view the HTML code, as shown in Figure 11.

   It is always helpful to learn what the HTML code means. As you edit and format your pages, read the code to see how it is written for each element. The more familiar you are with the code, the more comfortable you will feel with Dreamweaver and web design. A strong knowledge of HTML is a necessary skill for professional web designers.

4. Click the **Show Design view button** `Design` to return to Design view.

5. Save your work, then close the page.

*You changed the Property inspector options from CSS to HTML, then formatted the address and phone number for The Striped Umbrella by changing the font style to italic.*

## Save an image file in the assets folder

1. Open dw2_1.html from where you store your Data Files, save it as **spa.html** in the striped_umbrella folder, overwriting the existing file, then click **No** in the Update Links dialog box.

2. Select **The Striped Umbrella** banner.

   Updating links ties the image or hyperlink to the Data Files folder. Because you already copied su_banner.gif to the website, the banner image is visible. Notice that the Src text box shows the link is to the website assets folder, not to the Data Files folder.

3. Click the **Spa image broken link placeholder** to select it, click the **Browse for File icon** 📁 in the Property inspector next to the Src text box, navigate to the chapter_2 assets folder, click **the_spa.jpg**, then click **OK** (Win) or **Choose** (Mac).

   Because this image was not in the website, it appeared as a broken link. Using the Browse for File icon 📁 selects the source of the original image file. Dreamweaver automatically copies the file to the assets folder of the website and it is visible on the page. You may have to deselect the new image to see it replace the broken link.

4. Click the **Refresh button** 🔄 on the Files panel toolbar if necessary, then click the **plus sign** (Win) or **expander arrow** (Mac) next to the assets folder in the Files panel, (if necessary).

   A copy of the_spa.jpg file appears in the assets folder, as shown in Figure 12.

   *You opened a new file, saved it as the new spa page, and fixed a broken link by copying the image to the assets folder.*

**FIGURE 12**
*Image file added to The Striped Umbrella assets folder*

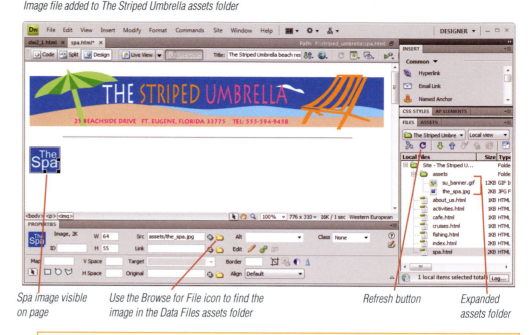

Spa image visible on page

Use the Browse for File icon to find the image in the Data Files assets folder

Refresh button

Expanded assets folder

### Choosing filenames for HTML web pages

When you choose a name for a web page, you should use a descriptive name that reflects the contents of the page. For example, if the page is about your company's products, you could name it products.html. You should also follow some general rules for naming web pages, such as naming the home page **index.html**. Most file servers look for the file named index.html to use as the initial page for a website. Do not use spaces, special characters, or punctuation in web page filenames or in the names of any images that will be inserted in your site. Spaces in filenames can cause errors when a browser attempts to read a file, and may cause your images to load incorrectly; use underscores in place of spaces. Forbidden characters include * & ^ % $ # @ ! / and \. You should also never use a number for the first character of a filename. To ensure that everything will load properly on all platforms, including UNIX, assume that filenames are case-sensitive and use lowercase characters. HTML web pages can be saved with the .htm or .html file extension. Although either file extension is appropriate, Dreamweaver uses the default file extension of .html.

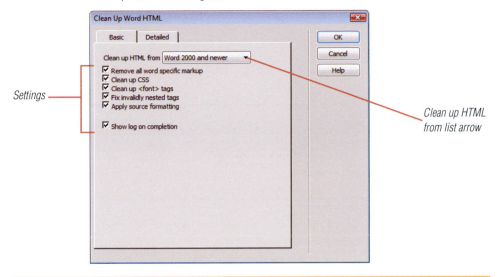

**FIGURE 13**
*Clean Up Word HTML dialog box*

Settings

Clean up HTML
from list arrow

## Importing and linking Microsoft Office documents (Windows)

Adobe makes it easy to transfer data between Microsoft Office documents and Dreamweaver web pages. When importing a Word or Excel document, click File on the Application bar, point to Import, then click either Word Document or Excel Document. Select the file want to import, then click the Formatting list arrow to choose between importing Text only; Text with structure (paragraphs, lists, and tables); Text, structure, basic formatting (bold, italic); Text, structure, full formatting (bold, italic, styles) before you click Open. The option you choose depends on the importance of the original structure and formatting. Always use the Clean Up Word HTML command after importing a Word file. You can also create a link to a Word or Excel document on your web page. To do so, drag the Word or Excel document from its current location to the location on the page where you would like the link to appear. (If the document is located outside the site, you can browse for it using the Site list arrow on the Files panel, Windows Explorer, or Mac Finder.) Next, select the Create a link option button in the Insert Document dialog box, then save the file in your root folder so it will be uploaded when you publish your site. If it is not uploaded, the link will be broken.

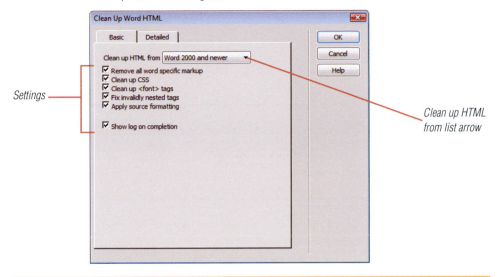

### Import text

1. With the insertion point to the right of the spa graphic on the spa.html page, press **[Enter]** (Win) or **[return]** (Mac).

2. Click **File** on the Application bar, point to **Import**, click **Word Document**, double-click the **chapter_2 folder** from where you store your Data Files, then double-click **spa.doc** (Win); or double-click **spa.doc** from where you store your Data Files, select all, copy, close spa.doc, then paste the copied text on the spa page in Dreamweaver (Mac).

3. Click **Commands** on the Application bar (Win) or Menu bar (Mac), then click **Clean Up Word HTML**.

   TIP  If a dialog box appears stating that Dreamweaver was unable to determine the version of Word used to generate this document, click OK, click the Clean up HTML from list arrow, then choose the Word 2000 and newer version of Word if it isn't already selected.

4. Make sure each check box in the Clean Up Word HTML dialog box is checked, as shown in Figure 13, click **OK**, then click **OK** again to close the results window.

*You imported a Word document, then used the Clean Up Word HTML command.*

## Set text properties

1. Click the Common category on the Insert panel if necessary, then scroll up and place the insertion point anywhere within the words "Spa Services."

2. Click the **Format list arrow** in the HTML Property inspector, click **Heading 4,** click the **Show Code and Design views button** ⊞ Split on the Document toolbar, then compare your screen to Figure 14.

   The Heading 4 format is applied to the paragraph. Even a single word is considered a paragraph if there is a hard return or paragraph break after it. The HTML code for a Heading 4 tag is <h4>. The tag is then closed with </h4>. The level of the heading tag follows the h, so the code for a Heading 1 tag is <h1>.

3. Click **Format** on the Application bar (Win) or Menu bar (Mac), point to **Align,** then click **Center**.

   When the paragraph is centered, the HTML code 'align="center"' is added to the <h4> tag.

*You applied a heading format to a heading, viewed the HTML code, then centered the heading.*

**FIGURE 14**

*Viewing the heading tag in Show Code and Design views*

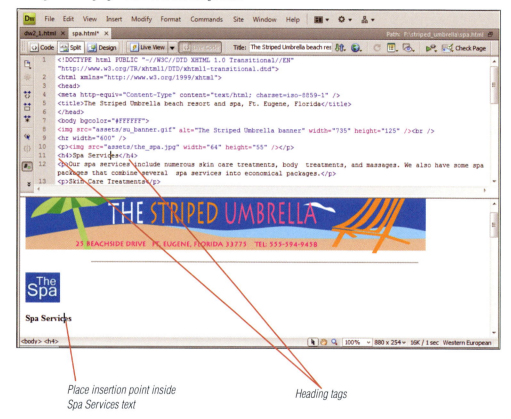

Place insertion point inside
Spa Services text

Heading tags

**FIGURE 15**
*Check Spelling dialog box*

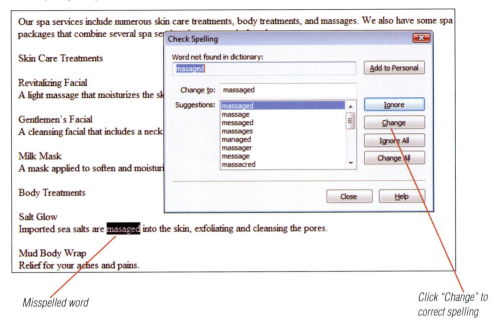

Misspelled word

Click "Change" to correct spelling

## Checking for spelling errors

It is very important to check for spelling and grammatical errors before publishing a page. A page that is published with errors will cause the viewer to immediately judge the site as unprofessional and carelessly made, and the accuracy of the data presented will be in question. If a file you create in a word processor will be imported into Dreamweaver, run a spell check in the word processor first. Then spell check the imported text again in Dreamweaver so you can add words such as proper names to the Dreamweaver dictionary so the program will not flag them again. Click the Add to Personal button in the Check Spelling dialog box to add a new word to the dictionary. Even though you may have checked a page using the spell check feature, you still must proofread the content yourself to catch usage errors such as "to," "too," and "two." Accuracy in both content and delivery is critical.

## Check spelling

1. Click the **Show Design view button** [Design] to return to Design view.

2. Place the insertion point in front of the text "Spa Services".

   It is a good idea to start a spelling check at the top of the document because Dreamweaver searches from the insertion point down. If your insertion point is in the middle of the document, you will receive a message asking if you want to check the rest of the document. Starting from the beginning just saves time.

3. Click **Commands** on the Application bar (Win) or Menu bar (Mac), then click **Check Spelling.**

   The word "masaged" is highlighted on the page as a misspelled word and suggestions are listed to correct it in the Check Spelling dialog box, as shown in Figure 15.

4. Click **massaged** in the Suggestions list if necessary, then click **Change.**

   The word is corrected on the page.

5. Click **OK** to close the Dreamweaver dialog box stating that the Spelling Check is completed.

6. Save and close the spa page, then close the dw2_1.html page.

*You checked the page for spelling errors.*

# ADD LINKS TO
## WEB PAGES

## What You'll Do

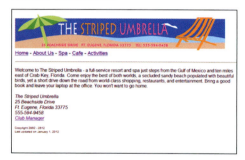

*In this lesson, you will open the home page and add links to the navigation bar that link to the About Us, Spa, Cafe, and Activities pages. You will then insert an email link at the bottom of the page.*

### Adding Links to Web Pages

Links provide the real power for web pages. Links make it possible for viewers to navigate all the pages in a website and to connect to other pages anywhere on the web. Viewers are more likely to return to websites that have a user-friendly navigation structure. Viewers also enjoy websites that have interesting links to other web pages or other websites.

To add links to a web page, first select the text or image that you want to serve as a link, and then specify a path to the page to which you want to link in the Link text box in the Property inspector.

When you create links on a web page, it is important to avoid **broken links**, or links that cannot find their intended destinations. You can accidentally cause a broken link by typing the incorrect address for the link in the Link text box. Broken links are often caused by companies merging, going out of business, or simply moving their website addresses.

In addition to adding links to your pages, you should provide a **point of contact**, or a place on a web page that provides viewers with a means of contacting the company. A common point of contact is a **mailto: link**, which is an email address that viewers with questions or problems can use to contact someone at the company's headquarters.

## Using Navigation Bars

A **navigation bar** is an area on a web page that contains links to the main pages of a website. Navigation bars are usually located at the top or side of the main pages of a website and can be created with text, images, or a combination of the two. To make navigating a website as easy as possible, you should place navigation bars in the same position on each page. Navigation bars are the backbone of a website's navigation structure, which includes all navigation aids for moving around a website. You can, however, include additional links to the main pages of the website elsewhere on the page. The web page in Figure 16 shows an example of a navigation bar that contains both text and image links that use JavaScript. Notice that when the mouse is placed on an item in the navigation bar, the image expands to include more information.

Navigation bars can also be simple and contain only text-based links to the pages in the site. You can create a simple navigation bar by typing the names of your website's pages at the top of your web page, formatting the text, and then adding links to each page name. It is always a good idea to provide plain text links for accessibility, regardless of the type of navigation structure you choose to use.

**FIGURE 16**

*The CIA website*

Additional information appears

Navigation bar with text links using JavaScript

## Create a navigation bar

1. Open **index.html**.

2. Position the insertion point to the left of "A" in About Us, then drag to select **About Us - Spa - Cafe**.

3. Type **Home - About Us - Spa - Cafe - Activities**, as shown in Figure 17.

   These five text labels will serve as a navigation bar. You will add the links later.

*You created a new navigation bar using text, replacing the original navigation bar.*

## Insert a horizontal rule

1. Click after the end of the word "Activities" if necessary, then press **[Shift][Enter]** (Win) **or [Shift][return]** (Mac).

2. Click **Horizontal Rule** in the Common category on the Insert panel to insert a horizontal rule under the navigation bar.

   A horizontal rule is a line used to separate page elements or to organize information on a page.

3. Compare your screen to Figure 18, then save your work.

   TIP   An asterisk after the filename in the title bar indicates that you have altered the page since you last saved it. After you save your work, the asterisk does not appear.

*You added a horizontal rule to separate the navigation bar from the page content.*

**FIGURE 17**
*Viewing the new navigation bar*

Home - About Us - Spa - Cafe - Activities

**FIGURE 18**
*Inserting a horizontal rule*

Asterisk indicates page has not been saved

Horizontal rule

Horizontal Rule command

FIGURE 19

*Selecting text for the Home link*

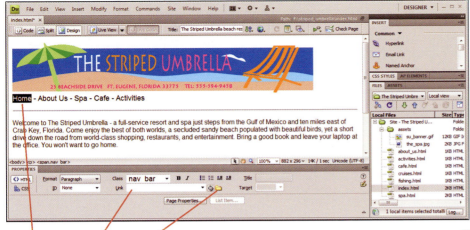

FIGURE 20

*Select File dialog box*

*The Striped Umbrella local root folder*

*index.html page*

*Click OK to set link*

*Relative to: list arrow*

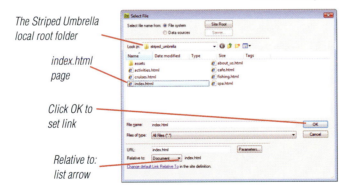

FIGURE 21

*Links added to navigation bar*

*Navigation bar with links added*

## Add links to web pages

1. Double-click **Home** to select it, as shown in Figure 19.

2. Click the **Browse for File icon** 🗀 next to the Link text box in the HTML Property inspector, then navigate to the striped_umbrella root folder (if necessary).

3. Verify that the link is set Relative to Document in the Relative to: list.

4. Click **index.html** as shown in Figure 20, click **OK** (Win) or **Choose** (Mac), then click anywhere on the page to deselect Home.

   TIP   Your file listing may differ depending on your view settings.

   Home now appears in blue with an underline, indicating it is a link. However, clicking Home will not open a new page because the link is to the home page. It might seem odd to create a link to the same page on which the link appears, but this will be helpful when you copy the navigation bar to other pages in the site. Always provide viewers a link to the home page.

5. Repeat Steps 1–4 to create links for About Us, Spa, Cafe, and Activities to their corresponding pages in the striped_umbrella root folder.

6. When you finish adding the links to the other four pages, deselect all, then compare your screen to Figure 21.

*You created a link for each of the five navigation bar elements to their respective web pages in The Striped Umbrella website.*

## Create an email link

1. Place the insertion point after the last digit in the telephone number, then insert a line break.

2. Click **Email Link** in the Common category on the Insert panel to insert an email link.

3. Type **Club Manager** in the Text text box, type **manager@stripedumbrella.com** in the E-Mail text box, as shown in Figure 22, then click **OK** to close the Email Link dialog box.

   If the text does not not retain the formatting from the previous line use the Edit, Undo command to undo Steps 1–3. Switch to Code view and place the insertion point immediately to the right of the telephone number, then repeat the steps again in Design view.

4. Save your work.

   The text "mailto:manager@striped_umbrella.com," appears in the Link text box in the HTML Property inspector. When a viewer clicks this link, a blank email message window opens in the viewer's default email software, where the viewer can type a message. See Figure 23.

   > TIP  You must enter the correct email address in the E-Mail text box for the link to work. However, you can enter any descriptive name, such as customer service or Bob Smith in the Text text box. You can also enter the email address as the text if you want to show the actual email address on the web page.

*You inserted an email link to serve as a point of contact for The Striped Umbrella.*

FIGURE 22
*Email Link dialog box*

Text for email link on the page (this could also be a person's name or position or the actual email link)

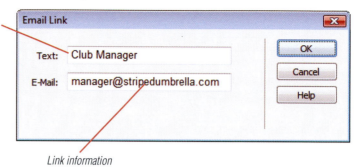

Link information

FIGURE 23
*mailto: link on the Property inspector*

mailto: link

**FIGURE 24**

*The Assets panel URL category*

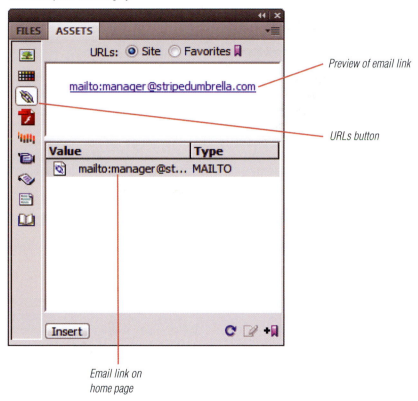

Preview of email link

URLs button

Email link on
home page

1. Click the **Assets panel tab** to view the Assets panel.

2. Click the **URLs button** to display the URLs in the website, as shown in Figure 24.

   **URL** stands for **Uniform Resource Locator**. The URLs listed in the Assets panel show all of the **external links,** or links pointing outside of the website. An email link is outside the website, so it is an external link. You will learn more about URLs and links in Chapter 4. The links you created to the site pages are internal links (inside the website), and are not listed in the Assets panel.

3. Click the **Files panel tab** to view the Files panel.

*You viewed the email link from the home page in the Assets panel.*

# USE THE HISTORY
## PANEL AND EDIT CODE

## What You'll Do

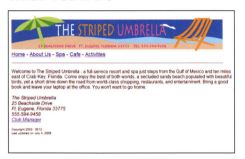

 *In this lesson, you will use the History panel to undo formatting changes you make to a horizontal rule. You will then use the Code Inspector to view the HTML code for the horizontal rule. You will also insert a date object and then view its code in the Code Inspector.*

### Using the History Panel

Throughout the process of creating a web page, it's likely that you will make mistakes along the way. Fortunately, you have a tool named the History panel to undo your mistakes. The **History panel** records each editing and formatting task performed and displays them in a list in the order in which they were completed. Each task listed in the History panel is called a **step**. You can drag the **slider** on the left side of the History panel to undo

or redo steps, as shown in Figure 25. You can also click in the bar to the left of a step to undo all steps below it. You click the step to select it. By default, the History panel records 50 steps. You can change the number of steps the History panel records in the General category of the Preferences dialog box. However, keep in mind that setting this number too high might require additional memory and could affect Dreamweaver's performance.

### Understanding other History panel features

Dragging the slider up and down in the History panel is a quick way to undo or redo steps. However, the History panel offers much more. It has the capability to "memorize" certain tasks and consolidate them into one command. This is a useful feature for steps that you perform repetitively on web pages. Some Dreamweaver features, such as drag and drop, cannot be recorded in the History panel and are noted by a red "x" placed next to them. The History panel does not show steps performed in the Files panel.

## Viewing HTML Code in the Code Inspector

If you enjoy writing code, you occasionally might want to make changes to web pages by entering the code rather than using the panels and tools in Design view. You can view the code in Dreamweaver using Code view, Code and Design views, or the Code Inspector. The **Code Inspector**, shown in Figure 26, is a separate window that displays the current page in Code view. The advantage of using the Code Inspector is that you can see a full-screen view of your page in Design view while viewing the underlying code in a floating window that you can resize and position wherever you want.

You can add advanced features, such as JavaScript functions, to web pages by copying and pasting code from one page to another in the Code Inspector. A **JavaScript** function is a block of code that adds dynamic content such as rollovers or interactive forms to a web page. A **rollover** is a special effect that changes the appearance of an object when the mouse moves over it.

### QUICK TIP

If you are new to HTML, you can use the Reference panel to find answers to your HTML questions. The Reference panel is accessed through the Code Inspector or the Results panel and contains many resources besides HTML help, such as JavaScript help.

**FIGURE 25**

*The History panel*

**FIGURE 26**

*The Code Inspector*

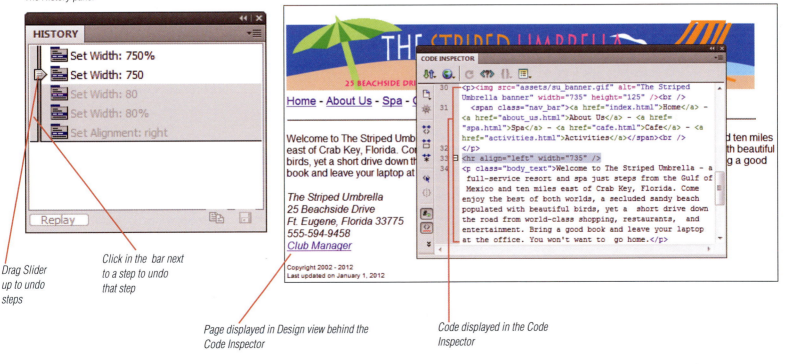

Drag Slider up to undo steps

Click in the bar next to a step to undo that step

Page displayed in Design view behind the Code Inspector

Code displayed in the Code Inspector

## Use the History panel

1. Click **Window** on the Application bar (Win) or Menu bar (Mac), then click **History**.

   The History panel opens and displays steps you have recently performed.

2. Click the **History panel options menu button** , click **Clear History**, as shown in Figure 27, then click **Yes** to close the warning box.

3. Select the **horizontal rule** on the home page.

   The Property inspector shows the properties of the selected horizontal rule.

4. Click the W text box in the Property inspector, type **750**, click the **Align list arrow**, click **Left**, then compare your Property inspector to Figure 28.

   > TIP  Horizontal rule widths can be set in pixels or as a percent of the width of the window. If the width is expressed in pixels, the code will only show the number without the word "pixels". Pixels is understood as the default width setting.

5. Using the Property inspector, change the W text box value to **80**, change the measurement unit to **%**, click the **Align list arrow**, then click **Right**.

6. Drag the **slider** on the History panel up to Set Alignment: Left, as shown in Figure 29.

   The bottom three steps in the History panel appear gray, indicating that these steps have been undone.

7. Right-click (Win) or Control-click (Mac) the **History panel title bar,** then click **Close** to close the History panel.

*You formatted the horizontal rule, made changes to it, then used the History panel to undo some of the changes.*

**FIGURE 27**
*Clearing the History panel*

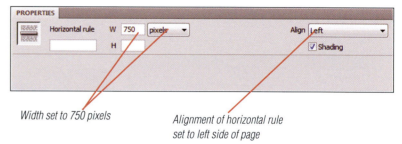

Options menu button

You will see a additional commands if your panel is displayed in a tab group

Clear History command

**FIGURE 28**
*Property inspector settings for horizontal rule*

Width set to 750 pixels

Alignment of horizontal rule set to left side of page

**FIGURE 29**
*Undoing steps using the History panel*

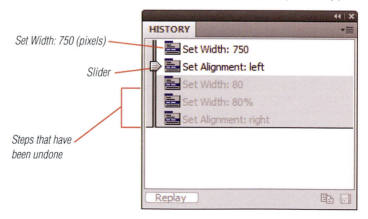

Set Width: 750 (pixels)

Slider

Steps that have been undone

**FIGURE 30**

*Viewing the Options menu in the Code Inspector*

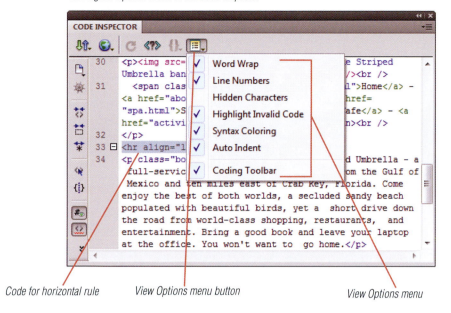

Code for horizontal rule    View Options menu button    View Options menu

### Use the Code Inspector

1. Click the **horizontal rule** to select it (if necessary), click **Window** on the Application bar (Win) or Menu bar (Mac), then click **Code Inspector**.

   Because the horizontal rule on the page is selected, the corresponding code is highlighted in the Code Inspector.

   TIP  You can also press [F10](Win) or [option][F10] (Mac) to display the Code Inspector.

2. Click the **View Options menu button** on the Code Inspector toolbar to display the View Options menu, then click **Word Wrap** (if necessary), to activate Word Wrap.

   The Word Wrap feature forces text to stay within the confines of the Code Inspector window, allowing you to read without scrolling sideways.

3. Click the **View Options menu button**, then verify that the Word Wrap, Line Numbers, Highlight Invalid Code, Syntax Coloring, Auto Indent, and the Coding Toolbar menu items are checked, as shown in Figure 30. If they are not checked, check them.

4. Select **750** in the horizontal rule width code, then type **735**.

*You changed the width of the horizontal rule by changing the code in the Code Inspector.*

## Use the Reference panel

1. Click the **Reference button** 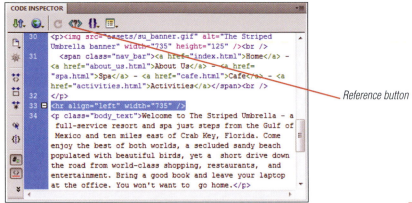 on the Code Inspector toolbar, as shown in Figure 31, to open the Results Tab Group with the Reference panel visible.

   TIP  Verify that the horizontal rule is still selected, or you will not see the horizontal rule description in the Reference panel.

2. Read the information about horizontal rules in the Reference panel, as shown in Figure 32, right-click in an empty area of the **Results Tab Group title bar**, then click **Close Tab Group** (Win) or click the **Panel Options menu button** then click **Close Tab Group** (Mac and Win) to close the Results Tab Group.

3. Close the Code Inspector.

*You read information about horizontal rule settings in the Reference panel.*

**FIGURE 31**
*Reference button on the Code Inspector toolbar*

Reference button

**FIGURE 32**
*Viewing the Reference panel*

Results tab group

Information on <HR> (horizontal rule tag)

## Inserting comments

A handy Dreamweaver feature is the ability to insert comments into HTML code. Comments can provide helpful information describing portions of the code, such as a JavaScript function. You can create comments in any Dreamweaver view, but you must turn on Invisible Elements to see them in Design view. Use the Edit (Win) or Dreamweaver (Mac), Preferences, Invisible Elements, Comments option to enable viewing of comments; then use the View, Visual Aids, Invisible Elements menu option to display them on the page. To create a comment, click the Common category on the Insert panel, click Comment, type a comment in the Comment dialog box, and then click OK. Comments are not visible in browser windows.

**FIGURE 33**

*Insert Date dialog box*

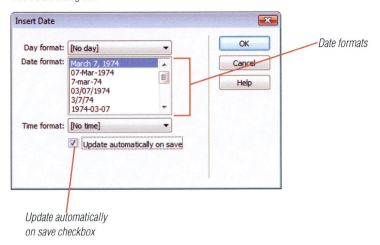

*Date formats*

*Update automatically
on save checkbox*

**FIGURE 34**

*Viewing the date object code*

```
35  <p class="body_text"><em>The Striped Umbrella<br />
36     25 Beachside Drive<br />
37     Ft. Eugene, Florida 33775<br />
38     555-594-9458<br />
39  <a href="mailto:manager@stripedumbrella.com">Club Manager</a></em></p>
40
41  <p class="small_text">Copyright 2002 - 2012 <br />
42  Last updated on
43     <!-- #BeginDate format:Am1 -->July 4, 2008<!-- #EndDate -->
44  </p>
45  </body>
46  </html>
47
```

*Code for date object*

1. Scroll down the page (if necessary) to select **January 1, 2012**, then press **[Delete]** (Win) or **[delete]** (Mac).

2. Click **Date** in the Common category in the Insert panel, then click **March 7, 1974** if necessary in the Date format list box.

3. Click the **Update automatically on save checkbox**, as shown in Figure 33, click **OK**, then deselect the text.

4. Change to Code and Design views.

   The code has changed to reflect the date object, which is set to today's date, as shown in Figure 34. (Your date will be different.) The new code is highlighted with a light yellow background, indicating that it is a date object, automatically coded by Dreamweaver, rather than a date that has been manually typed on the page by the designer.

5. Return to Design view, then save the page.

*You inserted a date object that will be updated automatically when you open and save the home page.*

# MODIFY AND TEST
## WEB PAGES

## What You'll Do

 *In this lesson, you will preview the home page in the browser to check for typographical errors, grammatical errors, broken links, and overall appearance. After previewing, you will make slight formatting adjustments to the page to improve its appearance.*

### Testing and Modifying web pages

Testing web pages is a continuous process. You never really finish a website, because there are always additions and corrections to make. As you add and modify pages, you must test each page as part of the development process. The best way to test a web page is to preview it in a browser window to make sure that all text and image elements appear the way you expect them to. You should also test your links to make sure they work properly. You also need to proofread your text to make sure it contains all the necessary information for the page with no typographical or grammatical errors. Designers typically view a page in a browser, return to Dreamweaver to make necessary changes, and then view the page in a browser again. This process may be repeated many times before the page is ready for publishing. In fact, it is sometimes difficult to stop making improvements to a page and move on to another project. You need to strike a balance among quality, creativity, and productivity.

> **DESIGN** TIP  **Using "Under Construction" or "Come back later" pages**
>
> Many people are tempted to insert an unfinished page as a placeholder for a page that will be finished later. Rather than have real content, these pages usually contain text or an image that indicates the page is not finished, or "under construction." You should not publish a web page that has a link to an unfinished page. It is frustrating to click a link for a page you want to open only to find an "under construction" note or image displayed. You want to make the best possible impression on your viewing audience. If you cannot complete a page before publishing it, at least provide enough information on it to make it "worth the trip."

## Testing a Web Page Using Different Browsers and Screen Sizes

Because users access the Internet using a wide variety of computer systems, it is important to design your pages so that all browsers and screen sizes can display them well. You should test your pages using different browsers and a wide variety of screen sizes to ensure the best view of your page by the most people possible. Although the most common screen size that designers use today is 1024 × 768, some viewers restore down (reduce) individual program windows to a size comparable to 800 × 600 to be able to have more windows open simultaneously on their screen. In other words, people use their "screen real estate" according to their personal work style. To view your page using different screen sizes, click the Window Size pop-up menu in the status bar, then choose the setting you want to use. Table 1 lists the Dreamweaver default window screen sizes. Remember also to check your pages using Windows and Macintosh platforms. Some page elements such as fonts, colors, table borders, layers, and horizontal rules may not appear consistently in both.

## Testing a Web Page as Rendered in a Mobile Device

Dreamweaver has another preview feature that allows you to see what a page would look like if it were viewed on a mobile hand-held device, such as a BlackBerry smartphone. To use this feature, click the Preview/Debug in Browser button on the Document toolbar, then click Preview in Device Central.

### TABLE 1: Dreamweaver default window screen sizes

| window size (inside dimensions of the browser window without borders) | monitor size |
|---|---|
| 592W | |
| 536 × 196 | 640 × 480, default |
| 600 × 300 | 640 × 480, maximized |
| 760 × 420 | 800 × 600, maximized |
| 795 × 470 | 832 × 624, maximized |
| 955 × 600 | 1024 × 768, maximized |

## Modify a web page

1. Click the **Restore Down button** on the index.html title bar to decrease the size of the home page window (Win) or skip to Step 2 (Mac).

   TIP You cannot use the Window Size options if your Document window is maximized (Win).

2. Click the current window size on the status bar, as shown in Figure 35, then click **600 × 300 (640 × 480, Maximized)**, (if necessary).

   A viewer using this setting will be forced to use the horizontal scroll bar to view the entire page.

3. Click the current window size on the status bar, then click **760 × 420 (800 × 600, Maximized)**.

4. Replace the period after the last sentence, "You won't want to go home." with an exclamation point.

5. Click the **Maximize button** on the index.html title bar to maximize the home page window.

6. Save your work.

*You viewed the home page using two different window sizes and you made simple formatting changes to the page.*

**FIGURE 35**
*Window screen sizes*

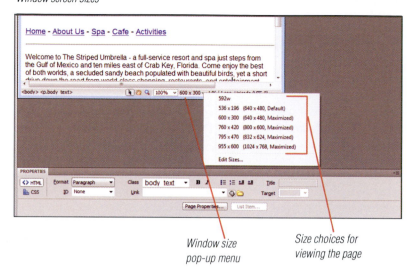

Window size pop-up menu

Size choices for viewing the page

### Using smart design principles in web page layout

As you view your pages in the browser, take a critical look at the symmetry of the page. Is it balanced? Are there too many images compared to text, or vice versa? Does everything "heavy" seem to be on the top or bottom of the page, or do the page elements seem to balance with the weight evenly distributed between the top, bottom, and sides? Use design principles to create a site-wide consistency for your pages. Horizontal symmetry means that the elements are balanced across the page. Vertical symmetry means that they are balanced down the page. Diagonal symmetry balances page elements along the invisible diagonal line of the page. Radial symmetry runs from the center of the page outward, like the petals of a flower. These principles all deal with balance; however, too much balance is not good, either. Sometimes it adds interest to place page elements a little off center or to have an asymmetric layout. Color, white space, text, and images should all complement each other and provide a natural flow across and down the page. The rule of thirds—dividing a page into nine squares like a tic-tac-toe grid—states that interest is increased when your focus is on one of the intersections in the grid. The most important information should be at the top of the page where it is visible without scrolling, or "above the fold," as they say in the newspaper business.

**FIGURE 36**

*Viewing The Striped Umbrella home page in the Firefox browser*

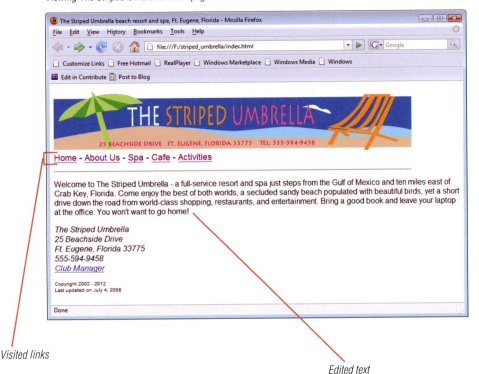

Visited links

Edited text

## Test web pages by viewing them in a browser

1. Click the **Preview/Debug in browser button** 🌐 on the Document toolbar, then choose your browser from the menu that opens.

   The Striped Umbrella home page opens in your default browser.

   TIP  If previewing the page in Internet Explorer 7, click the Information bar when prompted, click Allow Blocked Content, then click Yes to close the Security Warning dialog box.

2. Click each link on the navigation bar, then after each click, use the Back button on the browser toolbar to return to the home page.

   Pages with no content at this point will appear as blank pages. Compare your screen to Figure 36.

3. Close your browser window, then close all open pages in Dreamweaver.

*You viewed The Striped Umbrella home page in your browser and tested each link on the navigation bar.*

**DESIGN**TIP  **Choosing a window size**

Today, the majority of viewers are using a screen resolution of $1024 \times 768$ or higher. Because of this, more content can be displayed at one time on a computer monitor. Some people may use their whole screen to view pages on the Internet. Others may choose to allocate a smaller area of their screen to the browser window. In other words, people tend to use their "screen real estate" in different ways. The ideal web page will not be so small that it tries to spread out over a larger screen size or so large that the viewer has to use horizontal scroll bars to read the page content. Achieving the best balance is one of the design decisions that must be made during the planning process.

## Create head content and set page properties.

1. Open the blooms & bulbs website.
2. Open the index page and view the head content.
3. Add the word "Your" to the page title to read **blooms & bulbs - Your Complete Garden Center**.
4. Insert the following keywords: **garden**, **plants**, **nursery**, **flowers**, **landscape**, **blooms & bulbs**.
5. Insert the following description: **blooms & bulbs is a premier supplier of garden plants for both professional and home gardeners.**
6. Switch to Code view to view the HTML code for the head content, then switch back to Design view.
7. Open the Page Properties dialog box to view the current page properties.
8. Change the background color to a color of your choice.
9. Change the background color to white, then save your work.

## Create, import, and format text.

1. Create a new paragraph after the paragraph of text and type the following text, inserting a line break after each line.
   **blooms & bulbs**
   **Highway 43 South**
   **Alvin, Texas 77511**
   **(555) 248-0806**
2. Verify that the HTML button is selected in the Property inspector, and select it if it is not.
3. Italicize the address and phone number lines.
4. Change to Code view to view the formatting code for the italicized text.
5. Save your work, then close the home page.
6. Open dw2_2.html and save it as **tips.html** in the blooms & bulbs website, overwriting the existing file, but not updating links.
7. Click the broken image link below the blooms & bulbs banner, use the Property inspector to browse to the chapter_2 Data Files folder, select the file garden_tips.jpg in the assets folder, then click OK to save a copy of it in the blooms & bulbs website.
8. Place the insertion point under the Garden Tips graphic.
9. Import gardening_tips.doc from where you store your Data Files, using the Import Word Document command (Win) or copy and paste the text (Mac).
10. Use the Clean Up Word HTML command to correct or remove any unnecessary code.
11. Select the Seasonal Gardening Checklist heading, use the Application bar (Win) or Menu bar (Mac) to center the text, then delete the colon.
12. Use the Property inspector to format the selected text with a Heading 3 format.
13. Check the page for spelling errors by using the Check Spelling command.
14. Save your work and close the tips page and the data file.

## Add links to web pages.

1. Open the index page, then select the current navigation bar and replace it with **Home, Featured Plants, Garden Tips,** and **Classes**. Between each item, use a hyphen with a space on either side to separate the items.
2. Add a horizontal rule under the navigation bar, then remove any extra space between the navigation bar and the horizontal rule, so it looks like Figure 37.
3. Use the Property inspector to link Home on the navigation bar to the index.html page in the blooms & bulbs website.
4. Link Featured Plants on the navigation bar to the plants.html page.
5. Link Garden Tips on the navigation bar to the tips.html page.
6. Link Classes on the navigation bar to the classes.html page.
7. Using the Insert panel, create an email link under the telephone number.
8. Type **Customer Service** in the Text text box and **mailbox@blooms.com** in the E-Mail text box.
9. Save your work.
10. View the email link in the Assets panel, then view the Files panel. You may need to click the Refresh button to see the new link.

### Use the History panel and edit code.

1. Open the History panel, then clear its contents.
2. Select the horizontal rule under the navigation bar, then change the width to 700 pixels and the alignment to Left.
3. Change the width to 70% and the alignment to Center.
4. Use the History panel to restore the horizontal rule settings to 700 pixels wide, left aligned.
5. Close the History panel.
6. Open the Code inspector and verify that Word Wrap is selected.
7. Edit the code in the Code inspector to change the width of the horizontal rule to 735 pixels.
8. Open the Reference panel and scan the information about horizontal rules.

9. Close the Code inspector and close the Reference panel tab group.
10. Delete the current date in the Last updated on statement on the home page and replace it with a date that will update automatically when the file is saved.
11. Examine the code for the date at the bottom of the page to verify that the code that forces it to update on save is included in the code. (*Hint*: The code should be highlighted with a light yellow background.)
12. Save your work.

### Modify and test web pages.

1. Using the Window Size pop-up menu, view the home page at 600 × 300 (640 × 480, Maximized) and 760 × 420 (800 × 600, Maximized), then maximize the Document window.

2. View the page in your browser. (*Hint:* If previewing the page in Internet Explorer 7, click the Information bar when prompted to allow blocked content.)
3. Verify that all links work correctly, then close the browser.
4. On the home page, change the text "Stop by and see us soon!" to **We ship overnight**!
5. Save your work, then view the pages in your browser, comparing your pages to Figure 37 and Figure 38.
6. Close your browser.
7. Adjust the spacing (if necessary), save your work, then preview the home page in the browser again.
8. Close the browser, then save and close all open pages.

**FIGURE 37**

*Completed Skills Review, home page*

**FIGURE 38**

*Completed Skills Review, tips page*

Home - Featured Plants - Garden Tips - Classes

Welcome to blooms & bulbs. We carry a variety of plants and shrubs along with a large inventory of gardening supplies. Our four greenhouses are full of healthy young plants just waiting to be planted in your yard. Our staff includes a certified landscape architect, three landscape designers, and six master gardeners. We offer detailed landscape plans tailored to your location as well as planting and regular maintenance services. We ship overnight!

*blooms & bulbs*
*Highway 43 South*
*Alvin, Texas 77511*
*(555) 248-0806*
*Customer Service*

Copyright 2001 - 2012
Last updated on July 6, 2008

Garden Tips

We have some planting tips we would like to share with you as you prepare your gardens this season. Remember, there is always something to be done for your gardens, no matter what the season. Our experienced staff is here to help you plan your gardens, select your plants, prepare your soil, assist you in the planting, and maintain your beds. Check out our calendar for a list of our scheduled classes. All classes are free of charge and on a first-come, first-served basis!

**Seasonal Gardening Checklist**

Fall – The time to plant trees and spring blooming bulbs.
Winter – The time to prune fruit trees and finish planting your bulbs.
Spring – The time to prepare your beds, plant annuals, and apply fertilizer to established plants.
Summer – The time to supplement rainfall so that plants get one inch of water per week.

You have been hired to create a website for a TripSmart, a travel outfitter. You have created the basic framework for the website and are now ready to format and edit the home page to improve the content and appearance.

1. Open the TripSmart website, then open the home page.
2. Enter the following keywords: **TripSmart, travel**, **traveling**, **trips**, **vacations**, and **tours**.
3. Enter the following description: **TripSmart is a comprehensive travel store. We can help you plan trips**, **make travel arrangements**, **and supply you with travel gear**.
4. Change the page title to **TripSmart - Serving All Your Travel Needs**.

5. Select the existing navigation bar and replace it with the following text links: **Home**, **Catalog**, **Services**, **Destinations**, and **Newsletter**. Between each item, use a hyphen with a space on either side to separate the items.
6. Replace the date in the last updated statement with a date that will update automatically on save.
7. Type the following address two lines below the paragraph about the company, using line breaks after each line:
**TripSmart**
**1106 Beechwood**
**Fayetteville, AR 72704**
**555-848-0807**

8. Insert an email link in the line below the telephone number, using **Customer Service** for the Text text box and **mailbox@tripsmart.com** for the E-Mail text box in the Email Link dialog box.
9. Italicize TripSmart, the address, phone number, and email link.
10. Link the navigation bar entries to index.html, catalog.html, services.html, destinations.html, and newsletter.html.
11. View the HTML code for the page.
12. Insert a horizontal rule between the paragraph of text and the address.

**13.** Change the horizontal rule width to 720 pixels and align to the left side of the page.

**14.** Save your work.

**15.** View the page using two different window sizes, then test the links in your browser window.

**16.** Compare your page to Figure 39, close the browser, then close all open pages.

**FIGURE 39**
*Completed Project Builder 1*

Home - Catalog - Services - Destinations - Newsletter

Welcome to TripSmart - the smart choice for the savvy traveler. We're here to help you with all your travel needs. Choose customized trips to any location or our Five-Star Tours, recently rated number one in the country by Traveler magazine. With over 30 years of experience, we can bring you the best the world has to offer.

*TripSmart*
*1106 Beechwood*
*Fayetteville, AR 72704*
*555.848.0807*
Customer Service

Copyright 2002 - 2012
Last updated on July 6, 2008

*Developing a Web Page*

Your company has been selected to design a website for a catering business named Carolyne's Creations. You are now ready to add content to the home page and apply formatting options to improve the page's appearance, using Figure 40 as a guide.

1. Open the Carolyne's Creations website, then open the home page.
2. Edit the page title to read **Carolyne's Creations - Premier Gourmet Food Shop.**
3. Add the description **Carolyne's Creations is a full service gourmet food shop. We offer cooking classes, take-out meals, and catering services. We also have a retail shop that stocks gourmet treats and kitchen accessories.**

4. Add the keywords **Carolyne's Creations, gourmet, catering, cooking classes, kitchen accessories, take-out.**
5. Place the insertion point in front of the sentence beginning "Give us a call" and type **Feel like a guest at your own party**.
6. Add the following address below the paragraph using line breaks after each line:
   **Carolyne's Creations**
   **496 Maple Avenue**
   **Seven Falls, Virginia 52404**
   **555-963-8271**
7. Enter another line break after the telephone number and type **Email**, add a space, then add an email link using Carolyne Kate for the text and carolyne@carolynescreations.com for the email address.

8. Create links from each navigation bar element to its corresponding web page.
9. Replace the date that follows the text "Last updated on" with a date object, then save your work.
10. Insert a horizontal rule below the navigation bar.
11. Set the width of the horizontal rule to 360 pixels.
12. Left-align the horizontal rule.

13. Save your work, view the completed page in your default browser, then test each link. (*Hint*: If previewing the page in Internet Explorer 7, click the Information bar when prompted to allow blocked content.)

14. Close your browser.

15. Close all open pages.

**FIGURE 40**
*Completed Project Builder 2*

Home | Shop | Classes | Catering | Recipes

Let Carolyne's Creations be your personal chef, your one stop shop for the latest in kitchen items and fresh ingredients, and your source for new and innovative recipes. We enjoy planning and executing special events for all occasions - from children's birthday parties to corporate retreats. Feel like a guest at your own party. Give us a call or stop by our shop to browse through our selections.

Carolyne's Creations
496 Maple Avenue
Seven Falls, Virginia 52404
555-963-8271
Email Carolyne Kate

Copyright 2001 - 2012
Last updated on July 7, 2008

# DESIGN PROJECT

Angela Lou is a freelance photographer. She is searching the Internet looking for a particular type of paper to use in printing her digital images. She knows that websites use keywords and descriptions in order to receive "hits" with search engines. She is curious about how they work. Follow the steps below and write your answers to the questions.

1. Connect to the Internet, then go to *www.snapfish.com* to see the Snapfish website's home page, as shown in Figure 41.
2. View the page source by clicking View on the Application bar, then clicking Source (Internet Explorer) or Page Source (Mozilla Firefox).
3. Can you locate a description and keywords? If so, what are they?
4. How many keywords do you find?
5. Is the description appropriate for the website? Why or why not?
6. Look at the numbers of keywords and words in the description. Is there an appropriate number? Or are there too many or not enough?

7. Use a search engine such as Google at www.google.com, then type the words **photo quality paper** in the Search text box.

8. Click the first link in the list of results and view the source code for that page. Do you see keywords and a description? Do any of them match the words you used in the search?

## FIGURE 41
*Design Project*

*Snapfish website used with permission from Snapfish - www.snapfish.com*

# PORTFOLIO PROJECT

In this assignment, you will continue to work on the website you defined in Chapter 1. In Chapter 1, you created a storyboard for your website with at least four pages. You also created a local root folder for your site and an assets folder to store the site asset files. You set the assets folder as the default storage location for your images. You began to collect information and resources for your site and started working on the home page.

1. Think about the head content for the home page. Add the title, keywords, and a description.
2. Create the main page content for the home page and format it attractively.
3. Add the address and other contact information to the home page, including an email address.
4. Consult your storyboard and design the navigation bar.
5. Link the navigation bar items to the appropriate pages.
6. Add a last updated on statement to the home page with a date that will automatically update when the page is saved.
7. Edit and format the page content until you are satisfied with the results.
8. Verify that all links, including the email link, work correctly.
9. When you are satisfied with the home page, review the checklist questions shown in Figure 42, then make any necessary changes.
10. Save your work.

**FIGURE 42**
*Portfolio Project*

**Website Checklist**

1. Does the home page have a page title?
2. Does the home page have a description and keywords?
3. Does the home page contain contact information, including an email address?
4. Does the home page have a navigation bar that includes a link to itself?
5. Does the home page have a "last updated on" statement that will automatically update when the page is saved?
6. Do all paths for links and images work correctly?
7. Does the home page look good using at least two different browsers and screen resolutions?

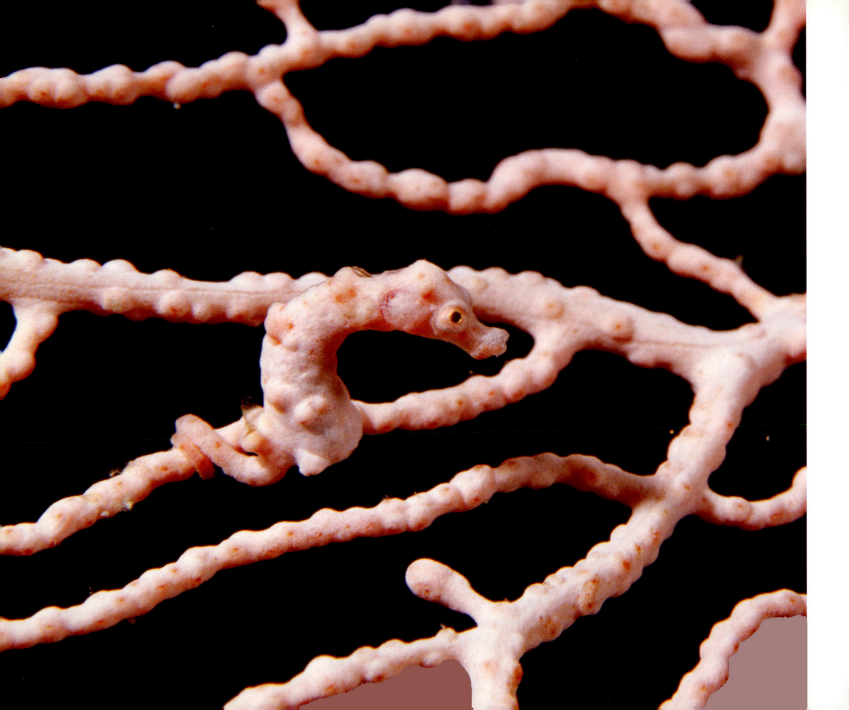

# WORKING WITH TEXT
## AND IMAGES

1. Create unordered and ordered lists

2. Create, apply, and edit Cascading Style Sheets

3. Add rules and attach Cascading Style Sheets

4. Insert and align graphics

5. Enhance an image and use alternate text

6. Insert a background image and perform site maintenance

# WORKING WITH TEXT
## AND IMAGES

## Introduction

Most web pages contain a combination of text and images. Dreamweaver provides many tools for working with text and images that you can use to make your web pages attractive and easy to read. Dreamweaver also has tools that help you format text quickly and ensure a consistent appearance of text elements across all your web pages.

## Formatting Text as Lists

If a web page contains a large amount of text, it can be difficult for viewers to digest it all. You can break up the monotony of large blocks of text by dividing them into smaller paragraphs or organizing them as lists. You can create three types of lists in Dreamweaver: unordered lists, ordered lists, and definition lists.

## Using Cascading Style Sheets

You can save time and ensure that all your page elements have a consistent appearance by using **Cascading Style Sheets (CSS)**. CSS are sets of formatting instructions, usually stored in a separate file, that control the appearance of content on a web page or throughout a website. You can use CSS to define consistent formatting attributes for page elements such as text and tables throughout your website. You can then apply the formatting attributes you define to any element in a single document or to all of the pages in a website.

## Using Images to Enhance Web Pages

Images make web pages visually stimulating and more exciting than pages that contain only text. However, you should use images sparingly. If you think of text as the meat and potatoes of a website, the images would be the seasoning. You should add images to a page just as you would add seasoning to food. A little seasoning enhances the flavor and brings out the quality of the dish. Too much seasoning overwhelms the dish and masks the flavor of the main ingredients. Too little seasoning results in a bland dish. There are many ways to work with images so that they complement the content of pages in a website. There are specific file formats used to save images for websites to ensure maximum quality with minimum file size. You should store images in a separate folder in an organized fashion.

# Tools You'll Use

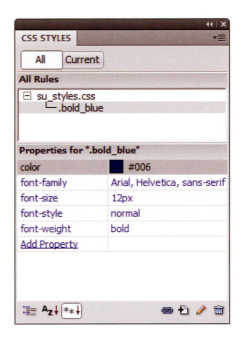

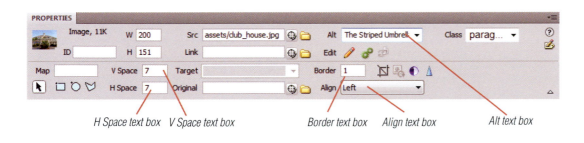

H Space text box    V Space text box        Border text box    Align text box      Alt text box

# CREATE UNORDERED AND
## ORDERED LISTS

## What You'll Do

Spa Packages

- Spa Sampler
  Mix and match any three of our services.
- Girl's Day Out
  One hour massage, a facial, a manicure, and a pedicure.

Call the Spa desk for prices and reservations. Our desk is open from 7:00 a.m. until 5:00 p.m.

Questions you may have

1. How do I schedule Spa services?
   Please make appointments by calling The Club desk at least 24 hours in advance. Please arrive 15 minutes before your appointment to allow enough time to shower or use the sauna.
2. Will I be charged if I cancel my appointment?
   Please cancel 24 hours before your service to avoid a cancellation charge. No-shows and cancellations without adequate notice will be charged for the full service.
3. Are there any health safeguards I should know about?
   Please advise us of medical conditions or allergies you have. Heat treatments like hydrotherapy and body wraps should be avoided if you are pregnant, have high blood pressure, or any type of heart condition or diabetes.
4. What about tipping?
   Gratuities are at your sole discretion, but are certainly appreciated.

*In this lesson, you will create an unordered list of spa services on the spa page. You will also import text with questions and format them as an ordered list.*

## Creating Unordered Lists

**Unordered lists** are lists of items that do not need to be placed in a specific sequence. A grocery list that lists items in a random order is a good example of an unordered list. Items in unordered lists are usually preceded by a **bullet**, or a small dot or similar icon. Unordered lists that contain bullets are sometimes called **bulleted lists**. Although you can use paragraph indentations to create an unordered list, bullets can often make lists easier to read. To create an unordered list, first select the text you want to format as an unordered list, then use the Unordered List button in the HTML Property inspector to insert bullets at the beginning of each paragraph of the selected text.

## Formatting Unordered Lists

In Dreamweaver, the default bullet style is a round dot. To change the bullet style to a square, click inside a bulleted item, expand the Property inspector to its full size, as shown in Figure 1, click the List Item button in the HTML Property inspector to open the List Properties dialog box, and then set the style for bulleted lists to Square. Be aware, however, that not all browsers display square bullets correctly, in which case the bullets will appear differently.

## Creating Ordered Lists

**Ordered lists**, which are sometimes called **numbered lists**, are lists of items that are presented in a specific sequence and that are preceded by sequential numbers or letters. An ordered list is appropriate for a list in which each item must be executed according to its specified order. A list that provides numbered directions for driving from Point A to Point B or a list that provides instructions for assembling a bicycle are both examples of ordered lists.

## Formatting Ordered Lists

You can format an ordered list to show different styles of numbers or letters by using the List Properties dialog box, as shown in Figure 2. You can apply numbers, Roman numerals, lowercase letters, or uppercase letters to an ordered list.

## Creating Definition Lists

Definition lists are similar to unordered lists but do not have bullets. They are often used with terms and definitions, such as in a dictionary or glossary. To create a definition list, select the text to use for the list, click Format on the Application bar (Win) or Menu bar (Mac), point to List, and then click Definition List.

**FIGURE 1**
*Expanded Property inspector*

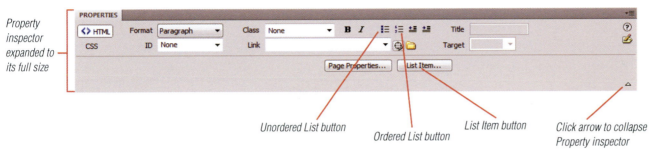

*Property inspector expanded to its full size*

Unordered List button    Ordered List button    List Item button    Click arrow to collapse Property inspector

List type list box

**FIGURE 2**
*Choosing a numbered list style in the List Properties dialog box*

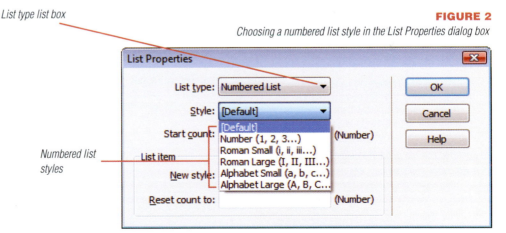

Numbered list styles

## Create an unordered list

1. Open the spa page in The Striped Umbrella website.

2. Select the three items under the Skin Care Treatments heading.

3. Click the **HTML button** in the Property inspector to switch to the HTML Property inspector if necessary, click the **Unordered List button** ⊞ to format the selected text as an unordered list, click anywhere to deselect the text, then compare your screen to Figure 3.

   Each spa service item and its description is separated by a line break. That is why each description is indented under its corresponding item, rather than formatted as a new list item. You must enter a paragraph break to create a new list item.

4. Repeat Step 3 to create unordered lists of the items under the Body Treatments, Massages, and Spa Packages headings, being careful not to include the contact information in the last sentence on the page as part of your last list.

   TIP  Pressing [Enter] (Win) or [return] (Mac) once at the end of an unordered list creates another bulleted item. To end an unordered list, press [Enter] (Win) or [return] (Mac) twice.

*You opened the spa page in Design view and formatted four spa services lists as unordered lists.*

**FIGURE 3**
*Creating an unordered list*

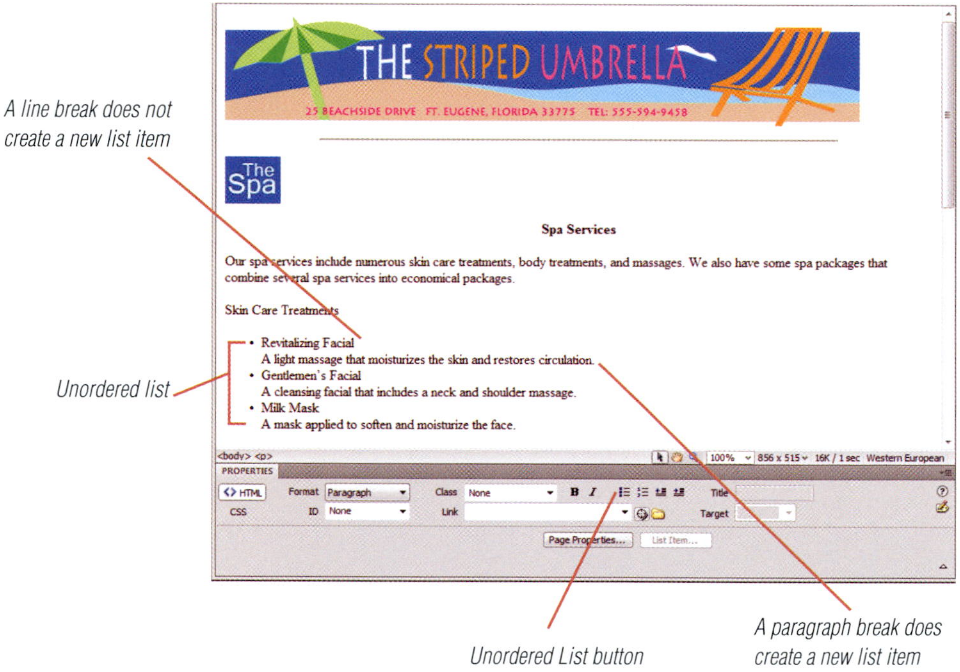

A line break does not create a new list item

Unordered list

Unordered List button

A paragraph break does create a new list item

**FIGURE 4**
*List Properties dialog box*

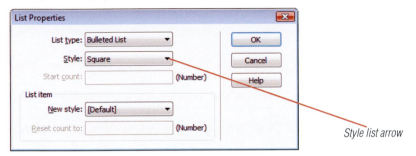

*Style list arrow*

**FIGURE 5**
*HTML tags in Code view for unordered list*

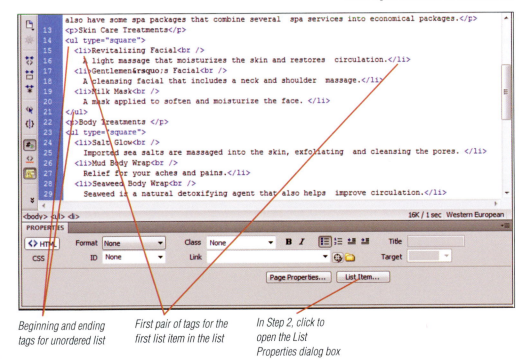

*Beginning and ending tags for unordered list*

*First pair of tags for the first list item in the list*

*In Step 2, click to open the List Properties dialog box*

## Format an unordered list

1. Click any of the items in the first unordered list to place the insertion point in the list.

2. Expand the Property inspector (if necessary), click **List Item** in the HTML Property inspector to open the List Properties dialog box, click the **Style list arrow**, click **Square**, as shown in Figure 4, then click **OK**.

   The bullets in the unordered list now have a square shape.

3. Repeat Step 2 to format the next three unordered lists.

4. Position the insertion point to the left of the first item in the first unordered list, then click the **Show Code view button** [Code] on the Document toolbar to view the code for the unordered list, as shown in Figure 5.

   Notice that there is a pair of HTML tags surrounding each type of element on the page. The first tag in each pair begins the code for a particular element, and the last tag ends the code for the element. For instance, the tags <ul></ul> surround the unordered list. The tags <li> and </li> surround each item in the list.

5. Click the **Show Design view button** [Design] on the Document toolbar.

6. Save your work.

*You used the List Properties dialog box to apply the Square bullet style to the unordered lists. You then viewed the HTML code for the unordered lists in Code view.*

## Create an ordered list

1. Place the insertion point at the end of the page, after the word "5:00 p.m."

2. Use the Import, Word Document command to import questions.doc from where you store your Data Files (Win) or open questions.doc from where you store your Data Files, select all, copy, then paste the copied text on the page (Mac).

   The inserted text appears on the same line as the existing text.

3. Use the Clean Up Word HTML command, place the insertion point to the left of the text "Questions you may have," then click **Horizontal Rule** in the Common category on the Insert panel.

   A horizontal rule appears and separates the unordered list from the text you just imported.

4. Select the text beginning with "How do I schedule" and ending with the last sentence on the page.

5. Click the **Ordered List button** 📑 in the HTML Property inspector to format the selected text as an ordered list.

6. Deselect the text, then compare your screen to Figure 6.

*You imported text on the spa page. You also added a horizontal rule to help organize the page. Finally, you formatted selected text as an ordered list.*

**FIGURE 6**

*Creating an ordered list*

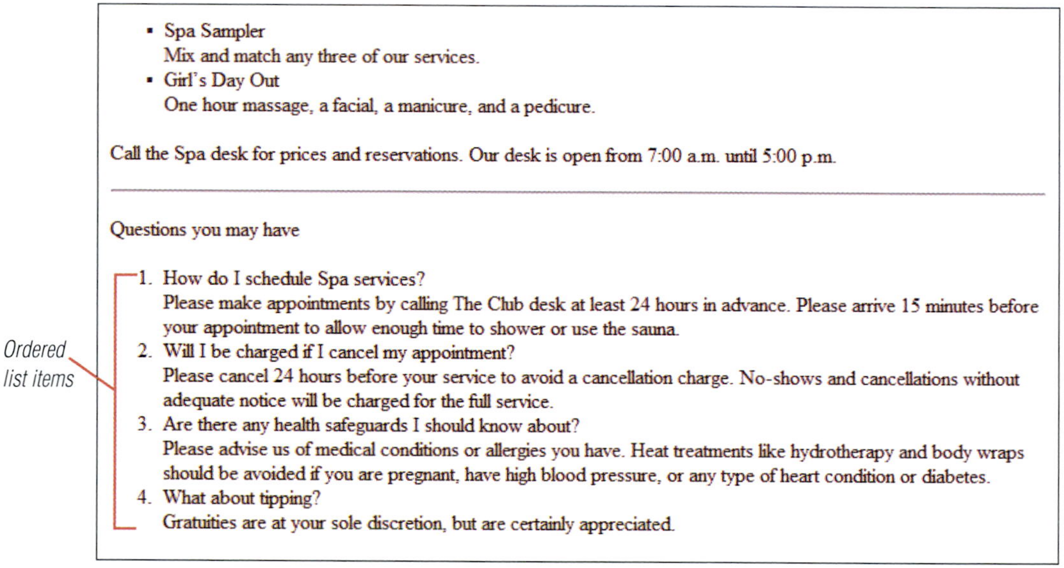

- Spa Sampler
  Mix and match any three of our services.
- Girl's Day Out
  One hour massage, a facial, a manicure, and a pedicure.

Call the Spa desk for prices and reservations. Our desk is open from 7:00 a.m. until 5:00 p.m.

Questions you may have

*Ordered list items*

1. How do I schedule Spa services?
   Please make appointments by calling The Club desk at least 24 hours in advance. Please arrive 15 minutes before your appointment to allow enough time to shower or use the sauna.
2. Will I be charged if I cancel my appointment?
   Please cancel 24 hours before your service to avoid a cancellation charge. No-shows and cancellations without adequate notice will be charged for the full service.
3. Are there any health safeguards I should know about?
   Please advise us of medical conditions or allergies you have. Heat treatments like hydrotherapy and body wraps should be avoided if you are pregnant, have high blood pressure, or any type of heart condition or diabetes.
4. What about tipping?
   Gratuities are at your sole discretion, but are certainly appreciated.

FIGURE 7

*Spa page with ordered list*

Formatted heading

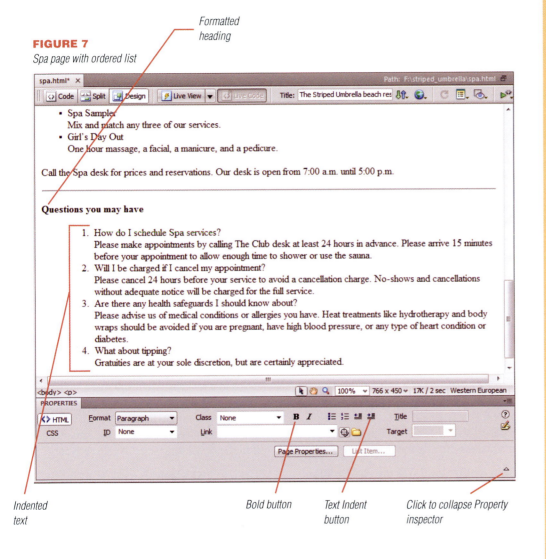

Indented text

Bold button

Text Indent button

Click to collapse Property inspector

**Format an ordered list**

**1.** Select the heading "Questions you may have," then click the **Bold button** B in the HTML Property inspector.

**2.** Select the four questions and answers text, click the **Text Indent button** in the HTML Property inspector, deselect the text, then compare your screen to Figure 7. The Text Indent and Text Outdent buttons are used to indent selected text or remove an indent from selected text.

> TIP If you want to see more of your web page in the Document window, you can collapse the Property inspector.

**3.** Save your work.

*You formatted the "Questions you may have" heading. You also indented the four questions and answers text.*

# CREATE, APPLY, AND EDIT
## CASCADING STYLE SHEETS

## What You'll Do

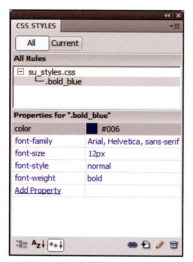

 *In this lesson, you will create a Cascading Style Sheet file for The Striped Umbrella website. You will also create a rule named bold_blue and apply it to text on the spa page.*

### Understanding Cascading Style Sheets

CSS are made up of sets of formatting attributes called **rules,** which define the formatting attributes for individual styles, and are classified by where the code is stored. Sometime "style" and "rule" are used interchangeably, but this is not technically accurate. The code can be saved in a separate file (**external style sheet**), as part of the head content of an individual web page (**internal or embedded styles**) or as part of the body of the HTML code (**inline styles**). External CSS style sheets are saved as files with the .css extension and are stored in the directory structure of a website. Figure 8 shows a style sheet named su_styles.css. This style sheet contains a rule called bold_blue. External style sheets are the preferred method for creating and using styles.

CSS are also classified by their type. A **Class type** can be used to format any page element. An **ID type** and a **Tag type** are used to redefine an HTML tag. A **Compound** type is used to format a selection. In this chapter, we will use class type stored in external style sheet files.

### Using the CSS Styles Panel

You use the buttons on the CSS Styles panel to create, edit, and apply rules. To add a rule, use the New CSS Rule dialog box to name the rule and specify whether to add it to a new or existing style sheet. You then use the CSS Rule definition dialog box to set the formatting attributes for the rule. Once you add a new rule to a style sheet, it appears in a list in the CSS Styles panel. To apply a rule, you select the text to which you want to apply the rule, and then choose a rule from the Targeted Rule list in the CSS Property inspector. You can apply CSS styles to elements on a single web page or to all of the pages in a website. When you make a change to a rule, all page elements formatted with that rule are automatically updated. Once you create a CSS style sheet, you can attach it to the remaining pages in your website.

The CSS Styles panel is used for managing your styles. The Properties pane displays properties for a selected rule at the bottom of the panel. You can easily change a property's value by clicking an option from a drop-down window.

## Comparing the Advantages of Using Style Sheets

You can use CSS styles to save an enormous amount of time. Being able to define a rule and then apply it to page elements on all the pages of your website means that you can make hundreds of formatting changes in a few minutes. In addition, style sheets create a more uniform look from page to page and they generate cleaner code. Using style sheets separates the development of content from the way the content is presented. Pages formatted with CSS styles are much more compliant with current accessibility standards than those with manual formatting.

QUICKTIP

For more information about Cascading Style Sheets, visit www.w3.org or play the audio/video tutorials at www.adobe.com/go/vid0152.

## Understanding CSS Style Sheet Code

You can see the code for a CSS rule by opening a style sheet file. A CSS style consists of two parts: the selector and the declaration. The **selector** is the name of the tag to which the style declarations have been assigned. The **declaration** consists of the property and the value. For example, Figure 9 shows the code for the su_styles.css style sheet. In this example, the first property listed for the .bold_blue rule is font-family. The value for this property is Arial, Helvetica, sans-serif. When you create a new CSS, you will see it as an open document in the Document window. Save this file as you make changes to it.

**FIGURE 8**

*Cascading Style Sheet file created in striped_umbrella root folder*

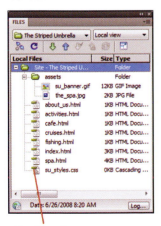

*New Cascading Style Sheet file*

Property · Value · **FIGURE 9**

*su_styles.css file*

```
1   .bold_blue {
2       font-family: Arial, Helvetica, sans-serif;
3       font-size: 14px;
4       font-style: normal;
5       font-weight: bold;
6       color: #306;
7   }
8   .heading {
9       font-family: Arial, Helvetica, sans-serif;
10      font-size: 16px;
11      font-style: normal;
12      font-weight: bold;
13      color: #036;
14      text-align: center;
15  }
16  .paragraph_text {
17      font-family: Arial, Helvetica, sans-serif;
18      font-size: 14px;
19      font-style: normal;
20  }
21
```

## Create a Cascading Style Sheet and a rule

1. Click the **CSS button**  in the Property inspector to switch to the CSS Property inspector, as shown in Figure 10.

   From this point forward, we will use CSS rather than HTML tags to format most text.

2. Click **Window** on the Application bar (Win) or Menu bar (Mac), then click **CSS Styles** to open the CSS Styles panel.

3. Click the **Switch to All (Document) Mode button**, click the **New CSS Rule button** in the CSS Styles panel to open the New CSS Rule dialog box, verify that Class (can apply to any HTML element) is selected under Selector Type, then type **bold_blue** in the Selector Name text box.

   > TIP   Class names are preceded by a period. If you don't enter a period when you type the name, Dreamweaver will add the period for you.

4. Click the **Rule Definition list arrow**, click **(New Style Sheet File)**, compare your screen with Figure 11, then click **OK**.

5. Type **su_styles** in the File name text box (Win) or the Save As text box (Mac), then click **Save** to open the CSS Rule Definition for .bold_blue in su_styles.css dialog box.

   The .bold_blue rule will be stored within the su_styles.css file.

   *(continued)*

CSS button

Options in the Proper... inspector change depending on whether the HTML or CSS button is selected

**FIGURE 11**
*New CSS Rule Dialog box*

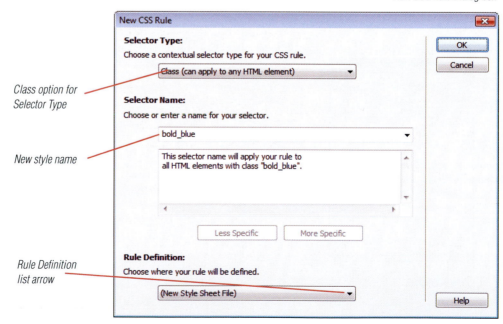

Class option for Selector Type

New style name

Rule Definition list arrow

FIGURE 12

*CSS Rule Definition for .bold_blue in the su_styles.css dialog box*

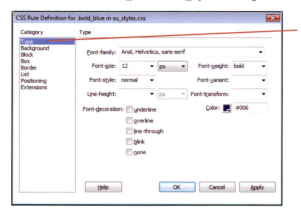

Type category
selected

**FIGURE 13**

*CSS Styles panel with bold_blue rule added*

bold_blue
rule

Properties for
bold_blue
rule

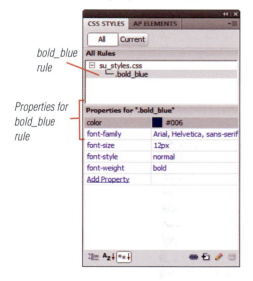

6. Verify that Type is selected in the Category list, set the Font-family to **Arial, Helvetica, sans-serif**, set the Font-size to **12 px**, set the Font-weight to **bold**, set the Font-style to **normal**, set the Color to **#006**, compare your screen to Figure 12, then click **OK**.

   TIP  You can modify the font combinations in the Font-family list by clicking Format on the Application bar (Win) or Menu bar (Mac), pointing to Font, then clicking Edit Font List.

7. Click the **plus sign** (Win) or the **expander arrow** (Mac) next to su_styles.css in the CSS Styles panel and expand the panel (if necessary) to list the bold_blue style, then select the **bold_blue style**.

   The CSS rule named .bold_blue and the properties appear in the CSS Styles panel, as shown in Figure 13.

   *You created a Cascading Style Sheet file named su_styles.css and a rule called .bold_blue.*

---

**DESIGN**TIP  **Choosing fonts**

There are two classifications of fonts: sans-serif and serif. Sans-serif fonts are block-style characters that are often used for headings and subheadings. The headings in this book use a sans-serif font. Examples of sans-serif fonts include Arial, Verdana, and Helvetica. Serif fonts are more ornate and contain small extra strokes at the beginning and end of the characters. Some people consider serif fonts easier to read in printed material, because the extra strokes lead your eye from one character to the next. This paragraph you are reading uses a serif font. Examples of serif fonts include Times New Roman, Times, and Georgia. Many designers feel that a sans-serif font is preferable when the content of a website is primarily intended to be read on the screen, but that a serif font is preferable if the content will be printed. When you choose fonts, you need to keep in mind the amount of text each page will contain and whether most viewers will read the text on-screen or print it. A good rule of thumb is to limit each website to no more than three font variations.

---

## Apply a rule in a Cascading Style Sheet

1. Click **View** on the Application bar (Win) or Menu bar (Mac), point to **Toolbars**, then click **Style Rendering**.

   TIP You can also right-click on an empty area on an open toolbar to see the displayed and hidden toolbars. The displayed toolbars have a check next to them. To display or hide a toolbar, click it.

2. Verify that the **Toggle Displaying of CSS Styles button** ![CSS] on the Style Rendering toolbar is active, as shown in Figure 14.

   TIP You can determine if the Toggle Displaying of CSS Styles button is active if it has an outline around the button. As long as this button is active, you do not have to display the toolbar on the screen.

   You use the Toggle Displaying of CSS Styles button to see how styles affect your page. If it is not active, you will not see the effects of your styles.

3. Select the text "Revitalizing Facial," as shown in Figure 15, click the **Targeted Rule text box** in the Property inspector, then click **bold_blue**, as shown in Figure 15.

4. Repeat Step 3 to apply the bold_blue style to each of the spa services bulleted items in the unordered lists, then compare your screen to Figure 16.

   TIP You can use the keyboard shortcut [Ctrl][Y] (Win) or [Command][Y] (Mac) to repeat the previous action.

   *You applied the bold_blue style to each item in the Spa Services category lists.*

**FIGURE 14**
*Style Rendering toolbar*

*Toggle Displaying of CSS Styles button*

**FIGURE 15**

*Applying a CSS rule to selected text*

*Toggle Displaying of CSS Styles button*

*Rule applied*

*Click to apply bold_blue rule to selected text*

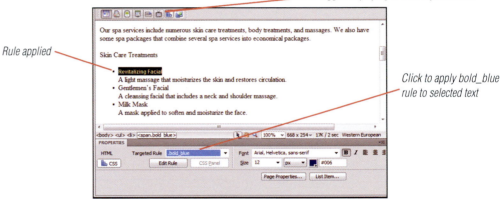

**FIGURE 16**

*Unordered list with bold_blue rule applied*

*bold_blue rule applied to each of the Spa Services items*

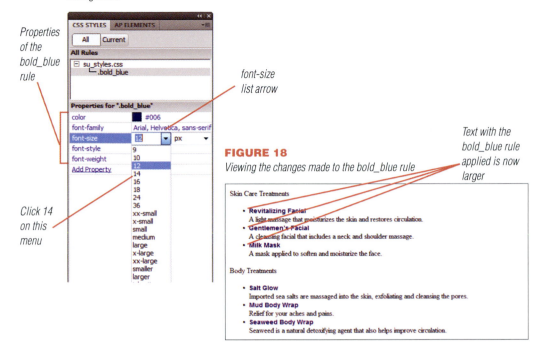

FIGURE 17
*Editing a rule*

Properties of the bold_blue rule

font-size list arrow

Click 14 on this menu

**FIGURE 18**
*Viewing the changes made to the bold_blue rule*

Text with the bold_blue rule applied is now larger

Skin Care Treatments

• **Revitalizing Facial**
  A light massage that moisturizes the skin and restores circulation.
• **Gentlemen's Facial**
  A cleansing facial that includes a neck and shoulder massage.
• **Milk Mask**
  A mask applied to soften and moisturize the face.

Body Treatments

• **Salt Glow**
  Imported sea salts are massaged into the skin, exfoliating and cleansing the pores.
• **Mud Body Wrap**
  Relief for your aches and pains.
• **Seaweed Body Wrap**
  Seaweed is a natural detoxifying agent that also helps improve circulation.

## Using the Style Rendering toolbar

The Style Rendering toolbar allows you to render your page as different media types, such as print, TV, or handheld. To display it when a page is open, click View on the Application bar (Win); or Menu bar (Mac), point to Toolbars, and then click Style Rendering. The buttons on the Style Rendering toolbar allow you to see how your page will look as you select different media types. The next to the last button on the toolbar is the Toggle Displaying of CSS Styles button, which you can use to view how a page looks with styles applied. It works independently of the other buttons. The last button is the Design-time Style Sheets button, which you can use to show or hide particular combinations of styles while you are working in the Document window.

## Edit a rule in a Cascading Style Sheet

**1.** Click **.bold_blue** in the CSS Styles panel.

The rule's properties and values appear in the Properties pane, the bottom part of the CSS Styles panel.

> TIP Click the plus sign (Win) or expander arrow (Mac) to the left of su_styles.css in the CSS Styles panel if you do not see .bold_blue. Click the plus sign (Win) or expander arrow (Mac) to the left of <style> if you do not see su_styles.css.

**2.** Click **12px** in the CSS Styles panel, click the **font-size list arrow**, click **14** as shown in Figure 17, then compare your screen to Figure 18.

All of the text to which you applied the bold_blue style is larger, reflecting the changes you made to the bold_blue rule. You can also click the **Edit Rule button** in the CSS Styles panel to open the CSS Rule Definition for .bold_blue dialog box.

> TIP If you position the insertion point in text that has a CSS rule applied to it, that rule is displayed in the Targeted Rule text box in the Property inspector.

**3.** Use the File, Save All command to save the spa page and the style sheet file.

**4.** Hide the Style Rendering toolbar.

*You edited the bold_blue style to change the font size to 14 pixels. You then viewed the results of the edited rule in the unordered list.*

## View code with the Code Navigator

1. Point to the text "Revitalizing Facial" and hover until the Click indicator to bring up the Code Navigator icon  is displayed, as shown in Figure 19.

2. Click the **Click indicator to bring up the Code Navigator icon** .

   A window opens, as shown in Figure 20, with the name of the style sheet that is linked to this page (su_styles.css) and the name of the rule in the style sheet that has been applied to this text (bold_blue).

   TIP  You can also [Alt]-click (Win) or [Command][Option]-click (Mac) the text on the page to display the Code Navigator.

3. Position your cursor over the bold_blue rule name to see the properties of the rule displayed, as shown in Figure 21.

   *You displayed the Code Navigator to view the properties of the bold_blue rule.*

**FIGURE 19**

*Viewing the Click indicator to bring up the Code Navigator icon*

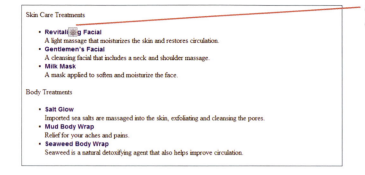

Click indicator to bring up the Code Navigator icon

**FIGURE 20**

*Viewing the Code Navigator*

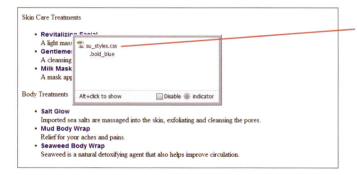

Window displays the name of the style sheet file and rule applied from the style sheet

**FIGURE 21**

*Viewing rule properties and values*

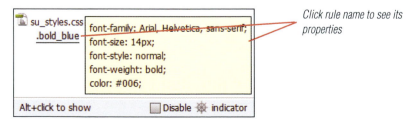

Click rule name to see its properties

FIGURE 22

*Using Code and Design views to view rule properties*

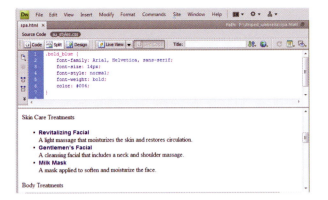

**FIGURE 23**

*Using Code and Design views to edit a rule*

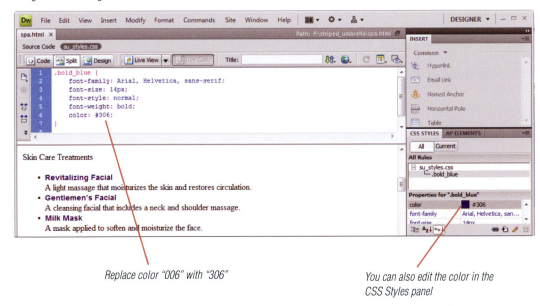

Replace color "006" with "306"

You can also edit the color in the
CSS Styles panel

**1.** Click **.bold_blue** in the Code Navigator.

The document window is split into two sections. The top section displays the code for the CSS file and the bottom section displays the page in Design view, as shown in Figure 22.

**2.** Type directly in the code to replace the color "006" with the color "306" as shown in Figure 23.

**3.** Save all files.

The font color has changed in Design view to reflect the new shade of blue in the rule.

TIP You can also edit the rule properties in the CSS Styles panel.

**4.** Click the Show Design view button [Design].

*You changed the color property in the .bold_blue rule.*

# ADD RULES AND ATTACH
## CASCADING STYLE SHEETS

*In this lesson, you will add a style to a Cascading Style Sheet. You will then attach the style sheet file to the index page and apply one of the styles to text on the page.*

### Understanding External and Embedded Style Sheets

When you are first learning about CSS, the terminology can be very confusing. In the last lesson, you learned that external style sheets are a separate file in a website saved with the .css file extension. You also learned that CSS can be part of an HTML file, rather than a separate file. These are called internal, or embedded, style sheets. External CSS files are created by the web designer. Embedded style sheets are created automatically if the designer does not create them, using default names for the rules. The code for these rules will reside in the head content for that page. These rules will be automatically named style1, style2, and so on. You can rename the rules as they are created to make them more recognizable for you to use, for example, paragraph_text, subheading, or address. Embedded style sheets apply only to a single page, although you can copy them into the code in other pages. Remember that style sheets can be used to format much more than text objects. They can be used to set the page background, link properties, tables, or determine the appearance of almost any object on the page. Figure 24 shows the code for some embedded rules. The code resides in the head content of the web page.

When you have several pages in a website, you will probably want to use the same CSS style sheet for each page to ensure that all your elements have a consistent appearance. To attach a style sheet to another document, click the Attach Style Sheet button on the CSS Styles panel to open the Attach External Style Sheet dialog box, make sure the Add as Link option is selected, browse to locate the file you want to attach, and then click OK. The rules contained in the attached style sheet will appear in the CSS Styles panel, and you can use them to apply rules to text on the page. External style sheets can be attached, or linked, to any page. This is an extremely powerful tool. If you decide to make a change in a rule, it will automatically be made to every object that it formats.

**FIGURE 24**

*Code for embedded rules shown in Code view*

*Rules are embedded in the head content rather than in an external style sheet file*

```
1   <!DOCTYPE html PUBLIC "-//W3C//DTD XHTML 1.0 Transitional//EN"
    "http://www.w3.org/TR/xhtml1/DTD/xhtml1-transitional.dtd">
2   <html xmlns="http://www.w3.org/1999/xhtml">
3   <head>
4   <meta http-equiv="Content-Type" content="text/html; charset=utf-8" />
5   <title>The Striped Umbrella beach resort and spa, Ft. Eugene, Florida</title>
6   <style type="text/css">
7   <!--
8   body {
9       background-color: #FFF;
10  }
11  .nav_bar {
12      font-size: large;
13      font-family: Arial, Helvetica, sans-serif;
14  }
15  .body_text {
16      font-size: medium;
17      font-family: Arial, Helvetica, sans-serif;
18  }
19  .small_text {
20      font-size: 10px;
21      font-family: Arial, Helvetica, sans-serif;
22  }
23  -->
24  </style>
```

## Add rules to a Cascading Style Sheet

1. Click the **New CSS Rule button** 🗗 in the CSS Styles panel.

2. Type **heading** in the Selector Name text box, as shown in Figure 25, then click **OK**.

3. Set the Font-family to **Arial**, **Helvetica**, **sans-serif**, set the Font-size to **16**, set the Font-style to **normal**, set the Font-weight to **bold**, set the Color to **#036**, compare your screen to Figure 26, then click **OK**.

4. Click the **Edit Rule button** 🖉.

5. Click the **Block category** in the CSS Rule Definition for .heading in su_styles.css dialog box, click the **Text align list arrow**, click **center**, as shown in Figure 27, then click **OK**.

6. Select the heading text "Spa Services," click the **HTML button** ⟨⟩ HTML in the Property inspector, set the Format to **Paragraph,** then click the **CSS button** 🖺 CSS in the Property inspector.

   **TIP**  Before you apply a style to selected text, you need to remove all formatting attributes such as font and color from that text, or the style will not be applied correctly.

7. Click the **Targeted Rule list arrow** in the Property inspector, then click **heading** to apply it to the Spa Services heading.

8. Repeat Steps 1 through 3 to add another rule called **paragraph_text** with the **Arial**, **Helvetica**, **sans-serif** Font-family, size **14**, and **normal** style.

9. Repeat Steps 6 and 7 to apply the paragraph_text style to the all the text on the page except for the blue text that already has the bold_blue style applied to it and the heading text "Questions you may have."

*(continued)*

**FIGURE 25**

*Adding a rule to a CSS Style sheet*

New rule name

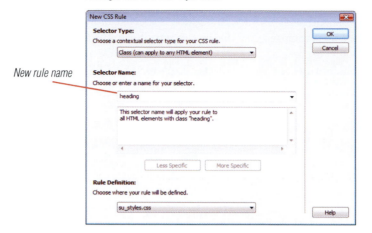

**FIGURE 26**

*Formatting options for heading rule*

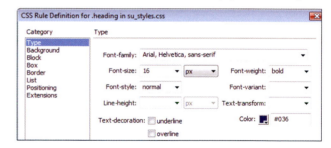

**FIGURE 27**

*Setting text alignment for heading rule*

Block category selected

Text align list arrow

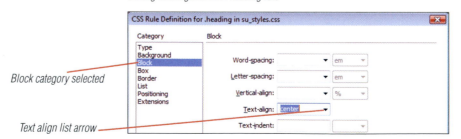

FIGURE 28
Spa page with style sheet applied to rest of text on page

heading rule
applied

paragraph_text
rule applied

Spa Services

Our spa services include numerous skin care treatments, body treatments, and massages. We also have some spa packages that combine several spa services into economical packages.

Skin Care Treatments

- **Revitalizing Facial**
  A light massage that moisturizes the skin and restores circulation.
- **Gentlemen's Facial**
  A cleansing facial that includes a neck and shoulder massage.
- **Milk Mask**
  A mask applied to soften and moisturize the face.

su_styles.css style sheet selected

**FIGURE 29**
Attaching a style sheet to a file

Link option
button

**FIGURE 30**
Viewing the code to link the CSS style sheet file

```
26  <meta name="Description" content="The Striped Umbrella is a full-service resort and spa
    just steps from the Gulf of Mexico in Ft. Eugene, Florida." />
27  <link href="su_styles.css" rel="stylesheet" type="text/css" />
28  </head>
29
30  <body>
31  <p><img src="assets/su_banner.gif" alt="The Striped Umbrella banner" width="735" height=
    "125" /><br />
32      <span class="nav_bar"><a href="index.html">Home</a> - <a href="about_us.html">About Us</a
    > - <a href="spa.html">Spa</a> - <a href="cafe.html">Cafe</a> - <a href="activities.html">
    Activities</a></a></span><br />
33  </p>
34  <hr align="left" width="735" />
35  <p class="paragraph_text">Welcome to The Striped Umbrella - a full-service resort and spa
    just steps from the Gulf of Mexico and ten miles east of Crab Key, Florida. Come enjoy the
    best of both worlds, a secluded sandy beach populated with beautiful birds, yet a  short
    drive down the road from world-class shopping, restaurants,  and entertainment. Bring a
    good book and leave your laptop at the office. You won't want to  go home!</p>
```

Code linking external style
sheet file to the index page

Code that applies the paragraph_text rule from the
external style sheet to the paragraph

**10.** Select the heading text **Questions you may have**, click the **HTML button** `<> HTML`, click the **Bold button** `B` to remove the bold setting, click the **CSS button** `CSS`, click the **Targeted Rule list arrow**, then click **heading** to apply the heading rule.

**11.** Click **File** on the Application bar (Win) or Menu bar (Mac), then click **Save All**, to save both the spa page and the su_styles.css file.

The styles are saved and applied to the text, as shown in Figure 28.

> TIP  You must save the open su_styles.css file after editing it, or you will lose your changes.

*You added two new rules called heading and paragraph_text to the su_styles.css file. You then applied the two rules to selected text.*

## Attach a style sheet

**1.** Close the spa page and open the index page.

**2.** Click the **Attach Style Sheet button** on the CSS Styles panel.

**3.** Browse to select the file su_styles.css (if necessary), click **OK** (Win) or click **Choose** (Mac), verify that the **Link option button** is selected, as shown in Figure 29, then click **OK**.

**4.** Select the opening paragraph text and the contact information paragraph, click the **HTML button** `<> HTML`, set the Format to **Paragraph**, click the **CSS button** `CSS`, click the **Targeted Rule text box**, then click **paragraph_text**.

**5.** Click the **Show Code view button** `Code` and view the code that links the su_styles.css file to the index page, as shown in Figure 30.

**6.** Click the **Show Design view button** `Design`, save your work, then close the index page.

*You attached the su_styles.css file to the index.html page and applied the paragraph_text rule to selected text on the page.*

# INSERT AND ALIGN
## GRAPHICS

## What You'll Do

*In this lesson, you will insert five images on the about_us page in The Striped Umbrella website. You will then stagger the alignment of the images on the page to make the page more visually appealing.*

### Understanding Graphic File Formats

When you add graphics to a web page, it's important to choose the appropriate file format. The three primary graphic file formats used in web pages are **GIF** (Graphics Interchange Format), **JPEG** (Joint Photographic Experts Group), and **PNG** (Portable Network Graphics). GIF files download very quickly, making them ideal to use on web pages. Though limited in the number of colors they can represent, GIF files have the ability to show transparent areas. JPEG files can display many colors. Because they often contain many shades of the same color, photographs are often saved in JPEG format. Files saved with the PNG format can display many colors and use various degrees of transparency, called **opacity**. While the GIF format is subject to licensing restrictions, the PNG format is free to use. However, not all older browsers support the PNG format.

### QUICKTIP

The status bar displays the download time for the page. Each time you add a new graphic to the page, you can see how much additional time is added to the total download time.

### Understanding the Assets Panel

When you add a graphic to a website, it is automatically added to the Assets panel. The **Assets panel**, located in the Files panel group, displays all the assets in a website. The Assets panel contains nine category buttons that you use to view your assets by category. These include Images, Colors, URLs, SWF, Shockwave, Movies, Scripts, Templates, and Library. To view a particular type of asset, click the appropriate category button. The Assets panel is split into two panes. When you click the Images button, as shown in Figure 31, the lower pane displays a list of all the images in your site and is divided into five columns. The top pane displays a thumbnail of the selected image in the list. You can view assets in each category in two ways. You can use the Site option button to view all the assets in a website, or you can use the Favorites option button to view those assets that you have designated as **favorites**, or assets that you expect to use repeatedly while you work on the site. You can use the Assets panel to add an asset to a web page by dragging the asset from the Assets panel to the page or by using the Insert button on the Assets panel.

### Inserting Files with Adobe Bridge

You can manage project files, including video and Camera Raw files, with a file-management tool called Adobe Bridge. Bridge is an easy way to view files outside the website before bringing them into the website. It is an integrated application, working with other Adobe programs such as Photoshop and Illustrator. You can also use Bridge to add meta tags and search text to your files. To open Bridge, click the Browse in Bridge command on the File menu or click the Browse In Bridge button on the Standard toolbar.

### Aligning Images

When you insert an image on a web page, you need to position it in relation to other elements on the page. Positioning an image is referred to as **aligning** an image. By default, when you insert an image in a paragraph, its bottom edge aligns with the baseline of the first line of text or any other element in the same paragraph. When you select an image, the Align text box in the Property inspector displays the alignment setting for the image. You can change the alignment setting using the options in the Align menu in the Property inspector.

**FIGURE 31**
The Assets panel

Drag title bar to undock tab group

Images button

Category buttons

Site option button

Favorites option button

Thumbnail of selected image

List of images in website

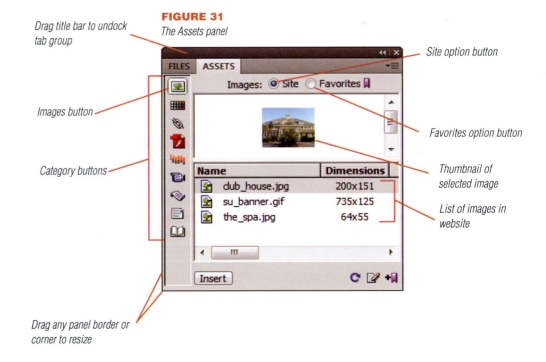

Drag any panel border or corner to resize

## Insert a graphic

1. Open dw3_1.html from where you store your Data Files, then save it as **about_us.html** in the striped_umbrella root folder.

2. Click **Yes** (Win) or **Replace** (Mac) to overwrite the existing file, click **No** to Update Links, then close dw3_1.html.

3. Click the **Attach Style Sheet button** in the CSS Styles panel, attach the su_styles.css style sheet, select the paragraphs of text on the page, click the **HTML button**, verify that the Style is set to **Paragraph**, click the **CSS button** then apply the paragraph_text rule to all of the paragraph text on the page.

4. Place the insertion point before "When" inthe first paragraph, click the **Images list arrow** in the Common category in the Insert panel if necessary, then click **Image** to open the Select Image Source dialog box.

5. Navigate to the assets folder where you store your Data Files, double-click **club_house.jpg**, type the alternate text **Club House** if prompted, click **OK**, open the Files panel if necessary, then verify that the file was copied to your assets folder in the striped_umbrella root folder.

   Compare your screen to Figure 32.

6. Click the **Assets panel tab** in the Files tab group, click the **Images button** in the Assets panel (if necessary), then click the **Refresh Site List button** in the Assets panel to update the list of images in The Striped Umbrella website.

   The Assets panel displays a list of all the images in The Striped Umbrella website, as shown in Figure 33.

*You inserted one image on the about_us page and copied it to the assets folder of the website.*

**FIGURE 32**

*The Striped Umbrella about_us page with inserted image*

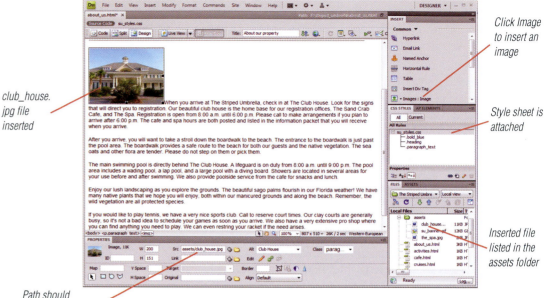

*Click Image to insert an image*

*Style sheet is attached*

*club_house. jpg file inserted*

*Path should begin with the word "assets"*

*Inserted file listed in the assets folder*

**FIGURE 33**

*Image files for The Striped Umbrella website listed in Assets panel*

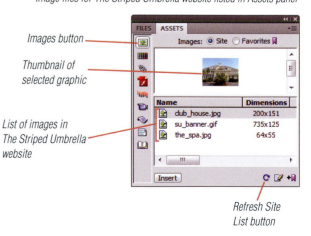

*Images button*

*Thumbnail of selected graphic*

*List of images in The Striped Umbrella website*

*Refresh Site List button*

*Working with Text and Images*

**FIGURE 34**

*Using Adobe Bridge*

*Your path may differ*

*Folders panel*

*Folders tab*

*boardwalk.jpg image is selected in Content panel*

*Preview panel*

*Metadata and Keywords panels*

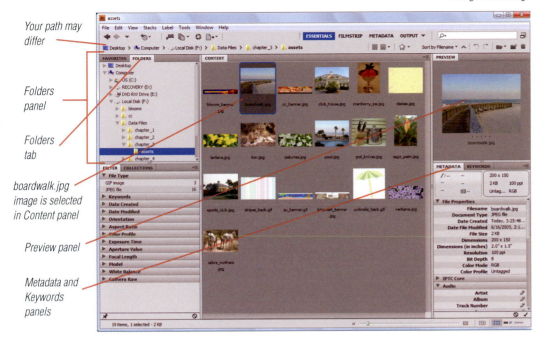

## Use Adobe Bridge

1. Click to place the insertion point before the word "After" at the beginning of the second paragraph.

2. Click **File** on the Application bar (Win) or Menu bar (Mac) click **Browse in Bridge,** close the dialog box asking if you want Bridge to start at login (if necessary), click the **Folders tab**, navigate to where you store your Data Files, then click the thumbnail image **board-walk.jpg** in the assets folder, as shown in Figure 34. If a dialog box opens asking if you want Bridge to launch at startup, click **Yes** or **No**, depending on your personal preference.

   Bridge is divided into several panels; files and folders are listed in the Folders Panel. The files in the selected folder appear in the Content Panel. A picture of the file appears in the Preview Panel. The Metadata and Keywords Panels list any tags that have been added to the file.

3. Click **File** on the Application bar (Win) or Menu bar (Mac), point to **Place**, then click **In Dreamweaver**.

4. Type the alternate text **Boardwalk to the beach,** if prompted, then click **OK**.

   The image appears on the page.

   TIP You can also click the Browse in Bridge button on the Standard toolbar to open Bridge.

*(continued)*

---

### Using Favorites in the Assets panel

The assets in the Assets panel can be listed two ways: Site and Favorites. The Site option lists all of the assets in the website in the selected category in alphabetical order. As your list of assets grows, you can designate some of the assets that are used more frequently as Favorites for quicker access. To add an asset to the Favorites list, right-click (Win) or [control]-click (Mac) the asset name in the Site list, and then click Add to Favorites. When an asset is placed in the Favorites list, it is still included in the Site list. To delete an asset from the Favorites list, click the Favorites option button in the Assets panel, select the asset you want to delete, and then press [Delete] or the Remove from Favorites button on the Assets panel. If you delete an asset from the Favorites list, it still remains in the Site list. You can further organize your Favorites list by creating folders for similar assets and grouping them inside the folders.

**5.** Repeat Steps 1–4 to place the **pool.jpg**, **sago_palm.jpg**, and **sports_club.jpg** files at the beginning of each of the succeeding paragraphs, adding appropriate alternate text if prompted for the pool, sago palm, and sports club images.

After refreshing, your Assets panel should resemble Figure 35.

*You inserted four images using Adobe Bridge on the about_us page and copied each image to the assets folder of The Striped Umbrella website.*

## Align an image

**1.** Scroll to the top of the page, click the **club house image**, then expand the Property inspector (if necessary).

Because an image is selected, the Property inspector displays tools for setting the properties of an image.

**2.** Click the **Align list arrow** in the Property inspector, then click **Left**.

The club house photo is now left-aligned with the text and the paragraph text flows around its right edge, as shown in Figure 36.

(continued)

**FIGURE 35**
*Assets panel with seven images*

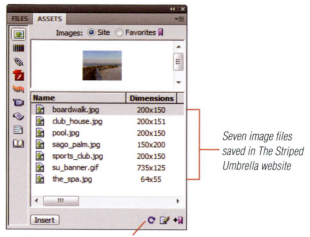

*Seven image files saved in The Striped Umbrella website*

*Click Refresh Site List button to refresh file list*

**FIGURE 36**
*Left-aligned club house image*

*Left-aligned club house image*

*Text wrapped around club house image*

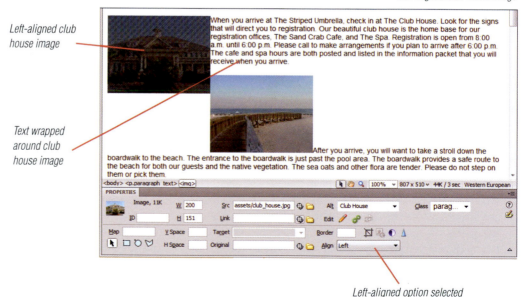

*Left-aligned option selected*

## FIGURE 37
*Aligned images on the about_us page*

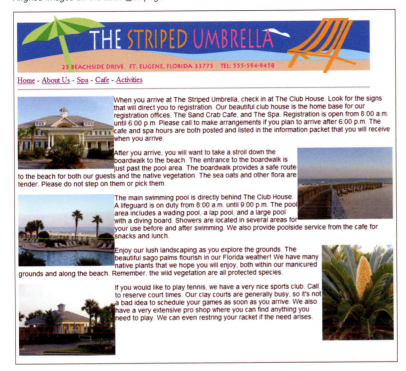

3. Select the boardwalk image, click the **Align list arrow** in the Property inspector, then click **Right**.

4. Align the pool image, using the **Left Align** option.

5. Align the sago palm image, using the **Right Align** option.

6. Align the sports club image, using the **Left Align** option.

7. Save your work.

8. Preview the web page in your browser, compare your screen to Figure 37, then close your browser.

9. Close Adobe Bridge.

*You used the Property inspector to set the alignment for the five images. You then previewed the page in your browser.*

## Graphics versus images

Two terms that sometimes seem to be used interchangeably are graphics and images. For the purposes of discussion in this text, we will use the term **graphics** to refer to the appearance of most non-text items on a web page such as photographs, logos, navigation bars, Flash animations, graphs, background images, and drawings. Files such as these are called graphic files. They are referred to by their file type, or graphic file format, such as JPEG (Joint Photographic Experts Group), GIF (Graphics Interchange Format), or PNG (Portable Network Graphics). We will refer to the actual pictures that you see on the pages as images. Don't worry about which term to use. Many people use one term or the other according to habit or region, or use them interchangeably.

# ENHANCE AN IMAGE AND
## USE ALTERNATE TEXT

## What You'll Do

*In this lesson, you will add borders to images, add horizontal and vertical space to set them apart from the text, and then add alternate text to each image on the page.*

### Enhancing an Image

After you place an image on a web page, you have several options for **enhancing** it, or improving its appearance. To make changes to the image itself, such as removing scratches from it, or erasing parts of it, you need to use an image editor such as Adobe Fireworks or Adobe Photoshop. To edit an image directly in Fireworks from Dreamweaver, first select the image, and then click Edit in the Property inspector. This will open the Fireworks program if it is installed on your computer.

Complete your editing, and then click Done to return to Dreamweaver.

**QUICK**TIP

You can copy a Photoshop PSD file directly into Dreamweaver. After inserting the image, Dreamweaver will prompt you to optimize the image for the web.

You can use Dreamweaver to enhance certain aspects of how images appear on a page. For example, you can add borders around an image or add horizontal and

**DESIGN**TIP  **Resizing graphics using an external editor**

Each image on a web page takes a specific number of seconds to download, depending on the size of the file. Larger files (in kilobytes, not width and height) take longer to download than smaller files. It's important to determine the smallest acceptable size for an image on your web page. Then, if you need to resize an image to reduce the file size, use an external image editor to do so, *instead* of resizing it in Dreamweaver. Although you can adjust the width and height settings of an image in the Property inspector to change the size of the image as it appears on your screen, these settings do not affect the file size. Decreasing the size of an image using the H (height) and W (width) settings in the Property inspector does *not* reduce the time it will take the file to download. Ideally you should use images that have the smallest file size and the highest quality possible, so that each page downloads as quickly as possible.

vertical space. **Borders** are frames that surround an image. Horizontal and vertical space is blank space above, below, and on the sides of an image that separates the image from text or other elements on the page. Adding horizontal or vertical space is the same as adding white space, and helps images stand out on a page. In the web page shown in Figure 38, the horizontal and vertical space around the images helps make these images more prominent. Adding horizontal or vertical space does not affect the width or height of the image. Spacing around web page objects can also be created by using "spacer" images, or clear images that act as placeholders.

## Using Alternate Text

One of the easiest ways to make your web page viewer-friendly and accessible to people of all abilities is to use alternate text. **Alternate text** is descriptive text that appears in place of an image while the image is downloading or when the mouse pointer is placed over it. You can program some browsers to display only alternate text and to download images manually. Alternate text can be "read" by a **screen reader**, a device used by persons with visual impairments to convert written text on a computer monitor to spoken words. Screen readers and alternate text make it possible for viewers who have visual impairments to have an image described to them in detail. One of the default preferences in Dreamweaver is to

prompt you to enter alternate text whenever you insert an image on a page.

The use of alternate text is the first checkpoint listed in the World Wide Web Consortium (W3C) list of Priority 1 accessibility checkpoints. The Priority 1 checkpoints dictate the most basic level of accessibility standards to be used by web developers today. The complete list of these and the other priority-level checkpoints are listed on the W3C website, www.w3.org (use the search "text accessibility level checkpoints"). You should always strive to meet these criteria for all web pages.

**FIGURE 38**
*National Park Service website*

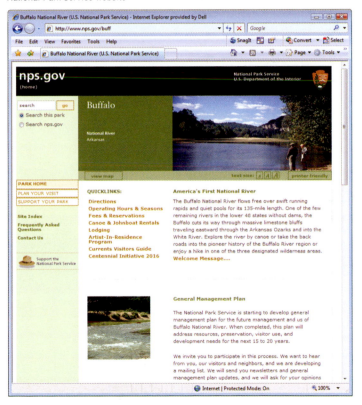

*National Park Service website – www.nps.gov*

## Add a border

1. Select the club house image, then expand the Property inspector (if necessary).

2. Type **1** in the Border text box, press **[Tab]** to apply the border to the club house image, then select the image, as shown in Figure 39.

   The border setting is not visible until you preview the page in a browser.

3. Repeat Step 2 to add borders to the other four images.

*You added a 1-pixel border to each image on the about_us page.*

## Add horizontal and vertical space

1. Select the club house image, type **7** in the V Space text box in the Property inspector, press **[Tab]**, type **7** in the H Space text box, press **[Tab]**, then compare your screen to Figure 40.

   The text is more evenly wrapped around the image and is easier to read, because it is not so close to the edge of the image.

2. Repeat Step 1 to set the V Space and H Space to 7 for the other four images.

   The spacing under each picture differs because of the difference in the lengths of the paragraphs.

*You added horizontal spacing and vertical spacing around each image on the about_us page.*

**FIGURE 39**

*Using the Property inspector to add a border*

Selected image with 1-pixel border

V Space text box          H Space text box          Border text box

**FIGURE 40**

*Comparing images with and without horizontal and vertical space*

Image with horizontal and vertical space

Image without horizontal and vertical space

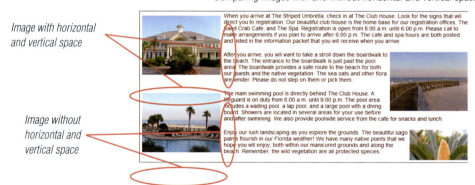

*Working with Text and Images*

FIGURE 41
Viewing the Image Preview dialog box

Options tab —

File tab —

Format list arrow

Format options

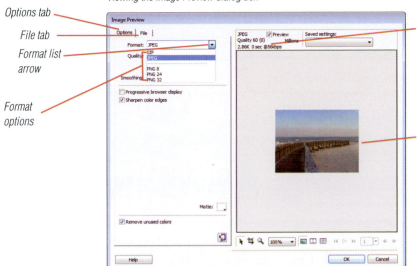

The file size and download time will increase or decrease as you edit the settings

Preview panel shows a thumbnail of the selected image

### Edit image settings

1. Select the **boardwalk image**.

2. Click the **Edit Image Settings button**  in the Property inspector, then click the **Format list arrow** on the Options tab, as shown in Figure 41.

   You can use this dialog box to save a copy of the image using a different file format. File property options will be displayed depending on which format you choose. It is important to note that no matter which settings you choose in this dialog box, the original file will not be altered. A duplicate copy of the file will be altered and saved when you finish editing the image.

3. Choose a PNG format, then notice the difference in file size displayed in the Preview panel.

4. Experiment with different file formats and settings, then click **Cancel** to close the dialog box without making any changes to the image.

   TIP In addition to being able to save an image using different file formats on the Options tab, you can also use the File tab to scale or resize an image.

*You experimented with file format settings in the Image Preview dialog box, then closed the dialog box without making any changes.*

### Integrating Photoshop CS4 with Dreamweaver

Dreamweaver has many functions integrated with Photoshop CS4. This new partnership includes the ability to copy and paste a Photoshop PSD file directly from Photoshop into Dreamweaver. After using the Paste command, Dreamweaver will prompt you to optimize the image by choosing a file format and settings for the web. After optimization, Dreamweaver will then paste the image on the page. If you want to edit the image later, simply double-click the image in Dreamweaver and it will open in Photoshop.

Photoshop users can set Photoshop as the default image editor in Dreamweaver. Click Edit on the Application bar, click Preferences, (Win) or click Dreamweaver, click Preferences (Mac) click File Types/Editors, click the Editors plus sign button, select a file format, then use the dialog box to browse to Photoshop (if you don't see it listed already), and then click Make Primary. Search the Adobe website for a tutorial on Photoshop and Dreamweaver integration.

## Edit alternate text

1. Select the club house image, select any existing text in the Alt text box in the Property inspector (if necessary), type **The Striped Umbrella Club House** as shown in Figure 42, then press **[Enter]** (Win) or **[return]** (Mac).

2. Save your work, preview the page in your browser, then point to the **club house image** until the alternate text appears, as shown in Figure 43. (*Hint*: You may not see the alternate text in some browsers.)

3. Close your browser.

4. Select the boardwalk image, type **The board-walk to the beach** in the Alt text box, replacing any existing text, then press **[Enter]** (Win) or **[return]** (Mac).

5. Repeat Step 4 to add the alternate text **The pool area** to the pool image.

6. Repeat Step 4 to add the alternate text **Lush sago palm** to the sago palm image.

7. Repeat Step 4 to add the alternate text **The Sports Club** to the sports club image.

8. Save your work.

9. Preview the page in your browser, view the alternate text for each image, then close your browser.

*You edited the alternate text for five images on the page, then you viewed the alternate text in your browser.*

**FIGURE 42**
*Alternate text setting in the Property inspector*

Alt text box

**FIGURE 43**
*Alternate text displayed in browser*

Alternate text appears
when triggered by the
mouse pointer

## FIGURE 44
*Preferences dialog box with Accessibility category selected*

Accessibility category

Check boxes for Form objects, Frames, Media, and Images

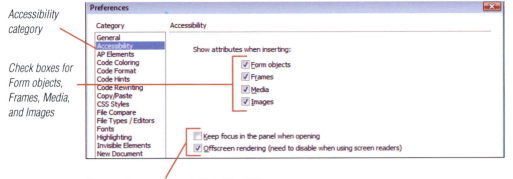

These options are not available in Mac OS X

1. Click **Edit** on the Application bar (Win) or **Dreamweaver** (Mac) on the Menu bar, click **Preferences** to open the Preferences dialog box, then click the **Accessibility category**.

2. Verify that the four attributes check boxes are checked, as shown in Figure 44, check them if they are not checked, then click **OK**.

   TIP   Once you set the Accessibility preferences, they will be in effect for all websites that you develop, not just the one that's open when you set them.

*You set the Accessibility preferences to prompt you to enter alternate text each time you insert a form object, frame, media, image, or object on a web page.*

## POWER USER SHORTCUTS

| to do this: | use this shortcut: |
|---|---|
| Switch views | [Ctrl][`] (Win) or [control][`] (Mac) |
| Insert image | [Ctrl][Alt][I] (Win) or ⌘ [option][I] (Mac) |
| Indent text | [Ctrl][Alt][]] (Win) or ⌘ [option][]] (Mac) |
| Outdent text | [Ctrl][Alt][[] (Win) or ⌘ [option][[] (Mac) |
| Align Left | [Ctrl][Alt][Shift][L] (Win) or ⌘ [option][shift][L] (Mac) |
| Align Center | [Ctrl][Alt][Shift][C] (Win) or ⌘ [option][shift][C] (Mac) |
| Align Right | [Ctrl][Alt][Shift][R] (Win) or ⌘ [option][shift][R] (Mac) |
| Align Justify | [Ctrl][Alt][Shift][J] (Win) or ⌘ [option][shift][J] (Mac) |
| Bold | [Ctrl][B] (Win) or ⌘ [B] (Mac) |
| Italic | [Ctrl][I] (Win) or ⌘ [I] (Mac) |
| Refresh | [F5] |
| Browse in Bridge | [Ctrl][Alt][O] (Win) or ⌘ [option][O] (Mac) |

# INSERT A BACKGROUND IMAGE
## AND PERFORM SITE MAINTENANCE

## What You'll Do

 *In this lesson, you will insert two types of background images. You will then use the Assets panel to delete them both from the website. You will also check for non-web-safe colors in the Assets panel.*

### Inserting a Background Image

You can insert a background image on a web page to provide depth and visual interest to the page, or to communicate a message or mood. **Background images** are image files used in place of background colors. Although you can use background images to create a dramatic effect, you should avoid inserting them on web pages where they would not provide the contrast necessary for reading page text. Even though they might seem too plain, standard white backgrounds are usually the best choice for web pages. If you choose to use a background image on a web page, it should be small in file size. You can insert either a small image file that is tiled, or repeated, across the page or a larger image that is not repeated across the page. A tiled image will download much faster than a large image. A **tiled image** is a small image that repeats across and down a web page, appearing as individual squares or rectangles. When you create a web page, you can use either a background color or a background image,

but not both, unless you have a need for the background color to be displayed while the background image finishes downloading. The background in the web page shown in Figure 45 uses an ocean-wave graphic, which ties to the restaurant name "Mermaids" and the ocean theme for the restaurant decor. This image background does not compete with the text on the page, however, because a solid black background is placed behind the text and in front of the image background. This can be done using tables or CSS blocks.

### Managing Images

As you work on a website, you might find that you accumulate files in your assets folder that the website does not use. To avoid accumulating unnecessary files, it's a good idea to look at an image first, before you place it on the page and copy it to the assets folder. If you inadvertently copy an unwanted file to the assets folder, you should delete it or move it to another location. This is a good website management practice that will prevent the assets folder from filling up with unwanted image files.

Removing an image from a web page does not remove it from the assets folder in the local root folder of the website. To remove an asset from a website, you first locate the file you want to remove in the Assets panel. You then use the Locate in Site command to open the Files panel with the unwanted file selected. You can then use the Delete command to remove the file from the site.

**QUICK**TIP

You cannot use the Assets panel to delete a file. You must use the Files panel to delete files and perform all file-management tasks.

## Removing Colors from a Website

You can use the Assets panel to locate non-web-safe colors in a website. **Non-web-safe** colors are colors that may not be displayed uniformly across computer platforms. After you replace a non-web-safe color with another color, you should use the Refresh Site List button on the Assets panel to verify that the color has been removed. Sometimes it's necessary to press [Ctrl] (Win) or ⌘ (Mac) while you click the Refresh Site List button. If refreshing the Assets panel does not work, try re-creating the site cache, and then refreshing the Assets panel.

**QUICK**TIP

To re-create the site cache, click Site on the Application bar (Win) or Menu bar (Mac), point to Advanced, then click Recreate Site Cache.

**FIGURE 45**

*Mermaids website*

*Mermaids website used with permission from Mermaids Restaurant and Catering - www.mermaids.ws*

## Insert a background image

1. Click **Modify** on the Application bar (Win) or Menu bar (Mac), then click **Page Properties** to open the Page Properties dialog box.

2. Click the **Appearance (CSS) category**, if necessary.

3. Click **Browse** next to the Background image text box, navigate to the assets folder where you store your Data Files, then double-click **umbrella_back.gif**.

4. Click **OK** to close the Page Properties dialog box, then click the **Refresh Site List button**  to refresh the file list in the Assets panel. The umbrella_back.gif file is automatically copied to The Striped Umbrella assets folder.

   A file with a single umbrella forms a background made up of individual squares, replacing the white background, as shown in Figure 46. It is much too busy and makes it difficult to read the page.

5. Repeat Steps 1–4 to replace the umbrella_back.gif background image with stripes_back.gif, located in the chapter_3 assets folder.

   As shown in Figure 47, the striped background is also tiled, but with vertical stripes, so you aren't aware of the small squares making up the pattern. It is still too busy, though.

*You applied a tiled background to the about_us page. Then you replaced the tiled background with another tiled background that was not as busy.*

**FIGURE 46**
*The About Us page with a busy tiled background*

*Each umbrella is a small square that forms a tiled background*

**FIGURE 47**
*The about_us page with a more subtle tiled background*

*It is harder to tell where each square ends*

*Working with Text and Images*

**FIGURE 48**

*Removing a background image*

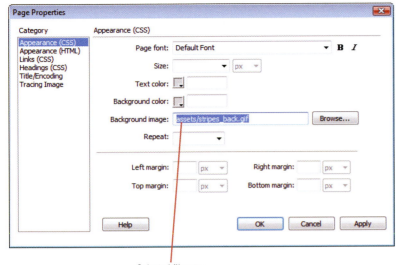

Selected filename

1. Click **Modify** on the Application bar (Win) or Menu bar (Mac), click **Page Properties**, then click **Appearance (CSS).**

2. Select the text in the Background image text box, as shown in Figure 48, press **[Delete]**, then click **OK**.

   The background of the about_us page is white again.

3. Save your work.

*You deleted the link to the background image file to change the about_us page background back to white.*

## Understanding HTML body tags

When you are setting page preferences, it is helpful to understand the HTML tags that are being generated. Sometimes it's much easier to make changes to the code, rather than use menus and dialog boxes. The <body> </body> tags define the beginning and end of the body section of a web page. The page content falls between these two tags. If you want to change the page properties, additional codes must be added to the <body> tag. Adding a color to the background will add a style to the page; for example, "body { Background-color:#000; }". If you insert an image for a background, the code will read "body { background-image: url assets/stripes.gif); }".

## Delete files from a website

1. Click the **Assets panel tab**, then click the **Images button** 🖼 (if necessary).

2. Refresh the Assets panel, right-click (Win) or [control]-click (Mac) **stripes_back.gif** in the Assets panel, click **Locate in Site** to open the Files panel, select **stripes_back.gif** on the Files panel (if necessary), press **[Delete]**, then click **Yes** in the dialog box that appears.

   TIP  Refresh the Assets panel if you still see the file listed.

3. Click the Assets panel tab, then repeat Step 2 to remove umbrella_back.gif from the website, open the Assets panel, then refresh the Assets panel.

   TIP  If you delete a file on the Files panel that has an active link to it, you will receive a warning message. If you rename a file on the Files panel that has a link to it, the Files panel will update the links to correctly link to the renamed file. To rename a file, right-click (Win) or [control]-click (Mac) the file you want to rename, point to Edit, click Rename, then type the new name.

   Your Assets panel should resemble Figure 49.

   *You removed two image files from The Striped Umbrella website, then refreshed the Assets panel.*

FIGURE 49
*Images listed in Assets panel*

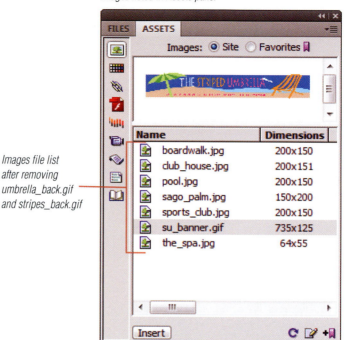

Images file list after removing umbrella_back.gif and stripes_back.gif

## Managing image files

It is a good idea to store original unedited copies of your website image files in a separate folder, outside the assets folder of your website. If you edit the original files, save them again using different names. Doing this ensures that you will be able to find a file in its original, unaltered state. You may have files on your computer that you are currently not using at all; however, you may need to use them in the future. Storing currently unused files also helps keep your assets folder free of clutter. Storing copies of original website image files in a separate location also ensures that you have back-up copies in the event that you accidentally delete a file from the website.

FIGURE 50
*Colors listed in Assets panel*

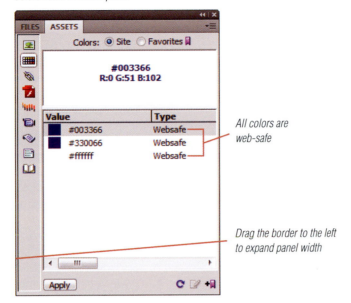

All colors are
web-safe

Drag the border to the left
to expand panel width

## Check for Non-web-safe colors

1. Click the **Colors button**  in the Assets panel to display the colors used in the website, then drag the left border of the Assets panel to display the second column, (if necessary), as shown in Figure 50.

   The two blue colors listed are not actually in the page code for the about_us page, but are in the attached style sheet.

   The Assets panel does not list any non-web-safe colors.

   > TIP  If you see a non-web-safe color listed, click Site on the Application bar (Win) or Menu bar (Mac), point to Advanced, then click Recreate Site Cache. The non-web-safe color should then be removed from the Assets panel. This should also remove any colors you have experimented with, unless you have saved a page with a color left on it. If you see an extra color, use the Find and Replace command to locate it, then remove it from the page and refresh the Assets panel again.

2. Save your work, preview the page in your browser, close your browser, then close all open files.

*You checked for non-web-safe colors in the Assets panel list of colors.*

## Using color in compliance with accessibility guidelines

The second guideline listed in the World Wide Web Consortium (W3C) list of Priority 1 Checkpoints is to not rely on the use of color alone. This means that if your website content is dependent on your viewer correctly seeing a color, then you are not providing for those people who cannot distinguish between certain colors or do not have monitors that display color.

Be especially careful when choosing color used with text to provide a good contrast between the text and the background. It is better to reference colors as numbers, rather than names. For example, use "#FFF" instead of "white." Using style sheets for specifying color formats is the preferred method for coding. For more information, see the complete list of priority level checkpoints listed on the W3C website, www.w3.org.

### Create unordered and ordered lists.

1. Open the blooms & bulbs website.
2. Open the tips page.
3. Select the four lines of text below the Seasonal Gardening Checklist heading and format them as an unordered list. (*Hint*: If each line does not become a separate list item, enter a paragraph break between each line, then remove any extra spaces.)
4. Select the lines of text below the Basic Gardening Tips heading and format them as an ordered list. (Refer to the Step 3 hint if each line does not become a separate list item.)
5. Indent the unordered list items one stop, then change the bullet format to square.
6. Save your work.

### Create, apply, and edit Cascading Style Sheets.

1. Create a new CSS rule named **bold_blue**, making sure that the Class option button is selected in the Selector Type section and that the (New Style Sheet File) option button is selected in the Rule Definition section of the New CSS Rule dialog box.
2. Click OK, name the style sheet file **blooms_styles** in the Save Style Sheet File As dialog box, then click Save.
3. Choose the following settings for the bold_blue style: Font-family = Arial, Helvetica, sans-serif; Font-size = large; Font-style = normal; Font-weight = bold; and Font-color = #036.

4. Apply the bold_blue style to the names of the seasons in the Seasonal Gardening Checklist: Fall, Winter, Spring, and Summer.
5. Edit the bold_blue style by changing the font size to 16 pixels.

### Add rules and attach Cascading Style Sheets.

1. Add an additional style called **headings** in the blooms_styles.css file and define this style choosing the following type settings: Font-family = Arial, Helvetica, sans-serif; Font-size = large; Font-style = normal; Font-weight = bold; and Font-color = #036.
2. Apply the headings style to the two sub-headings on the page: Seasonal Gardening Checklist and Basic Gardening Tips. (*Hint*: Make sure you remove any manual formatting before applying the style.)
3. Create a new rule named **paragraph_text** in the blooms_styles.css file with the Arial, Helvetica, sans-serif, size 14 font.
4. Apply the paragraph_text rule to the rest of the text on the page that has not been previously formatted with a rule, then save the page.
5. Open the index page and attach the blooms_styles.css file.
6. Select both the introductory paragraph and the contact information paragraph, remove the body_text rule from the text, and apply the paragraph_text rule. If necessary, add a paragraph break after the introductory paragraph.
7. Click File on the Application bar (Win) or Menu bar (Mac), click Save All, then view

both pages in the browser. (*Hint:* If previewing the page in Internet Explorer 7, click the Information bar when prompted to allow blocked content.)
8. Close the browser and all open pages.

### Insert and align graphics.

1. Open dw3_2.html from where you store your Data Files, then save it as **plants.html** in the blooms & bulbs website, overwriting the existing plants.html. Do not update links.
2. Verify that the path of the blooms & bulbs banner is set correctly to the assets folder in the blooms root folder.
3. Set the Accessibility preferences to prompt you to add alternate text to images (if necessary).
4. Use Adobe Bridge to insert the petunias.jpg file from the assets folder where you store your Data Files to the left of the words "Pretty petunias" and add **Petunias** as alternate text.
5. Use Bridge to insert the verbena.jpg file from assets folder where you store your Data Files in front of the words "Verbena is one" and add **Verbena** as alternate text.
6. Insert the lantana.jpg file from the assets folder where you store your Data Files in front of the words "Dramatic masses" and add **Lantana** as alternate text.
7. Refresh the Files panel to verify that all three images were copied to the assets folder.
8. Left-align the petunias image.
9. Right-align the verbena image.
10. Left-align the lantana image.
11. Save your work.

### Enhance an image and use alternate text.

1. Apply a 1-pixel border, vertical spacing of 10 pixels, and horizontal spacing of 20 pixels around the petunias image.

2. Apply a 1-pixel border, vertical spacing of 10 pixels, and horizontal spacing of 20 pixels around the verbana image.

3. Apply a 1-pixel border, vertical spacing of 10 pixels, and horizontal spacing of 20 pixels around the lantana image.

4. Attach the blooms_styles.css file to the page, then apply the headings style to the heading at the top of the page and the paragraph_text to the rest of the text on the page.

5. Save your work, preview it in the browser, then compare your screen to Figure 51.

6. Close the browser and open the tips page and add V Space of 10 and H Space of 10 to the garden_tips.jpg image.

7. Left-align the garden tips image, then compare your screen to Figure 52.

8. Save your work.

### Insert a background image and perform site maintenance.

1. Switch to the plants page, then insert the **daisies.jpg** file as a background image from the assets folder where you store your Data Files.

2. Save your work.

3. Preview the web page in your browser, then close your browser.

4. Remove the daisies.jpg file from the background.

5. Open the Assets panel, then refresh the Files list.

6. Use the Files panel to delete the daisies.jpg file from the list of images.

7. Refresh the Assets panel, then verify that the daisies.jpg file has been removed from the website.

8. View the colors used in the site in the Assets panel, then verify that all are web-safe.

9. Save your work, then close all open pages.

**FIGURE 51**
*Completed Skills Review*

**FIGURE 52**
*Completed Skills Review*

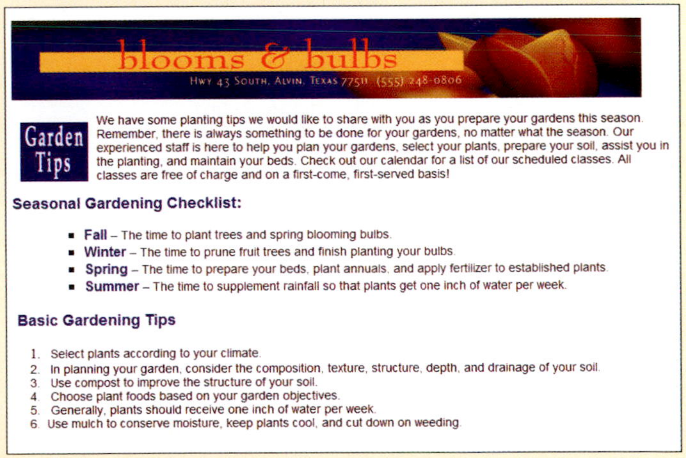

Use Figures 53 and 54 as guides to continue your work on the TripSmart website that you began in Project Builder 1 in Chapter 1, and continued to work on in Chapter 2. You are now ready to format text on the newsletter page and begin work on the destinations page that showcases one of the featured tours to Kenya. You want to include some colorful pictures and attractively formatted text on the page.

1. Open the TripSmart website.
2. Open dw3_3.html from where you store your Data Files and save it in the tripsmart root folder as **newsletter.html**, overwriting the existing newsletter.html file and not updating the links.
3. Verify that the path for the banner is correctly set to the assets folder of the TripSmart website. Create an unordered list from the text beginning "Expandable clothesline" to the end of the page.
4. Create a new CSS rule called **paragraph_text** making sure that the Class option is selected in the Selector Type section and that the (New Style Sheet File) option is selected in the Rule Definition section of the New CSS Rule dialog box.
5. Save the style sheet file as **tripsmart_styles.css** in the TripSmart website root folder.

6. Choose a font, size, style, color, and weight of your choice for the paragraph_text style.
7. Apply the **paragraph_text** style to all of the text on the page except the "Ten Packing Essentials" heading.
8. Create another style called **heading** with a font, size, style, color, and weight of your choice and apply it to the "Ten Packing Essentials" heading.
9. Type **Travel Tidbits** in the Title text box on the Document toolbar, save and close the newsletter page and the tripsmart_styles file, then close the dw3_3.html page.

10. Open dw3_4.html from where you store your Data Files and save it in the tripsmart root folder as **destinations.html**, overwriting the existing destinations.html file. Do not update links.
11. Attach the tripsmart_styles.css style sheet to the page.
12. Insert **zebra_mothers.jpg** from the assets folder where you store your Data Files to the left of the sentence beginning "Our next," then add appropriate alternate text.

**FIGURE 53**

*Sample Project Builder 1*

13. Insert lion.jpg from the assets folder where you store your Data Files to the left of the sentence beginning "This lion", then add appropriate alternate text.

14. Align both images using the Align list arrow in the Property inspector with alignments of your choice, then add horizontal spacing, vertical spacing, or borders if desired.

15. Apply the heading style to the "Destination: Kenya" heading and the paragraph_text style to the rest of the text on the page. Add any necessary paragraph breaks to separate the paragraphs of text.

16. Apply any additional formatting to enhance the page appearance, then add the page title **Destination: Kenya**.

17. Save your work, then preview the destinations page in your browser. (*Hint:* If previewing the page in Internet Explorer 7, click the Information bar when prompted to allow blocked content.)

18. Close your browser, then close all open files.

**FIGURE 54**
*Sample Project Builder 2*

**Destination: Kenya**

Our next Photo Safari to Kenya has now been scheduled with a departure date of May 5 and a return date of May 23. Come join us and take some beautiful pictures like these two Grevy's zebras nursing their young at Samburu National Reserve. Our flight will leave New York for London, where you will have dayrooms reserved before flying all night to Nairobi, Kenya. To provide the finest in personal attention, this tour will be limited to no more than sixteen persons. Game drives will take place early each morning and late afternoon to provide maximum opportunity for game viewing, as the animals are most active at these times. We will visit five game reserves to allow for a variety of animal populations and scenery.

This lion is relaxing in the late afternoon sun. Notice the scar under his right ear. He might have received that when he was booted out of his pride as a young lion. We will be spending most nights in tented camps listening to the night sounds of hunters such as this magnificent animal. Enjoy visiting native villages and trading with the local businessmen. Birding enthusiasts will enjoy adding to their bird lists with Kenya's over 300 species of birds. View the beginning of the annual migration of millions of wildebeest, a spectacular sight. The wildebeest are traveling from the Serengeti Plain to the Mara in search of water and grass. Optional excursions include ballooning over the Masai Mara, fishing on Lake Victoria, camel rides at Amboseli Serena Lodge, and golfing at the Aberdare Country Club. Lake Victoria is the largest freshwater lake in the world.

In this exercise, you continue your work on the Carolyne's Creations website that you started in Project Builder 2 in Chapter 1, and continued to build in Chapter 2. You are now ready to add two new pages to the website. One page will display featured items in the kitchen store and one will be used to showcase a recipe. Figures 55 and 56 show possible solutions for this exercise. Your finished pages will look different if you choose different formatting options.

1. Open the Carolyne's Creations website.
2. Open dw3_5.html from where you store your Data Files, save it to the website root folder as **recipes.html**, overwriting the existing file and not updating the links.
3. Format the list of ingredients as an unordered list.
4. Create a CSS rule named **paragraph_text** and save it in a style sheet filenamed **cc_styles.css** in the website root folder. Use any formatting options that you like, and then apply the paragraph_text rule to all text except the navigation bar and the text "Cranberry Ice" and "Directions."

**FIGURE 55**
*Completed Project Builder 2*

**FIGURE 56**
*Completed Project Builder 2*

5. Create another rule called **heading** using appropriate formatting options and apply it to the text "Cranberry Ice" and "Directions."

6. Create another rule called **nav_bar** using appropriate formatting options and apply it to the navigation bar.

7. Insert the file cranberry_ice.jpg from where you store your Data Files, then place it on the page, using alignment, horizontal space, and vertical space settings. (*Hint*: In Figure 55 the align setting is set to left, H space is set to 30, and V space is set to 10.

8. Add appropriate alternate text to the banner, then save and close the page and the style sheet file.

9. Open dw3_6.html from where you store your Data Files and save it as **shop.html**, overwriting the existing file and not updating the links.

10. Attach the cc_styles.css style sheet and create a new rule named **sub_head** to use in formatting the text "January Specials - Multifunctional Pot and Cutlery Set." Use any formatting options that you like. Apply the nav_bar rule to the navigation bar. Apply the **paragraph_text** rule to the rest of the text on the page.

11. Insert the pot_knives.jpg image from the assets folder where you store your Data Files next to the paragraph beginning

"We try," choosing your own alignment and spacing settings and adding appropriate alternate text.

12. Save the shop page and the style sheet file, then preview both new pages in the browser, (*Hint:* If previewing the page in Internet Explorer 7, click the Information bar when prompted to allow blocked content.)

13. Close your browser, then close all open pages.

# DESIGN PROJECT

Don Chappell is a new sixth-grade history teacher. He is reviewing educational websites for information he can use in his classroom.

1. Connect to the Internet, then navigate to the Library of Congress website at www.loc.gov. The Library of Congress website is shown in Figure 57.
2. Which fonts are used for the main content on the home—serif or sans-serif? Are the same fonts used consistently on the other pages in the site?
3. Do you see ordered or unordered lists on any pages in the site? If so, how are they used?
4. Use the Source command on the View menu to view the source code to see if a style sheet was used.
5. Do you see the use of Cascading Style Sheets noted in the source code?

**FIGURE 57**
*Design Project*

*The Library of Congress website - www.loc.gov*

# PORTFOLIO PROJECT

In this assignment, you will continue to work on the website that you started in Chapter 1, and continued to build in Chapter 2. No Data Files are supplied. You are building this site from chapter to chapter, so you must do each Portfolio Project assignment in each chapter to complete your website.

You continue building your website by designing and completing a page that contains a list, headings, paragraph_text, images, and a background. During this process, you will develop a style sheet and add several rules to it. You will insert appropriate images on your page and enhance them for maximum effect. You will also check for non-web-safe colors and remove any that you find.

1. Consult your storyboard and decide which page to create and develop for this chapter.
2. Plan the page content for the page and make a sketch of the layout. Your sketch should include at least one ordered or unordered list, appropriate headings, paragraph text, several images, and a background color or image. Your sketch should also show where the paragraph text and headings should be placed on the page and what rules should be used for each type of text. You should plan on creating at least two rules.

3. Create the page using your sketch for guidance.
4. Create a Cascading Style Sheet for the site and add to it the rules you decided to use. Apply the rules to the appropriate content.
5. Access the images you gathered in Chapter 2, and place them on the page so that the page matches the sketch you created in Step 2. Add a background image if you want, and appropriate alternate text for each image.
6. Remove any non-web-safe colors.
7. Identify any files in the Assets panel that are currently not used in the site. Decide which of these assets should be removed, then delete these files.

8. Preview the new page in a browser, then check for page layout problems and broken links. Make any necessary corrections in Dreamweaver, then preview the page again in the browser. Repeat this process until you are satisfied with the way the page looks in the browser. (*Hint:* If previewing the page in Internet Explorer 7, click the Information bar when prompted to allow blocked content.)
9. Use the checklist in Figure 58 to check all the pages in your site.
10. Close the browser, then close the open pages.

**FIGURE 58**
*Portfolio Project checklist*

---

**Website Checklist**

1. Does each page have a page title?
2. Does the home page have a description and keywords?
3. Does the home page contain contact information?
4. Does every page in the site have consistent navigation links?
5. Does the home page have a last updated statement that will automatically update when the page is saved?
6. Do all paths for links and images work correctly?
7. Do all images have alternate text?
8. Are all colors web-safe?
9. Are there any unnecessary files you can delete from the assets folder?
10. Is there a style sheet with at least two rules?
11. Did you apply the rules to all text blocks?
12. Do all pages look good using at least two different browsers?

---

# 4

# WORKING WITH
## LINKS

1. Create external and internal links

2. Create internal links to named anchors

3. Create, modify, and copy a navigation bar

4. Create an image map

5. Manage website links

# 4 WORKING WITH
## LINKS

### Introduction

What makes websites so powerful are the links that connect one page to another within a website or to any page on the web. Although you can add graphics, animations, movies, and other enhancements to a website to make it visually attractive, the links you include are often a site's most essential components. Links that connect the pages within a site are always very important because they help viewers navigate between the pages of the site. However, if one of your goals is to keep viewers from leaving your website, you might want to avoid including links to other websites. For example, most e-commerce sites include only links to other pages in the site to discourage shoppers from leaving the site. In this chapter, you will create links to other pages in The Striped Umbrella website and to other sites on the web. You will also insert a navigation bar that contains images instead of text, and check the links in The Striped

Umbrella website to make sure they all work correctly.

### Understanding Internal and External Links

Web pages contain two types of links: internal links and external links. **Internal links** are links to web pages in the same website, and **external links** are links to web pages in other websites or to email addresses. Both internal and external links have two important parts that work together. The first part of a link is the element that viewers see and click on a web page, for example, text, an image, or a button. The second part of a link is the **path**, or the name and location of the web page or file that will open when the element is clicked. Setting and maintaining the correct paths for all your links is essential to avoid having broken links in your site, which can easily cause a visitor to click away immediately.

# Tools You'll Use

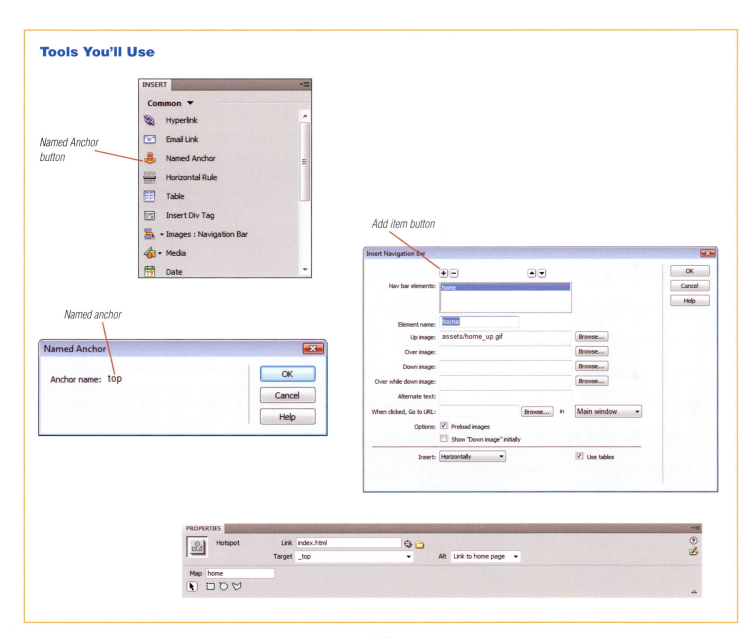

*Named Anchor button*

*Named anchor*

*Add item button*

# CREATE EXTERNAL AND
## INTERNAL LINKS

### What You'll Do

 *In this lesson, you will create external links on The Striped Umbrella activities page that link to websites related to area attractions. You will also create internal links to other pages within The Striped Umbrella website.*

### Creating External Links

A good website often includes a variety of external links to other related websites so that viewers can get more information on a particular topic. To create an external link, you first select the text or object that you want to serve as a link, then you type the absolute path to the destination web page in the Link text box in the Property inspector. An **absolute path** is a path used for external links that includes the complete address for the destination page, including the protocol (such as http://)

and the complete **URL** (Uniform Resource Locator), or address, of the destination page. When necessary, the web page filename and folder hierarchy are also part of an absolute path. Figure 1 shows an example of an absolute path showing the protocol, URL, and filename. An example for the code for an external link would be <a href="http://www.adobe.com"> Adobe website</a>.

### FIGURE 1
*An example of an absolute path*

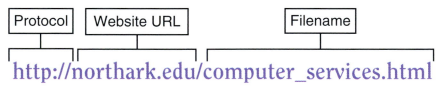

## Creating Internal Links

Each page in a website usually focuses on an individual category or topic. You should make sure that the home page provides links to each major page in the site, and that all pages in the site contain numerous internal links so that viewers can move easily from page to page. To create an internal link, you first select the text element or image that you want to use to make a link, and then use the Browse for File icon next to the Link text box in the HTML Property inspector to specify the relative path to the destination page. A **relative path** is a type of path used to reference web pages and image files within the same website. Relative paths include the filename and folder location of a file. Figure 2 shows an example of a relative path. Table 1 describes absolute paths and relative paths. Relative paths can either be site-root relative or document-relative. You can also use the Point to File icon in the HTML Property inspector to point to the file you want to use for the link, or drag the file you want to use for the link from the Files panel into the Link text box in the Property inspector.

You should take great care in managing your internal links to make sure they work correctly and are timely and relevant to the page content. You should design the navigation structure of your website so that viewers are never more than three or four clicks away from the page they are seeking. An example for the code for a relative internal link would be <a href="activities.html"> Activities</a>.

**FIGURE 2**
*An example of a relative path*

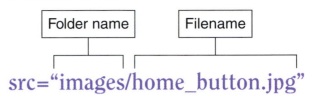

src="images/home_button.jpg"

| TABLE 1: Description of absolute and relative paths | | |
|---|---|---|
| **type of path** | **description** | **examples** |
| Absolute path | Used for external links and specifies protocol, URL, and filename of destination page | http://www.yahoo.com/recreation |
| Relative path | Used for internal links and specifies location of file relative to the current page | spa.html or assets/heron.gif |
| Root-relative path | Used for internal links when publishing to a server that contains many websites or where the website is so large it requires more than one server | /striped_umbrella/activities.html |
| Document-relative path | Used in most cases for internal links and specifies the location of file relative to current page | cafe.html or assets/heron.gif |

## Create an external link

1. Open The Striped Umbrella website, open dw4_1.html from where you store your Chapter 4 Data Files, then save it as **activities** in the striped_umbrella root folder, overwriting the existing activities page, but not updating links.

2. Attach the su_styles.css file, then apply the **paragraph_text rule** to the paragraphs of text on the page (not to the navigation bar).

3. Select the first broken image link, click the **Browse for File icon** next to the Src text box, then select the **heron_waiting_small.jpg** in the Data Files assets folder to save the image in your assets folder.

4. Click on the page next to the broken image link to see the heron_waiting_small image, as shown in Figure 3.

*(continued)*

**FIGURE 3**
*Saving an image file in the assets folder*

Broken image is replaced when file is saved in the assets folder

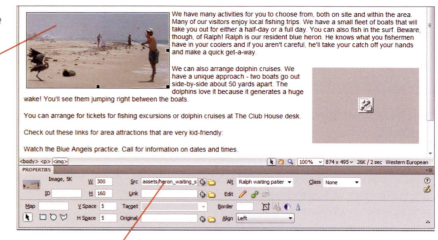

Image is saved in assets folder

## Typing URLs

Typing URLs in the Link text box in the Property inspector can be very tedious. When you need to type a long and complex URL, it is easy to make mistakes and create a broken link. You can avoid such mistakes by copying and pasting the URL from the Address text box (Internet Explorer) or Location bar (Mozilla Firefox) to the Link text box in the Property inspector. Copying and pasting a URL ensures that the URL is entered correctly.

FIGURE 4

*Assets panel with two new images added*

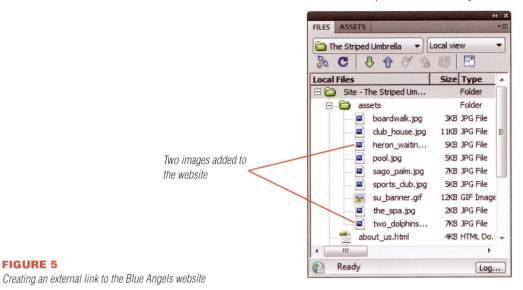

Two images added to
the website

FIGURE 5

*Creating an external link to the Blue Angels website*

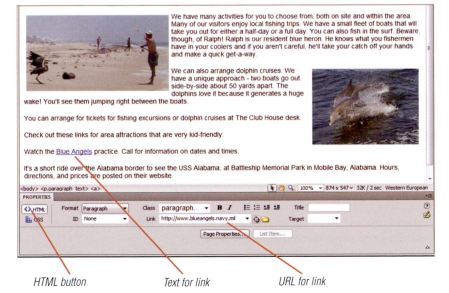

HTML button          Text for link          URL for link

5. Repeat Step 3 for the second image, **two_dolphins_small.jpg**. The two new files are copied into the assets folder, as shown in Figure 4.

6. Scroll down, then select the text "Blue Angels."

7. Click the **HTML button** ⟨⟩ HTML in the Property inspector to switch to the HTML Property inspector, click in the Link text box, type **http://www.blueangels.navy.mil**, press [**Enter**] (Win) or [**return**] (Mac), deselect the link, then compare your screen to Figure 5.

8. Repeat Steps 6 and 7 to create a link for the USS Alabama site in the next paragraph: **http://www.ussalabama.com**.

9. Save your work, preview the page in your browser, test all the links to make sure they work, then close your browser.

> TIP   You must have an active Internet connection to test the links. If clicking a link does not open a page, make sure you typed the URL correctly in the Link text box.

*You opened The Striped Umbrella website, replaced the existing activities page, attached the su_styles.css.file, applied the paragraph_text style to the text, then imported the new images into the site. You added two external links to other sites on the page, then tested each link in your browser.*

## Create an internal link

1. Select the text "fishing excursions" in the third paragraph.

2. Click the **Browse for File icon** 📁 next to the Link text box in the HTML Property inspector, then double-click **fishing.html** in the Select File dialog box to set the relative path to the fishing page.

    Notice that fishing.html appears in the Link text box in the Property inspector, as shown in Figure 6.

    TIP Pressing [F4] will hide or redisplay all panels, including the ones on the right side of the screen.

3. Select the text "dolphin cruises" in the same sentence.

4. Click the **Browse for File icon** 📁 next to the Link text box in the HTML Property inspector, then double-click **cruises.html** in the Select File dialog box to specify the relative path to the cruises page.

    The words "dolphin cruises" are now a link to the cruises page.

5. Save your work, preview the page in your browser to verify that the internal links work correctly, then close your browser.

    The fishing and cruises pages do not have page content yet, but serve as placeholders until they do.

    *You created two internal links on the activities page, and then tested the links in your browser.*

**FIGURE 6**
*Creating an internal link on the activities page*

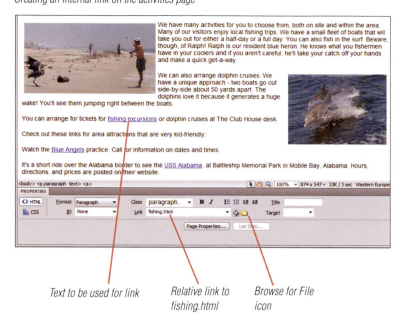

Text to be used for link

Relative link to fishing.html

Browse for File icon

## Using case-sensitive links

When text is said to be "case sensitive," it means that the text will be treated differently when it is typed using uppercase letters rather than lowercase letters, or vice-versa. With some operating systems, such as Windows, it doesn't matter which case you use when you enter URLs. However, with other systems, such as UNIX, it does matter. To be sure that your links will work with all systems, use lowercase letters for all links. This is another good reason to select and copy a URL from the browser address bar, and then paste it in the link text box or code in Dreamweaver when creating an external link. You won't have to worry about missing a case change.

## FIGURE 7
*Assets panel with three external links*

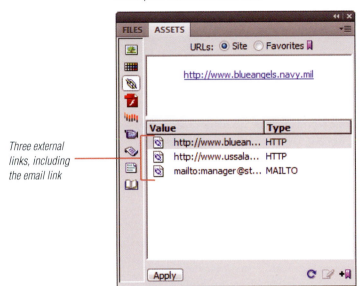

*Three external links, including the email link*

1. Click the **Assets panel tab** to view the Assets panel.

2. Click the **URLs button** 🖉 in the Assets panel.

3. Click the **Refresh Site List button** 🔁 .

   Three links are listed in the Assets panel: one external link for the email link and two external links to the Blue Angels and USS Alabama websites, as shown in Figure 7. Notice that the internal links are not displayed in the Assets panel.

4. Click the **Files panel tab** to view the Files panel.

5. Close the activities page and the dw4_1.html page.

*You viewed the external links on the activities page in the Assets panel.*

# CREATE INTERNAL LINKS
## TO NAMED ANCHORS

## What You'll Do

 *In this lesson, you will insert five named anchors on the spa page: one for the top of the page and four for each of the spa services lists. You will then create internal links to each named anchor.*

### Inserting Named Anchors

Some web pages have so much content that viewers must scroll repeatedly to get to the bottom of the page and then back up to the top of the page. To make it easier for viewers to navigate to specific areas of a page without scrolling, you can use a combination of internal links and named anchors. A **named anchor** is a specific location on a web page that has a descriptive name. Named anchors act as targets for internal links and make it easy for viewers to jump to a particular place on the same page quickly. A **target** is the location on a web page that a browser displays when an internal link is clicked. For example, you can insert a named anchor called "top" at the top of a web page, and then create a link to it from the bottom of the page.

You can also insert named anchors in strategic places on a web page, such as at the beginning of paragraph headings.

You insert a named anchor using the Named Anchor button in the Common category on the Insert panel, as shown in Figure 8. You then enter the name of the anchor in the Named Anchor dialog box. You should choose short names that describe the named anchor location on the page. Named anchors are represented by yellow anchor icons on a web page when viewed in Design view. Selected anchors are represented by blue icons. You can show or hide named anchor icons by clicking View on the Application bar (Win) or Menu bar (Mac), bar, pointing to Visual Aids, and then clicking Invisible Elements.

## Creating Internal Links to Named Anchors

Once you create a named anchor, you can create an internal link to it using one of two methods. You can select the text or image on the page that you want to use to make a link, and then drag the Point to File icon from the Property inspector to the named anchor icon on the page. Or, you can select the text or image to which you want to use to make a link, then type # followed by the named anchor name (such as "#top") in the Link text box in the Property inspector.

**QUICK**TIP

To avoid possible errors, you should create a named anchor before you create a link to it.

**FIGURE 8**

*Using the Point to File icon*

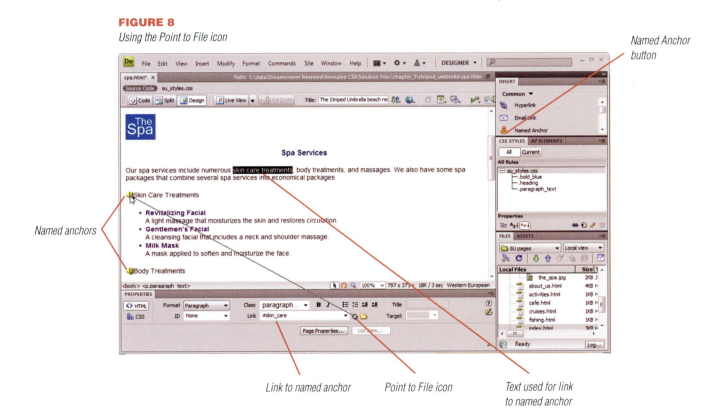

Named Anchor button

Named anchors

Link to named anchor          Point to File icon          Text used for link to named anchor

## Insert a named anchor

1. Open the spa page, click the **banner image** to select it, then press [←] to place the insertion point to the left of the banner.

2. Click **View** on the Application bar (Win) or Menu bar (Mac), point to **Visual Aids**, then verify that Invisible Elements is checked.

   TIP If there is no check mark next to Invisible Elements, this feature is turned off. Click Invisible Elements to turn this feature on.

3. Click the **Common** category on the Insert panel (if necessary).

4. Click **Named Anchor** on the Insert panel to open the Named Anchor dialog box, type **top** in the Anchor name text box, compare your screen with Figure 9, then click **OK**.

   An anchor icon now appears before The Striped Umbrella banner.

   TIP Use lowercase letters, no spaces, and no special characters in named anchor names. You should also avoid using a number as the first character in a named anchor name.

   *(continued)*

**FIGURE 9**
*Named Anchor dialog box*

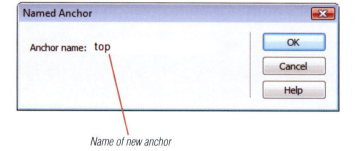

*Name of new anchor*

**FIGURE 10**

*Named anchors on the activities page*

Named anchor icons

Selected named anchor icon

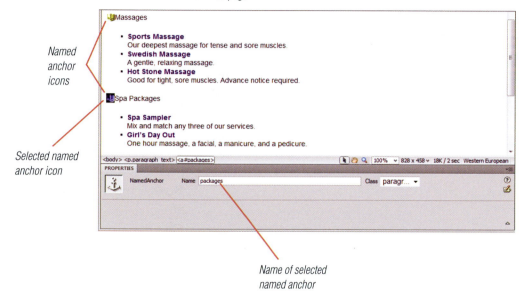

Name of selected named anchor

5. Click to the left of the Skin Care Treatments heading, then insert a named anchor named **skin_care**.

6. Insert named anchors to the left of the Body Treatments, Massages, and Spa Packages headings using the following names: **body_treatments**, **massages**, and **packages**.

Your screen should resemble Figure 10.

*You created five named anchors on the activities page; one at top of the page, and four that will help viewers quickly access the Spa Services headings on the page.*

## Create an internal link to a named anchor

1. Select the words "skin care treatments" in the first paragraph, then drag the **Point to File icon** ⊙ from the Property inspector to the anchor named skin_care, as shown in Figure 11.

   The words "skin care treatments" are now linked to the skin_care named anchor. When viewers click the words "skin care treatments" the browser will display the Skin Care Treatments heading at the top of the browser window.

   TIP   The name of a named anchor is always preceded by a pound (#) sign in the Link text box in the Property inspector.

2. Create internal links for body treatments, massages, and spa packages in the first paragraph by first selecting each of these words or phrases, then dragging the **Point to File icon** ⊙ to the appropriate named anchor icon.

   The words "body treatments," "massages," and "spa packages" are now links that connect to the Body Treatments, Massages, and Spa Packages headings.

   TIP   Once you select the text on the page you want to link, you might need to scroll down to view the named anchor on the screen. Once you see the named anchor on your screen, you can drag the Point to File icon on top of it. You can also move the pointer to the edge of the page window (still in the white area of the page) to scroll the page.

   *(continued)*

**FIGURE 11**

*Dragging the Point to File icon to a named anchor*

*Text to link to named anchor*

*Point to File icon dragged to named anchor*

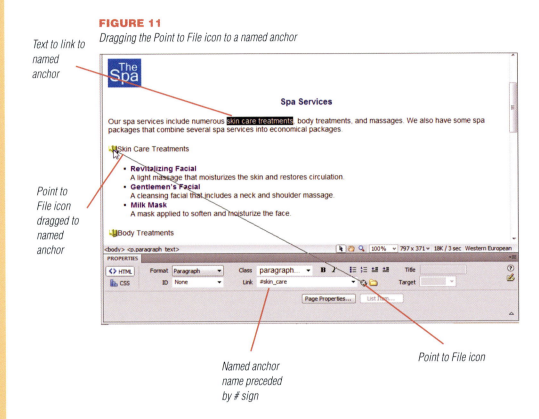

*Named anchor name preceded by # sign*

*Point to File icon*

**FIGURE 12**

*Spa page in Mozilla Firefox with internal links to named anchors*

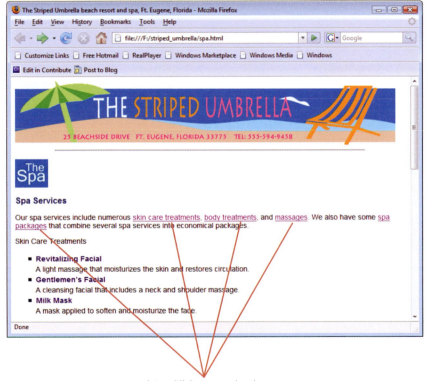

*Internal links to named anchors*

3. Scroll down to the bottom of the page, then place the insertion point at the end of the last sentence on the page.

4. Press [**Enter**] (Win) or [**return**] (Mac) twice to insert two paragraph breaks, then type **Top of page**.

5. Click the **CSS button** 🔲 CSS to switch to the CSS Property inspector, then apply the paragraph_text rule to "Top of Page."

6. Click the **HTML button** <> HTML to switch to the HTML Property inspector, then use the Point to File icon to link the text to the top named anchor.

7. Save your work, preview the page in your browser, as shown in Figure 12, then test the links to each named anchor.

    Notice that when you click the spa packages link in the browser, the associated named anchor appears in the middle of the page instead of at the top. This happens because the spa page is not long enough to position this named anchor at the top of the page.

8. Close your browser.

*You created internal links to the named anchors next to the Spa Services headings and to the top of the spa page. You then previewed the page in your browser and tested each link.*

<br>

**LESSON 3**

# CREATE, MODIFY, AND COPY
## A NAVIGATION BAR

## What You'll Do

*In this lesson, you will create a navigation bar on the spa page that can be used to link to each major page in the website. The navigation bar will have five elements: home, about _us, cafe, spa, and activities. You will also copy the new navigation bar to other pages in the website. On each page you will modify the appropriate element state to reflect the current page.*

### Creating a Navigation Bar Using Images

To make your website more visually appealing, you can create a navigation bar with images rather than text. Any images you use in a navigation bar must be created in a graphics software program, such as Adobe Fireworks or Adobe Illustrator. For a browser to display a navigation bar correctly, all image links in the navigation bar must be exactly the same size. You insert a navigation bar by clicking Insert on the Application bar (Win) or Menu bar (Mac), pointing to Image Objects, then clicking Navigation Bar. The Insert Navigation Bar dialog box appears. You use this dialog box to specify the appearance of each link, called an **element**, in each of four possible states. A **state** is the condition of the element relative to the mouse pointer. The four states are as follows: **Up image** (the state when the mouse pointer is not on top of the element), **Over image** (the state when the mouse pointer is positioned on top of the element), **Down image** (the state when you click the element), and **Over while down image** (the state when the mouse

pointer is positioned over an element that has been clicked). You can create a rollover effect by using different colors or images to represent each element state. You can add many special effects to navigation bars or to links on a web page. For instance, the website shown in Figure 13 contains a navigation bar that uses rollovers and also contains images that link to featured items in the website.

When a navigation bar is inserted on a web page using the Insert Navigation Bar command, JavaScript code is added to the page to make the interaction work with the navigation bar elements. Dreamweaver also creates a Scripts folder and adds it to the root folder to store the newly created AC-RunActiveContent.js file. When a viewer views a web page with one of these navigation bars, the JavaScript that runs is stored on the user's, or client's, computer.

**QUICK**TIP

You can insert only one navigation bar using the Insert, Image Objects, Navigation Bar command or by clicking the Common category in the Insert panel and then selecting Navigation Bar from the Images menu.

## Copying and Modifying a Navigation Bar

After you create a navigation bar, you can reuse it and save time by copying and pasting it to the other main pages in your site. Make sure you place the navigation bar in the same position on each page. This practice ensures that the navigation bar will look the same on each page, making it much easier for viewers to navigate to all the pages in your website. If you are even one line or one pixel off, the navigation bar will appear to "jump" as it changes position from page to page.

You use the Modify Navigation Bar dialog box to customize the appearance of the copied navigation bar on each page. For example, you can change the appearance of the spa navigation bar element on the spa page so that it appears in a different color. Highlighting the navigation element for the current page provides a visual reminder so that viewers can quickly tell which page they are viewing. This process ensures that the navigation bar will not only look consistent across all pages, but will be customized for each page.

**FIGURE 13**
*NASA website*

Navigation bar
with rollovers

Navigation links
with rollovers

Rollover images
serving as links

1. Select the banner on the spa page, press the **right arrow key,** then press **[Shift][Enter]** (Win) or **[Shift][return]** (Mac) to enter a line break after the banner.

   The insertion point is now positioned between the banner and the horizontal rule.

2. Click the **Common** category on the Insert panel (if necessary), click the **Images list arrow,** then click **Navigation Bar.**

3. Type **home** in the Element name text box, in the Insert Navigation Bar dialog box, click the **Insert list arrow** as shown in Figure 14, click **Horizontally** (if necessary), to specify that the navigation bar be placed horizontally on the page.

   Be sure to choose Horizontally for the navigation bar orientation. The two options below the horizontal rule will not be available in the Modify Navigation Bar dialog box. If you miss these settings now, you will either have to make your corrections directly in the code or start over.

4. Click **Browse** next to the Up image text box, navigate to the assets folder where you store your Data Files, then double-click **home_up.gif.**

   The path to the file home_up.gif appears in the Up image text box, as shown in Figure 14.

5. Click **Browse** next to the Over image text box to specify a path to the file home_down.gif located in the chapter_4 Data Files assets folder.

6. Click **Browse** next to the Down image text box to specify a path to the file home_down.gif

   *(continued)*

**FIGURE 14**

*Insert Navigation Bar dialog box*

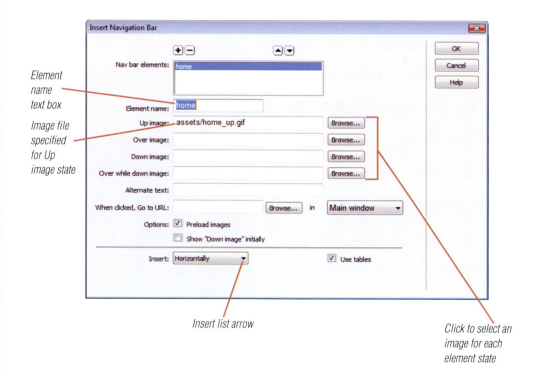

Element name text box

Image file specified for Up image state

Insert list arrow

Click to select an image for each element state

**FIGURE 15**

*Insert Navigation Bar dialog box*

*All states now have an image specified*

*These options will not be available in the Modify Navigation Bar dialog box*

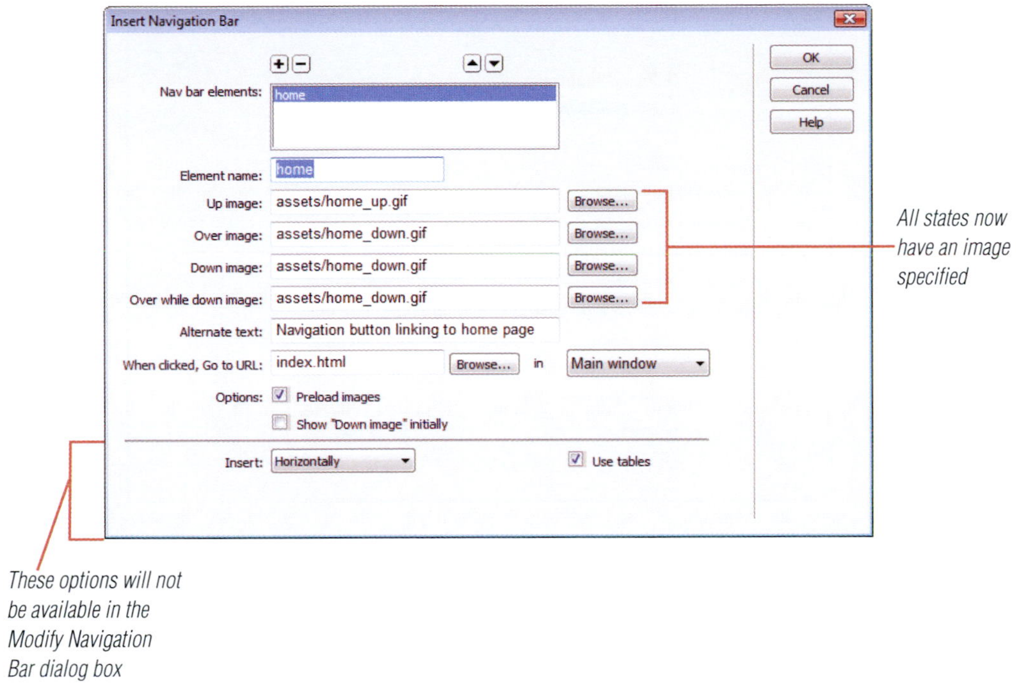

located in the chapter_4 Data Files assets folder, overwriting the existing file.

Because this is a simple navigation bar, you use the home_down.gif image for the Over, Down, and Over while down image states.

> TIP  Instead of clicking Browse in Steps 6 and 7, you could copy the path of the home_down.gif file in the Over image text box and paste it to the Down image and Over while down image text boxes. You could also reference the home_down.gif file in The Striped Umbrella assets folder once it is copied there in Step 5.

**7.** Click **Browse** next to the Over while down image text box to specify a path to the file home_down.gif located in the chapter_4 Data Files assets folder, overwriting the existing file.

By specifying one graphic for the Up image state, and another graphic for the Over image, Down image, and Over while down image states, you will create a rollover effect.

**8.** Type **Navigation button linking to home page** in the Alternate text text box, click **Browse** next to the When clicked, Go to URL text box, double-click **index.html** in the striped_umbrella root folder, then compare your screen to Figure 15.

*You used the Insert Navigation Bar dialog box to create a navigation bar for the spa page and added the home element to it. You used one image for the Up state and one for the other three states.*

## Add elements to a navigation bar

1. Click the **Add item button** ⊞ in the Insert Navigation Bar dialog box, then type **about_us** in the Element name text box.

   TIP You use the Add item button ⊞ to add a new navigation element to the navigation bar, and the Delete item button ⊟ to delete a selected navigation bar element from the navigation bar.

2. Click **Browse** next to the Up image text box, navigate to the chapter_4 assets folder, click **about_us_up.gif**, then click **OK** (Win) or **Choose** (Mac).

3. Click **Browse** next to the Over image text box to specify a path to the file **about_us_down.gif** located in the chapter_4 assets folder.

4. Click **Browse** next to the Down image text box to specify a path to the file **about_us_down.gif** located in the chapter_4 assets folder, over-writing the existing file.

5. Repeat Step 4 for the Over while down image.

6. Type **Navigation button linking to about_us page** in the Alternate text text box, click **Browse** next to the When clicked, Go to URL text box, double-click **about_us.html**, then compare your screen to Figure 16.

*(continued)*

**FIGURE 16**

*Add elements to a navigation bar*

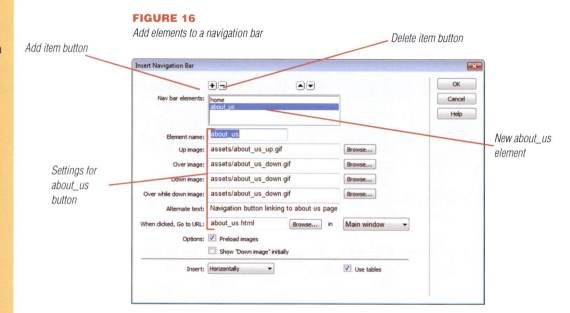

Add item button

Delete item button

New about_us element

Settings for about_us button

## FIGURE 17
*Navigation bar with all elements added*

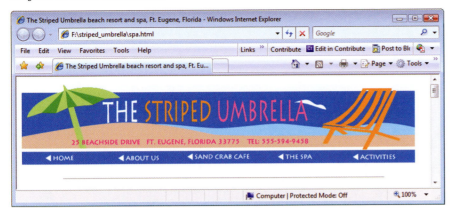

## TABLE 2: Settings to use in the Insert Navigation Bar dialog box for each new element

| dialog box item | cafe element | spa element | activities element |
|---|---|---|---|
| Up image file | cafe_up.gif | spa_up.gif | activities_up.gif |
| Over image file | cafe_down.gif | spa_down.gif | activities_down.gif |
| Down image file | cafe_down.gif | spa_down.gif | activities_down.gif |
| Over while down image file | cafe_down.gif | spa_down.gif | activities_down.gif |
| Alternate text | Navigation button linking to cafe page | Navigation button linking to spa page | Navigation button linking to activities page |
| When clicked, Go to URL | cafe.html | spa.html | activities.html |

7. Using the information provided in Table 2, add three more navigation bar elements in the Insert Navigation Bar dialog box called **cafe**, **spa**, and **activities**.

   TIP  All files listed in the table are located in the assets folder of the chapter_4 folder where you store your Data Files.

8. Click **OK** to close the Insert Navigation Bar dialog box.

9. Save your work, preview the page in your browser, compare your screen to Figure 17, check each link to verify that each element works correctly, then close your browser.

*You completed The Striped Umbrella navigation bar by adding four more elements to it, each of which contain links to four pages in the site. All images added to the navigation bar are now stored in the assets folder of The Striped Umbrella website.*

## Copy and paste a navigation bar

1. Place the insertion point to the left of the navigation bar, press and hold **[Shift]**, then click to the right of the navigation bar. Since this navigation bar was created using the tables option in the Insert Navigation Bar dialog box, table tags are used to place the navigation bar. To make sure you have selected the entire table that formats the navigation bar, verify in the Tag selector that the <table> tag is selected, as shown in Figure 18.

2. Click **Edit** on the Application bar (Win) or Menu bar (Mac) then click **Copy**.

3. Double-click **activities.html** on the Files panel to open the activities page.

4. Select the original navigation bar on the page, click **Edit** on the Application bar (Win) or Menu bar (Mac) click **Paste**, then compare your screen to Figure 19.

*You copied the navigation bar from the spa page and pasted it on the activities page.*

## Modify a navigation bar

1. Click **Modify** on the Application bar (Win) or Menu bar (Mac), then click **Navigation Bar** to open the Modify Navigation Bar dialog box.

2. Scroll down and click **activities** in the Nav bar elements list box, then click the **Show "Down image" initially check box**, as shown in Figure 20.

   An asterisk appears next to activities in the Nav bar elements list box, indicating that this element will be displayed in the Down image state initially. The sand-colored activities navigation

*(continued)*

**FIGURE 18**
*Table tag selected in Tag selector*

Table tag is selected

**FIGURE 19**
*Navigation bar copied to the activities page*

**FIGURE 20**
*Changing settings for the activities element*

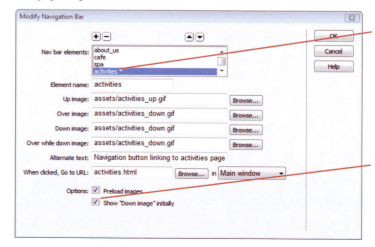

Asterisk is placed next to the element name

Show "Down image" initially is selected

**FIGURE 21**

*About Us page with the modified navigation bar*

When you arrive at The Striped Umbrella, check in at The Club House. Look for the signs that will direct you to registration. Our beautiful club house is the home base for our registration offices, The Sand Crab Cafe, and The Spa. Registration is open from 8:00 a.m. until 6:00 p.m. Please call to make arrangements if you plan to arrive after 6:00 p.m. The cafe and spa hours are both posted and listed in the information packet that you will receive when you arrive.

After you arrive, you will want to take a stroll down the boardwalk to the beach. The entrance to the boardwalk is just past the pool area. The boardwalk provides a safe route to the beach for both our guests and the native vegetation. The sea oats and other flora are tender. Please do not step on them or pick them.

The main swimming pool is directly behind The Club House. A lifeguard is on duty from 8:00 a.m. until 9:00 p.m. The pool area includes a wading pool, a lap pool, and a large pool with a diving board. Showers are located in several areas for your use before and after swimming. We also provide poolside service from the cafe for snacks and lunch.

Enjoy our lush landscaping as you explore the grounds. The beautiful sago palms flourish in our Florida weather! We

element normally used for the Down image state of the activities navigation bar element will remind viewers that they are on the activities page.

3. Click **OK** to save the new settings and close the Modify Navigation Bar dialog box, then save and close the activities page.

4. Repeat Steps 1 through 3 to modify the navigation bar on the spa page to show the Down image initially for the spa element, then save and close the spa page.

> TIP  The Show "Down image" initially check box should be checked only for the element that links to the current page.

5. Open the home page, paste the navigation bar on top of the original navigation bar, then modify the navigation bar to show the Down image initially for the home element.

6. Save and close the home page.

7. Open the about_us page, paste the navigation bar on top of the original navigation bar, then use the Modify Navigation Bar dialog box to specify that the Down image be displayed initially for the about_us element, then compare your screen to Figure 21.

8. Save your work, preview the current page in your browser, test the navigation bar on the home, about_us, spa, and activities pages, then close your browser.

The cafe page is blank at this point, so use the Back button when you test the cafe link to return to the page you were viewing previously.

*You modified the navigation bar on the activities page to show the activities element in the Down state initially. You then copied the navigation bar to two additional pages in The Striped Umbrella website, modifying the navigation bar elements each time to show the Down image state initially.*

# CREATE AN
## IMAGE MAP

**What You'll Do**

*In this lesson, you will create an image map by placing a hotspot on The Striped Umbrella banner that will link to the home page.*

Another way to create links for web pages is to combine them with images by creating an image map. An **image map** is an image that has one or more hotspots placed on top of it. A **hotspot** is a clickable area on an image that, when clicked, links to a different location on the page or to another web page. For example, a map of the United States could have a hotspot placed on each individual state so that viewers could click a state to link to information about that state. The National Park Service website is shown in Figure 22. As you place your mouse over a state, the state name, a photo, and introductory sentences from that state's page are displayed. When you click a state, you will be linked to information about national parks in that state. You

can create hotspots by first selecting the image on which you want to place a hotspot, and then using one of the hotspot tools in the Property inspector to define its shape.

There are several ways to create image maps to make them user-friendly and accessible. One way is to be sure to include alternate text for each hotspot. Another is to draw the hotspot boundaries a little larger than they need to be to cover the area you want to set as a link. This allows viewers a little leeway when they place their mouse over the hotspot by creating a larger target area for them.

The hotspot tools in Dreamweaver make creating image maps a snap. In addition to the Rectangle Hotspot Tool, there is a

Circle Hotspot Tool and a Polygon Hotspot Tool for creating different shapes. These tools can be used to create any shape hotspot that you need. For instance, on a map of the United States, you can draw an outline around each state with the Polygon Hotspot Tool.

You can then make each state "clickable." Hotspots can be easily changed and rearranged on the image. Use the Pointer Hotspot Tool to select the hotspot you would like to edit. You can drag one of the hotspot selector handles to change the size or shape of a hotspot. You can also

move the hotspot by dragging it to a new position on the image. It is a good idea to limit the number of complex hotspots in an image because the code can become too lengthy for the page to download in a reasonable length of time.

**FIGURE 22**
*Viewing an image map on the National Park Service website*

*The pointer is over Hawaii, which causes a window with a photo and introductory text about Hawaii to display*

*Clicking on an individual state will link to information about parks in that state*

National Park Service website - www.nps.gov

## Create an image map

1. Open the activities page, if necessary, select the banner, then click the **Rectangle Hotspot Tool** 🔲 in the Property inspector.

2. Drag the **pointer** to create a rectangle over the umbrella in the banner, as shown in Figure 23, then click **OK** to close the dialog box that reminds you to supply alternate text for the hotspot.

   > TIP  To adjust the shape of a hotspot, click the Pointer Hotspot Tool 🔍 in the Property inspector, then drag a sizing handle on the hotspot.

3. Drag the **Point to File icon** 🌐 in the Property inspector to the index.html file on the Files panel to link the index page to the hotspot.

4. Replace the default text "Map" with **home** in the Map text box in the Property inspector to give the image map a unique name.

5. Click the **Target list arrow** in the Property inspector, then click **_top**.

   When the hotspot is clicked, the _top option causes the home page to open in the same window. See Table 3 for an explanation of the four target options.

   *(continued)*

FIGURE 23
*Properties of the rectangular hotspot on the banner*

Hotspot

Rectangle Hotspot Tool

---

### TABLE 3: Options in the Target list

| target | result |
| --- | --- |
| _blank | Displays the destination page in a separate browser window |
| _parent | Displays the destination page in the parent frameset (replaces the frameset) |
| _self | Displays the destination page in the same frame or window |
| _top | Displays the destination page in the whole browser window |

FIGURE 24

*Hotspot properties*

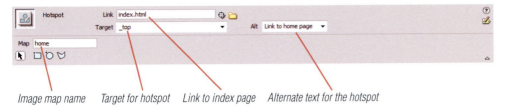

*Image map name*     *Target for hotspot*     *Link to index page*     *Alternate text for the hotspot*

**FIGURE 25**

*Image map preview on the activities page in the browser*

*Alternate text for hotspot*

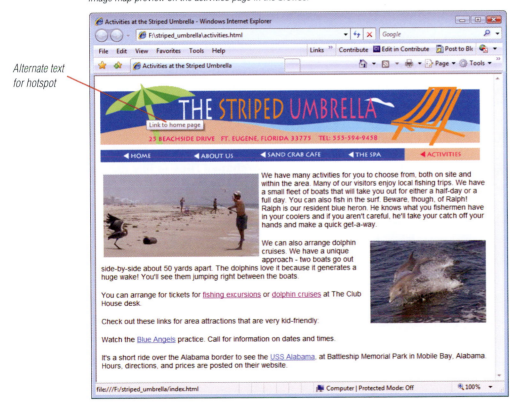

6. Type **Link to home page** in the Alt text box in the Property inspector, as shown in Figure 24. then press **[Enter]** (Win) or **[return]** (Mac).

7. Save your work, preview the page in your browser, then place the pointer over the image map.

   As you place the pointer over the hotspot, you see the alternate text displayed and the pointer indicates the link (Win), as shown in Figure 25.

8. Click the link to test it, close the browser, then close all open pages.

*You created an image map on the banner of the activities page using the Rectangle Hotspot Tool. You then linked the hotspot to the home page.*

*Lesson 4   Create an Image Map*

# MANAGE WEBSITE
## LINKS

## What You'll Do

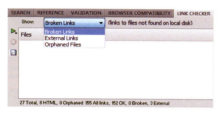

*In this lesson, you will use some of Dreamweaver's reporting features to check The Striped Umbrella website for broken links and orphaned files.*

### Managing Website Links

Because the World Wide Web changes constantly, websites may be up one day and down the next. If a website changes server locations or goes down due to technical difficulties or a power failure, the links to it become broken. Broken links, like misspelled words on a web page, indicate that a website is not being maintained diligently.

Checking links to make sure they work is an ongoing and crucial task you need to perform on a regular basis. You must check external links manually by reviewing your website in a browser and clicking each link to make sure it works correctly. The Check Links Sitewide feature is a helpful tool for managing internal links. You can use it to check your entire website for the total number of links and the number of links that are okay, external, or broken, and then view the results in the Link Checker panel. The Link Checker panel also provides a list of all of the files used in a website, including those that are **orphaned files**, or files that are not linked to any pages in the website.

---

**DESIGN**TIP   **Considering navigation design issues**

As you work on the navigation structure for a website, you should try to limit the number of links on each page to no more than is necessary. Too many links may confuse visitors to your website. You should also design links so that viewers can reach the information they want within a few clicks. If finding information takes more than three or four clicks, the viewer may become discouraged or lost in the site. It's a good idea to provide visual clues on each page to let viewers know where they are, much like a "You are here" marker on a store directory at the mall, or a bread crumbs trail. A **bread crumbs trail** is a list of links that provides a path from the initial page you opened in a website to the page that you are currently viewing.

---

## FIGURE 26

*Link Checker panel displaying external links*

*List of external links*   *Show list arrow*

## FIGURE 27

*Link Checker panel displaying no orphaned files*

*No orphaned files shown*

*Show list arrow*

## FIGURE 28

*Assets panel displaying links*

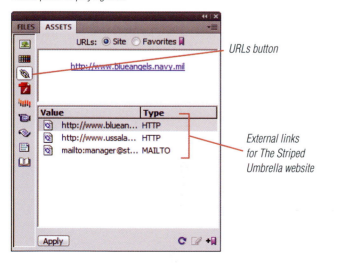

*URLs button*

*External links for The Striped Umbrella website*

### Manage website links

1. Click **Site** on the Application bar (Win) or Menu bar (Mac), point to **Advanced**, then click **Recreate Site Cache**.

2. Click **Site** on the Application bar (Win) or Menu bar (Mac), then click **Check Links Sitewide**.

   The Results tab group opens with the Link Checker panel displayed. By default, the Link Checker panel initially displays any broken internal links found in the website. The Striped Umbrella website has no broken links.

3. Click the **Show list arrow** in the Link Checker panel, click **External Links**, then compare your screen to Figure 26.

4. Click the **Show list arrow**, then click **Orphaned Files** to view the orphaned files in the Link Checker panel, as shown in Figure 27.

   The Striped Umbrella website has no orphaned files.

5. Right-click in an empty area of the Results tab group title bar, then click **Close tab group**.

6. Display the Assets panel (if necessary), then click the **URLs button** 🖎 in the Assets panel if necessary to display the list of links in the website.

   The Assets panel displays the external links used in the website, as shown in Figure 28.

*You used the Link Checker panel to check for broken links, external links, and orphaned files in The Striped Umbrella website. You also viewed the external links in the Assets panel.*

## Update a page

1. Open dw4_2.html from where you store your Data Files, then save it as **fishing.html** in the striped_umbrella root folder, overwriting the existing fishing page, but not updating the links.

2. Click the broken link image placeholder, click the **Browse for File icon** 📁 next to the Src text box in the Property inspector, then browse to the chapter_4 Data Files folder and select the file **heron_small.jpg** to copy the file to the striped_umbrella assets folder.

3. Deselect the image placeholder and the image will appear as shown in Figure 29.

   Notice that the text is automatically updated with the paragraph_text style. The code was already in place on the page linking the su_styles.css to the file.

4. Save and close the fishing page, then close the dw4_2.html page.

   *(continued)*

*(continued)*

**FIGURE 29**
*Fishing page updated*

### POWER USER SHORTCUTS

| to do this: | use this shortcut: |
| --- | --- |
| Close a file | [Ctrl][W] (Win) or ⌘[W] (Mac) |
| Close all files | [Ctrl][Shift][W] (Win) or ⌘[Shift][W] (Mac) |
| Print Code | [Ctrl][P] (Win) or ⌘[P] (Mac) |
| Check page links | [Shift][F8] |
| Undo | [Ctrl][Z], [Alt][BkSp] (Win) or ⌘[Z], [option][delete] (Mac) |
| Redo | [Ctrl][Y], [Ctrl][Shift][Z] (Win) or ⌘[Y], ⌘[Shift][Z] (Mac) |
| Refresh Design View | [F5] |
| Hide all Visual Aids | [Ctrl][Shift][I] (Win) or ⌘[Shift][I] (Mac) |
| Insert a Named Anchor | [Ctrl][Alt][A] (Win) or ⌘[option][A] (Mac) |
| Make a Link | [Ctrl][L] (Win) or ⌘[L] (Mac) |
| Remove a Link | [Ctrl][Shift][L] (Win) or ⌘[Shift][L] (Mac) |
| Check Links Sitewide | [Ctrl][F8] (Win) or ⌘[F8] (Mac) |
| Show Files tab group | [F8] (Win) or ⌘[Shift][F] (Mac) |

**FIGURE 30**

*Cruises page updated*

This is the Dolphin Racer at dock. We leave daily at 4:00 p.m. and 6:30 p.m. for 1 1/2 hour cruises. There are snacks and restrooms available on board. We welcome children of all ages. Our ship is a U.S. Coast Guard approved vessel and our captain is a former member of the Coast Guard. Call The Club desk for reservations.

5. Open dw4_3.html from where you store your Data Files, then save it as **cruises.html** in the striped_umbrella root folder, overwriting the existing cruises page, but not updating the links.

6. Click the broken link graphic placeholder, click the **Browse for File icon** next to the Src text box in the Property inspector, then browse to the chapter_4 Data Files folder and select the file **boats.jpg** to copy the file to the striped_umbrella assets folder.

7. Deselect the image placeholder and the image will appear as shown in Figure 30.

   Notice that the text is automatically updated with the paragraph_text style. The code was already in place on the page linking the su_styles.css to the file.

8. Save and close the page.

9. Open each page that has a horizontal rule under the navigation bar, delete the horizontal rule, then save each page.

   Each page did not have a horizontal rule. By deleting each existing horizontal rule after the navigation bars were added, all pages now have a consistent look.

10. Preview each page in the browser, close the browser, then close all open pages.

*You added content to two previously blank pages in the website, then deleted horizontal rules under navigation bars to provide a consistent look for each page in the site.*

## Create external and internal links.

1. Open the blooms & bulbs website.
2. Open dw4_4.html from where you store your Data Files, then save it as **newsletter.html** in the blooms & bulbs website, overwriting the existing file without updating the links. Close dw4_4.html.
3. Verify that the banner path is set correctly to the assets folder in the website and correct it, if it is not.
4. Scroll to the bottom of the page, then link the National Gardening Association text to http://www.garden.org.
5. Link the Organic Gardening text to http://www.organicgardening.com.
6. Link the Southern Living text to http://www.southernliving.com/southern.
7. Save the file, then preview the page in your browser, verifying that each link works correctly.
8. Close your browser, then return to the newsletter page in Dreamweaver.
9. Scroll to the paragraph about gardening issues, select the gardening tips text in the last sentence, then link the selected text to the tips.html file in the blooms root folder.
10. Apply the paragraph_text rule from the blooms_styles.css file to all of the text on the page except the subheadings and heading.

11. Apply the headings rule to the text "Gardening Matters," and the bold_blue rule to the sub-headings on the page.
12. Change the page title to **Gardening Matters**, then save your work.
13. Open the plants page and add the following sentence to the end of the last paragraph: **We have many annuals, perennials, and water plants that have just arrived**.
14. Link the "annuals" text to the annuals.html file, link the "perennials" text to the perennials.html file, and the "water plants" text to the water_plants.html file.
15. Save your work, test the links in your browser, then close your browser. (*Hint*: These pages do not have content yet, but are serving as placeholders.)

## Create internal links to named anchors.

1. Show Invisible Elements (if necessary).
2. Click the Common category in the Insert panel.
3. Switch to the newsletter page, then insert a named anchor in front of the Grass heading named **grass**.
4. Insert a named anchor in front of the Plants heading named **plants**.
5. Insert a named anchor in front of the Trees heading named **trees**.

6. Use the Point to File icon in the Property inspector to create a link from the word "grass" in the Gardening Issues paragraph to the anchor named "grass."
7. Create a link from the word "trees" in the Gardening Issues paragraph to the anchor named "trees."
8. Create a link from the word "plants" in the Gardening Issues paragraph to the anchor named "plants."
9. Save your work, view the page in your browser, test all the links to make sure they work, then close your browser.

## Create, modify, and copy a navigation bar.

1. Select the banner, press the right arrow key, click the Images list arrow on the Insert panel, then click Navigation Bar to insert a horizontal navigation bar at the top of the newsletter page below the banner. Verify that the option to use tables is selected.

2. Type **home** as the first element name, then use the **b_home_up.jpg** file for the Up image state. This file is in the assets folder where you store your Data Files.

3. Specify the file **b_home_down.jpg** for the three remaining states. This file (and all files for the remainder of this exercise) are in the assets folder where you store your Data Files.

4. Enter **Link to home page** as the alternate text, then set the index.html file as the link for the home element.

5. Create a new element named **plants** and use the **b_plants_up.jpg** file for the Up image state and the **b_plants_down.jpg** file for the remaining three states.

6. Enter **Link to plants page** as the alternate text, then set the **plants.html** file as the link for the plants element.

7. Create a new element named **tips** and use the **b_tips_up.jpg** file for the Up image state and the **b_tips_down.jpg** file for the remaining three states.

8. Enter **Link to tips page** as the alternate text, then set the **tips.html** file as the link for the tips element.

9. Create a new element named **classes** and use the **b_classes_up.jpg** file for the Up image state and the **b_classes_down.jpg** file for the remaining three states.

10. Enter **Link to classes page** as the alternate text, then set the **classes.html** file as the link for the classes element.

11. Create a new element named **newsletter**, then use the **b_newsletter_up.jpg** file for the Up image state and the **b_newsletter_down.jpg** file for the remaining three states.

12. Enter the alternate text **Link to newsletter page**, then set the **newsletter.html** file as the link for the newsletter element.

13. Save the page and test the links in your browser, then close the browser.

14. Select and copy the navigation bar, then open the home page.

15. Delete the current navigation bar on the home page, paste the new navigation bar under the banner, then delete the horizontal rule under the navigation bar. Remove any space between the banner and navigation bar if necessary. (*Hint*: The easiest way to remove any extra space is to go to Code view and delete any space between the end of the banner code and the beginning table tag for the navigation bar.)

16. Modify the home element on the navigation bar to show the Down image state initially.

17. Save the page, test the links in your browser, then close the browser and the page.

18. Modify the navigation bar on the newsletter page so the Down image is shown initially for the newsletter element.

19. Paste the navigation bar on the plants page and the tips page, making the necessary modifications so that the Down image is shown initially for each element.

**20.** Save your work, preview all the pages in your browser, compare your newsletter page to Figure 31, test all the links, then close your browser.

### Create an image map.

**1.** Use the Rectangle Hotspot Tool to draw an image map across the left side of the banner on the newsletter page that will link to the home page.

**2.** Name the image map **home** and set the target to **_top**.

**3.** Add the alternate text **Link to home page**, save the page, then preview it in the browser to test the link. (*Hint*: In the Internet Explorer browser, you may see a space between the banner and the navigation bar that is caused by the image map on the banner. Mozilla Firefox will display the page correctly without the space.)

**4.** Close the page.

### Manage website links.

**1.** Use the Link Checker panel to view and fix broken links and orphaned files in the blooms & bulbs website.

**2.** Open dw4_5.html from where you store your Data Files, then save it as **annuals.html**, replacing the original file. Do not update links, but save the file **fuschia.jpg** in the assets folder of the website. Close dw4_5.html.

**3.** Repeat Step 2 using **dw4_6.html** to replace **perennials.html**, saving the **iris.jpg** file in

the assets folder and using **dw4_7.html** to replace **water_plants.html**, saving the **water_hyacinth.jpg** file in the assets folder.

**4.** Save your work, then close all open pages.

**FIGURE 31**
*Completed Skills Review*

**Gardening Matters**

Welcome, fellow gardeners. My name is Cosie Simmons, and I am the owner of blooms & bulbs. My passion has always been my gardens. Ever since I was a small child, I was drawn to my back yard where all varieties of beautiful plants flourished. A lush carpet of thick grass bordered with graceful beds is truly a haven for all living creatures. With proper planning and care, your gardens will draw a variety of birds and butterflies and become a great pleasure to you.

**Gardening Issues**
There are several areas to concentrate on when formulating your landscaping plans. One is your grass. Another is the number and variety of trees you plant. The third is the combination of plants you select. All of these decisions should be considered in relation to the climate in your area. Be sure and check out our gardening tips before you begin work.

**Grass**
Lawn experts classify grass into two categories: cool-climate and warm-climate. The northern half of the United States would be considered cool-climate. Examples of cool-climate grass are Kentucky bluegrass and ryegrass. Bermuda grass is a warm-climate grass. Before planting grass, whether by seeding, sodding, sprigging, or plugging, the ground must be properly prepared. The soil should be tested for any nutritional deficiencies and cultivated. Come by or call to make arrangements to have your soil tested.

**Plants**
There are so many types of plants available that it can become overwhelming. Do you want border plants, shrubs, ground covers, annuals, perennials, vegetables, fruits, vines, or bulbs? In reality, a combination of several of these works well. Water plants are quite popular now. We will be happy to help you sort out your preferences and select a harmonious combination of plants for you.

**Trees**
Before you plant trees, you should evaluate your purpose. Are you interested in shade, privacy, or color? Do you want to attract wildlife? Attract birds? Create a shady play area? Your purpose will determine what variety of tree you should plant. Of course, you also need to consider your climate and available space. We carry many varieties of trees and are happy to help you make your selections to fit your purpose.

**Further Research**
These are some of my favorite gardening links. Take the time to browse through some of the information they offer, then give me a call at (555) 248-0806 or e-mail me at cosie@blooms&bulbs.com

National Gardening Association
Organic Gardening
Southern Living

Use Figure 32 as a guide to continue your work on the TripSmart website that you began in Project Builder 1 in Chapter 1 and developed in the previous chapters. You have been asked to create a new page for the website that lists helpful links for customers. You will also add content to the destinations, kenya, and amazon pages.

1. Open the TripSmart website.
2. Open dw4_8.html from where you store your Data Files, then save it as **services.html** in the TripSmart website root folder, replacing the existing file and not updating links. Close dw4_8.html.
3. Verify that the TripSmart banner is in the assets folder of the root folder.
4. Apply the paragraph_text rule to the paragraphs of text and the heading rule to the four main paragraph headings.
5. Create named anchors named **reservations, outfitters, tours**, and **links** in front of the respective headings on the page, then link each named anchor to "Reservations," "Travel Outfitters," "Escorted Tours," and "Helpful Links in Travel Planning" in the first paragraph.

6. Link the text "on-line catalog" in the Travel Outfitters paragraph to the catalog.html page.
7. Link the text "CNN Travel Channel" under the heading Travel Information Sites to http://www.cnn.com/TRAVEL.
8. Repeat Step 7 to create links for the rest of the websites listed:
   US Department of State:
   http://travel.state.gov
   Yahoo!:
   http://yahoo.com/Recreation/Travel
   MapQuest:
   http://www.mapquest.com
   Rand McNally:
   http://www.randmcnally.com
   AccuWeather:
   http://www.accuweather.com
   The Weather Channel:
   http://www.weather.com
9. Save the services page, then open the index page.
10. Reformat the navigation bar on the home page with a style of your choice. If you decide to use graphics for the navigation bar, you will have to create your own graphic files using a graphics program. There are no Data Files for you to use.

(*Hint*: If you create your own graphic files, be sure to create two graphic files for each element: one for the Up image state and one for the Down image state.) To design a navigation bar using text, you simply type the text for each navigation bar element, format the text appropriately using styles, and insert links to each text element as you did in Chapter 2. The navigation bar should contain the following elements: Home, Catalog, Services, Destinations, and Newsletter. In Figure 32, the navigation bar style was edited to incorporate letter spacing to spread the text slightly. Indents were then used to center the navigation bar under the banner. (Letter spacing and indents are in the Block category in the CSS Rule definition dialog box. You can also use the Text Indent button on the HTML Property inspector.)
11. Copy the navigation bar, then place it on each completed page of the website.

12. Save each page, then check for broken links and orphaned files. (*Hint*: The two orphaned files will be removed after completing the next steps.)

13. Open the destinations.html file in your root folder and save it as **kenya.html**, overwriting the existing file, then close the file.

14. Open dw4_9.html from where you store your Data Files, then save it as **amazon.html**, overwriting the existing file. Do not update links, but save the **water_lily.jpg** and **sloth.jpg** files in the assets folder of the website, then save and close the file. Close dw4_9.html.

15. Open dw4_10.html from where you store your Data Files, then save the file as **destinations.html**, overwriting the existing file. Do not update links, but save the **parrot.jpg** and **giraffe.jpg** files in the assets folder of the website. Close dw4_10.html.

16. Link the text "Amazon" in the second sentence of the first paragraph to the **amazon.html** file.

17. Link the text "Kenya" in the first sentence in the second paragraph to the **kenya.html** file.

18. Copy your customized navigation bar to the two new pages so they will match the other pages.

19. Check all text on all pages to make sure each text block uses a style for formatting. Correct those that don't.

20. Save all files.

21. Test all links in your browser, close your browser, then close all open pages.

**FIGURE 32**

*Sample Project Builder 1*

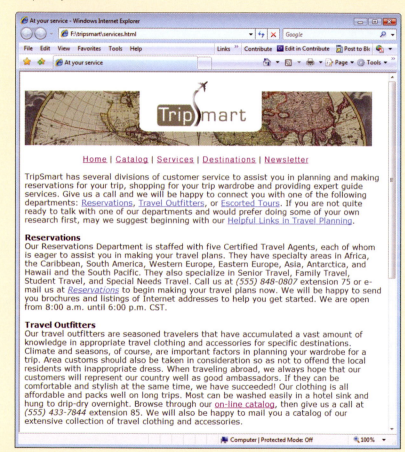

You are continuing your work on the Carolyne's Creations website, that you started in Project Builder 2 in Chapter 1 and developed in the previous chapters. Chef Carolyne has asked you to create a page describing her cooking classes offered every month. You will create the content for that page and individual pages describing the children's classes and the adult classes. Refer to Figures 33-36 for possible solutions.

1. Open the Carolyne's Creations website.
2. Open dw4_11.html from where you store your Data Files, save it as **classes.html** in the root folder of the Carolyne's Creations website, overwriting the existing file and not updating the links. Close dw4_11.html.
3. Check the path of the banner to make sure it is linking to the banner in the assets folder of the website. Notice that styles have already been applied to the text, because the CSS code was already in the Data File.
4. Select the text "adults' class" in the last paragraph, then link it to the adults.html page. (*Hint*: This page has not been developed yet.)
5. Select the text "children's class" in the last paragraph and link it to the children.html page. (*Hint*: This page has not been developed yet.)

6. Create an email link from the text "Sign me up!" that links to **carolyne@carolynescreations.com**
7. Insert the file **fish.jpg** from the assets folder where you store your Data Files at the beginning of the second paragraph, add

appropriate alternate text, then choose your own alignment and formatting settings.
8. Add the file **children_cooking.jpg** from the assets folder where you store your Data Files at the beginning of the third paragraph.

**FIGURE 33**
*Completed Project Builder 2*

### Cooking Classes are fun!

Chef Carolyne loves to offer a fun and relaxing cooking school each month in her newly refurbished kitchen. She teaches an **adult class** on the fourth Saturday of each month from 6:00 to 8:00 pm. Each class will learn to cook a complete dinner and then enjoy the meal at the end of the class with a wonderful wine pairing. This is a great chance to get together with friends for a fun evening.

Chef Caroline also teaches a **children's class** on the second Tuesday of each month from 4:00 to 5:30 pm. Our young chefs will learn to cook two dishes that will accompany a full meal served at 5:30 pm. Kids aged 5–8 years accompanied by an adult are welcome. We also host small birthday parties where we put the guests to work baking and decorating the cake! Call for times and prices.

We offer several special adult classes throughout the year. The **Valentine Chocolate Extravaganza** is a particular favorite. You will learn to dip strawberries, make truffles, and bake a sinful Triple Chocolate Dare You Torte. We also host the **Not So Traditional Thanksgiving** class and the **Super Bowl Snacks** class each year with rave reviews. Watch the Web site for details!

Prices are $40.00 for each adults' class and $15.00 for each children's class. Sign up for classes by calling 555-963-8271 or by emailing us: Sign me up!

See what's cooking this month for the adults' class and children's class.

9. Compare your work to Figure 33 for a possible solution, then save and close the file.

10. Open dw4_12.html from where you store your Data Files, then save it as **children.html,** overwriting the existing file and not updating links. Save the image **cookies_oven.jpg** from the assets folder where you store your Data Files to the website assets folder. Close dw4_12.html.

11. Use your own alignment and formatting settings, compare your work to Figure 34 for a possible solution, then save and close the file.

**FIGURE 35**
*Completed Project Builder 2*

**Adult Cooking Class for March: Chinese Cuisine**

The class in March will be cooking several traditional Chinese dishes: Peking dumplings, wonton soup, fried rice, Chinese vegetables, and shrimp with lobster sauce. For dessert: banana spring rolls.

This looks easier than it is! Chef Carolyne is demonstrating the first steps in making Chinese dumplings, known as *jiaozi* (pronounced geeow dz). Notice that she is using a traditional wooden rolling pin to roll out the dough. These dumplings were stuffed with pork and then steamed, although other popular fillings are made with chicken and leeks or vegetables with spiced tofu and cellophane noodles. Dumplings can be steamed, boiled, or fried, and have unique names depending on the preparation method.

**FIGURE 34**
*Completed Project Builder 2*

**Children's Cooking Class for March: Oven Chicken Fingers, Chocolate Chip Cookies**

This month we will be baking oven chicken fingers that are dipped in a milk and egg mixture, then coated with breadcrumbs. The chocolate chip cookies are based on a famous recipe that includes chocolate chips, M&Ms, oatmeal, and pecans. Yummy! We will be learning some of the basics like how to cream butter and crack eggs without dropping shells into the batter.

We will provide French fries, green beans, fruit salad, and a beverage to accompany the chicken fingers.

12. Repeat Steps 10 and 11 to open the dw4_13.html file and save it as **adults.html**, overwriting the existing file and saving the files **dumplings1.jpg, dumplings2.jpg,** and **dumplings3.jpg** in the assets folder, then use alignment settings of your choice. Compare your work to Figure 35 for a possible solution, then save and close the file.

13. Open the index page and delete the banner, navigation bar, and horizontal rule.

14. Insert the file **cc_banner_with_text.jpg** from where you store your Data Files in

place, of what you just deleted adding appropriate alternate text.

15. Create an image map for each word at the bottom of the navigation bar to be used as a link to that page, as shown in Figure 36. Use **_top** as the target, the names of the "buttons" as the image map names, and appropriate alternate text. Link each image map to its corresponding page.

16. Copy the new banner with the navigation bar to each completed page, deleting existing navigation bars and banners.

17. Save all the pages, then check for broken links and orphaned files. You will see one orphaned file, the original version of the banner.

18. Apply a rule from the style sheet to any text that is not formatted with a style.

19. Preview all the pages in your browser, check to make sure the links work correctly, close your browser, then close all open pages.

**FIGURE 36**
*Completed Project Builder 2*

Let Carolyne's Creations be your personal chef, your one stop shop for the latest in kitchen items and fresh ingredients, and your source for new and innovative recipes. We enjoy planning and executing special events for all occasions - from children's birthday parties to corporate retreats. Feel like a guest at your own party. Give us a call or stop by our shop to browse through our selections.

Carolyne's Creations
496 Maple Avenue
Seven Falls, Virginia 52404
555-963-8271
E-mail Carolyne Kate

Copyright 2001 - 2012
Last updated on July 29, 2008

## DESIGN PROJECT

Grace Keiko is a talented young watercolor artist who specializes in botanical works. She wants to develop a website to advertise her work, but isn't sure what she would like to include in a website or how to tie the pages together. She decides to spend several hours looking at other artists' websites to help her get started.

1. Connect to the Internet, then navigate to the Kate Nessler website pictured in Figure 37, www.katenessler.com.
2. Spend some time looking at several of the pages in the site to get some ideas.
3. What categories of page content would you include on your website if you were Grace?
4. What external links would you consider including?
5. Describe how you would place external links on the pages and list examples of ones you would use.
6. Would you use text or images for your navigation bar?
7. Would you include rollover effects on the navigation bar elements? If so, describe how they might look.
8. How could you incorporate named anchors on any of the pages?
9. Would you include an image map on a page?
10. Sketch a website plan for Grace, including the pages that you would use as links from the home page.

11. Refer to your website sketch, then create a home page for Grace that includes a navigation bar, a short introductory paragraph about her art, and a few external links.

**FIGURE 37**
*Design Project*

# PORTFOLIO PROJECT

In this assignment, you will continue to work on the website that you started in Chapter 1 and developed in the previous chapters.

You will continue building your website by designing and completing a page with a navigation bar. After creating the navigation bar, you will copy it to each completed page in the website. In addition to the navigation bar, you will add several external links and several internal links to other pages as well as to named anchors. You will also link text to a named anchor. After you complete this work, you will check for broken links and orphaned files.

1. Consult your storyboard to decide which page or pages you would like to develop in this chapter. Decide how to design and where to place the navigation bar, named anchors, and any additional page elements you decide to use. Decide which reports should be run on the website to check for accuracy.

2. Research websites that could be included on one or more of your pages as external links of interest to your viewers. Create a list of the external links you want to use. Using your storyboard as a guide, decide where each external link should be placed in the site.

3. Add the external links to existing pages or create any additional pages that contain external links.

4. Create named anchors for key locations on the page, such as the top of the page, then link appropriate text on the page to them.

5. Decide on a design for a navigation bar that will be used on all pages of the website.

6. Create the navigation bar and copy it to all finished pages on the website. If you decided to use graphics for the navigation bar, create the graphics that will be used.

7. Think of a good place to incorporate an image map, then add it to a page.

8. Use the Link Checker panel to check for broken links and orphaned files.

9. Use the checklist in Figure 38 to make sure your website is complete, save your work, then close all open pages.

**FIGURE 38**
*Portfolio Project checklist*

**Website Checklist**

1. Do all pages have a page title?
2. Does the home page have a description and keywords?
3. Does the home page contain contact information?
4. Does every page in the website have consistent navigation links?
5. Does the home page have a last updated statement that will automatically update when the page is saved?
6. Do all paths for links and images work correctly?
7. Do all images have alternate text?
8. Are all colors web-safe?
9. Are there any unnecessary files that you can delete from the assets folder?
10. Is there a style sheet with at least two styles?
11. Did you apply the style sheet to page content?
12. Does at least one page contain links to one or more named anchors?
13. Does at least one page contain an internal link?
14. Do all pages look good using at least two different browsers?

chapter

# 5 POSITIONING OBJECTS
## WITH CSS AND TABLES

1. Create a page using CSS layouts

2. Add content to CSS layout blocks

3. Edit content in CSS layout blocks

4. Create a table

5. Resize, split, and merge cells

6. Insert and align images in table cells

7. Insert text and format cell content

# 5 POSITIONING OBJECTS
## WITH CSS AND TABLES

### Introduction

To create an organized, attractive web page, you need precise control of the position of text and graphic elements. CSS page layouts can provide this control. **CSS page layouts** consist of containers formatted with CSS styles in which you place web page content. These containers can accommodate images, blocks of text, Flash movies, or any other page element. The appearance and position of the containers are set through the use of HTML tags known as **div tags**. Using div tags, you can position elements next to each other as well as on top of each other in a stack. Another option for controlling the placement of page elements is through the use of tables. **Tables** are placeholders made up of small boxes called cells, into which you can insert text and graphics. Cells in a table are arranged horizontally in **rows** and vertically in **columns**. Using tables on a web page gives you control over the placement of each object on the page, similar to the way CSS blocks control placement. In this chapter, you will use a CSS predefined page layout with div tags to place text and graphics on a page. You will then add a table to one of the CSS blocks on the page to place some of the page elements.

### Using Div Tags Versus Tables for Page Layout

Div tags and tables both enable you to control the appearance of content in your web pages. But unlike tables, div tags allow you to stack your information in a vertical pile, allowing for just one piece of information to be visible at a time. Tables are static, which makes it difficult to change them quickly as a need arises. Div tags can be dynamic, changing in response to variables such as a mouse click. You can create dynamic div tags using JavaScript **behaviors**, simple action scripts that let you incorporate interactivity by modifying style or content based on variables like user actions. For example, you could add a JavaScript behavior to a block of text in a div tag to make it become larger or smaller when a viewer places the pointer over it.

There has been much discussion since the inception of CSS about which tool is better—CSS layouts or table layouts. Both have advantages and disadvantages, but designers tend to prefer CSS layouts. In actual practice, many designers use a combination of both tools, choosing the tool that is the best suited to the current design challenge. No matter which tool or tools you plan to use, it is important to complete a rough sketch of a page before you actually begin working on it.

# Tools You'll Use

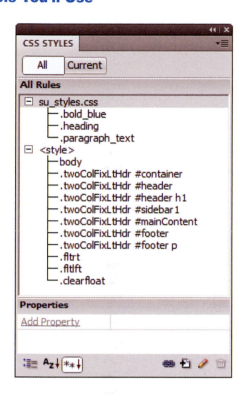

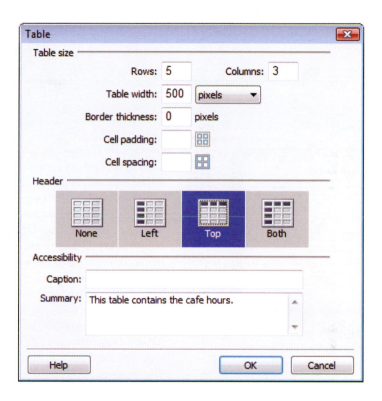

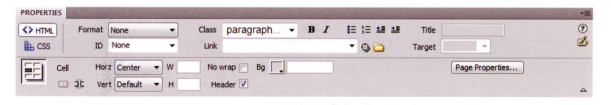

# CREATE A PAGE
## USING CSS LAYOUTS

## What You'll Do

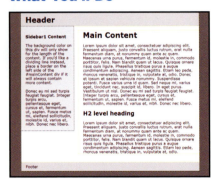

*In this lesson, you will create a new page based on a predefined CSS layout to become the new cafe page for the website.*

### Understanding Div Tags

Div tags are HTML tags that define how areas of content are formatted or positioned on a web page. For example, when you center an image on a page or inside a table cell, Dreamweaver automatically inserts a div tag in the HTML code. In addition to using div tags to align page elements, designers also use them to assign colors to content blocks, CSS styles to text, and many other properties to page elements. One type of div tag is an **AP div tag**. AP stands for absolutely positioned, so an **AP div tag** creates a container that has a specified, fixed position on a web page. The resulting container that an AP div tag creates on a page is called an **AP element**.

### Using CSS Page Layouts

Because building a web page using div tags can be tedious for beginning designers, Dreamweaver provides 32 predesigned layouts in the New Document dialog box, as shown in Figure 1. These layouts contain div tags that control the placement of page content using placeholders. You can

use these layouts to create web pages with attractive and consistent layouts. Placeholder text is displayed in each div tag container until you replace it with your own content. Because div tags use CSS for formatting and positioning, they are the preferred method for building content for web pages. As you become more comfortable using the predesigned layouts, you will begin to build your own CSS-based pages from scratch. You must be careful, however, to test pages with CSS layouts in multiple browsers; some CSS layouts will not render correctly in all browsers. When you use the Dreamweaver predesigned layouts, you can be sure that your pages will appear as you intended in all browsers.

**QUICK**TIP

The Browser Compatibility Check feature flags code that might present a CSS rendering issue in some browsers by underlining code in green. To see this feature, simply switch to Code view and browse through the code.

## Viewing CSS Layout Blocks

As you design web pages using div tags for page layout, you can use Design view to see and adjust CSS content blocks. In Design view, text or images that have been aligned or positioned using div tags have a dotted border, as shown in Figure 2. You can use options on the View/Visual Aids menu to display borders, backgrounds, padding, and margins of various AP elements. In the Visual Aids list on the View menu, you can select options such as CSS Layout Backgrounds, CSS Layout Box Model, CSS Layout Outlines, and AP Element Outlines. The CSS Layout Box Model displays the padding and margins of a block element.

FIGURE 1
*New Document dialog box*

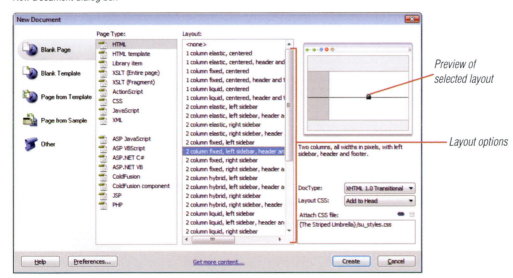

Preview of selected layout

Layout options

FIGURE 2
*CSS blocks defined by dotted borders*

*Dotted-line borders surround the CSS content blocks*

---

## Using Tracing Images for Page Design

Another design option for creating a page layout is the use of a tracing image. A **tracing image** is an image that is placed in the background of a document. By adjusting the transparency (opacity) of the image, you can then use it to create page elements on top of it, similar to the way you would place a piece of tracing paper on top of a drawing and trace over it. To insert a tracing image, Use the Modify, Page Properties, Tracing Image text box or the View, Tracing Image, Load command. Browse to select the image you want to use for the tracing image, then adjust the transparency as desired.

## Create a page with a CSS layout

1. Open The Striped Umbrella website.

2. Click **File** on the Application bar (Win) or Menu bar (Mac), click **New**, verify that Blank Page is highlighted in the first category of the New Document dialog box, click **HTML** in the Page Type category if necessary, then click **2 column fixed, left sidebar, header and footer** in the Layout category, as shown in Figure 3.

   A fixed layout will remain the same size regardless of the size of the browser window.

   *(continued)*

FIGURE 3

*Pre-defined layout selected for new page*

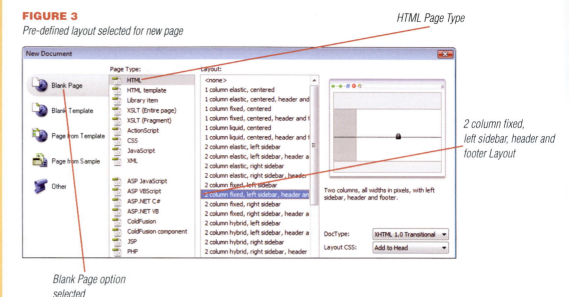

*HTML Page Type*

*2 column fixed, left sidebar, header and footer Layout*

*Blank Page option selected*

---

## Using XML and XSL to create and format web page content

Another option you have with Dreamweaver is to create containers of information with XML, Extensible Markup Language, and XSL, Extensible Stylesheet Language. **XML** is a language that you use to create the structure of blocks of information, similar to HTML. It uses opening and closing tags and the nested tag structure that is used by HTML documents. However, XML tags do not determine how the information is formatted. This is done through XSL. **XSL** is similar to CSS; the XSL stylesheet information formats the containers created by XML. One more term to learn is **XSLT**, Extensible Stylesheet Language Transformations. XSLT displays the information on a web page and transforms it through the use of the style sheet. XSL transformations can be written as client-side or server-side transformations. To create XML documents, use the XML page type in the New Document dialog box.

*Positioning Objects with CSS and Tables*

**FIGURE 4**

The su_styles.css file is attached to the new page

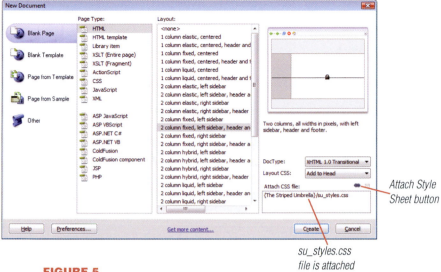

su_styles.css
file is attached

Attach Style
Sheet button

**FIGURE 5**

New page based on CSS layout

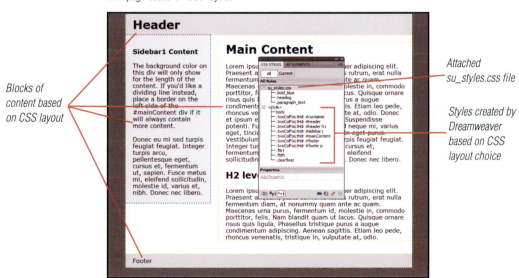

Blocks of
content based
on CSS layout

Attached
su_styles.css file

Styles created by
Dreamweaver
based on CSS
layout choice

**3.** Click the **Attach Style Sheet button** in the bottom-right corner of the dialog box, then click **Browse** in the Attach External Style Sheet dialog box.

The Select Style Sheet File dialog box opens.

**4.** Select the **su_styles.css file** in the Select Style Sheet File dialog box, click **OK**, then click **OK** to close the information box.

The links will not be relative until the page is saved in the website.

**5.** Verify that the Link option is selected in the Attach External Style Sheet dialog box, then click **OK** to close the Attach External Style Sheet dialog box.

The su_styles.css file is attached to the new page, as shown in Figure 4.

**6.** Click **Create** in the New Document dialog box, open the CSS Styles panel, then expand the styles if necessary.

A new page is created based on the CSS predefined layout with placeholder text, as shown in Figure 5, that will be replaced with content for The Striped Umbrella website. We will use this new page to create the cafe page.

*You created a new page based on a predefined CSS layout, attaching the style sheet for The Striped Umbrella website.*

# ADD CONTENT
## TO CSS LAYOUT BLOCKS

### What You'll Do

 *In this lesson, you will copy the text and banner from the index page and paste it into the new page. You will then overwrite the old cafe page with this new one.*

### Understanding Div Tag Content

As you learned in Lesson 1, a div tag is a container that formats blocks of information on a web page, such as background colors, images, links, tables, and text.

Also, as with formatting text on a web page, you should use CSS styles to format your text when using div tags. You can also add all other properties such as text indent, padding, margins, and background color using CSS styles.

In this lesson, you will use a CSS layout to create a new cafe page that arranges the page content into defined areas on the page.

### Using Dreamweaver sample pages

You can use either the Welcome Screen or the New command on the File menu to create several different types of pages. The predesigned CSS page layouts make it very easy to design accessible web pages based on Cascading Style Sheets without an advanced level of expertise in writing HTML code. Predesigned templates are another time-saving feature that promotes consistency across a website. Framesets, CSS Style Sheets, and Starter Pages are a few of the other options. It is worth the time to explore each category to understand what is available to you as a designer. Once you have selected a sample page, you can customize it to suit your client's content and design needs.

## Understanding CSS Code

When you view a page based on a predesigned CSS layout in Code view, you will notice helpful comments that explain sections of the code, as shown in Figure 6. The comments are in gray to differentiate them from the rest of the code. The CSS rules reside in the Head section. The code for a CSS container begins with the class, or name of the rule, and is followed by the ID, or the name of the container. A pound sign (#) precedes the ID. For example, in Figure 6, the container described on line 32 begins with the class name .twoColFixLtHdr, which is followed by its ID name, #sidebar. The code that links the rules to the content is located in the body section.

**FIGURE 6**

*Code view for CSS in head content*

*ID preceded by # sign*

*Comments in gray text*

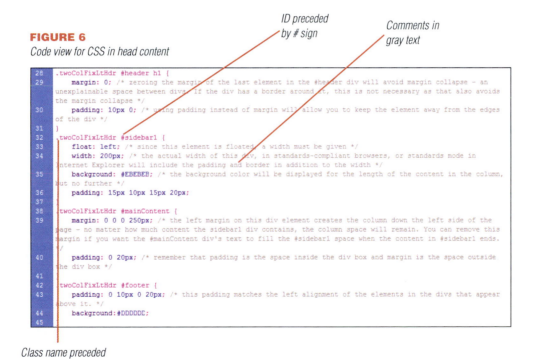

*Class name preceded by period*

## Add text to a CSS container

1. Select the content between the Header and Footer in the main section of the page, as shown in Figure 7, then press [**Delete**].

2. Import the file **cafe.doc** from the location where you store your Data Files (Win) or copy and paste it (Mac) in the blank container, then delete any extra space after the paragraph.

3. Delete the placeholder content in the left column, delete any extra space at the insertion point, then type **Reservations are recommended for The Dining Room during the peak summer season**.

   TIP  If your text appears in bold, it is picking up the original placeholder H1 tag. To remove it, select the bold text and change the format setting in the HTML Property inspector from Heading 3 to Paragraph.

4. Delete the word "Footer" in the footer block, then type **Copyright 2002 - 2012 The Striped Umbrella** as shown in Figure 8.

5. Save the page as **cafe.html** in The Striped Umbrella website, overwriting the existing file.

*You imported text and typed text in the CSS blocks, replacing the placeholder text, then saved the page as the new cafe.html page.*

FIGURE 7

*Text selected in main section of new page*

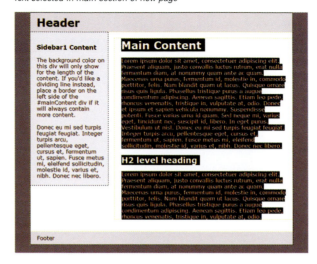

FIGURE 8

*Text pasted into mainContent layout block of new page*

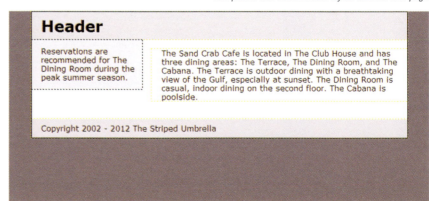

*Positioning Objects with CSS and Tables*

## FIGURE 9

*Editing code in the header section*

*Delete these heading tags*

```
132
133   <div id="container">
134     <div id="header">
135       <h1><img src="assets/su_banner.gif" alt="The Striped Umbrella banner" width="735" height="125" /><br />
136       </h1>
137       <table border="0" cellpadding="0" cellspacing="0">
138         <tr>
139           <td><a href="index.html" target="_top" onclick=
      "MM_nbGroup('down','group1','home','assets/home_down.gif',1)" onmouseover=
      "MM_nbGroup('over','home','assets/home_down.gif','assets/home_down.gif',1)" onmouseout="MM_nbGroup('out')"><img
      src="assets/home_down.gif" alt="Navigation bar linking to home page" name="home" border="0" id="home" onload=
      "MM_nbGroup('init','group1','home','assets/home_up.gif',1)" /></a></td>
140           <td><a href="about_us.html" target="_top" onclick=
      "MM_nbGroup('down','group1','about_us','assets/about_us_down.gif',1)" onmouseover=
      "MM_nbGroup('over','about_us','assets/about_us_down.gif','assets/about_us_down.gif',1)" onmouseout=
      "MM_nbGroup('out')"><img src="assets/about_us_up.gif" alt="Navigation button linking to about_us page" name=
```

## FIGURE 10

*Images placed on page*

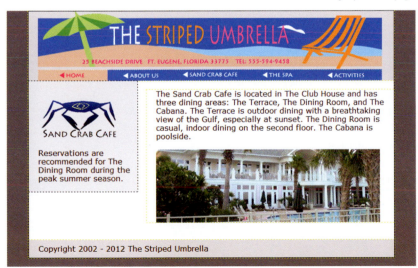

## Add images to a CSS container

1. Open the Striped Umbrella index page and copy both the banner and the navigation bar.

2. Switch back to the cafe page, delete the word "Header", and paste the banner and navigation bar into the header section of the page.

   TIP  Press [Ctrl][Tab] (Win) or [⌘][`](Mac) to switch between two open pages.

3. Close the index page.

4. Select the banner, switch to Code View and delete the pair of <H1> tags around the banner, as shown in Figure 9, then switch back to Design view.

   These tags were in the original placeholder text. They are affecting the spacing between the navigation bar and the banner.

   TIP  If you still see a space between the banner and navigation bar, place the insertion point in the space, then press [Delete].

5. Place the insertion point immediately in front of the word "Reservations", insert a paragraph break, press the up arrow on your keyboard, insert **cafe_logo.gif** from where you store your Data Files, then type **Sand Crab Cafe logo** as the alternate text.

6. Place the insertion point after the period after the word "poolside", insert a paragraph break, insert **cafe_photo.jpg** from where you store your Data Files, then type **Sand Crab Cafe photo** as the alternate text.

7. Save your file, then compare your screen to Figure 10.

*You copied the banner and navigation bar from the index page, pasted it onto the new cafe page, then added the cafe logo and photo to the page.*

# EDIT CONTENT
## IN CSS LAYOUT BLOCKS

## What You'll Do

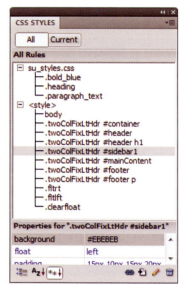

 In this lesson, you will center the two images you have added to the page. You will then view the div tag properties and edit the background colors. You will also change the body background color.

### Edit Content in CSS Layout Blocks

It is unlikely that you will find a preformatted CSS page layout that is exactly what you have in mind for your website. However, once you have created a page with a predefined CSS layout, it is easy to modify the individual style properties to change content formatting or placement to better fit your needs. You can easily change the properties to fit the color scheme of your website.

During the process of creating a page, you can attach an external style sheet to the page. If you choose to do this, you will see both the external style sheet and any internal styles for the page layout in the CSS Styles panel. Click the plus sign, if necessary, to see the rules listed in each section, and then select the rule you want to

modify. The properties and values for the selected rule appear in the Properties pane, as shown in Figure 11, where you can modify them.

**FIGURE 11**
*Viewing the CSS Styles panel*

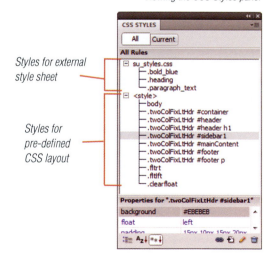

*Styles for external style sheet*

*Styles for pre-defined CSS layout*

FIGURE 12
*Centering content in layout blocks*

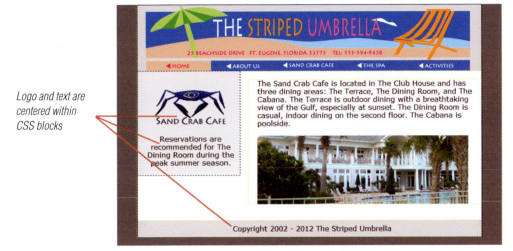

Logo and text are
centered within
CSS blocks

## Format content in CSS layout blocks

1.  Place the insertion point in front of the cafe logo.
2.  Change to the CSS Property inspector if necessary, then click the **Align Center button** 🔳.

    The logo and text are now centered in the left sidebar.
3.  Repeat Steps 1 and 2 to center the copyright statement, then compare your page to Figure 12.

    *(continued)*

### Using the Adobe CSS Advisor for cross-browser rendering issues

You can use the Browser Compatibility Check (BCC) feature to check for problems in the HTML code for CSS features that may render differently in multiple browsers. It flags and rates code on three levels: an error that could cause a serious display problem; an error that probably won't cause a serious display problem; or a warning that it has found code that is unsupported, but won't cause a serious display problem. Each bug is linked to the CSS Advisor, a part of the Adobe website, that offers solutions for that particular bug and other helpful information for resolving any issues with your pages. To check for browser compatibility, click File, point to Check Page, and then click Browser Compatibility or click the Check browser compatibility button on the Document toolbar.

**4.** Move the pointer over the top of the mainContent block (the block containing the cafe description and picture), click the **yellow border** to select the block, (the border turns red after it is selected), then move the pointer on the block border until the floating window shown in Figure 13 appears.

The properties of the div tag are displayed in a floating window. The Property inspector displays the div tag properties.

> TIP You can change the border color of div tags when the mouse is positioned over them in the Preferences dialog box. Select the Highlighting category, then click the Mouse-Over color box and select a different color. You can also disable highlighting by deselecting the Show checkbox for Mouse-Over.

**5.** Save your work.

*You centered the logo, reservations text, and copyright statement. You also viewed the properties of the div tag.*

**FIGURE 13**
*Viewing the div tag properties*

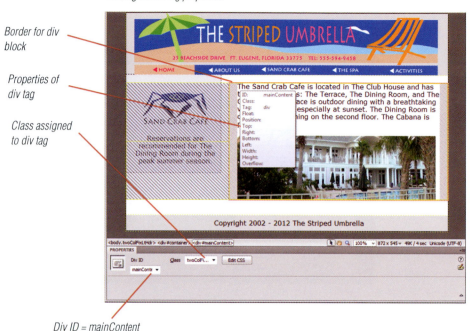

Border for div block

Properties of div tag

Class assigned to div tag

Div ID = mainContent

---

**Viewing options for CSS layout blocks**

There are several options for viewing your layout blocks in Design view. You can choose to show or hide outlines, temporarily assign different background colors to each individual layout block, or view the CSS Layout Box Model (padding and margins) of a selected layout. To change these options, use the View/Visual Aids menu, and then select or deselect the CSS Layout Outlines, CSS Layout Backgrounds, or CSS Layout Box Model menu choice. You can also use the Visual Aids button on the Document toolbar.

**FIGURE 14**

*Applying rules from the su_styles.css style sheet*

Text with bold_blue
rule applied

Text with paragraph_
text rule applied

1. Place the insertion point at the beginning of the paragraph in front of the words "The Sand Crab Cafe" in the introductory paragraph, press and hold **[Shift]**, then click the space at the end of the paragraph.

2. Click the **Targeted Rule list arrow** in the CSS Property inspector, then click **paragraph_text.**

   The paragraph_text rule is applied to the paragraph.

3. Repeat Steps 1 and 2 to apply the **paragraph_text** rule to the copyright statement and the **bold_blue** rule to the reservation information, as shown in Figure 14.

4. Save your work.

*You formatted three text blocks with rules from the style sheet.*

## Edit CSS layout block properties

1. Click the **twoColFixLtHdr #mainContent rule** in the CSS Styles panel to select it.

   The values of the margin and padding properties are displayed in the Properties pane. The mainContent block has a 250 pixel left margin with 20 px padding on the right and left sides of the block.

   *(continued)*

2. Click the **margin text box** to place the insertion point, replace 250 with **230**, then press **[Enter]** (Win) or **[return]** (Mac) as shown in Figure 15.

   TIP   You can also create more room for content by increasing the width of the container in the CSS Styles panel Properties pane.

   This will give more room for the text in the main paragraph to expand across the page.

3. Select the **cafe photo image**, click the **H space text box** in the Property inspector, type **10** to indent the image in the block, then press **[Tab]**.

4. Click the **twoColFixLtHdr #header** rule in the CSS Styles panel to select it.

5. Click to select the background color #DDDDDD, type **#FFFFFF** as shown in Figure 16, then press **[Enter]** (Win) or **[return]** (Mac).

   The header background color is now white.

   TIP   You only need to use the abbreviated hexadecimal color code, such as #FFF, when specifying colors. However, in the Dreamweaver predesigned CSS layouts, the color codes are shown with the full 6-character codes. Either code will work. You can also specify colors by their names. For example, the color magenta can be specified as "magenta", #FF00FF, or #F0F.

6. Repeat Steps 4 and 5 to change the footer and sidebar1 background colors to **#FFFFFF**.

7. Save your work, then compare your screen to Figure 17.

*You changed the margin width of a CSS layout block, indented the cafe photo, then changed the background color of three CSS layout blocks to white.*

**FIGURE 15**
*Editing the properties of the twoColFixLtHdr #mainContent rule*

Select the twoColFixLtHdr #mainContent rule

Change the margin settings for the block to 0 0 0 230px

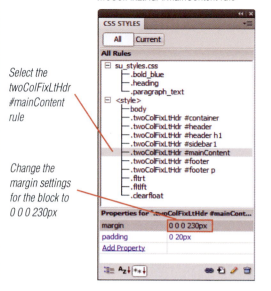

**FIGURE 16**
*Editing the properties of the twoColFixLtHdr #header rule*

Select the twoColFixLtHdr #header rule

Change the background color value to #FFFFFF

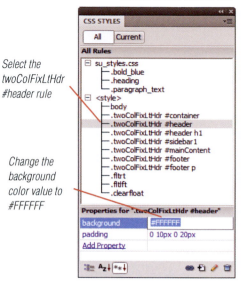

**FIGURE 17**
*The four layout blocks now have a white background*

The four blocks have the same background color

**FIGURE 18**

*Changing the body background value to #FFFFFF*

Select the body rule

Change the background
color value to #FFFFFF

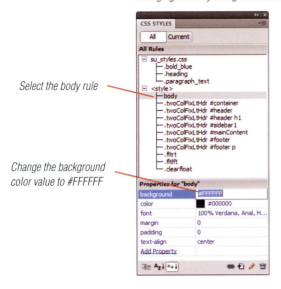

1. Select the **body tag** in the CSS Styles panel.

2. Click to select the background color **#666666**, type **#FFFFFF**, as shown in Figure 18, then press **[Enter]** (Win) or **[return]** (Mac).

   The body tag for the page is now set to display a white background. The body background color is the color of the page behind the CSS container.

3. Save your work, preview the page in your browser, compare your screen to Figure 19, then close the browser.

*You changed the value for the background color to white.*

**FIGURE 19**

*Viewing the cafe page in the browser*

# CREATE A
## TABLE

## What You'll Do

*In this lesson, you will create a table for the cafe page in The Striped Umbrella website to provide a grid for the cafe hours.*

### Understanding Table Modes

Now that you have learned how CSS can act as containers to hold information in place on web pages, let's look at tables as another layout tool. Tables are great when you have a need for a grid layout on a page, such as a chart with text and numbers. Some web pages are based entirely on tables for their page layouts and some pages contain tables inside CSS layout blocks. To create a table, click the Table button on the Insert panel. When the Layout category of the Insert panel is displayed, you can choose Standard mode or Expanded Table mode by clicking the appropriate button on the Insert panel after selecting a table on the page.

### Creating a Table

To create a table in Standard mode, click the Table button on the Insert panel to open the Table dialog box. Enter values for the number of rows and columns, the border thickness, table width, cell padding, and cell spacing. The **border** is the outline or frame around the table and the individual cell and is measured in pixels. The table width can be specified in pixels or as a percentage. When the table width is specified as a percentage, the table width will expand to fill up its container (the browser window, a CSS container, or another table). A table placed inside another table is called a **nested table**. Figure 20 could either be a page based on a table set to 100% width (of the browser window or container), or it could be a page that is not based on a table at all. The content spreads across the entire browser window, without a container to set boundaries, such as the pages you created in the first four chapters. When the table width is specified in pixels, the table width stays the same, regardless of the size of the browser window or container. The page in Figure 21 is an example of a page based on a table with a fixed width of 750 pixels. The content will not spread outside the table borders unless it contains images that are wider than the table. **Cell padding** is the distance between the cell content and the **cell walls**, the lines inside the cell borders. **Cell spacing** is the distance between cells.

## Using Expanded Tables Mode

Expanded Tables mode is a feature that allows you to change to a table view with expanded table borders and temporary cell padding and cell spacing. This mode makes it much easier to actually see how many rows and columns you have in your table. Often, especially after splitting empty cells, it is difficult to place the insertion point precisely in a table cell. The Expanded Tables mode allows you to see each cell clearly. However, most of the time you will want to work in Standard mode to maintain the WYSIWYG environment. **WYSIWYG** is the acronym for What You See Is What You Get. This

means that your page should look the same in the browser as it does in the web editor. Before you create a table, you should sketch a plan for it that shows its location on the page and the placement of text and graphics in its cells. You should also decide whether to include borders around the tables and cells. Setting the border value to 0 causes the table to appear invisible, so that viewers will not realize that you used a table for the layout unless they look at the code. Figure 22 shows a sketch of the table you will create on The Striped Umbrella cafe page to organize the cafe hours.

## Setting Table Accessibility Preferences

You can make a table more accessible to visually handicapped viewers by adding a table caption and a table summary that screen readers can read. The table caption appears on the screen. The table summary does not. These features are especially useful for tables that are used for tabular data. **Table headers** are another way to provide accessibility. Table headers can be placed at the top or sides of a table with data. They are automatically centered and bold and are used by screen readers to help viewers identify the table content. Table captions, summaries, and headers are all created in the Table dialog box.

**FIGURE 20**

*Page shown without using tables or using a table based on a 100% width*

Content spreads across the browser window

**FIGURE 21**

*Same page shown using a fixed-width table for layout*

Table confines content; leftover white space displayed outside table borders

**FIGURE 22**

*Sketch of table on cafe page*

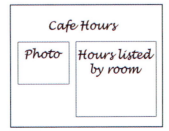

## Create a table

1. Click to place the insertion point in the white space between the cafe photo and the footer.

2. Click **Table** in the Common group on the Insert panel.

    The Table dialog box opens.

3. Type **5** in the Rows text box, type **3** in the Columns text box, type **500** in the Table width text box, click the **Table width list arrow**, click **pixels** if necessary, type **0** in the Border thickness text box, then click the **Top** Header.

    TIP  It is better to add more rows than you think you will need when you create your table. After they are filled with content, it is far easier to delete rows than to add rows if you decide later to split or merge cells in the table.

4. In the Summary text box, type **This table contains the cafe hours**, then compare your screen to Figure 23.

5. Click **OK**.

    The table appears on the page, but the table summary is not visible. The summary will not appear in the browser but will be read by screen readers.

    TIP  To edit accessibility preferences for a table, switch to Code view to edit the code directly.

*(continued)*

**FIGURE 23**
*Table dialog box*

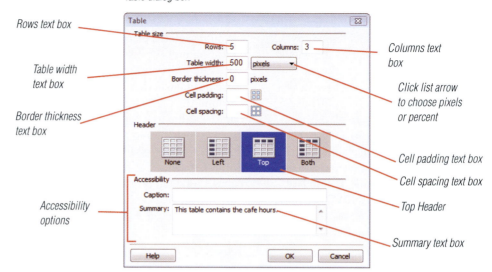

Rows text box

Table width text box

Border thickness text box

Columns text box

Click list arrow to choose pixels or percent

Cell padding text box

Cell spacing text box

Top Header

Accessibility options

Summary text box

---

**DESIGN**TIP  **Setting table and cell widths when using tables for page layout**

If you use a table to place all the text and graphics contained on a web page, it is wise to set the width of the table in pixels. This ensures that the table will not resize itself proportionately if the browser window size is changed. If you set the width of a table using pixels, the table will remain one size, regardless of the browser window size. For instance, if the width of a table is set to slightly less than 800, the table will stretch across the whole width of a browser window set at a resolution of $800 \times 600$. The same table would be the same size on a screen set at $1024 \times 768$ and therefore would not stretch across the entire screen. Most designers use a resolution of $800 \times 600$ or higher. Be aware, however, that if you set the width of your table at 800 pixels, your table will be too wide to print the entire width of the page, and part of the right side of the page will be cut off. If you are designing a table layout for a page that is likely to be printed by the viewer, you should make your table narrower to fit on a printed page. If you set a table width as a percentage, however, the table would resize itself proportionately in any browser window, regardless of the resolution. You can also set each cell width as either a percentage of the table or as fixed pixels.

**FIGURE 24**

*Expanded Tables mode*

Click "exit" to
return to
Standard
mode

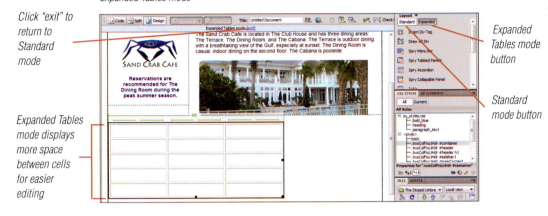

Expanded
Tables mode
button

Standard
mode button

Expanded Tables
mode displays
more space
between cells
for easier
editing

**FIGURE 25**

*Property inspector showing properties of selected table*

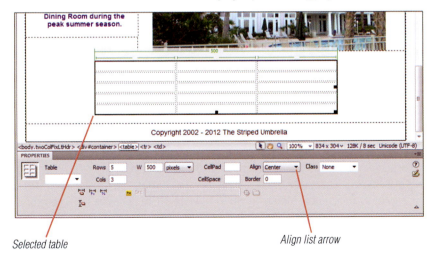

Selected table

Align list arrow

6. Click the **Insert panel list arrow**, click **Layout**, click the **Expanded Tables mode button** Expanded , click **OK** in the Getting Started in Expanded Tables Mode dialog box, then compare your screen to Figure 24.

The Expanded Tables mode makes it easier to select and edit tables.

7. Click the **Standard mode button** Standard to return to Standard mode.

TIP  You can also return to Standard mode by clicking [exit] in the blue bar below the Document toolbar.

*You created a table on the cafe page that will display the cafe hours with five rows and three columns and a width of 500 pixels. You used a top header and added a table summary that will be read by screen readers.*

## Set table properties

1. Move the pointer slowly to the top or bottom edge of the table until you see the pointer change to a Table pointer ⌖ , then click the **table border** to select the table, if necessary.

2. Expand the Property inspector (if necessary) to display the current properties of the new table.

TIP  The Property inspector will display information about the table only when the table is selected.

3. Click the **Align list arrow** in the Property inspector, then click **Center** to center the table on the page, as shown in Figure 25.

The center alignment formatting will center the table inside the CSS container.

*You selected and center-aligned the table.*

# RESIZE, SPLIT, AND
## MERGE CELLS

## What You'll Do

 *In this lesson, you will set the width of the table cells to be split across the table in predetermined widths. You will then split one cell. You will also merge some cells to provide space for the table header.*

### Resizing Table Elements

You can resize the rows or columns of a table manually. To resize a table, row, or column, you must first select the table, then drag one of the table's three selection handles. To change all the columns in a table so that they are the same size, drag the middle-right selection handle. To resize the height of all rows simultaneously, drag the middle-bottom selection handle. To resize the entire table, drag the right-corner selection handle. To resize a row or column individually, drag the interior cell borders up, down, to the left, or to the right. You can also resize selected columns, rows, or individual cells by entering specific measurements in the W and H text boxes in the Property inspector specified either in pixels or as a percentage. Cells whose width or height is specified as a percentage will maintain that percentage in relation to the width or height of the entire table if the table is resized.

### Adding or deleting a row

As you add new content to your table, you might find that you have too many or too few rows or columns. You can add or delete one row or column at a time or several at once. You use commands on the Modify menu to add and delete table rows and columns. When you add a new column or row, you must first select the existing column or row to which the new column or row will be adjacent. The Insert Rows or Columns dialog box lets you choose how many rows or columns you want to insert or delete, and where you want them placed in relation to the selected row or column. The new column or row will have the same formatting and number of cells as the selected column or row. After you have split and merged cells, it can be challenging to add or delete rows.

Using the Table button creates a new table with evenly spaced columns and rows. Sometimes you will want to adjust the cells in a table by splitting or merging them. To **split** a cell means to divide it into multiple rows or columns. To **merge** cells means to combine multiple cells into one cell. Using split and merged cells gives you more flexibility and control in placing page elements in a table and can help you create a more visually exciting layout. When you merge cells, the HTML tag used to describe the merged cell changes from a width size tag to a column span or row span tag. For example, <td colspan="2"> is the code for two cells that have been merged into one cell that spans two columns.

**QUICK**TIP
You can split merged cells and merge split cells.

---

**DESIGN**TIP **Using nested tables**

A nested table is a table inside a table. To create a nested table, you place the insertion point in the cell where you want to insert the nested table, then click the Table button on the Insert panel. A nested table is a separate table that can be formatted differently from the table in which it is placed. Nested tables are useful when you want part of your table data to have visible borders and part to have invisible borders. For example, you can nest a table with red borders inside a table with invisible borders. You need to plan carefully when you insert nested tables. It is easy to get carried away and insert too many nested tables, which makes it more difficult to apply formatting and rearrange table elements. Before you insert a nested table, consider whether you could achieve the same result by adding rows and columns or by splitting cells.

## Resize columns

1. Click inside the **first cell** in the bottom row.

2. Type **30%** in the W text box in the Property inspector, then press **[Enter]** (Win) or **[return]** (Mac) to change the width of the cell to 30 percent of the table width.

   Notice that the column width is shown as a percentage at the top of the first column in the table, along with the table width of 500 pixels.

   > TIP  You need to type the % sign next to the number you type in the W text box. Otherwise, the width will be expressed in pixels.

3. Repeat Steps 1 and 2 for the next two cells in the last row, using **30%** for the middle cell and **40%** for the last cell, then compare your screen to Figure 26.

   The combined widths of the three cells add up to 100 percent. As you add content to the table, the columns will remain in this proportion unless you insert an image that is larger than the table cell. If a larger image is inserted, the cell width will expand to display it.

   > TIP  Changing the width of a single cell changes the width of the entire column.

*You set the width of each of the three cells in the bottom row to set the column sizes for the table. This will keep the table from resizing when you add content.*

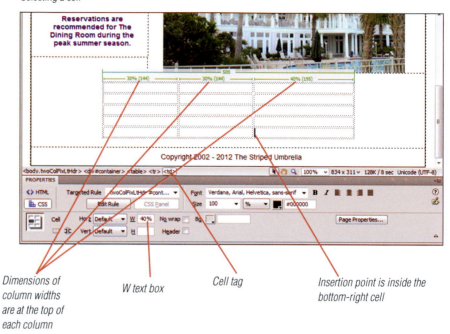

FIGURE 26
*Selecting a cell*

Dimensions of column widths are at the top of each column

W text box

Cell tag

Insertion point is inside the bottom-right cell

---

### Resetting table widths and heights

After resizing columns and rows in a table, you might want to change the sizes of the columns and rows back to their previous sizes. To reset columns and rows to their previous widths and heights, select the table, click Modify on the Application bar (Win) or Menu bar (Mac), point to Table, then click Clear Cell Heights or Clear Cell Widths. Using the Clear Cell Heights command also forces the cell border to snap to the bottom of any inserted graphics, so you can also use this command to tighten up extra white space in a cell. This menu also has choices for converting table widths and heights from pixels to percents and vice versa.

---

*Positioning Objects with CSS and Tables*

**FIGURE 27**

*Resizing the height of a row*

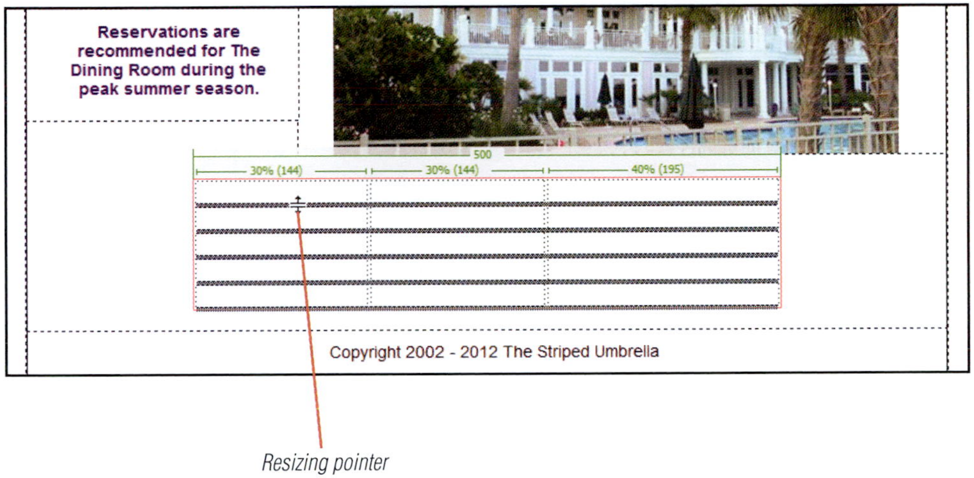

*Resizing pointer*

1. Place the pointer over the bottom border of the first row until it changes to a resizing pointer ⬍, as shown in Figure 27, then click and drag down about ¼ of an inch to increase the height of the row.

   The border turns darker when you select and drag it.

2. Click **Window** on the menu bar, click **History**, then drag the **slider** in the History panel up one line to the **Set Width**: **40%** mark to return the row to its original height.

3. Close the History panel.

*You changed the height of the top row, then used the History panel to change it back to its original height.*

## HTML table tags

When formatting a table, it is important to understand the basic HTML table tags. The tags used for creating a table are <table> </table>. The tags used to create table rows are <tr></tr>. The tags used to create table cells are <td></td>. Dreamweaver places the   code into each empty table cell at the time it is created. The   code represents a nonbreaking space, or a space that a browser will display on the page. Some browsers will collapse an empty cell, which can ruin the look of a table. The nonbreaking space will hold the cell until content is placed in it, at which time it will be automatically removed.

## Split cells

1. Click inside the first cell in the fifth row, then click the **<td>** in the tag selector.

   TIP  You can click the cell tag <td> (the HTML tag for that cell) on the tag selector to select the corresponding cell in the table. To select the entire table, click the <table> tag on the tag selector.

2. Click the **Splits cell into rows or columns button** ⊐⊏ in the Property inspector.

3. Click the **Split cell into Rows option button** (if necessary), type **2** in the Number of rows text box (if necessary), as shown in Figure 28, click **OK,** then click in the cell to deselect it.

   The cell is split, as shown in Figure 29.

   TIP  To create a new row identical to the one above it, place the insertion point in the last cell of a table, then press [Tab].

*You split a cell into two rows.*

**FIGURE 28**
*Splitting a cell into two rows*

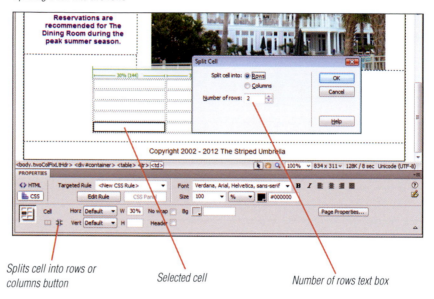

Splits cell into rows or columns button

Selected cell

Number of rows text box

**FIGURE 29**
*Resulting split cells*

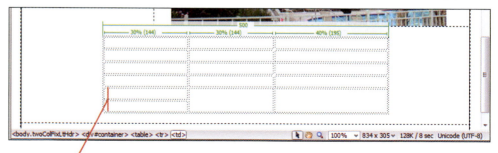

Two cells split from one cell

## FIGURE 30
*Merging selected cells into one cell*

Resulting merged cell

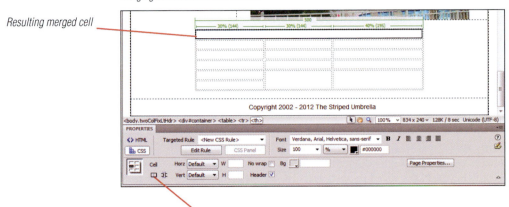

Merges selected cells using spans button

1. Click to set the insertion point in the first cell in the top row, then drag to the right to select the second and third cells in the top row.

2. Click the **Merges selected cells using spans button** in the Property inspector.

   The three cells are merged into one cell, as shown in Figure 30. Merged cells are good placeholders for banners or headings.

   TIP   You can only merge cells that are adjacent to each other.

3. Click the **Show Code view button** ⟨⟩ Code, then view the code for the merged cells, as shown in Figure 31.

   Notice the table tags denoting the column span (th colspan="3") and the nonbreaking spaces ( ) inserted in the empty cells.

   The nonbreaking space is a special character that is inserted automatically in an empty cell to serve as a placeholder until content is added. A nonbreaking space will override automatic word wrap, or prevent a line break from being inserted in HTML code.

4. Click the **Show Design view button** Design, select and merge the first cells in rows 2, 3, 4, and 5 in the left column, then save your work.

*You merged three cells in the first row to make room for the table header. You then merged four cells in the left column to make room for an image.*

## FIGURE 31
*Code for merged cells*

```
159        </p>
160        <p><img src="assets/cafe_photo.jpg" alt="Sand Crab Cafe photo" width="480" height="155" hspace="10" />
     </p>
161    </div>
162    <!-- This clearing element should immediately follow the #mainContent div in order to force the
     #container div to contain all child floats -->
163    <table width="500" border="0" align="center" summary="This table contains the cafe hours.">
164        <tr>
165            <th colspan="3" scope="col"> </th>
166        </tr>
167        <tr>
168            <td> </td>
169            <td> </td>
170            <td> </td>
```

Nonbreaking spaces          colspan tag

# INSERT AND ALIGN
## IMAGES IN TABLE CELLS

## What You'll Do

*In this lesson, you will insert an image of a cheesecake in the left column of the table. After placing the image, you will align it within the cell.*

### Inserting Images in Table Cells

You can insert images in the cells of a table using the Image command in the Images menu on the Insert panel. If you already have images saved in your website that you would like to insert in a table, you can drag them from the Assets panel into the table cells. When you add a large image to a cell, the cell expands to accommodate the inserted image. If you select the Show attributes when inserting Images check box in the Accessibility category of the Preferences dialog box, the Image Tag Accessibility Attributes dialog box will open after you insert an image, prompting you to enter alternate text. Figure 32 shows the John Deere website, which uses several tables for page layout and contains images in its table cells. Notice that some images appear in cells by themselves, and some appear in cells containing text or other graphics. Some cells have a white background, and some have a green background.

## Aligning Images in Table Cells

You can align images both horizontally and vertically within a cell. You can align an image horizontally using the Horz (horizontal) alignment options in the Property inspector, as shown in Figure 33. This option is used to align the entire contents of the cell, whether there is one object or several. You can also align an image vertically by the top, middle, bottom, or baseline of a cell. To align an image vertically within a cell, use the Vert (vertical) Align list arrow in the Property inspector, then choose an alignment option. To control spacing between cells, you can use cell padding and cell spacing. **Cell padding** is the space between a cell's border and its contents. **Cell spacing** is the distance between adjacent cells.

### FIGURE 32
*John Deere website*

*John Deere website used with permission from Deere & Company – www.johndeere.com*

### FIGURE 33
*Horizontally aligning cell contents*

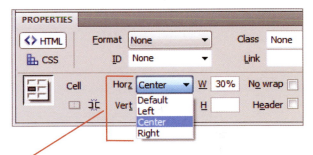

*Horizontal alignment options*

## Insert images in table cells

1. Click in the merged cells in the left column of the table (under the merged cells in the top row) to place the insertion point.

2. Insert **cheesecake.jpg** from where you store your Data Files, then type **Banana Chocolate Cheesecake** for the alternate text.

   TIP    You may have to click out of the cell if you see extra space around the image.

3. Compare your screen to Figure 34.

4. Refresh the Assets panel to verify that the new image was copied to The Striped Umbrella website assets folder.

5. Save your work, then preview the page in your browser.

6. Close your browser.

*You inserted an image into a table cell on the cafe page.*

**FIGURE 34**
*Image inserted into table cell*

*cheesecake.jpg*

## Using rulers, grids, and guides for positioning page content

There are some other options available to help you position your page content that are available through the View menu. **Grids** provide a graph paper-like view of a page. Horizontal and vertical lines fill the page when this option is turned on. You can edit the line colors, the distance between them, whether they are displayed using lines or dots, and whether or not objects "snap" to them. **Guides** are horizontal or vertical lines that you drag onto the page from the rulers. You can edit both the colors of the guides and the color of the distance, a feature that shows you the distance between two guides. You can lock the guides so you don't accidentally move them and you can set them either to snap to page elements or have page elements snap to them. To display grids or guides, click View on the Application bar (Win) or Menu bar (Mac), point to Grid, then click Show Grid or point to Guides and then click Show Guides.

*Positioning Objects with CSS and Tables*

**FIGURE 35**
*Aligning image in cell*

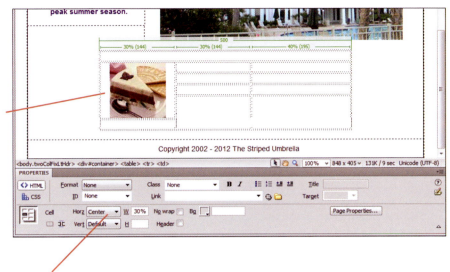

*Cheesecake photo is centered within cell*

*Horizontal alignment is set to center*

1. Click to the right side of the **cheesecake image** to place the insertion point.

2. Click the **Horz list arrow** in the Property inspector, then click **Center**. (Both the HTML and CSS Property inspectors have the alignment options.)

   The cheesecake image is centered in the cell. The alignment will be applied to all content inserted into this cell. The effect of the alignment, however, may not be apparent until more content is added to the table.

3. Compare your screen to Figure 35.

4. Save your work.

5. Preview the page in your browser, view the aligned image, then close your browser.

*You center-aligned cell content.*

## Working with div tags

Div tags are used for formatting blocks of content, similar to the way P tags are used to format paragraphs of text. Div tags, however, are more flexible in that they can be used as a container for any type of block content. They are used in various ways, such as centering content on a page or applying color to an area of a web page. One of the benefits of using div tags is that they are combined easily with Cascading Style Sheets for formatting and positioning. When alignment is assigned to a block of content, Dreamweaver will automatically add a div tag. Div tags are frequently used in style sheets to specify formatting attributes.

# INSERT TEXT AND FORMAT
## CELL CONTENT

## What You'll Do

*In this lesson, you will type the cafe hours in the table. You will also format the text to enhance its appearance on the page. Last, you will add formatting to some of the cells and cell content.*

### Inserting Text in a Table

You can enter text in a table either by typing it in a cell, copying it from another source and pasting it into a cell, or importing it from another program. Once you place text in a table cell, you can format it to make it more readable and more visually appealing on the page.

### Formatting Cell Content

To format the contents of a cell, select the contents in the cell, then apply formatting to it. For example, you can select an image in a cell and center it, add a border, or add V space. Or, you can select text in a cell and apply a style or use the Text Indent or Text Outdent buttons in the HTML Property inspector to move the text farther away from or closer to the cell walls.

If a cell contains multiple objects of the same type, such as text, you can either format each item individually or select the entire cell and apply formatting that will be applied identically to all items. You can tell whether you have selected the cell contents or the cell by looking to see what options are showing in the Property inspector. Figure 36 shows a selected image in a cell. Notice that the Property inspector displays options for formatting the object, rather than options for formatting the cell.

## Formatting Cells

Formatting a cell is different from formatting a cell's contents. Formatting a cell can include setting properties that visually enhance the cell's appearance, such as setting a cell width and assigning a background color. You can also set global alignment properties for the cell content, using the Horz or Vert list arrows on the Property inspector. These options set the alignment for cell content horizontally or vertically. To format a cell, you need to either select the cell or place the insertion point inside the cell you want to format, then choose the cell formatting options you want in the Property inspector. For example, to choose a fill color for a selected cell, click the Background Color button in the Property inspector, then choose a color from the color picker.

### QUICKTIP

Cell and table formatting can also be specified through rules in a Cascading Style Sheet. Some options, such as using an image for a cell background, cannot be set using the Property inspector.

To format a cell, you must expand the Property inspector to display the cell formatting options. In Figure 37, notice that the insertion point is positioned in the cheesecake cell, but the **image** is not selected. The Property inspector displays the formatting options for cells.

### FIGURE 36
*Property inspector showing options for selected image*

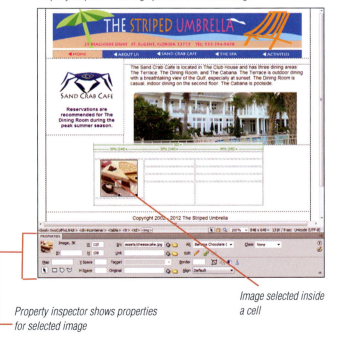

*Property inspector shows properties for selected image*

*Image selected inside a cell*

### FIGURE 37
*Property inspector showing options for formatting a cell*

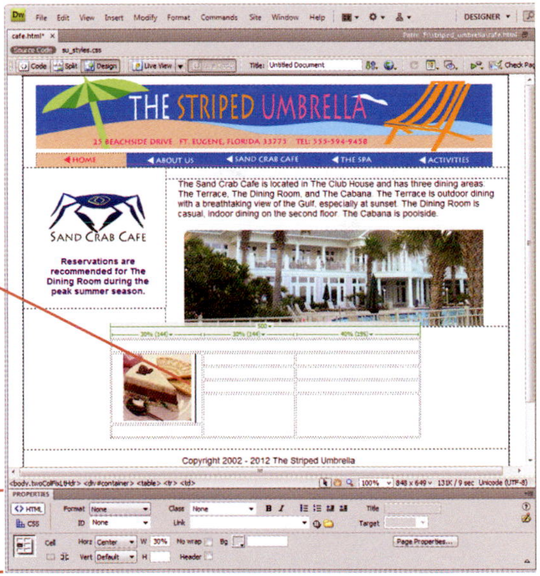

*Insertion point in cell*

*Property inspector shows cell properties, not image properties*

## Insert text

1. Click in the cell below the cheesecake photo, type **Banana Chocolate**, press **[Shift][Enter]** (Win) or **[shift][return]** (Mac), type **Cheesecake**, press **[Shift][Enter]** (Win) or **[shift][return]** (Mac), then type **Our signature dessert**.

2. Click in the top row of the table to place the insertion point, then type **Sand Crab Cafe Hours**.

   The text is automatically bolded because the top row header was chosen when you created the table.

3. Merge the two bottom-right cells in the last row, then enter the cafe dining area names, hours, and room service information as shown in Figure 38. Use line breaks after the first two lines of text.

   > TIP   If your table cells seem to have extra space in them, click the <table> tag to tighten it up.

*You entered text in the table to provide information about the dining room hours.*

FIGURE 38
*Typing text into cells*

Text typed into cells

### Importing and exporting data from tables

You can import and export tabular data into and out of Dreamweaver. Tabular data is data that is arranged in columns and rows and separated by a **delimiter**: a comma, tab, colon, semicolon, or similar character. **Importing** means to bring data created in another software program into Dreamweaver, and **exporting** means to save data created in Dreamweaver in a special file format that can be opened by other programs. Files that are imported into Dreamweaver must be saved as delimited files. **Delimited files** are database or spreadsheet files that have been saved as text files with delimiters such as tabs or commas separating the data. Programs such as Microsoft Access and Microsoft Excel offer many file formats for saving files. To import a delimited file, click File on the Application bar (Win) or Menu bar (Mac), point to Import, then click Tabular Data. The Import Tabular Data dialog box opens, offering you formatting options for the imported table. To export a table that you created in Dreamweaver, click File on the Application bar (Win) or Menu bar (Mac), point to Export, then click Table. The Export Table dialog box opens, letting you choose the type of delimiter you want for the delimited file.

**FIGURE 39**

*Formatting text using a Cascading Style Sheet*

paragraph_text style

paragraph_text style

bold_blue style

## Format cell content

1.  Select the text "Banana Chocolate Cheesecake," then apply the **bold_blue** rule.

2.  Select the text "Our Signature dessert" and apply the **paragraph_text** rule, then select all of the text about the cafe hours and apply the **paragraph_text** rule.

3.  Repeat Step 2 to apply the **paragraph_text** rule to the room service text.

    Your screen should resemble Figure 39.

4.  Modify the navigation bar to show the cafe button, rather than the home button, in the down state.

*You formatted text in table cells using a Cascading Style Sheet, and modified the navigation bar to show the cafe button in the down state.*

## POWER USER SHORTCUTS

| to do this: | use this shortcut: |
|---|---|
| Insert table | [Ctrl][Alt][T] (Win) or ⌘[option][T] (Mac) |
| Select a cell | [Ctrl][A] (Win) or ⌘[A] (Mac) |
| Merge cells | [Ctrl][Alt][M] (Win) or ⌘[option][M] (Mac) |
| Split cell | [Ctrl][Alt][S] (Win) or ⌘[option][S] (Mac) |
| Insert row | [Ctrl][M] (Win) or ⌘[M] (Mac) |
| Insert column | [Ctrl][Shift][A] (Win) or ⌘[Shift][A] (Mac) |
| Delete row | [Ctrl][Shift][M] (Win) or ⌘[Shift][M] (Mac) |
| Delete column | [Ctrl][Shift][-] (Win) or ⌘[Shift][-] (Mac) |
| Increase column span | [Ctrl][Shift][]] (Win) or ⌘[Shift][]] (Mac) |
| Decrease column span | [Ctrl][Shift][[] (Win) or ⌘[Shift][[] (Mac) |

## Format cells

1. Click to place the insertion point in the cell with the cheesecake text.

2. Click the **Horz list arrow** in the Property inspector, then click **Center** to center the cell contents.

   You do not need to select the text because you are setting the alignment for all contents in the cell.

3. Repeat Steps 1 and 2 for the cell with the table header and the cell with the room service information.

   TIP   Click to the right of the nested table to easily select the cell.

4. Click in the cell with the room service text, click the **Vert text box**, then click **Bottom**, as shown in Figure 40.

   TIP   Setting alignment can be helpful if you need to troubleshoot a page later.

5. Save your work.

*You formatted table cells by adding horizontal and vertical alignment.*

**FIGURE 40**

*Formatting cells using horizontal and vertical alignment*

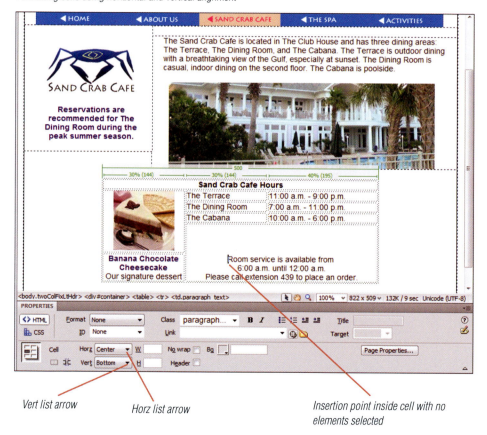

Vert list arrow

Horz list arrow

Insertion point inside cell with no elements selected

**FIGURE 41**

*Hiding visual aids*

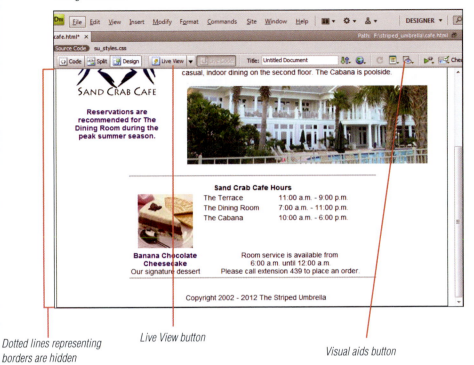

Dotted lines representing borders are hidden

Live View button

Visual aids button

## Using visual aids

Dreamweaver has an option for turning on and off various features, such as table borders, that are displayed in Design view but are not displayed in the browser. This tool is called Visual Aids and can be accessed through the View menu or through the Visual Aids button on the Document toolbar. Most of the time, these features are very helpful while you are editing and formatting a page. However, turning them off is a quick way to see how the page will appear in the browser without having to open it in the browser window.

### Modify cell content

1. Click after the word "dessert" in the bottom left cell, then press [Tab].

    Pressing the tab key while the insertion point is in the last cell of the table creates a new row. Even though it looks like the cell with the room service information is the last cell, it is not because of the merged cells.

2. Merge the cells in the new row, click **Insert** on the Application bar (Win) or Menu bar (Mac), point to **HTML**, then click **Horizontal Rule**.

3. Click in front of the table header, then insert another horizontal rule.

4. Save your work.

*You added two horizontal rules to the table to set the table off from the rest of the page.*

### Check layout

1. Click the **Visual Aids button** 🖻 on the Document toolbar, then click **Hide All Visual Aids**, as shown in Figure 41.

    The borders around the table, table cells, and CSS blocks are all hidden, allowing you to see more clearly how the page will look in the browser.

2. Repeat Step 1 to show the visual aids again. (*Hint*: You can also click the Live View button on the Document toolbar to see how the page will look in the browser.)

3. Save your work, preview the cafe page in the browser, close the browser, then close Dreamweaver.

*You used the Hide All Visual Aids command to hide the table borders and layout block outlines, then showed them again.*

**Create a page using CSS layouts.**

1. Open the blooms & bulbs website, then create a new blank HTML page with the 2 column elastic, left sidebar, header and footer style, linking the blooms_styles.css file to the page.

2. Save the file as **classes.html**, overwriting the existing classes page.

**Add content to CSS layout blocks.**

1. Open the index page, copy the banner and navigation bar, then close the index page. (*Hint*: If you have space between your banner and navigation bar, place the insertion point between them and press [Delete].)

2. Delete the placeholder text in the header on the classes page (including the <h1> tags), then paste the banner and navigation bar in the header container.

3. Modify the navigation bar to show the classes button as the down image.

4. Delete the footer placeholder text, type **Copyright 2001 - 2012 blooms & bulbs** in the footer container, apply the paragraph_text rule, then center it.

5. Delete the placeholder content from the #mainContent block, including any <h1> tags.

6. Type **Master Gardener Classes Beginning Soon!**, enter a paragraph break, then import the text gardeners.doc.

7. Enter a paragraph break, then insert the flower_bed.jpg from your Data Files folder. Add the alternate text **Flower bed in downtown Alvin** to the image when prompted.

8. Save your work.

**Edit content in CSS layout blocks.**

1. Select the twoColElsLtHdr #container style in the CSS Styles panel.

2. Edit the rule by changing the width of the container to **48em**, and the float to **Left**. (*Hint*: The Float setting is in the Box category.)

3. Select the twoColElsLtHdr #header style in the CSS panel and change the background color to #FFF.

4. Repeat Step 3 to change the background color of the footer to #FFF and the background color of the sidebar1 to #FFF.

5. Repeat Step 3 to change the body background to #FFF.

6. Place the insertion point in front of the banner, then center the banner.

7. Select the text Master Gardener Classes Beginning Soon! and apply the bold_blue rule.

8. Select the paragraphs of Master Gardener information in the mainContent block and format it with the paragraph_text rule.

9. Save your work.

**Create a table.**

1. Delete the placeholder text in the left sidebar, then insert a table with the following settings: Rows: **10**, Columns: **2**, Table width: **150 pixels**, Border thickness: **0**, Cell padding: **5**, Cell spacing: **5**, and Header: **Top**. In the Summary text box, enter the text **This table is used to list the class dates and hours.**

2. Center-align the table in the sidebar.

3. Replace the existing page title with the title **Master Gardener classes begin soon!**, then save your work.

**Resize, split, and merge cells.**

1. Select the first cell in the last row, then set the cell width to **25%**.

2. Select the second cell in the last row, then set the cell width to **75%**.

3. Merge the two cells in the first row.

4. Merge the two cells in the last row.

5. Save your work.

## Insert and align images in table cells.

1. Use the Insert panel to insert gardening_gloves.gif in the last row of the table. You can find this image in the assets folder where you store your Data Files. Add the alternate text **Gardening gloves** to the image when prompted, then center the image in the merged cell.

2. Save your work.

## Insert text and format cell content.

1. Type **Schedule** in the merged cell in the first row, then center align the cell.

2. Type the dates and times for the classes from Figure 42 in each row of the table.

3. Select Schedule and apply the bold_blue rule.

4. Select the dates and times in the table and apply the paragraph_text rule, then add a horizontal rule under the image at the bottom of the page.

5. Save your work, preview the page in your browser, then close your browser.

6. Close all open pages.

**FIGURE 42**
*Completed Skills Review*

# PROJECT BUILDER 1

In this exercise, you will continue your work on the TripSmart website that you began in Project Builder 1 in Chapter 1 and developed in the previous chapters. You are ready to begin work on a page that will feature catalog items. You plan to use a CSS layout with a table to place the information on the page.

1. Open the TripSmart website.

2. Create a new page based on the 1 column elastic, centered, header and footer CSS page layout, attaching the tripsmart_styles.css file, then save the file as **catalog.html**, replacing the placeholder catalog page in the website.

3. Open the index page, copy the banner and navigation bar, then close the index page.

4. Paste the banner and navigation bar in the header block, replacing the placeholder text.

5. Edit the oneColElsCtrHdr #container width to **48 em**.

6. Edit the oneColElsCtrHdr #header background to **#FFF**.

7. Edit the oneColElsCtrHdr #footer to have a white background.

8. Save your work.

9. Delete the placeholder content in the oneColElsCtrHdr #mainContent block.

10. Insert a table into the #mainContent block with the following settings: Rows: **5**, Columns: **3**, Table width: **725 pixels**, Border thickness: **0**, Header: **Top**. Enter an appropriate table summary, then center-align the table.

11. Set the cell widths in the bottom row to **33%**, **33%**, and **34%**.

12. Merge the three cells in the first row, type **Our products are backed with a 100% guarantee.**

13. In the three cells in the second row, type **Protection from UV rays; Cool, light-weight, versatile;** and **Pockets for everything** then center the text in each cell.

14. Place the files hat.jpg, pants.jpg, and vest.jpg from the assets folder where you store your Data Files in the three cells in the third row, adding the following alternate text to the images: **Safari hat**, **Kenya convertible pants**, and **Photographer's vest**; center the three images.

15. Type **Safari Hat**, **Kenya Convertible Pants**, and **Photographer's Vest** in the three cells in the fourth row, then center each label.

16. Type **Item number 50501** and **$29.00** with a line break between them in the first cell in the fifth row.

17. Repeat Step 16 to type **Item number 62495** and **$39.50** in the second cell in the fifth row.

18. Repeat Step 16 to type **Item number 52301** and **$54.95** in the third cell in the fifth row, then center each item number and price in the cells.

19. Apply the paragraph_text rule to the three descriptions in the second row.

20. Create a new class rule in the tripsmart_styles.css style sheet named **reverse_text** with the following settings: Font-family, Verdana, Geneva, sans-serif; Font-size, 14 px; Font-style, normal; Font-weight, bold; Color, #FFF. (*Hint*: Be sure to choose Class under Selector Type.)

21. Apply the reverse_text rule to the text "Our products are backed by a 100% guarantee.", then change the cell background color to **#666666**.

22. Apply the reverse_text rule to the three item names under the images, then change the cell background color to **#999**.

**23.** Create a new rule called **item_numbers** with the following settings: Font: Verdana, Geneva, sans-serif; Size: 10 px; Style: normal; Weight: bold.

**24.** Apply the item_numbers rule to the three items' numbers and prices.

**25.** Delete the #footer block placeholder text, then type **TripSmart Copyright 2002 - 2012.**

**26.** Create a new class rule named **small_ centered_text** with the following settings: Font-family: Verdana, Geneva, sans-serif; Font-size: 12 pixels; Font-style: Normal; Text-align: Center. (*Hint*: the Text-align property is in the Block category.)

**27.** Apply the small_centered_text rule to the copyright statement.

**28.** Save your work, view the page in your browser, compare your screen with Figure 43, then close the browser. (*Hint*: You may need to delete the H1 tags from the #mainContent block if you have too much space between the navigation bar and the table.)

**29.** Save your work, then close all open pages.

**FIGURE 43**
*Sample Project Builder 1*

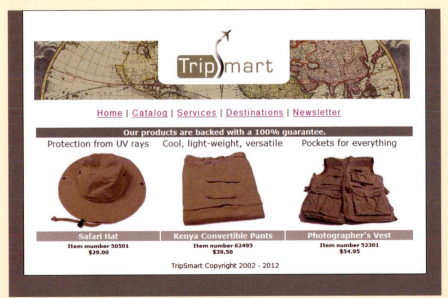

Use Figure 44 as a guide to continue your work on the Carolyne's Creations website that you started in Chapter 1 and developed in the previous chapters. You are now ready to begin work on a page that will showcase the company's catering services. You decide to use CSS with a table for page layout.

1. Open the Carolyne's Creations website, then create a new page based on the 1 column fixed, centered, header and footer layout, attach the cc_styles.css file, and save the page as **catering.html**, overwriting the existing page.

2. Copy the banner that includes the navigation bar from one of the other pages, then paste it on the page, replacing the placeholder content. (*Hint*: If the banner is too wide for the container you're placing it in, edit the width of the container in the CSS styles panel properties to accommodate it.)

3. Edit the container properties with values of your choice to format the page to blend with the existing pages in the website.

4. Use the main area of the page to insert a table that will showcase the catering services, with the following settings: Rows: **10**, Columns: **3**, Table width: **770 pixels**, Border thickness: **0**, Cell padding: **3**, Cell spacing: **0**, adding an appropriate table summary.

5. Center-align the table and set the width of the three cells to **33%**, **33%**, and **34%**.

6. Type **Catering for All Occasions** in the second cell in the second row and **Dinner to Go** in the second cell in the sixth row.

7. Apply the **sub_head** rule to the text you typed in Step 6 and center the text.

8. Merge the cells in the 5th and 9th rows, then Insert rules in the merged cells. (*Hint*: Change the view to Expanded Tables mode to be able to see the cells more easily.)

9. Type **Lunch Boxes**, **Brunch Boxes**, and **Gift Baskets** in the three cells in the third row.
10. Type **Soups**, **Entrees**, and **Desserts** in the three cells in the seventh row.
11. Apply the nav_bar rule to the text you typed in Steps 9 and 10.
12. Use a color of your choice for the background for each cell in the third and seventh rows.
13. Type the text **Call/fax by 9:00 a.m. for lunch orders, Call/fax by 1:00 p.m. for dinner orders, Fax number: 555-963-5938** in the first cell in the last row using a line break to separate each line.
14. Apply the paragraph_text rule to the text you typed in Step 13.
15. Use your word processor to open the file menu items.doc from your Data Files folder. Copy and paste each text block into the cells in the fourth and eighth rows, apply the paragraph_text rule to each text block, then center align each text block in the cells, using Figure 44 as a guide.
16. Merge the last two cells in the last row, then insert the image muffins.jpg with alternate text and any additional formatting of your choice.
17. Delete the footer placeholder text and change the background color of the footer to white.
18. Save your work, preview the page in your browser, make any adjustments that you feel would improve the page appearance, then close all open files.

**FIGURE 44**
*Completed Project Builder 2*

Jon Bishop is opening a new restaurant and wants to have the restaurant website launched two weeks before his opening. He has hired you to create the site and has asked for several design proposals. You begin by looking at some restaurant sites with pleasing designs.

1. Connect to the Internet, then go to www.jamesatthemill.com, as shown in Figure 45.

2. How are CSS used in this site?

3. How are CSS used to prevent an overload of information in one area of the screen?

4. View the source code for the page and locate the html tags that control the CSS on the page.

5. Use the Reference panel in Dreamweaver to look up the code used in this site to place the content on the page. (To do this, make note of a tag that you don't understand, then open the Reference panel and find that tag the Tag list box in the Reference panel. Select it from the list and read the description in the Reference panel.)

6. Do you see any tables on the page? If so, how are they used?

**FIGURE 45**
*Design Project*

*James at the Mill website used with permission from Miles James – www.jamesatthemill.com*

*Positioning Objects with CSS and Tables*

# PORTFOLIO PROJECT

For this assignment, you will continue to work on the portfolio project that you have been developing since Chapter 1. There will be no Data Files supplied. You are building this website from chapter to chapter, so you must do each Portfolio Project assignment in each chapter to complete your website.

You will continue building your website by designing and completing a page that uses layers rather than tables to control the layout of information.

1. Consult your storyboard to decide which page to create and develop for this chapter. Draw a sketch of the page to show how you will use CSS to lay out the content.

2. Create the new page for the site and set the default preferences for div tags. Add the appropriate number of div tags to the new page and configure them appropriately, making sure to name them and set the properties for each.

3. Add text, background images, and background colors to each container.

4. Create the navigation links that will allow you to add this page to your site.

5. Update the other pages of your site so that each page includes a link to this new page.

6. Add images in the containers (where appropriate), making sure to align them with text so they look good.

7. Review the checklist in Figure 46 and make any necessary modifications.

8. Save your work, preview the page in your browser, make any necessary modifications to improve the page appearance, close your browser, then close all open pages.

**FIGURE 46**
*Portfolio Project checklist*

| Website Checklist |
|---|
| 1. Do all pages have titles? |
| 2. Do all navigation links work correctly? |
| 3. Are all colors in your layers web-safe? |
| 4. Does the use of CSS in your website improve the site navigation? |
| 5. Do your pages look acceptable in at least the two major browsers? |
| 6. Do all images in your CSS containers appear correctly? |

chapter

# 6

# MANAGING A WEB
## SERVER AND FILES

1. Perform website maintenance

2. Publish a website and transfer files

3. Check files out and in

4. Cloak files

5. Import and export a site definition

6. Evaluate web content for legal use

chapter **6** MANAGING A WEB
SERVER AND FILES

## Introduction

Once you have created all the pages of your
website, finalized all the content, and performed site maintenance, you are ready to
publish your site to a remote server so the
rest of the world can access it. In this chapter, you will start by running some reports to
make sure the links in your site work properly, that the colors are web-safe, and that
orphaned files are removed. Next, you will
set up a connection to the remote site for
The Striped Umbrella website. You will then
transfer files to the remote site and learn
how to keep them up to date. You will also
check out a file so that it is not available to
other team members while you are editing it
and you will learn how to cloak files. When a
file is **cloaked**, it is excluded from certain
processes, such as being transferred to the
remote site. Next, you will export the site
definition file from The Striped Umbrella
website so that other designers can import
the site. Finally, you will research important
copyright issues that affect all websites.

## Preparing to Publish a Site

Before you publish a site, it is extremely
important that you test it regularly to

make sure the content is accurate and up
to date and that everything is functioning
properly. When viewing pages over the
Internet, it is very frustrating to click a
link that doesn't work or have to wait for
pages that load slowly because of large
graphics and animations. Remember that
the typical viewer has a short attention
span and limited patience. Before you
publish your site, make sure to use the
Link Checker panel to check for broken
links and orphaned files. Make sure that
all image paths are correct and that all
images load quickly and have alternate
text. Verify that all pages have titles, and
remove all non-web-safe colors. View the
pages in at least two different browsers
and different versions of the same
browser to ensure that everything works
correctly. The more frequently you test,
the better the chance that your viewers
will have a positive experience at your site
and want to return. *Before you publish
your pages, verify that all content is
original to the website, has been
obtained legally, and is used properly
without violating the copyright of someone else's work.*

# Tools You'll Use

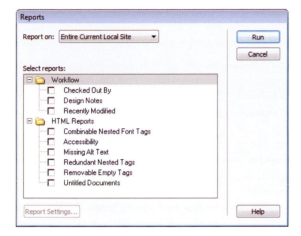

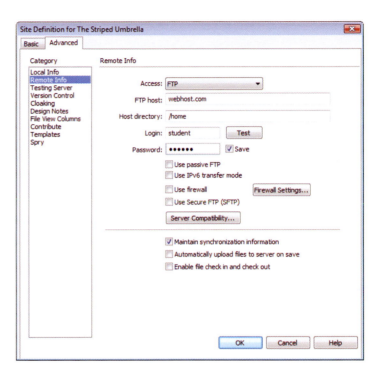

# PERFORM WEBSITE MAINTENANCE

## What You'll Do

*In this lesson, you will use some Dreamweaver site management tools to check for broken links, orphaned files, and missing alternate text. You will also verify that all colors are web-safe. You will then correct any problems that you find.*

### Maintaining a Website

As you add pages, links, and content to a website, it can quickly become difficult to manage. It's easier to find and correct errors as you go, rather than waiting until the end of the design phase. It's important to perform maintenance tasks frequently to make sure your website operates smoothly and remains "clean." You have already learned about some of the tools described in the following paragraphs. Although it is important to use them as you create and modify your pages, it is also important to run them at periodic intervals after publishing your website to make sure it is always error-free.

### Using the Assets Panel

You should use the Assets panel to check the list of images and colors used in your website. If you see images listed that are not being used, you should move them to a storage folder outside the website until you need them. You should also check to see if all of the colors used in the site are web-safe. If there are non-web-safe colors in the list, locate the elements to which

these colors are applied and apply web-safe colors to them.

### Checking Links Sitewide

Before and after you publish your website, you should use the Link Checker panel to make sure all internal links are working. If the Link Checker panel displays any broken links, you should repair them. If the Link Checker panel displays any orphaned files, you should evaluate whether to delete them or link them with existing pages.

### Using Site Reports

You can use the Reports command in the Site menu to generate six different HTML reports that can help you maintain your website. You choose the type of report you want to run in the Reports dialog box, shown in Figure 1. You can specify whether to generate the report for the current document, the entire current local site, selected files in the site, or a selected folder. You can also generate workflow reports to see files that have been checked out by others or recently modified or you can view the Design Notes attached to files.

**Design Notes** are separate files in a website that contain additional information about a page file or a graphic file. In a collaborative situation, designers can record notes to exchange information with other designers. Design Notes can also be used to record sensitive information that would not be included in files that could be viewed on the website. Information about the source files for graphic files, such as Flash files or Fireworks files, are also stored in Design Notes.

### Validating Markup

One of the report features in Dreamweaver is the ability to validate markup. This means that Dreamweaver will go through the code to look for errors that could occur with different language versions, such as XHTML or XML. To validate code for a page, click File on the Application bar (Win) or Menu bar (Mac) point to Validate, and then click Markup. The Results tab group displaying the Validation panel opens and lists any pages with errors, the line numbers where the errors occur, and an explanation of the errors. The Validate button on the Validation panel offers the choice of validating a single document, an entire local website, or selected files in a local website.

### Testing Pages

Finally, you should test your website using many different types and versions of browsers, platforms, and screen resolutions. You can use the Check Page button on the Document toolbar to check browser

compatibility. This feature lists issues with the pages in your site that may cause problems when the pages are viewed using certain browsers, such as the rendering of square bullets in Mozilla Firefox. If you find such issues, you then have the choice to make changes to your page to eliminate the problems. The Results Tab group's Browser Compatibility window includes a URL that you can visit to find the solutions to problems. You should test every link to make sure it connects to a valid, active website.

Pages that download slowly should be reduced in size to improve performance. You should analyze all user feedback on the website objectively, saving both positive and negative comments for future reference to help you make improvements to the site.

**FIGURE 1**

*Reports dialog box*

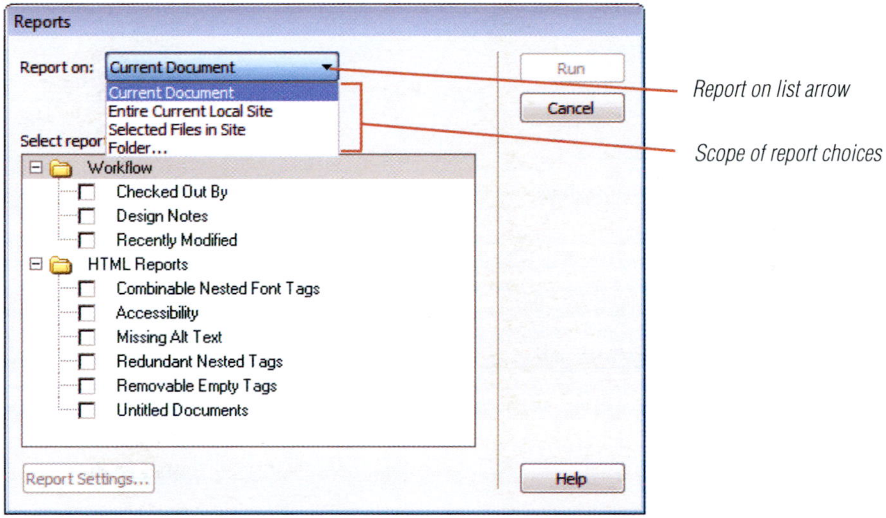

## Check for broken links

1. Open The Striped Umbrella website.
2. Show the Files panel (if necessary).
3. Click **Site** on the Application bar (Win) or Menu bar (Mac), point to **Advanced**, then click **Recreate Site Cache**.
4. Click **Site** on the Application bar (Win) or Menu bar (Mac), then click **Check Links Sitewide**.

   No broken links are listed in the Link Checker panel of the Results tab group, as shown in Figure 2.

*You verified that there are no broken links in the website.*

## Check for orphaned files

1. On the Link Checker panel, click the **Show list arrow**, then click **Orphaned Files**.

   There are no orphaned files, as shown in Figure 3.
2. Close the Results tab group.

*You verified that there are no orphaned files in the website.*

**FIGURE 2**
*Link Checker panel displaying no broken links*

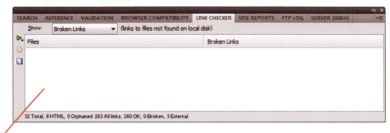

No broken links listed

**FIGURE 3**
*Link Checker panel displaying no orphaned files*

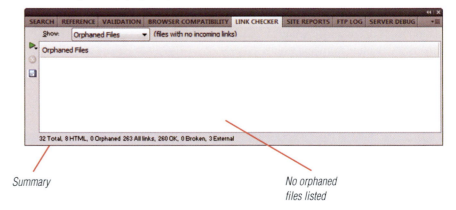

Summary

No orphaned files listed

**FIGURE 4**

*Assets panel displaying web-safe colors*

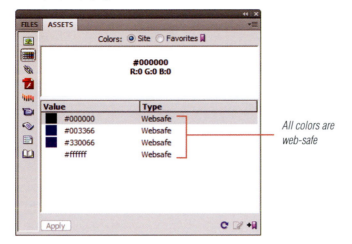

All colors are
web-safe

1. Click the **Assets panel tab**, then click the **Colors button** ▦ to view the website colors, as shown in Figure 4.

   The Assets panel shows that all colors used in the website are web-safe.

   *You verified that the website contains all web-safe colors.*

### Using Find and Replace to locate non-web-safe colors

As with many software applications, Dreamweaver has a Find and Replace feature that can be used both in Design view and in Code view on the Edit menu. This command can be used to search the current document, selected files, or the entire current local site. If you are looking for a particular non-web-safe color, you will probably save time by using the Find and Replace feature to locate the hexadecimal color code in Code view. If a site has many pages, this will be the fastest way to locate it. The Find and Replace feature can also be used to locate other character combinations, such as a phrase that begins or ends with a particular word or tag. These patterns of character combinations are referred to as **regular expressions**. To find out more, search for "regular expressions" in Dreamweaver Help.

## Check for untitled documents

1. Click **Site** on the Application bar (Win) or Menu bar (Mac), then click **Reports** to open the Reports dialog box.

2. Click the **Report on list arrow**, click **Entire Current Local Site**, click the **Untitled Documents check box**, as shown in Figure 5, then click **Run**.

   The Site Reports panel opens in the Results tab group, and shows that the cafe page does not have a page title, as shown in Figure 6.

3. Open the cafe page, replace the current page title "Untitled Document" with the title **The Sand Crab Cafe**, then save the file.

4. Close the cafe page.

5. Run the report again to check the entire site for untitled documents.

   No files should appear in the Site Reports panel.

*You ran a report for untitled documents, then added a page title to the cafe page.*

### FIGURE 5
*Reports dialog box with Untitled Documents option selected*

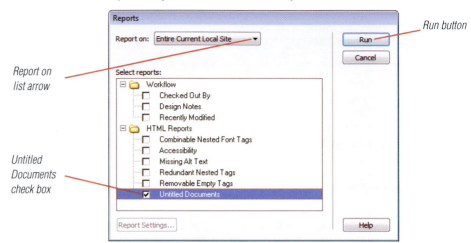

Run button

Report on list arrow

Untitled Documents check box

### FIGURE 6
*Site Reports panel showing one page without a page title*

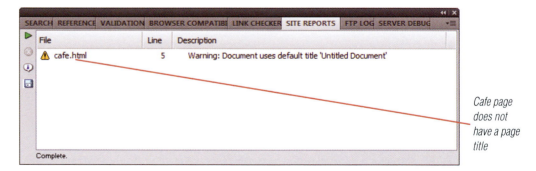

Cafe page does not have a page title

**FIGURE 7**

*Reports dialog box with Missing Alt text option selected*

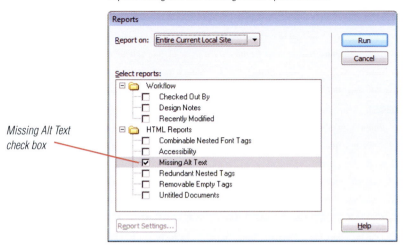

Missing Alt Text
check box

**FIGURE 8**

*Site Reports panel displaying missing "alt" tag*

Line number in code
with missing "alt" tag

One missing "alt" tag
found on one page

## Check for missing alternate text

1. Using Figure 7 as a guide, run another report that checks the entire current local site for missing alternate text.

   The results show that the spa page contains an image that is missing alternate text, as shown in Figure 8.

2. Open the spa page, then find the image that is missing alternate text.

   TIP The Site Reports panel documents the code line number where the missing alt tag occurs. Sometimes it is faster to locate the errors in Code view, rather than in Design view.

3. Add appropriate alternate text to the image.

4. Save your work, then run the report again to check the entire site for missing alternate text.

   No files should appear in the Site Reports panel.

5. Close the Results tab group, then close all open pages.

*You ran a report to check for missing alternate text in the entire site. You then added alternate text for one image and ran the report again.*

## Validating Accessibility Standards

There are many accessibility issues to consider to ensure that your website conforms to current accessibility standards. HTML Reports provide an easy way to check for missing alternate text, missing page titles, and other accessibility concerns such as improper markup, deprecated features, or improper use of color or images. HTML Reports can be run on the current document, selected files, or the entire local site. You can also use the Check Page, Accessibility command under the File menu to check for accessibility issues on an open page. After the report is run, a list of issues will open in the Site Reports panel with the line number and description of each problem. If you right-click a description, you will see the option "More Info. . ." Click on this option to read a more detailed description and solutions to correct the issue.

## Enable Design Notes

1. Click **Site** on the Application bar (Win) or Menu bar (Mac), click **Manage Sites**, verify that The Striped Umbrella site is selected, click **Edit**, click the **Advanced tab** (if necessary), then click the **Design Notes category**.

2. Click the **Maintain Design Notes check box**, to select it (if necessary), as shown in Figure 9.

   Selecting this option enables the designer to record notes about a page in a separate file linked to the page. For instance, a Design Note for the index.html file would be saved in a file named index.html.mno. This file would be automatically saved in a folder that is created by Dreamweaver named _notes. This folder does not appear in the Files panel, but can be seen using Windows Explorer (Win) or Finder (Mac).

3. Click the **File View Columns category**, then click **Notes** in the File View Columns list.

4. Click the **Options: Show check box**, to select it (if necessary).

   The Notes column now displays the word "Show" in the Show column, as shown in Figure 10, indicating that the Notes column will be visible in the Files panel.

5. Click **OK**, then click **Done** in the Manage Sites dialog box.

   *You set the preference to use Design Notes in the website. You also set the option to display the Notes column in the Files panel.*

**FIGURE 9**

*Design Notes category in the Site Definition for The Striped Umbrella*

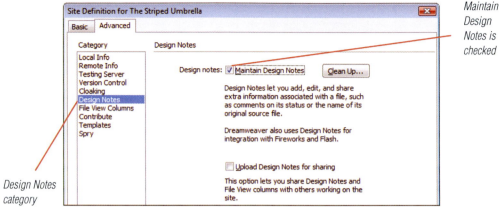

Maintain Design Notes is checked

Design Notes category

**FIGURE 10**

*File View Columns category in the Site Definition for The Striped Umbrella*

File View Columns category

Notes column will appear in Files panel

Options: Show checkbox

**FIGURE 11**
*Design Notes dialog box*

Status list arrow

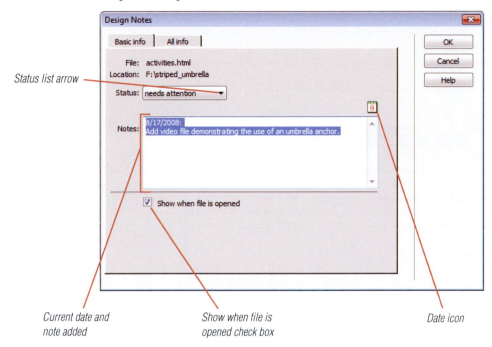

Current date and note added

Show when file is opened check box

Date icon

1. Open the activities page, click **File** on the Application bar (Win) or Menu bar (Mac), click **Design Notes**, then click the **Basic info tab** (if necessary).

   The Design Notes dialog box opens with a text box to record a note related to the open file, the option to display the note each time the file is opened, an option to include the current date, and a status indicator.

2. Click the **Date icon** above the Notes text box on the right.

   The current date is added to the Notes text box.

3. Type **Add video file demonstrating the use of an umbrella anchor.** in the Notes text box beneath the date.

4. Click the **Status list arrow**, then click **needs attention**.

5. Click the **Show when file is opened** check box to select it, as shown in Figure 11, then click **OK**.

*You added a design note to the activities page with the current date and a status indicator. The note will open each time the file is opened.*

---

**Using Version Cue to manage assets**

Another way to collaborate with team members is through Adobe Version Cue, a workgroup collaboration system that is included in Adobe Creative Suite 4. You can perform such functions such as managing security, backing up data, and using metadata to search files. **Metadata** includes information about a file such as key-words, descriptions, and copyright information. Adobe Bridge also organizes files with metadata.

## Edit a Design Note

1. Click **File** on the Application bar (Win) or Menu bar (Mac), then click **Design Notes** to open the Design Note associated with the activities page.

   You can also right-click (Windows) or control-click (Mac) the filename in the Files panel, then click Design Notes, or double-click the yellow Design Notes icon in the Files panel next to the filename to open a Design Note, as shown in Figure 12.

   > TIP    You may have to click the Refresh button [refresh icon] to display the Notes icon.

2. Edit the note by adding the sentence **Ask Jane Pinson to send the file.** after the existing text in the Notes section, then click **OK** to close it.

   A file named activities.html.mno has been created in a new folder called _notes. This folder and file will not display in the Files panel unless you have the option to show hidden files and folders selected. However, you can switch to Windows Explorer to see them without selecting this option.

   *(continued)*

*(continued)*

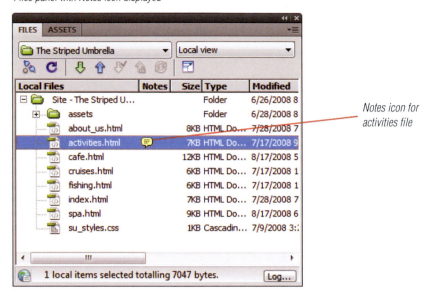

**FIGURE 12**
*Files panel with Notes icon displayed*

Notes icon for activities file

## Deleting a Design Note

There are two steps to deleting a Design Note that you don't need anymore. The first step is to delete the Design Note file. To delete a Design Note, right-click the filename in the Files panel that is associated with the Design Note you want to delete, and then click Explore (Win) or Reveal in Finder (Mac) to open your file management system. Open the _notes folder, then delete the .mno file in the files list, and then close Explorer (Win) or Finder (Mac). The second step is done in Dreamweaver. Click Site on the Application bar (Win) or Menu bar (Mac), click Manage Sites, click Edit, and then select the Design Notes category. Click the Clean Up button. (*Note*: Don't do this if you deselect Maintain Design Notes first or it will delete all of your design notes!) The Design Notes icon will be removed from the Notes column in the Files panel.

**FIGURE 13**

*Windows Explorer displaying the _notes file and folder*

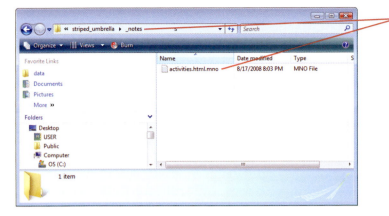

Notes file
in _notes folder

3. Right-click (Win) or control-click (Mac) **activities.html** in the Files panel, then click **Explore** (Win) or **Reveal in Finder** (Mac).

4. Double-click the folder **_notes** to open it, then double-click the file **activities.html.mno**, shown in Figure 13, to open the file in Dreamweaver.

   The notes file opens in Code view in Dreamweaver, as shown in Figure 14.

5. Read the file, close it, close Explorer (Win) or Finder (Mac), then close the activities page.

*You opened the Design Notes dialog box and edited the note in the Notes text box. Next, you viewed the .mno file that Dreamweaver created when you added the Design Note.*

**FIGURE 14**

*Code for the activities.html.mno file*

```
1   <?xml version="1.0" encoding="utf-8" ?>
2   <info>
3       <infoitem key="notes" value="8/17/2008: &#xD;Add video file demonstrating the use of an
    umbrella anchor. Ask Jane Pinson to send the file." />
4       <infoitem key="status" value="needs attention" />
5       <infoitem key="showOnOpen" value="true" />
6   </info>
7
```

# PUBLISH A WEBSITE
## AND TRANSFER FILES

## What You'll Do

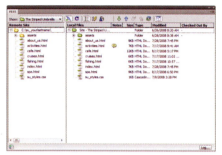

 *In this lesson, you will set up remote access to either an FTP folder or a local/network folder for The Striped Umbrella website. You will also view a website on a remote server, upload files to it, and synchronize the files.*

### Defining a Remote Site

As you learned in Chapter 1, publishing a site means transferring all the site's files to a web server. A **web server** is a computer that is connected to the Internet with an IP (Internet Protocol) address so that it is available on the Internet. Before you can publish a site to a web server, you must first define the remote site by specifying the Remote Info settings on the Advanced tab of the Site Definition dialog box. You can specify remote settings when you first create a new site and define the root folder (as you did in Chapter 1 when you defined the remote access settings for The Striped Umbrella website), or you can do it after you have completed all of your pages and are confident that your site is ready for public viewing. To specify the remote settings for a site, you must first choose an Access setting, which specifies the type of server you will use. The most common Access setting is FTP (File Transfer Protocol). If you specify FTP, you will need to specify an address for the server and the name of the folder on the FTP site in which your root folder will be stored. You can also use **Secure FTP (SFTP)**, an FTP option that enables you to encrypt file transfers. This option will pro-

tect your files, user names, and passwords. To use SFTP, check the Use Secure FTP (SFTP) check box in the Site Definition dialog box. You will also need to enter login and password information. Figure 15 shows an example of FTP settings in the Remote Info category of the Site Definition dialog box.

### QUICKTIP

If you do not have access to an FTP site, you can publish a site to a local/network folder. This is referred to as a **LAN**, or a Local Area Network. Use the alternate steps provided in this lesson to publish your site to a local/network folder.

### Viewing a Remote Site

Once you have defined a site to a remote location, you can then view the remote folder in the Files panel by choosing Remote view from the View list. If your remote site is located on an FTP server, Dreamweaver will connect to it. You will see the File Activity dialog box showing the progress of the connection. You can also use the Connects to remote host button on the Files panel toolbar to connect to the remote site. If you defined your site on a local/network folder, then you don't need to use the Connects to remote host button; the root folder and any files and folders it contains will appear in the Files panel when you switch to Remote view.

## Transferring Files to and from a Remote Site

After you define a remote site, you will need to transfer or **upload** your files from the local version of your site to the remote host. To do this, view the site in Local view, select the files you want to upload, and then click the Put File(s) button on the Files panel toolbar. Once you click this button, the files will be transferred to the remote site. To view the uploaded files, switch to Remote view, as shown in Figure 16. Or, you can expand the Files panel to view both the Remote Site and the Local Files panes by clicking the Expand to show local and remote sites button in the Files panel.

If a file you select for uploading requires additional files, such as graphics, a dialog box will open after you click the Put File(s) button and ask if you want those files (known as **dependent files**) to be uploaded. By clicking Yes, all dependent files in the selected page will be uploaded to the appropriate folder in the remote site. If a file that you want to upload is located in a folder in the local site, the folder will be automatically transferred to the remote site.

**QUICK**TIP

To upload an entire site to a remote host, select the root folder, then click the Put File(s) button.

If you are developing or maintaining a website in a group environment, there might be times when you want to transfer or **download** files that other team members have created from the remote site to your local site. To do this, switch to Remote view, select the files you want to download, then click the Get File(s) button on the Files panel toolbar.

**FIGURE 15**

*FTP settings in the Site Definition for The Striped Umbrella dialog box*

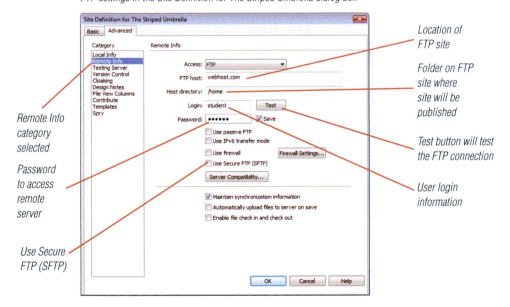

*Remote Info category selected*

*Password to access remote server*

*Use Secure FTP (SFTP)*

*Location of FTP site*

*Folder on FTP site where site will be published*

*Test button will test the FTP connection*

*User login information*

**FIGURE 16**

*Files panel with Remote view selected*

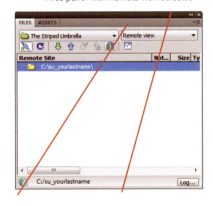

*Expand to show local and remote sites button*

*Remote view*

## Synchronizing Files

To keep a website up to date—especially one that contains several pages and involves several team members—you will need to update and replace files. Team members might make changes to pages on the local version of the site or make additions to the remote site. If many people are involved in maintaining a site, or if you are constantly making changes to the pages, ensuring that both the local and remote sites have the most up-to-date files could get confusing. Thankfully, you can use the Synchronize command to keep things straight. The Synchronize command instructs Dreamweaver to compare the dates of the saved files in both versions of the site, then transfers only the files that have changed. To synchronize files, use the Synchronize Files dialog box, as shown in Figure 17. You can synchronize an entire site or selected files. You can also specify whether to upload newer files to the remote site, download newer files from the remote site, or both.

**FIGURE 17**

*Synchronize Files dialog box*

Specifies to synchronize
all files in the site

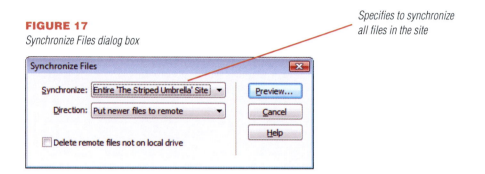

### Understanding Dreamweaver connection options for transferring files

The connection types with which you are probably the most familiar are FTP and Local/Network. Other connection types that you can use with Dreamweaver are Microsoft Visual SafeSource **(VSS)**, WebDav, and RDS. VSS is used only with the Windows operating system with Microsoft Visual SafeSource Client version 6. **WebDav** stands for Web-based Distributed Authoring and Versioning. This type of connection is used with the WebDav protocol. An example would be a website residing on an Apache web server. The **Apache web server** is a public domain, open source web server that is available using several different operating systems including UNIX and Windows. **RDS** stands for Remote Development Services, and is used with web servers using Cold Fusion.

FIGURE 18

*FTP settings specified in the Site Definition for The Striped Umbrella dialog box*

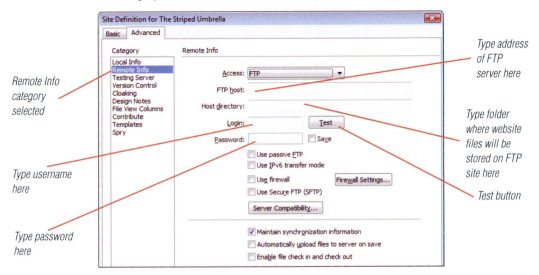

Remote Info category selected

Type username here

Type password here

Type address of FTP server here

Type folder where website files will be stored on FTP site here

Test button

## Comparing two files for differences in content

There are situations where it would be helpful to be able to compare the contents of two files, such as a local file and the remote version of the same file; or an original file and the same file that has been saved with a different name. Once the two files are compared and differences are detected, you can merge the information in the files. A good time to compare files is before you upload them to a remote server to prevent accidentally writing over a file with more recent information. To compare files, you must first locate and install a third-party file comparison utility, or "dif" tool, such as Araxis Merge or Beyond Compare. (Dreamweaver does not have a file comparison tool included as part of the software. You will have to download one. If you are not familiar with these tools, find one using your favorite search engine.)

After installing the files comparison utility, use the Preferences command on the Edit menu, and then select the File Compare category. Next, browse to select the application to compare files. After you have set your Preferences, click the Compare with Remote command on the File menu to compare an open file with the remote version.

## Set up web server access on an FTP site

NOTE: Complete these steps only if you know you can store The Striped Umbrella files on an FTP site and you know the login and password information. If you do not have access to an FTP site, complete the exercise called Set up web server access on a local or network folder on Page 6-18.

1. Click **Site** on the Application bar (Win) or Menu bar (Mac), then click **Manage Sites**.

2. Click **The Striped Umbrella** in the Manage Sites dialog box (if necessary), then click **Edit**.

3. Click the **Advanced tab**, click **Remote Info** in the Category list, click the **Access list arrow**, click **FTP**, then compare your screen to Figure 18.

4. Enter the FTP host, Host directory, Login, and Password information in the dialog box.

   TIP  You must have file and folder permissions to use FTP. The server administrator will also tell you the folder name and location to use to publish your files.

5. Click the **Test button** to test the connection to the remote site.

6. If the connection is successful, click **Done** to close the dialog box; if it is not successful, verify that you have the correct settings, then repeat Step 4.

7. Click **OK**, click **OK** to restore the cache, then click **Done** to close the Manage Sites dialog box.

*You set up remote access information for The Striped Umbrella website using FTP settings.*

## Set up web server access on a local or network folder

NOTE: Complete these steps if you do not have the ability to post files to an FTP site and could not complete the previous lesson.

1. Using Windows Explorer (Win) or Finder (Mac), create a new folder on your hard drive or on a shared drive named **su_yourlastname** (e.g., if your last name is Jones, name the folder **su_jones**.)

2. Switch back to Dreamweaver, open The Striped Umbrella website, then open the Manage Sites dialog box.

   TIP   You can also double-click the site name in the Site Name list box in the Files panel to open the Advanced tab in the Site Definition dialog box.

3. Click **The Striped Umbrella**, click **Edit** to open the Site Definition for The Striped Umbrella dialog box, click the **Advanced tab**, then click **Remote Info** in the Category list.

4. Click the **Access list arrow**, then click **Local/Network**.

5. Click the **Browse for File icon** 📁 next to the Remote folder text box to open the Choose remote root folder for site The Striped Umbrella dialog box, navigate to the folder you created in Step 1, select the folder, click **Open**, then click **Select** (Win) or **Choose** (Mac).

6. Compare your screen to Figure 19, click **OK**, click **OK** in the message window about the site cache, then click **Done**.

You created a new folder and specified it as the remote location for The Striped Umbrella website, then set up remote access to a local or network folder.

**FIGURE 19**

Local/Network settings specified in the Site Definition for The Striped Umbrella dialog box

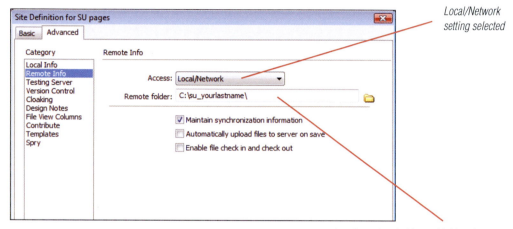

Local/Network setting selected

Local or network drive and folder where remote site will be published (your folder name should end with your last name)

## FIGURE 20
Connecting to the remote site

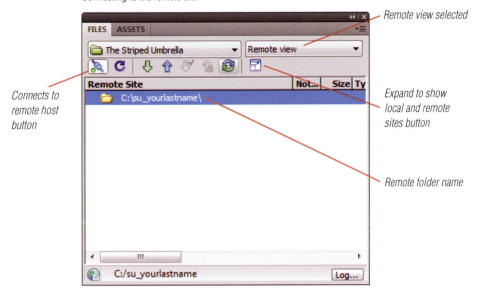

Remote view selected

Connects to remote host button

Expand to show local and remote sites button

Remote folder name

1. Click the **View list arrow** in the Files panel, then click **Remote view**, as shown in Figure 20.

   If you specified your remote access to a local or network folder, then the su_yourlastname folder will now appear in the Files panel. If your remote access is set to an FTP site, Dreamweaver will connect to the host server to see the remote access folder.

2. Click the **Expand to show local and remote sites button** to view both the Remote Site and Local Files panes. The su_yourlast-name folder appears in the Remote Site portion of the expanded Files panel.

   TIP  If you don't see your remote site files, click the Connects to remote host button or the Refresh button  If you don't see two panes, one with the remote site files and one with the local files, drag the panel border to enlarge the panel.

*You used the Files panel to set the view for The Striped Umbrella site to Remote view. You then connected to the remote server to view the contents of the remote folder you specified.*

## Using a site usability test to test your site

Once you have at least a prototype of the website ready to evaluate, it is a good idea to conduct a site usability test. This is a process that involves asking unbiased people, who are not connected to the design process, to use and evaluate the site. A comprehensive usability test will include pre-test questions, participant tasks, a post-test interview, and a post-test survey. This will provide much-needed information as to how usable the site is to those unfamiliar with it. Typical questions include: "What are your overall impressions?"; "What do you like the best and the least about the site?"; and "How easy is it to navigate inside the site?" For more information, go to www.w3.org and search for "site usability test."

## Upload files to a remote server

1. Click the **about_us.html file**, then click the **Put File(s) button** ⬆ on the Files panel toolbar.

   The Dependent Files dialog box opens, asking if you want to include dependent files.

2. Click **Yes**.

   The about_us file, the style sheet file, and the image files used in the about_us page are copied to the remote server. The Background File Activity dialog box appears and flashes the names of each file as they are uploaded.

3. Expand the assets folder in the remote site (if necessary), then compare your screen to Figure 21.

   The remote site now contains the about_us page as well as the images on that page, and the striped_umbrella external style sheet file, all of which are needed by the about_us page.

   TIP   You might need to expand the su_yourlastname folder in order to view the assets folder.

*You used the Put File(s) button to upload the about_us file and all files that are dependent files of the about_us page.*

**FIGURE 21**
*Remote view of the site after uploading the about_us page*

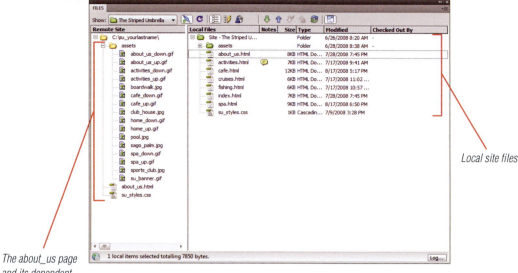

*Local site files*

*The about_us page and its dependent files in remote site*

## Continuing to work while transferring files to a remote server

During the process of uploading files to a remote server, there are many Dreamweaver functions that you can continue to use while you wait. For example, you can create a new site, create a new page, edit a page, add files and folders, and run reports. However, there are some functions that you cannot use while transferring files, many of which involve accessing files on the remote server or using Check In/Check Out.

**FIGURE 22**
*Synchronize Files dialog box*

## Synchronize files

1. Click the **Synchronize button** on the Files panel toolbar to open the Synchronize Files dialog box.

2. Click the **Synchronize list arrow**, then click **Entire 'The Striped Umbrella' Site**.

3. Click the **Direction list arrow**, click **Put newer files to remote** (if necessary), then compare your screen to Figure 22.

4. Click **Preview**.

   The Background File Activity dialog box might appear and flash the names of all the files from the local version of the site that need to be uploaded to the remote site. The Synchronize dialog box shown in Figure 23 then opens and lists all the files that need to be uploaded to the remote site.

5. Click **OK**.

   All the files from the local The Striped Umbrella site are now contained in the remote version of the site. Notice that the remote folders are yellow and the local folders are green.

*You synchronized The Striped Umbrella website files to copy all remaining files from the local root folder to the remote root folder.*

**FIGURE 23**
*Files that need to be uploaded to the remote site*

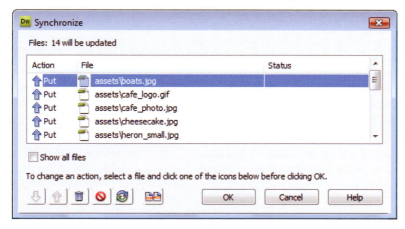

# CHECK FILES
## OUT AND IN

 *In this lesson, you will use the Site Definition dialog box to enable the Check In/Check Out feature. You will then check out the cafe page, make a change to it, and then check it back in.*

### Managing a Website with a Team

When you work on a large website, chances are that many people will be involved in keeping the site up to date. Different individuals will need to make changes or additions to different pages of the site by adding or deleting content, changing graphics, updating information, and so on. If everyone had access to the pages at the same time, problems could arise. For instance, what if you and another team member both made edits to the same page at the same time? If you post your edited version of the file to the site after the other team member posts his edited version of the same file, the file that you upload will overwrite his version and none of his changes will be incorporated.

Not good! Fortunately, you can avoid this scenario by using Dreamweaver's collaboration tools.

### Checking Out and Checking In Files

Checking files in and out is similar to checking library books in and out or video/DVD rentals. No one else can read the same copy that you have checked out. Using Dreamweaver's Check In/Check Out feature ensures that team members cannot overwrite each other's pages. When this feature is enabled, only one person can work on a file at a time. To check out a file, click the file you want to work on in the Files panel, and then click the Check Out File(s) button on the Files panel toolbar. Files that you have checked out are marked with green check marks in the Files panel. Files that have been checked in are marked with padlock icons.

After you finish editing a checked-out file, you need to save and close the file, and then click the Check In button to check the file back in and make it available to other users. When a file is checked in, you cannot make

edits to it unless you check it out again. Figure 24 shows the Check Out File(s) and Check In buttons on the Files panel toolbar.

## Enabling the Check In/Check Out Feature

To use the Check In/Check Out feature with a team of people, you must first enable

it. To turn on this feature, check the Enable file check in and check out check box in the Remote Info settings of the Site Definition dialog box.

**FIGURE 24**

Check Out File(s) and Check In buttons on the Files Panel toolbar

*Check Out File(s) button*     *Check In button*

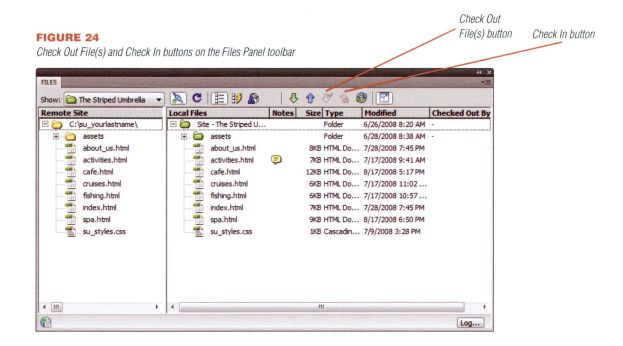

## Enable the Check In/Check Out feature

1. Verify that the Site panel is in expanded view, click **Site** on the menu bar, click **Manage Sites** to open the Manage Sites dialog box, click **The Striped Umbrella** in the list, then click **Edit** to open the Site Definition for The Striped Umbrella dialog box.

2. Click **Remote Info** in the Category list, then click the **Enable file check in and check out check box** to select it.

3. Check the **Check out files when opening check box** to select it (if necessary).

4. Type your name using all lowercase letters and no spaces in the Check out name text box.

5. Type your email address in the Email address text box.

6. Compare your screen to Figure 25, click **OK** to close the Site Definition for The Striped Umbrella dialog box, then click **Done** to close the Manage Sites dialog box. Your dialog box will look different if you are using FTP access.

*You used the Site Definition for The Striped Umbrella dialog box to enable the Check In/Check Out feature to let team members know when you are working with a file in the site.*

## Check out a file

1. Click the **cafe page** in the Local Files list in the Files panel to select it.

*(continued)*

**FIGURE 25**

*Enabling the Check In/Check Out feature*

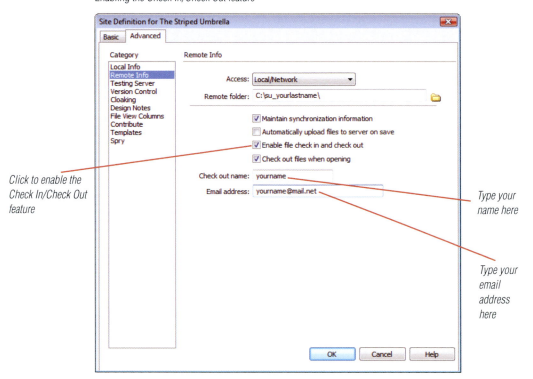

*Click to enable the Check In/Check Out feature*

*Type your name here*

*Type your email address here*

## FIGURE 26
Files panel in Local view after checking out cafe page

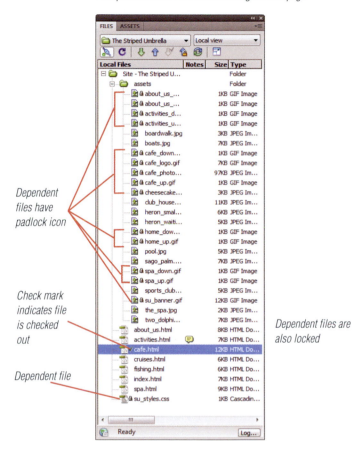

Dependent files have padlock icon

Check mark indicates file is checked out

Dependent file

## FIGURE 27
Files panel after checking in cafe page

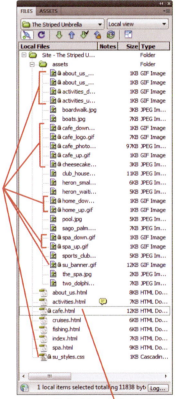

Dependent files are also locked

Padlock icon indicates file is read-only and cannot be edited unless it is checked out

2. Click the **Check Out File(s) button** 🗹 on the Files panel toolbar.

   The Dependent Files dialog box appears, asking if you want to include all files that are needed for the cafe page.

3. Click **Yes**, expand the assets folder if necessary, collapse the Files panel, click the **View list arrow**, click **Local view**, then compare your screen to Figure 26.

   The cafe file has a check mark next to it indicating you have checked it out. The dependent files have a padlock icon.

   TIP  If a dialog box appears asking "Do you wish to overwrite your local copy of cafe.html?", click Yes.

*You checked out the cafe page so that no one else can use it while you work on it.*

## Check in a file

1. Open the cafe page, change the closing hour for the The Cabana in the table to **7:00 p.m.**, then save your changes.

2. Close the cafe page, then click the **cafe page** in the Files panel to select it.

3. Click the **Check In button** 🔒 on the Files panel toolbar.

   The Dependent Files dialog box opens, asking if you want to include dependent files.

4. Click **Yes**, click another file in the Files panel to deselect the cafe page, then compare your screen to Figure 27.

   A padlock icon appears instead of a green check mark next to the cafe page on the Files panel.

*You made a content change on the cafe page, then checked in the cafe page, making it available for others to check it out.*

# CLOAK
## FILES

### What You'll Do

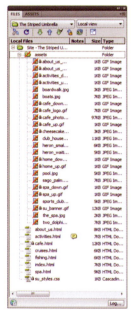

 *In this lesson, you will cloak the assets folder so that it is excluded from various operations, such as the Put, Get, Check In, and Check Out commands. You will also use the Site Definition dialog box to cloak all .gif files in the site.*

### Understanding Cloaking Files

There may be times when you want to exclude a particular file or files from being uploaded to a server. For instance, suppose you have a page that is not quite finished and needs more work before it is ready to be viewed by others. You can exclude such files by **cloaking** them, which marks them for exclusion from several commands, including Put, Get, Synchronize, Check In, and Check Out. Cloaked files are also excluded from site-wide operations, such as checking for links or updating a template or library item. You can cloak a folder or specify a type of file to cloak throughout the site.

**QUICK**TIP

By default, the cloaking feature is enabled. However, if for some reason it is not turned on, open the Site Definition dialog box, click the Advanced tab, click the Cloaking category, then click the Enable cloaking check box.

### Cloaking a Folder

There may be times when you want to cloak an entire folder. For instance, if you are not concerned with replacing outdated image files, you might want to cloak the assets folder of a website to save time when synchronizing files. To cloak a folder, select the folder, click the Options menu button in the Files panel, point to Site, point to Cloaking, and then click Cloak. The folder you cloaked and all the files it contains appear with red slashes across them, as shown in Figure 28. To uncloak a folder, click the Options menu button on the Files panel, point to Site, point to Cloaking, and then click Uncloak.

**QUICK**TIP

To uncloak all files in a site, click the Files panel Options menu button, point to Site, point to Cloaking, then click Uncloak All.

## Cloaking Selected File Types

There may be times when you want to cloak a particular type of file, such as a .jpg file. To cloak a particular file type, open the Site Definition dialog box, click the Cloaking category, click the Cloak files ending with check box, and then type a file extension in the text box below the check box. All files throughout the site that have the specified file extension will be cloaked.

**FIGURE 28**
*Cloaked assets folder in the Files panel*

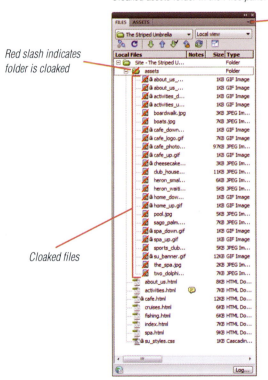

Options menu button

Red slash indicates folder is cloaked

Cloaked files

## Cloak and uncloak a folder

1. Verify that Local view is displayed in the Files panel, then open the Manage Sites dialog box.

2. Click **The Striped Umbrella** (if necessary), click **Edit** to open the Site Definition for The Striped Umbrella dialog box, click **Cloaking** in the Category list, verify that the Enable cloaking check box is checked, click **OK**, then click **Done**.

3. Click the **assets folder** in the Files panel, click the **Options menu button** ▼☰ , point to **Site**, point to **Cloaking**, click **Cloak**, then compare your screen to Figure 29.

   A red slash now appears on top of the assets folder in the Files panel, indicating that all files in the assets folder are cloaked and will be excluded from putting, getting, checking in, checking out, and many other operations.

   TIP  You can also cloak a folder by right-clicking (Win) or [control]-clicking (Mac) the folder, pointing to Cloaking, then clicking Cloak.

4. Right-click (Win) or [control]-click (Mac) the **assets folder**, point to **Cloaking**, then click **Uncloak**.

   The assets folder and all the files it contains no longer appear with red slashes across them, indicating they are no longer cloaked.

*You cloaked the assets folder so that this folder and all the files it contains would be excluded from many operations, including uploading and down-loading files. You then uncloaked the assets folder.*

**FIGURE 29**
*Assets folder after cloaking*

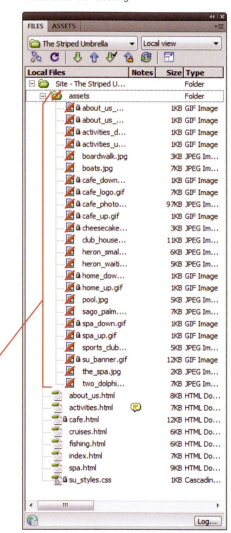

Red slashes indicate folder and files in it are cloaked

*Managing a Web Server and Files*

**FIGURE 30**

*Specifying a file type to cloak*

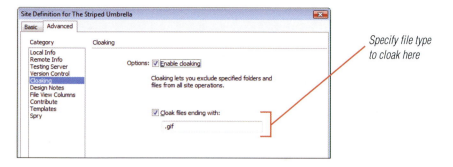

Specify file type
to cloak here

**FIGURE 31**

*Assets folder in Files panel after cloaking .gif files*

Assets folder
is not cloaked

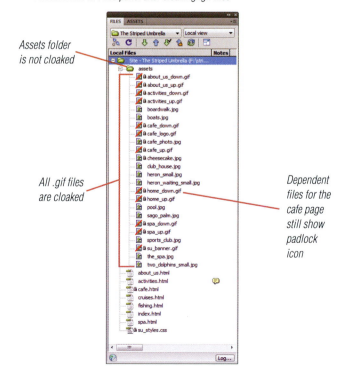

All .gif files
are cloaked

Dependent
files for the
cafe page
still show
padlock
icon

## Cloak selected file types

1. Right-click (Win) or [control]-click (Mac) the **assets folder** in the Files panel, point to **Cloaking**, then click **Settings** to open the Site Definition for The Striped Umbrella dialog box with the Cloaking category selected.

2. Click the **Cloak files ending with check box**, select the text in the text box that appears, type **.gif** in the text box, then compare your screen to Figure 30.

3. Click **OK**.

   A dialog box opens, indicating that the site cache will be re-created.

4. Click **OK**, expand the assets folder (if necessary), then compare your screen to Figure 31.

   All of the .gif files in the assets folder appear with red slashes across them, indicating that they are cloaked. Notice that the assets folder is not cloaked.

*You cloaked all the .gif files in The Striped Umbrella website.*

# IMPORT AND EXPORT
## A SITE DEFINITION

### What You'll Do

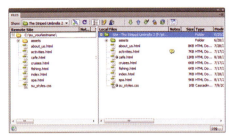

*In this lesson, you will export the site definition file for The Striped Umbrella website. You will then import The Striped Umbrella website.*

### Exporting a Site Definition

When you work on a website for a long time, it's likely that at some point you will want to move it to another machine or share it with other collaborators who will help you maintain it. The site definition for a website contains important information about the site, including its URL, preferences that you've specified, and other secure information, such as login and password information. You can use the Export command to export the site definition file to another location. To do this, open the Manage Sites dialog box, click the site you want to export, and then click Export. Because the site definition file contains password information that you will want to keep secret from other site users, you should never save the site definition file in the website. Instead, save it in an external folder.

### Importing a Site Definition

If you want to set up another user with a copy of your website, you can import the site definition file. To do this, click Import in the Manage Sites dialog box to open the Import Site dialog box, navigate to the .ste file you want to import, then click Open.

**FIGURE 32**

*Saving The Striped Umbrella.ste file in the su_site_definition folder*

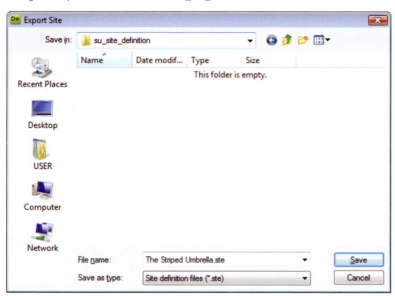

1. Use Windows Explorer (Win) or Finder (Mac) to create a new folder on your hard drive or external drive named **su_site_definition**.

2. Switch back to Dreamweaver, open the Manage Sites dialog box, click **The Striped Umbrella**, then click **Export** to open the Export Site dialog box. If you see a message asking if you are exporting the site to back up your settings or to share your settings with other users, choose the Back up my settings option, then click **OK**.

3. Navigate to and double-click to open the **su_site_definition folder** that you created in Step 1, as shown in Figure 32, click **Save**, then click **Done**.

*You used the Export command to create the site definition file and saved it in the su_site_definition folder.*

## Import a site definition

1. Open the Manage Sites dialog box, click **The Striped Umbrella**, then click **Import** to open the Import Site dialog box.

2. Navigate to the su_site_definition folder, compare your screen to Figure 33, select **The Striped Umbrella.ste**, then click **Open**.

   A dialog box opens and says that a site named The Striped Umbrella already exists. It will name the imported site The Striped Umbrella 2 so that it has a different name.

3. Click **OK**.

4. Click **The Striped Umbrella 2** (if necessary), click **Edit**, then compare your screen to Figure 34.

   The settings show that the The Striped Umbrella 2 site has the same root folder and default images folder as the The Striped Umbrella site. Both of these settings are speci- fied in the The Striped Umbrella.ste file that you imported. Importing a site in this way makes it possible for multiple users with differ- ent computers to work on the same site.

   > TIP Make sure you know who is responsi- ble for which files to keep from overwriting the wrong files when they are published. The Synchronize Files and Check In/Check Out features are good procedures to use with multiple designers.

5. Click **OK**, click **OK** to close the warning mes- sage, then click **Done**.

   > TIP If a dialog box opens warning that the root folder chosen is the same as the folder for the site "The Striped Umbrella," click OK.

*You imported The Striped Umbrella.ste file and created a new site, The Striped Umbrella 2.*

**FIGURE 33**
*Import Site dialog box*

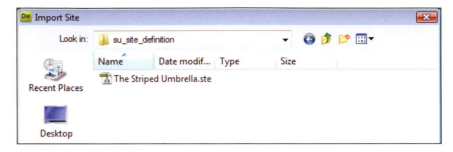

**FIGURE 34**
*Site Definition for the The Striped Umbrella 2 dialog box*

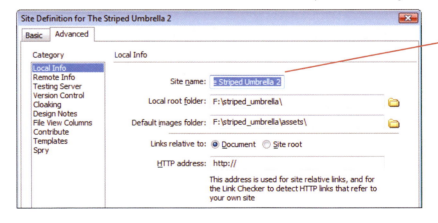

Name of imported site

**FIGURE 35**

Viewing The Striped Umbrella 2 website files

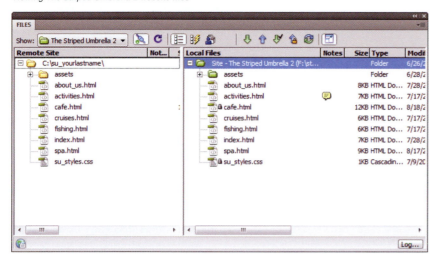

## POWER USER SHORTCUTS

| to do this: | use this shortcut: |
| --- | --- |
| Validate Markup | [Shift][F6] |
| Get | [Ctrl][Shift][D] (Win) or ⌘ [Shift][D] (Mac) |
| Check Out | [Ctrl][Alt][Shift][D] (Win) or ⌘ [option][Shift][D] (Mac) |
| Put | [Ctrl][Shift][U] (Win) or ⌘ [Shift][U] (Mac) |
| Check In | [Ctrl][Alt][Shift][U] (Win) or ⌘ [option][Shift][U] (Mac) |
| Check Links | [Shift][F8] |
| Check Links Sitewide | [Ctrl][F8] (Win) or ⌘ [F8] (Mac) |

## View the imported site

1. Click the **Expand to show local and remote sites button** 🖻 on the Files panel toolbar to expand the Files panel.

2. Expand the Site root folder to view the contents (if necessary).

3. Click the **Refresh button** 🔃 to view the files in the Remote Site pane.

   As shown in Figure 35, the site looks identical to the original The Striped Umbrella site, except the name has been changed to The Striped Umbrella 2.

   TIP  If you don't see your remote site files, click the Connects to remote host button.

4. Click the **Collapse to show only local or remote site button** 🖻 to collapse the Files panel.

5. Open the Manage Sites dialog box, verify that The Striped Umbrella 2 site is selected, click **Remove**, click **Yes** to clear the warning dialog box, then click **Done** to delete The Striped Umbrella 2 website.

6. Close all open pages, then close Dreamweaver.

*You viewed the expanded Files panel for The Striped Umbrella 2 website and then deleted The Striped Umbrella 2 website.*

# EVALUATE WEB CONTENT FOR
## LEGAL USE

## What You'll Do

*In this lesson, you will examine copyright issues in the context of using content gathered from sources such as the Internet.*

### Can I Use Downloaded Media?

The Internet has made it possible to locate compelling and media-rich content to use in websites. A person who has learned to craft searches can locate a multitude of interesting material, such as graphics, animations, sounds, and text. But just because you can find it easily does not mean that you can use it however you want or under any circumstance. Learning about copyright law can help you decide whether or how to use content created and published by someone other than yourself.

### Understanding Intellectual Property

Intellectual property is a product resulting from human creativity. It can include inventions, movies, songs, designs, clothing, and so on.

The purpose of copyright law is to promote progress in society, not expressly to protect the rights of copyright owners. However, the vast majority of work you might want to download and use in a project is protected by either copyright or trademark law.

**Copyright** protects the particular and tangible *expression* of an idea, not the idea itself. If you wrote a story using the idea of aliens crashing in Roswell, New Mexico, no one could copy or use your story without permission. However, anyone could write a story using a similar plot or characters—the *idea* of aliens crashing in Roswell is not copyright-protected. Generally, copyright lasts for the life of the author plus 70 years.

**Trademark** protects an image, word, slogan, symbol, or design used to identify goods or services. For example, the Nike swoosh, Disney characters, or the shape of a classic Coca-Cola bottle are works protected by trademark. Trademark protection lasts for 10 years with 10-year renewal terms, lasting indefinitely provided the trademark is in active use.

## What Exactly Does the Copyright Owner Own?

Copyright attaches to a work as soon as you create it; you do not have to register it with the U.S. Copyright Office. A copyright owner has a "bundle" of six rights, consisting of:

1) reproduction (including downloading)
2) creation of **derivative works** (for example, a movie version of a book)
3) distribution to the public
4) public performance
5) public display
6) public performance by digital audio transmission of sound recordings

By default, only a copyright holder can create a derivative work of his or her original by transforming or adapting it.

## Understanding Fair Use

The law builds in limitations to copyright protection. One limitation to copyright is **fair use**. Fair use allows limited use of copyright-protected work. For example, you could excerpt short passages of a film or song for a class project or parody a television show. Determining if fair use applies to a work depends on the *purpose* of its use, the *nature* of the copyrighted work, *how much* you want to copy, and the *effect* on the market or value of the work. However, there is no clear formula on what constitutes fair use. It is always decided on a case-by-case basis.

## How Do I Use Work Properly?

Being a student doesn't mean you can use any amount of any work for class.

On the other hand, the very nature of education means you need to be able to use or reference different work in your studies. There are many situations that allow you to use protected work.

In addition to applying a fair use argument, you can obtain permission, pay a fee, use work that does not have copyright protection, or use work that has a flexible copyright license, where the owner has given the public permission to use the work in certain ways. For more information about open-access licensing, visit www.creativecommons.org. Work that is no longer protected by copyright is in the **public domain**; anyone can use it however

### FIGURE 36
*The Library of Congress home page*

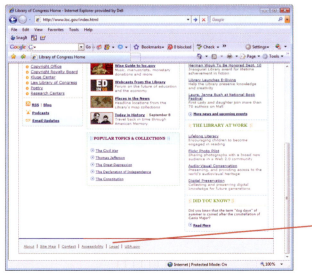

*Library of Congress website – www.loc.gov*

they wish for any purpose. In general, the photos and other media on federal government websites are in the public domain.

## Understanding Licensing Agreements

Before you decide whether to use media you find on a website, you must decide whether you can comply with its licensing agreement. A **licensing agreement** is the permission given by a copyright holder that conveys the right to use the copyright holder's work under certain conditions.

Websites have rules that govern how a user may use its text and media, known as **terms of use**. Figures 36, 37, and 38 are great

*Link to legal information regarding the use of content on the website*

examples of clear terms of use for the Library of Congress website.

A site's terms of use do not override your right to apply fair use. Also, someone cannot compile public domain images in a website and then claim they own them or dictate how the images can be used. Conversely, someone can erroneously state in their terms of use that you can use work on the site freely, but they may not know the work's copyright status. The burden is on you to research the veracity of anyone claiming you can use work.

## Obtaining Permission or a License

The **permissions process** is specific to what you want to use (text, photographs, music, trademarks, merchandise, and so on) and how you want to use it (school term paper, personal website, fabric pattern). How you want to use the work will determine the level and scope of permissions you need to secure. The fundamentals, however, are the same. Your request should contain the following:

- Your full name, address, and complete contact information.
- A specific description of your intended use. Sometimes including a sketch, storyboard, or link to a website is helpful.
- A signature line for the copyright holder.
- A target date when you would like the copyright holder to respond. This can be important if you're working under deadline.

## Posting a Copyright Notice

The familiar © symbol or "Copyright" is no longer required to indicate copyright, nor does it automatically register your work,

## FIGURE 37
*Library of Congress website legal page*

*Library of Congress website – www.loc.gov*

## FIGURE 38
*Library of Congress website copyright page*

### About Copyright and the Collections

Whenever possible, the Library of Congress provides factual information about copyright owners and related matters in the catalog records, finding aids and other texts that accompany collections. As a publicly supported institution, the Library generally does not own rights in its collections. Therefore, it does not charge permission fees for use of such material and generally does not grant or deny permission to publish or otherwise distribute material in its collections. Permission and possible fees may be required from the copyright owner independently of the Library. It is the researcher's obligation to determine and satisfy copyright or other use restrictions when publishing or otherwise distributing materials found in the Library's collections. Transmission or reproduction of protected items beyond that allowed by fair use requires the written permission of the copyright owners. Researchers must make their own assessments of rights in light of their intended use.

If you have any more information about an item you've seen on our website or if you are the copyright owner and believe our website has not properly attributed your work to you or has used it without permission, we want to hear from you. Please contact OGC@loc.gov with your contact information and a link to the relevant content.

but it does serve a useful purpose. When you post or publish it, you are stating clearly to those who may not know anything about copyright law that this work is claimed by you and is not in the public domain. Your case is made even stronger if someone violates your copyright and your notice is clearly visible. That way, violator can never claim ignorance of the law as an excuse for infringing. Common notification styles include:

Copyright 2013
Delmar, Cengage Learning
or
© 2013 Delmar, Cengage Learning

Giving proper attribution for text excerpts is a must; giving attribution for media is excellent practice, but is never a substitute for applying a fair use argument, buying a license, or simply getting permission.

You must provide proper citation for materials you incorporate into your own work, such as the following:

**References**

Waxer, Barbara M., and Baum, Marsha L. 2006. *Internet Surf and Turf – The Essential Guide to Copyright, Fair Use, and Finding Media.* Boston: Thomson Course Technology.

This expectation applies even to unsigned material and material that does not display the copyright symbol (©). Moreover, the expectation applies just as certainly to ideas you summarize or paraphrase as to words you quote verbatim.

Guidelines have been written by the American Psychological Association (APA) to establish an editorial style to be used to present written material. These guidelines include the way citations are referenced.

Here's a list of the elements that make up an APA-style citation of web-based resources:
- Author's name (if known)
- Date of publication or last revision (if known), in parentheses
- Title of document
- Title of complete work or website (if applicable), underlined
- URL, in angled brackets
- Date of access, in parentheses

Following is an example of how you'd reference the APA Home page on the Reference page of your paper:

APA Style.org. Retrieved August 22, 2012, from APA Online website: http://www.apastyle.org/electext.html

Another set of guidelines used by many schools and university and commercial presses is the Modern Language Association (MLA) style. For more information, go to http://www.mla.org.

## Perform website maintenance.

1. Open the blooms & bulbs website, then re-create the site cache.
2. Use the Link Checker panel to check for broken links, then fix any broken links that appear.
3. Use the Link Checker to check for orphaned files. If any orphaned files appear in the report, take steps to link them to appropriate pages or remove them.
4. Use the Assets panel to check for non-web-safe colors. (*Hint*: If you do see any non-web-safe colors, recreate the site cache again, then refresh the Assets panel.)
5. Run an Untitled Documents report for the entire local site. If the report lists any pages that have no titles, add page titles to the untitled pages. Run the report again to verify that all pages have page titles.
6. Run a report to look for missing alternate text. Add alternate text to any graphics that need it, then run the report again to verify that all images contain alternate text.

7. Enable the Design Notes preference and add a Design Note to the classes page as follows: **Shoot a video of the hanging baskets class to add to the page**. Add the status **needs attention** and check the Show when file is opened option.

## Publish a website and transfer files.

1. Set up web server access for the blooms & bulbs website on an FTP server or a local/network server (whichever is available to you) using blooms_yourlastname as the remote folder name.
2. View the blooms & bulbs remote site in the Files panel.
3. Upload the iris.jpg file to the remote site, then view the remote site.
4. Synchronize all files in the blooms & bulbs website, so that all files from the local site are uploaded to the remote site.

## Check files out and in.

1. Enable the Check In/Check Out feature.
2. Check out the plants page and all dependent pages.
3. Open the plants page, then change the heading style of "Drop by to see our Featured Spring Plants" to bold_blue, then save the file.
4. Check in the plants page and all dependent files.

## Cloak files.

1. Verify that cloaking is enabled in the blooms & bulbs website.
2. Cloak the assets folder, then uncloak it.
3. Cloak all the .jpg files in the blooms & bulbs website.

**Import and export a site definition.**

1. Create a new folder named **blooms_site_ definition** on your hard drive or external drive.

2. Export the blooms & bulbs site definition to the blooms_site_definition folder.

3. Import the blooms & bulbs site definition to create a new site called **blooms & bulbs 2**.

4. Make sure that all files from the blooms & bulbs website appear in the Files panel for the imported site, then compare your screen to Figure 39.

5. Remove the blooms & bulbs 2 site.

6. Close all open files.

**FIGURE 39**
*Completed Skills Review*

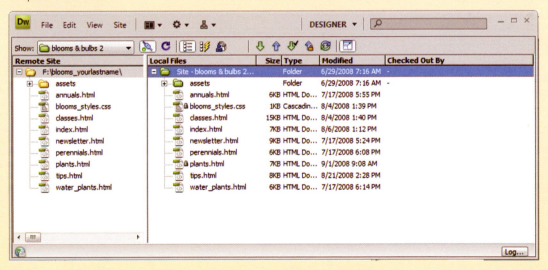

In this Project Builder, you will publish the TripSmart website that you have developed throughout this book to a local/network folder. Mike Andrew, the owner, has asked that you publish the site to a local folder as a backup location. You will first run several reports on the site, specify the remote settings for the site, upload files to the remote site, check files out and in, and cloak files. Finally, you will export and import the site definition.

1. Use the TripSmart website that you began in Project Builder 1 in Chapter 1 and developed in previous chapters.

2. Use the Link Checker panel to check for broken links, then fix any broken links that appear.

3. Use the Link Checker to check for orphaned files. If any orphaned files appear in the report, take steps to link them to appropriate pages or remove them.

4. Use the Assets panel to check for non-web-safe colors.

5. Run an Untitled Documents report for the entire local site. If the report lists any pages that lack titles, add page titles to the untitled pages. Run the report again to verify that all pages have page titles.

6. Run a report to look for missing alternate text. Add alternate text to any graphics that need it, then run the report again to verify that all images contain alternate text.

7. Enable the Design Notes preference, if necessary, and add a design note to the newsletter page as follows: **Add a Flash video showing the river route**. Add the status **needs attention** and check the Show when file is opened option.

8. If you did not do so in Project Builder 1 in Chapter 1, use the Site Definition dialog box to set up web server access for a remote site using a local or network folder.

9. Upload the index page and all dependent files to the remote site.

10. View the remote site to make sure that all files uploaded correctly.

11. Synchronize the files so that all other files on the local TripSmart site are uploaded to the remote site.

12. Enable the Check In/Check Out feature.

13. Check out the index page in the local site and all dependent files.

14. Open the index page, close the index page, then check in the index page and all dependent pages.

15. Cloak all .jpg files in the website.

16. Export the site definition to a new folder named **tripsmart_site_definition**.

17. Import the TripSmart.ste file to create a new site named TripSmart 2.

18. Expand the assets folder in the Files panel (if necessary), then compare your screen to Figure 40.

19. Remove the TripSmart 2 site.

20. Close any open files.

**FIGURE 40**

*Sample Project Builder 1*

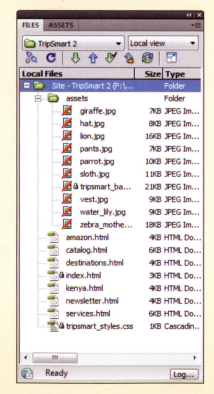

In this Project Builder, you will finish your work on the Carolyne's Creations website. You are ready to publish the website to a remote server and transfer all the files from the local site to the remote site. First, you will run several reports to make sure the website is in good shape. Next, you will enable the Check In/Check Out feature so that other staff members may collaborate on the site. Finally, you will export and import the site definition file.

1. Use the Carolyne's Creations website that you began in Project Builder 1 in Chapter 1 and developed in previous chapters.

2. If you did not do so in Project Builder 2 in Chapter 1, use the Site Definition dialog box to set up web server access for a remote site using either an FTP site or a local or network folder.

3. Run reports for broken links and orphaned files, correcting any errors that you find. The cc_banner.jpg file is no longer needed, so delete the file.

4. Run reports for untitled documents and missing alt text, correcting any errors that you find.

5. Check for non-web-safe colors.

6. Upload the classes.html page and all dependent files to the remote site.

7. View the remote site to make sure that all files uploaded correctly.

8. Synchronize the files so that all other files on the local Carolyne's Creations site are uploaded to the remote site.

9. Enable the Check In/Check Out feature.

10. Check out the classes page and all its dependent files.

11. Open the classes page, then change the price of the adult class to **$45.00**.

12. Save your changes, close the page, then check in the classes page and all dependent pages.

13. Export the site definition to a new folder named **cc_site_definition**.

14. Import the Carolyne's Creations.ste file to create a new site named Carolyne's Creations 2.

15. Expand the root folder in the Files panel (if necessary), compare your screen to Figure 41, then remove the Carolyne's Creations2 site.

**FIGURE 41**

*Completed Project Builder 2*

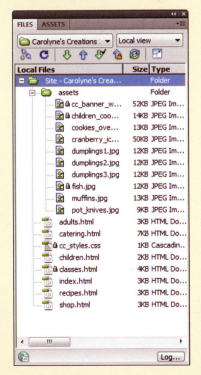

# DESIGN PROJECT

Throughout this book you have used Dreamweaver to create and develop several websites that contain different elements, many of which are found in popular commercial websites. For instance, Figure 42 shows the National Park Service website, which contains photos and information on all the national parks in the United States. This website contains many types of interactive elements, such as image maps and tables—all of which you learned to create in this book.

1. Connect to the Internet, then go to the National Park Service website at www.nps.gov.
2. Spend some time exploring the pages of this site to familiarize yourself with its elements.
3. Type a list of all the elements in this site that you have learned how to create in this book. After each item, write a short description of where and how the element is used in the site.
4. Print the home page and one or two other pages that contain some of the elements you described and attach it to your list.

**FIGURE 42**
*Design Project*

National Park Service website – www.nps.gov

## PORTFOLIO PROJECT

In this project, you will finish your work on the website that you created and developed throughout this book.

You will publish your site to a remote server or local or network folder.

1. Before you begin the process of publishing your website to a remote server, make sure that it is ready for public viewing. Use Figure 43 to assist you in making sure your website is complete. If you find problems, make the necessary changes to finalize the site.

2. Decide where to publish your site. The folder where you will publish your site can be either an FTP site or a local/network folder. If you are publishing to an FTP site, be sure to write down all the information you will need to publish to the site, including the URL of the FTP host, the directory on the FTP server where you will publish your site's root folder, and the login and password information.

3. Use the Site Definition dialog box to specify the remote settings for the site using the information that was decided upon in Step 2.

4. Transfer one of the pages and its dependent files to the remote site, then view the remote site to make sure the appropriate files were transferred.

5. Synchronize the files so that all the remaining local pages and dependent files are uploaded to the remote site.

6. Enable the Check In/Check Out feature.

7. Check out one of the pages. Open the checked-out page, make a change to it, save the change, close the page, then check the page back in.

8. Cloak a particular file type.

9. Export the site definition for the site to a new folder on your hard drive or on an external drive.

10. Import the site to create a new version of the site.

11. Close the imported site, save and close all open pages (if necessary), then exit Dreamweaver.

### FIGURE 43
*Portfolio Project checklist*

---

**Website Checklist**

1. Are you satisfied with the content and appearance of every page?
2. Are all paths for all links and images correct?
3. Does each page have a title?
4. Do all images appear?
5. Are all colors web-safe?
6. Do all images have appropriate alternate text?
7. Have you eliminated any orphaned files?
8. Have you deleted any unnecessary files?
9. Have you viewed all pages using at least two different browsers?
10. Does the home page have keywords and a description?

---

chapter

# 7

# USING STYLES AND
## STYLE SHEETS
## FOR DESIGN

1. Create and use embedded styles

2. Modify embedded styles

3. Work with external CSS style sheets

4. Work with conflicting styles

5. Use coding tools to view and edit styles

### Introduction

In Chapter 3, you learned how to create, apply, and edit Cascading Style Sheets. Using CSS styles is the best and most powerful way to ensure that all elements in a website are formatted consistently. The advantage of using CSS styles is that all of your formatting rules are kept in a separate or **external style sheet** file, so that you can change the appearance of every page to which the style sheet is attached by modifying the style sheet file. For instance, suppose your external style sheet contains a style called headings that is applied to all top-level headings in your website. If you want to change the heading color to blue, you simply change the color attribute to blue in the style sheet file, and all headings in the website are updated instantly. Because style sheets separate the formatting from the content, the site is formatted automatically from the style sheet information.

You can also create **embedded CSS styles**, which are styles whose code is located within the head section of the HTML code of a web page. The advantage of embedded

styles is that you can use them to override an external style. For instance, if all headings in your website are blue because the external style applied to them specifies blue as the color attribute, you could change the color of one of those headings to a different color by creating and apply ing an embedded style that specifies a different color as the color attribute. However, in general, you should avoid using embedded styles to format all the pages of a website; it is a better practice to keep formatting rules in a separate file from the content. External CSS styles also reduce the overall file sizes of your pages; most formatting code can be stored in a single file, rather than in individual page files.

In this chapter, you will import a redesigned Striped Umbrella website. Each page has been redesigned using CSS styles for page layout to provide consistency. You will replace your current site with this new one. You will then create and apply embedded styles and work with external CSS style sheets to format the pages in the site.

# Tools You'll Use

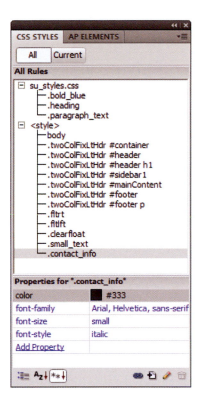

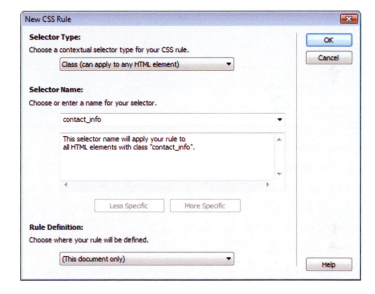

# CREATE AND USE
## EMBEDDED STYLES

### What You'll Do

 *In this lesson, you will replace your Striped Umbrella files by importing a revised website. Next, you will create and apply an embedded style to the home page.*

### Understanding Embedded Styles

In Chapter 3, you learned how to create and use an external style sheet to apply consistent formatting to the elements of a website. An external style sheet is a separate file with a .css extension that contains a collection of rules that create styles for formatting elements of a website. External style sheets can be applied to multiple pages, and are, therefore, a great tool to help ensure formatting consistency across all pages of a website. Sometimes, however, you might want to create a style that is used only on a single page in your site. You can do this using **embedded styles**, or styles whose code is embedded in the code of an individual page. Embedded styles are handy when you want a particular page in your site to use formatting that is different from the styles specified in an external style sheet. If both an external style and embedded style are applied to a single element, the embedded style overrides the external style. There is also a type of style similar to an embedded style called an inline style. Like an embedded style, the **inline style** is part of the individual page code, but it is written in the body section, rather than the head section. Inline styles refer to a specific instance of a tag, rather than a global tag style on a page. The ID selector type creates an inline style. These rule names are preceded by a # sign. To apply an inline style to a page element, use the ID list box on the HTML Property inspector.

### Creating and Applying a Custom Style

To create an embedded style, you use the New CSS Rule button in the CSS Styles panel to open the New CSS Rule dialog box, as shown in Figure 1. You use this dialog box to create both embedded styles as well as styles that are added to external style sheets. To specify the new style as an embedded style, click the (This document only) option in the Rule Definition section. If you click the (New Style Sheet File) option you will need to name and save a new CSS style sheet file using the Save Style Sheet File As dialog box. You also have the choice of creating a new style in an existing CSS style sheet, such as the one you have already created for The Striped Umbrella website.

You use the New CSS Rule dialog box to create a **custom style** (also known as a **class style**), which contains a combination of formatting attributes that can be applied to a block of text or other page elements. When you name a class style, you begin the name with a period (.).

After you name the rule and click OK, the CSS Rule definition dialog box will open with settings for the Type category displayed, as shown in Figure 2. This dialog box contains eight different categories whose settings can be defined. To specify the settings for a category, click the category, then enter the settings. When you finish specifying settings for all of the desired categories, click OK.

Once you create a class style, it appears in the CSS Styles panel and as a choice in the Class list box in the HTML Property inspector or in the Targeted Rule list box in the CSS Property inspector. To apply a class style to an element on a web page, select the element, and then click the style from the list.

**FIGURE 1**

*New CSS Rule dialog box*

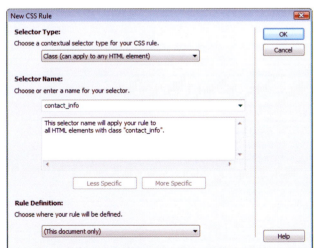

**FIGURE 2**

*CSS Rule definition for .heading in su_styles.css*

*Choose a category to see property options for that category*

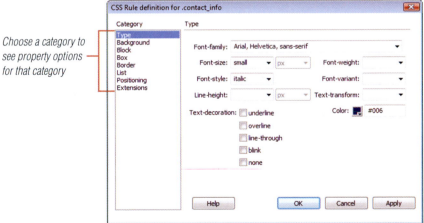

## Import the revised Striped Umbrella website (Win)

1. Open Windows Explorer, then navigate to where you store your Data Files for this chapter, so that the files appear in the right pane.

2. In the left pane, navigate to where you store your striped_umbrella folder, as shown in Figure 3, right-click it, then click **Delete**. Confirm the deletion if a confirmation dialog box opens.

3. Copy the **striped_umbrella folder** from the chapter_7 Data Files folder in the right pane to the folder where you save your files in the left pane.

    The redesigned pages in the new folder replace your previous root folder.

4. Close Windows Explorer, then start Dreamweaver.

5. Click **Site** on the Application bar, click **Manage Sites**, verify that The Striped Umbrella website is selected, click **Remove**, then click **Yes** in the warning dialog box.

    It is better to remove the previous site, because the site you will be importing has the same name. Remember that deleting a website in the Manage Sites dialog box does not actually delete the files. It just deletes the site definition.

6. Click **Import**.

    The Import Site dialog box opens.

7. Click the **Look in list arrow** to navigate to the chapter_7 Data Files folder, click **The Striped Umbrella.ste**, as shown in Figure 4, then click **Open**.

*(continued)*

### FIGURE 3
*Dragging the striped_umbrella folder to create a folder with revised files*

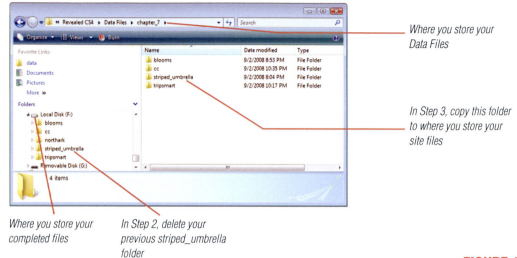

*Where you store your Data Files*

*In Step 3, copy this folder to where you store your site files*

*Where you store your completed files*

*In Step 2, delete your previous striped_umbrella folder*

### FIGURE 4
*Import Site dialog box*

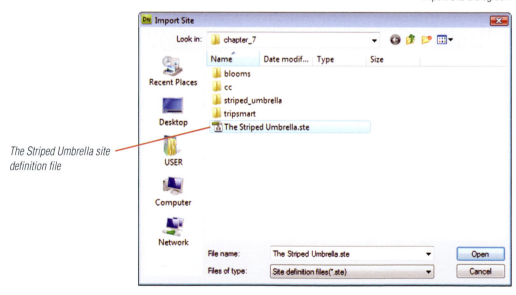

*The Striped Umbrella site definition file*

**FIGURE 5**

*Site Definition for The Striped Umbrella dialog box (Win)*

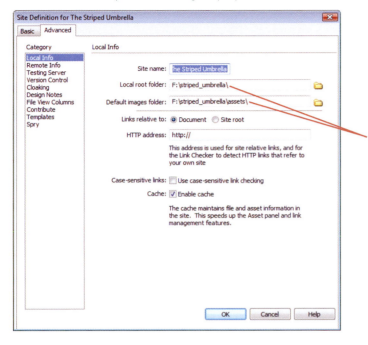

*Your paths will be different depending on the location you chose for the striped_umbrella folder and will probably be the same locations you chose for the original files*

The .ste file is an XML file that contains information about the website, including any information entered in the Manage Sites dialog box.

8.  Navigate to the striped_umbrella folder that you moved in Step 3, click the folder, click **Open**, then click **Select**.

    The Choose local images folder for site The Striped Umbrella dialog box opens.

9.  Click the **assets folder** in the striped_umbrella folder, click **Open**, then click **Select**.

    This sets the Default Images Folder path to the assets folder located in the striped_umbrella folder.

10. Verify that The Striped Umbrella site is selected in the Manage Sites dialog box, then click **Edit**.

11. Verify that the striped_umbrella folder is the root folder for the website and the assets folder under the striped_umbrella folder is the default location for images, as shown in Figure 5.

12. Click **OK**, then click **Done**.

    TIP  If you do not see the files listed in the Files panel, click the plus sign next to the root folder.

*You copied the striped_umbrella folder from the chapter_7 Data Files folder to a different drive or folder on your computer or external drive. You then imported the revised Striped Umbrella site and verified that the root folder was set to the striped_umbrella folder that you copied. You also verified that the default images folder is still the assets folder of the striped_umbrella folder.*

---

**DESIGN**TIP  **Designing media-dependent style sheets**

One challenge web designers have is to provide alternate versions of web pages that will display attractively on hand-held devices. Because of the vast difference in the size of screens, a page designed for viewing on a computer screen will not work well when viewed on a hand-held device, such as a smart phone. **Media-dependent style sheets** are tools for identifying the device being used and formatting the page. There are two methods that can be used: by adding code to a style sheet such as "@media" or "@import at-rules" or by adding code to the head section of a document that specifies the target medium. For more information, go to www.w3.org and search for "media-dependent style sheets."

---

## Import the revised Striped Umbrella website (Mac)

1. Open Finder, then navigate to the folder where you want to store the revised Striped Umbrella website, then delete your original root folder.

2. Click **File** on the Menu bar, click **New Finder Window** to open another instance of Finder, then open the chapter_7 Data Files folder.

3. Drag the **striped_umbrella folder** from the chapter_7 folder to where you want to store The Striped Umbrella website, as shown in Figure 6.

4. Close the Finder windows, start Dreamweaver (if necessary), click **Site** on the Menu bar, click **Manage Sites**, verify that The Striped Umbrella website is selected, click **Remove**, then click **Yes** in the Warning dialog box.

   It is better to remove the previous site, since the site you will be importing has the same name. Remember that deleting a website in the Manage Sites dialog box does not actually delete the files. It just deletes the site definition.

5. Click **Import**.

   The Import Site dialog box opens.

6. Navigate to the chapter_7 Data Files folder, click **The Striped Umbrella**.ste, then click **Open**.

   The Choose Local Root Folder for site The Striped Umbrella opens.

   *(continued)*

### FIGURE 6
*Dragging the striped-umbrella folder to replace the old folder (Mac)*

*Using Styles and Style Sheets for Design*

**FIGURE 7**

*Site Definition for The Striped Umbrella dialog box (Mac)*

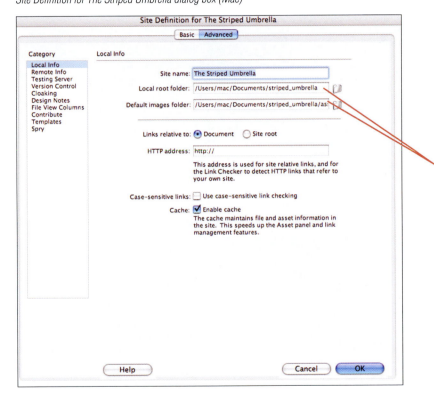

*Your paths will be different depending on the location you chose for the striped_umbrella folder and will probably be the same locations you chose for the original files*

7. Navigate to the striped_umbrella folder that you moved in Step 3, then click **Choose**.

   The Choose local images folder for site The Striped Umbrella dialog box opens.

8. Click the **assets folder** in the striped_umbrella folder, then click **Choose**.

   This sets the Default images Folder path to the assets folder located in the striped_umbrella folder.

9. Verify that The Striped Umbrella site is selected in the Manage Sites dialog box, then click **Edit**.

10. Click the **Advanced tab** (if necessary), then click the **Local Info category** (if necessary).

11. Compare your screen with Figure 7, click **OK**, then click **Done**.

*You copied the striped_umbrella folder from the chapter_7 Data Files folder to a different drive or folder on your computer or external drive. You then imported The Striped Umbrella site and verified that the default images folder is still the assets folder of the striped_umbrella folder.*

## Create a custom style

1.  Open the index page in The Striped Umbrella website, expand the CSS Styles panel, then click the **Switch to All (Document) Mode button** [All] (if necessary).

    The new, redesigned home page is now based on a CSS layout. The CSS block elements are outlined with dotted borders.

2.  Click the **New CSS Rule button** [icon] in the CSS Styles panel to open the New CSS Rule dialog box.

3.  Click the **Selector Type list arrow**, click **Class (can apply to any HTML element)**, click in the **Selector Name text box**, type **contact_info** click the **Rule Definition list arrow**, click **(This document only)**, then compare your screen to Figure 8.

4.  Click **OK** to open the CSS Rule definition for .contact_info dialog box, and verify that the Type category is selected.

5.  Set the Font-family to **Arial, Helvetica, sans-serif**; set the Font-size to **small**; set the Font-style to **italic**; set the Color to **#033**, then compare your screen to Figure 9.

6.  Click **OK**.

    The contact_info style appears in the CSS Styles panel.

    > TIP    If you do not see the contact_info style, click the plus sign (Win) or the triangle (Mac) next to <style> in the CSS Styles panel.

*You created a new custom style named contact_info and set the properties for it.*

**FIGURE 8**

*New CSS Rule dialog box with settings for contact_info style*

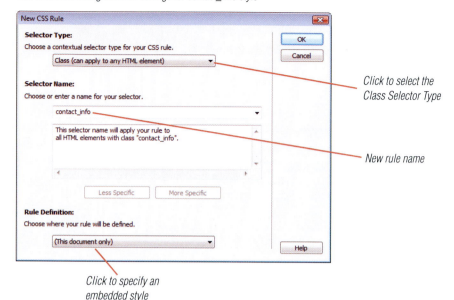

Click to select the Class Selector Type

New rule name

Click to specify an embedded style

**FIGURE 9**

*CSS Rule definition for .contact_info dialog box with Type category selected*

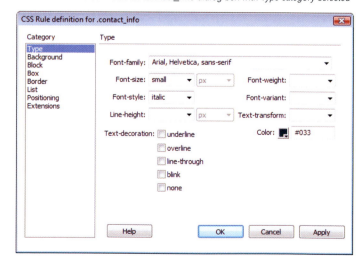

FIGURE 10

*Applying the contact_info style using the Property inspector*

Selected text

Class list arrow

Italic button

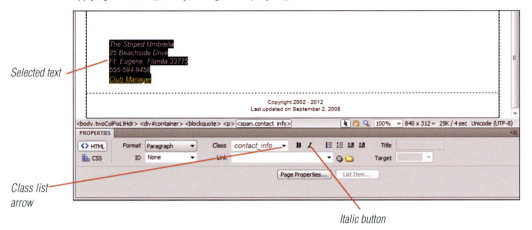

**FIGURE 11**

*Viewing the external and embedded styles*

External styles created to format text

Embedded styles include the CSS layout rules and the rules created to format text

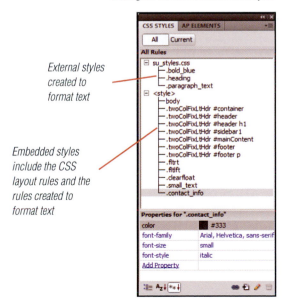

## Apply a custom style

1.  Select the paragraph with The Striped Umbrella contact information.

2.  Click the **Italic button** *I* in the HTML Property inspector to remove the italic formatting.

    You must remove manual formatting before applying a CSS style.

3.  Click the **Class list arrow** in the Property inspector, click **contact_info** as shown in Figure 10, then deselect the text.

    The selected text is now a dark gray, the color specified by the contact_info rule.

4.  Scroll down in the CSS Styles panel if necessary to view the contact_info rule, as shown in Figure 11.

    The contact_info rule is displayed in the CSS Styles panel, but not as a part of the su_styles.css style sheet. The contact_info rule is an embedded rule, along with the rules that are used to define the CSS layout and the other rule created to format text. The bold_blue, heading, and paragraph_text rules are external styles that reside in the su_styles.css file.

5.  Save your work.

*You used the Property inspector to apply the contact_info rule to selected text.*

# MODIFY EMBEDDED
## STYLES

### What You'll Do

 *In this lesson, you will modify the contact_info style, redefine an HTML tag, edit an embedded style, and then delete an embedded style.*

### Editing Embedded Styles

To edit a style, click the rule you want to edit in the CSS Styles panel, click the Edit Rule button in the CSS Styles panel, then use the CSS Rule Definition dialog box to change the settings as you wish, or simply enter the new settings in the CSS properties panel. Any changes that you make to the style are automatically reflected on the page; all elements to which the style is attached will update to reflect the change.

### Redefining HTML Tags

When you use the Property inspector to format a web page element, a predefined HTML tag is added to that element. Sometimes, you might want to change the definition of an HTML tag to add more "pizzazz" to elements that have that tag. For instance, perhaps you want all text that has the <em> tag, which is the tag used for italic formatting, to appear in bold purple. To change the definition of an HTML tag, click the Tag (redefines an HTML element) Selector type in the New CSS Rule dialog box, click the Selector Name list arrow to view all available HTML tags, click the tag you want to redefine, then click OK to open the CSS Rule definition dialog box, where you specify the desired formatting settings. Once you save the rule and apply it, the tags you target will be formatted according to the altered settings you specified.

### Using the CSS Styles Panel

There are two modes in the CSS Styles panel: All mode and Current mode. When All mode is selected, you will see style sheet rules listed in the top half of the panel, which is called the **All Rules pane**. When you click one of the rules, the bottom half, which is called the **Properties pane**, lists that rule's properties, as shown in Figure 12.

When Current mode is selected, the top half of the panel is called the Summary for Selection pane. When an object with a style is selected on an open web page, the Summary for Selection pane will display the properties for that style, as shown in Figure 13. The bottom half of the CSS Styles panel is called the

Properties pane in either mode. The small pane between the Summary for selection pane and the Properties pane in Current mode is called the Rules pane. The **Rules pane** displays the location of the current selected rule in the open document.

**QUICK**TIP

To delete an embedded rule, click the rule you wish to delete, then click the Delete CSS Rule button in the CSS Styles panel.

**FIGURE 12**
*CSS Styles panel in All mode*

**FIGURE 13**
*CSS Styles panel in Current mode*

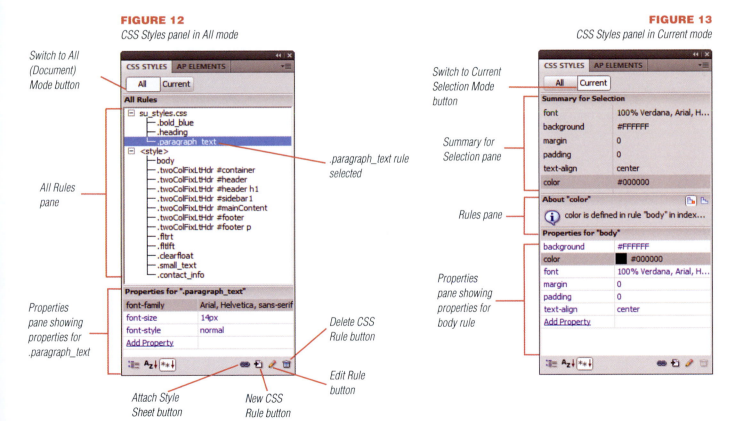

Switch to All (Document) Mode button

All Rules pane

Properties pane showing properties for .paragraph_text

Attach Style Sheet button

New CSS Rule button

.paragraph_text rule selected

Delete CSS Rule button

Edit Rule button

Switch to Current Selection Mode button

Summary for Selection pane

Rules pane

Properties pane showing properties for body rule

## Modify a custom style

1. Click the **contact_info rule** in the CSS Styles panel, then click the **Edit Rule button** .

2. Change the Color to **#006,** then compare your screen to Figure 14.

3. Click **OK**, compare your screen to Figure 15, then save and close the index page.

   The text with the contact_info style applied to it automatically changed to reflect the changes that you made to the rule.

   *You made a formatting change to the Type category of the contact_info rule. You then saw this change reflected in text with the contact_info style applied to it.*

**FIGURE 14**
*CSS Rule definition for .contact_info dialog box with modified type settings*

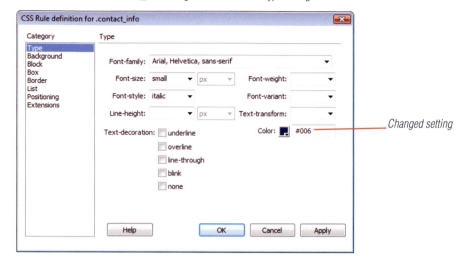

*Changed setting*

**FIGURE 15**
*Contact information shown with updated rule*

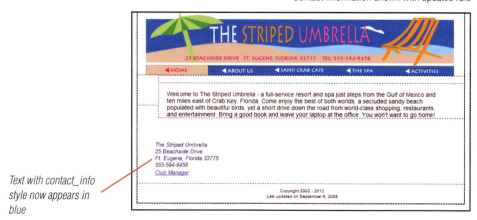

*Text with contact_info style now appears in blue*

**FIGURE 16**

Creating a new CSS Rule to redefine the hr HTML tag

Tag selector type

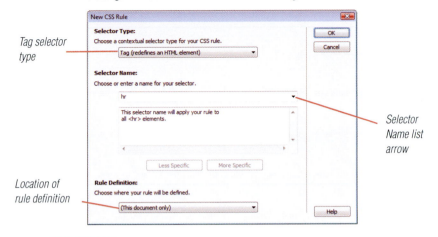

Selector Name list arrow

Location of rule definition

**FIGURE 17**

Redefining the hr HTML tag

Color is changed from the default color to blue

**FIGURE 18**

Redefining the body HTML tag

Background category

Change the page background color to #FFC

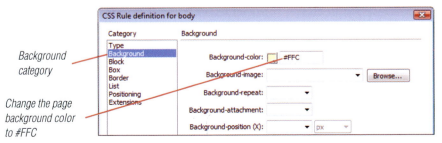

## Redefine an HTML tag

1. Open the about_us page, then click the **New CSS Rule button** 🗐 in the CSS Styles panel to open the New CSS Rule dialog box.

2. Click the **Selector Type list arrow**, click the **Tag (redefines an HTML element)**, click the **Selector Name list arrow**, scroll down, click **hr**, click the **Rule Definition list arrow**, then click **(This document only)**, as shown in Figure 16.

   The hr tag is the tag that creates a horizontal rule.

   TIP   To scroll quickly to the tags that begin with the letter h, type h after you click the Tag list arrow.

3. Click **OK** to open the CSS Rule definition for hr dialog box, set the Color to **#006**, compare your screen to Figure 17, then click **OK**.

   The horizontal rule in the middle of the page changed to blue because the rule definition has changed the way a horizontal rule is rendered.

4. Using Steps 1 through 3 as a guide, create a new CSS rule that redefines the body HTML tag, by using the Background category rather than the Type category to set the Background color to **#FFC**, as shown in Figure 18, then click **OK**.

   The page now has a yellow background. (The page background is behind the CSS container with all of the page content. You may need to collapse your panels to see it.)

*(continued)*

5. Switch to Code view to view the code that changes the properties for the horizontal rule, as shown in Figure 19.

Because these are embedded styles, the code for the styles is embedded into the page in the head section of the code. The style changing the background page color to yellow overrode the white page background color that you defined earlier by using the Page Properties dialog box.

6. Scroll up in the code, if necessary, to find the code that links the external style sheet file, as shown in Figure 20.

You cannot see the individual rule properties, because the file is linked, not embedded. If you open the su_styles.css file, however, you will see the rules and properties listed.

> TIP   If you have two embedded styles, you can tell which style takes precedence by its position in the tag selector. Tags with greater precedence are positioned to the right of other tags in the tag selector.

You used the New CSS Rule dialog box to redefine the hr and body HTML tags. You also viewed the code for the new embedded styles and the code that links the external style sheet file.

FIGURE 19
Viewing the code for embedded styles

```
60      }
61      .clearfloat { /* this class should be placed on a div or break element and should be the final element
        before the close of a container that should fully contain a float */
62          clear:both;
63          height:0;
64          font-size: 1px;
65          line-height: 0px;
66      }
67      hr {
68          color: #006;
69      }
70      body {
71          background-color: #FFC;
72      }
```

Code redefining the hr and body HTML
tags is part of head section

The code linking the
file resides in the head
section of the code

FIGURE 20
Viewing the code linking an external style sheet file

```
2       <html xmlns="http://www.w3.org/1999/xhtml">
3       <head>
4       <meta http-equiv="Content-Type" content="text/html; charset=utf-8" />
5       <title>The Striped Umbrella</title>
6       <link href="su_styles.css" rel="stylesheet" type="text/css" />
7       <style type="text/css">
8       <!--
9       body  {
10          font: 100% Verdana, Arial, Helvetica, sans-serif;
11          background: #FFFFFF;
12          margin: 0; /* it's good practice to zero the margin and padding of the body element to account for
        differing browser defaults */
13          padding: 0; /* this centers the container in IE 5* browsers. The text is then set to the left
        aligned default in the #container selector */
```

Code linking the
su_styles.css file to
the about_us page

**FIGURE 21**

*Changing the color property of the hr HTML tag*

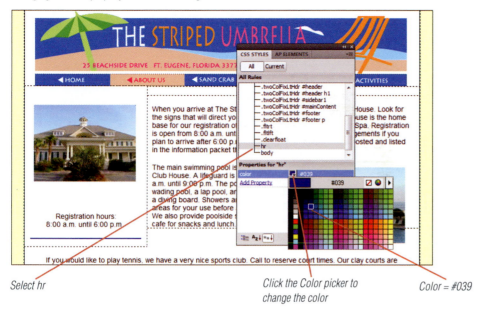

Select hr

Click the Color picker to change the color

Color = #039

**FIGURE 22**

*CSS Rules panel after deleting body style*

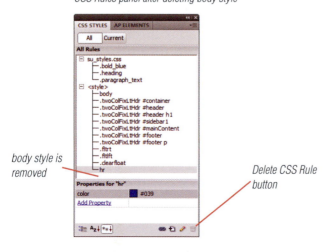

body style is removed

Delete CSS Rule button

## Edit an embedded style

1. Switch to Design view, then view the external and embedded styles for the about_us page in the CSS Styles panel.

2. Click the **hr style** in the CSS Styles panel.

   The properties of the hr rule are displayed in the Properties pane.

3. Click the **color picker** in the Properties pane, click color swatch **#039** to change the horizontal rule to a lighter blue, then compare your screen to Figure 21.

*You used the CSS Styles panel to change the color settings for the hr embedded style.*

## Delete an embedded style

1. Click the **.body rule** at the bottom of the list of rules in the CSS Styles panel to select it.

2. Click the **Delete CSS Rule button** 🗑, then compare your screen to Figure 22.

   The body rule is removed from the CSS Styles panel. The page background changes back to white.

   TIP   You can also delete an embedded style by right-clicking (Win) or [control]-clicking (Mac) the rule in the CSS Styles panel, then clicking Delete.

3. Save your changes, then close the about_us page.

*You used the CSS Styles panel to delete the body rule.*

# WORK WITH EXTERNAL
## CSS STYLE SHEETS

### What You'll Do

*In this lesson, you will make formatting changes in the style sheet and see those changes reflected on pages. You will also add hyperlink styles and custom code to the su_styles style sheet. Finally, you will delete a style from the su_styles style sheet.*

### Using External CSS Style Sheets

If you want to ensure consistent formatting across all elements of a website, it's a good idea to use external CSS style sheets instead of HTML styles or embedded styles. Most web developers prefer to use external CSS style sheets so they can make changes to the appearance of a website without opening each page. Using embedded styles requires you to make changes to the styles on each page, which takes more time and leaves room for error and inconsistency.

### Attaching an External CSS Style Sheet to a Page or Template

One of the big advantages of using external CSS style sheets is that you can attach them to pages that you've already created. When you do this, all of the rules specified in the style sheet are applied to the HTML tags on the page. So for instance, if your external style sheet specifies that all first-level headings are formatted in Arial 14-point bold blue, then all text in your web page that has the <h1> tag will change to reflect these settings when you attach the style sheet to the page. To attach an external style sheet to a page, open the page, and then use the Attach Style Sheet button in the CSS Styles panel to open the Attach External Style Sheet dialog box, as shown in Figure 23. Use this dialog box to browse for the external style sheet file you want to attach and to specify whether to link or import the file. In most cases, you should choose to link the file so that the content of the page is kept separate from the style sheet file.

If all the pages in your site are based on a template, you can save an enormous amount of time and development effort by attaching an external style sheet to the template. Doing this saves you from having to attach the style sheet to every page in the site; you have to attach it only to the template file. Then, when you make changes to the style sheet, those changes will be reflected in the template and will be updated in every page based on the template, when you save the template.

### Adding Hyperlink Rules to a CSS Style Sheet

You can use an external style sheet to create rules for all links in a website. To do this, open the style sheet so it appears in the document window, and then click the New CSS Rule button to open the New CSS Rule dialog box. Click the Selector Type list arrow, click Compound (based on your selection) and then choose one of the selectors from the Selector Name list, as shown in Figure 24. After you choose a selector and click OK, the CSS Rule Definition dialog box opens, where you can specify the formatting of the selected link. In addition to adding hyperlink rules, you can also create rules for other types of tags using the Compound selector type. By default, the Selector Name text box will display the name of the tag at the insertion point on an open page. In Figure 24, the insertion point was in the body tag, so the body tag is listed in the Selector Name text box as a choice. But you can type any tag name in the text box to modify any tag other than the one that is selected.

### Adding Custom Code to a CSS Style Sheet

You can make changes to a style sheet by editing the code in the style sheet file rather than through the CSS Styles panel. To do this, open the style sheet file so that it appears in the document window, click to place the insertion point where you want to add code, and then type the code you want. For instance, you can add code to the body tag of the style sheet that changes the colors of a viewer's scroll bar to match the colors of your website.

**FIGURE 23**
*Attach External Style Sheet dialog box*

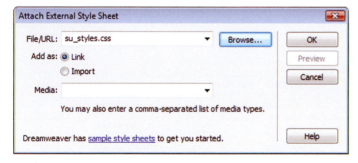

**FIGURE 24**
*New CSS Rule dialog box with Compound Selector Type displayed*

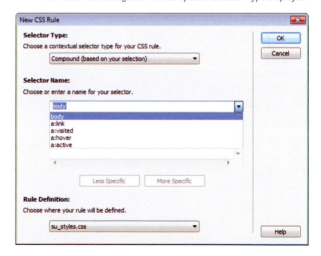

## Modify an external CSS style sheet

1. Open the activities page, then click **OK** to close the Design Notes dialog box.

2. Double-click the **su_styles.css file** in the root folder in the Files panel.

   The su_styles.css file opens in the Document window.

3. Switch back to the activities page, then click the **New CSS Rule button** 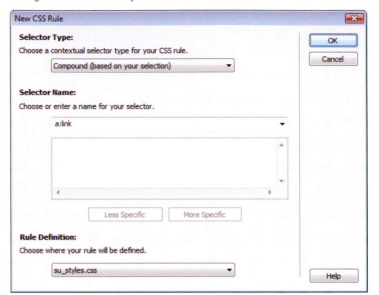 in the CSS Styles panel to open the New CSS Rule dialog box.

4. Click the **Selector Type list arrow**, then click **Compound (based on your selection)**.

5. Click the **Selector Name list arrow**, click **a:link**, click the **Rule Definition list arrow**, click **su_styles.css** if necessary, as shown in Figure 25, then click **OK**.

6. Set the Font-family to **Arial, Helvetica, sans-serif**; set the Font-size to **small**; set the Font-weight to **bold**; set the Color to **#036**; compare your screen to Figure 26; then click **OK**.

7. Click the **su_styles.css tab** to view the file in the Document window.

   The su_styles.css page now contains new code that reflects the font settings you specified for the a:link style.

8. Save your changes, switch to the activities page, scroll down the page, then notice that the fishing excursions and dolphin cruises page links now appear a different shade of blue, reflecting the formatting changes that you made to the a:link rule.

*You opened the su_styles.css file and made modifications to the a:link rule using the CSS Rule Definition dialog box.*

**FIGURE 25**

*Adding the a:link rule to the style sheet*

**FIGURE 26**

*Modifying the a:link rule*

**FIGURE 27**

*About_us page after modifying a:hover style*

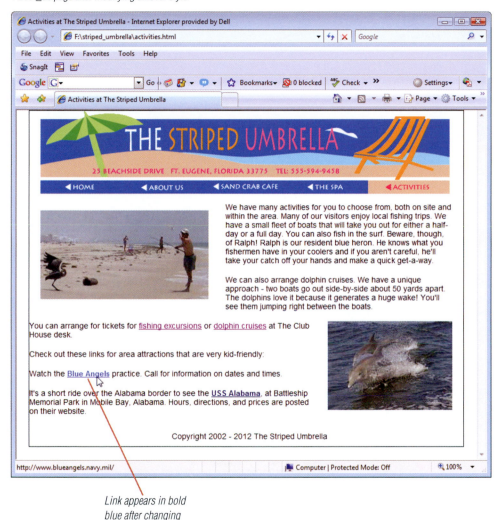

*Link appears in bold blue after changing a:hover style*

## Add hyperlink styles

1. Click the **New CSS Rule button** in the CSS Styles panel to open the New CSS Rule dialog box.

2. Click the **Selector Type list arrow**, click **Compound (based on your selection)**, click the **Selector Name list arrow**, then click **a:hover**.

3. Click the **Rule Definition list arrow**, click **su_styles.css**, then click **OK** to open the CSS Rule definition for a:hover in the su_styles.css dialog box.

4. Set the Font-family to **Arial, Helvetica, sans-serif**; set the Font-size to **small**; set the Font-weight to **bold**; set the Color to **#06C**; then click **OK**.

   The su_styles.css page now contains new code that reflects the font specifications you set for the a:hover style.

5. Click **File** on the Application bar (Win) or Menu bar (Mac), click **Save All** to save both pages, preview the page in your browser, position the mouse pointer over the Blue Angels link, then compare your screen to Figure 27.

   The links in the paragraph text appear in medium blue when the mouse pointer hovers over them, reflecting the formatting changes that you made to the a:hover style.

6. Close your browser, then close the activities page.

*You modified the a:hover style using the CSS Rule definition dialog box.*

## Add custom code to a style sheet

1. Open the spa page, then switch to the su_styles.css file.

2. Locate the .bold_blue style code in the style sheet, then replace the font size with **small**, as shown in Figure 28.

3. Switch to the spa page, then compare your screen to Figure 29.

   The text with the .bold_blue style is smaller now and looks better on the page.

4. Close the spa page, then save the su_styles.css page.

   *You opened the su_styles.css file and made changes to the bold_blue rule directly in the code.*

FIGURE 28

*su_styles.css file after changing the font-size for the bold_blue rule*

```
1   .bold_blue {
2       font-family: Arial, Helvetica, sans-serif;
3       font-size: small;
4       font-style: normal;
5       font-weight: bold;
6       color: #306;
7   }
8   .heading {
9       font-family: Arial, Helvetica, sans-serif;
10      font-size: 16px;
11      font-style: normal;
12      font-weight: bold;
13      color: #036;
14      text-align: center;
15  }
```

Font-size changed to small

FIGURE 29

*Spa page after rule has been modified*

Text with .bold-blue rule is smaller now

*Using Styles and Style Sheets for Design*

**FIGURE 30**
*Selected a:link code in su_styles.css file*

```
1    .bold_blue {
2        font-family: Arial, Helvetica, sans-serif;
3        font-size: small;
4        font-style: normal;
5        font-weight: bold;
6        color: #306;
7    }
8    .heading {
9        font-family: Arial, Helvetica, sans-serif;
10       font-size: 16px;
11       font-style: normal;
12       font-weight: bold;
13       color: #036;
14       text-align: center;
15   }
16   .paragraph_text {
17       font-family: Arial, Helvetica, sans-serif;
18       font-size: 14px;
19       font-style: normal;
20   }
21   a:link {
22       font-family: Arial, Helvetica, sans-serif;
23       font-size: small;
24       font-weight: bold;
25       color: #036;
26   }
27   a:hover {
28       font-family: Arial, Helvetica, sans-serif;
29       font-size: small;
30       font-weight: bold;
31       color: #06C;
32   }
33
```

*Selected a:link code*

## Use Code view to delete external styles from a style sheet

1. Open the css_styles.css file if necessary, select the **a:link tag** and the **five lines of code** below it, then compare your screen to Figure 30.

2. Press **[Delete]** (Win) or **[delete]** (Mac), then save your changes.

   The a:link style no longer appears in the CSS Styles panel.

3. Open the activities page, close the Design Notes dialog box, then preview the page in your browser.

   The activities page text links no longer appear as bold, indicating that the a:link style has been deleted from the style sheet.

   TIP  You can detach a style sheet from a template or web page by clicking the style sheet file in the CSS Styles panel, then clicking the Unlink CSS Stylesheet button. When you do this, the file is no longer linked to the web page, but it is not actually deleted; it remains in its original location on your computer.

4. Close the browser, then close all open files.

*You deleted the a:link style from the su_styles.css file and then saved your changes.*

# WORK WITH
## CONFLICTING STYLES

### What You'll Do

In this lesson, you will discover that embedded styles have precedence over styles redefining HTML tags.

When you have a mixture of embedded styles, external styles, and styles redefining HTML tags, you need to understand what happens when the styles conflict. In general, embedded styles override external styles and styles redefining HTML tags. Styles can also conflict with HTML formatting applied using the Property inspector. If you try to use the Property inspector to format text that already has a style applied to it, Dreamweaver will ask you to create a new style. Using styles to format text is better than using the Property inspector. Styles ensure consistency, cleaner code, and allow you to work more efficiently. While you are just beginning to understand Cascading Style Sheets, it might be wise to stick to external style sheets until you build up your experience base and confidence.

## FIGURE 31

Text with rule applied from redefined body tag

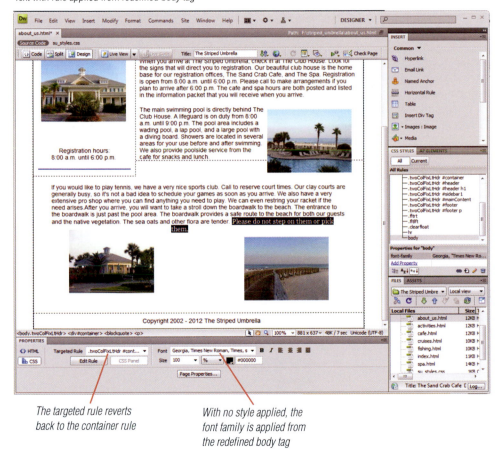

The targeted rule reverts
back to the container rule

With no style applied, the
font family is applied from
the redefined body tag

## Compare conflicting styles

1. Open the about_us page.

2. Click the **New CSS Rule button** on the CSS Styles panel, click the **Selector Type list arrow**, click **Tag (redefines an HTML element)**, click the **Selector Name list arrow**, click **body**, click the **Rule Definition list arrow**, click **(This document only)**, then click **OK**.

3. Click the **Font-family list arrow**, click **Georgia, Times New Roman, Times, serif**, then click **OK**.

   The body style is listed in the CSS Styles panel as an embedded style, specifying that all text in the body of the page be displayed using the Georgia, Times New Roman, Times, serif font family. However, the text on the page did not change because the body_text style from the su_styles.css file takes precedence over the style that changed the body tag.

4. Select the last sentence on the page beginning "Please do not step . . .", click the **CSS button** on the Property inspector if necessary, click the **Targeted Rule list arrow**, then click **<Remove Class>**.

   When the paragraph_text style is removed, the style from the body tag is applied, as shown in Figure 31.

5. Click **Edit** on the Application bar (Win) or Menu bar (Mac), then click **Undo Apply <span>** (Win) or **Undo** (Mac) to apply the paragraph_text style again.

6. Delete the body style from the CSS Styles panel.

*You found that an embedded style has precedence over a style redefining an HTML tag.*

# USE CODING TOOLS
## TO VIEW AND EDIT STYLES

## What You'll Do

 *In this lesson, you will collapse, then expand the code for the about_us page to view the code for the styles. You will then move the embedded style for the horizontal rule to the external style sheet file.*

### Coding Tools in Dreamweaver

There are several tools you can use on the Coding toolbar while you are in Code view. The Coding toolbar buttons include Open Documents, Show Code Navigator, Collapse Full Tag, Collapse Selection, Expand All, Select Parent Tag, Balance Braces, Line Numbers, Highlight Invalid Code, Syntax Error Alerts in Info Bar, Apply Comment, Remove Comment, Wrap Tag, Recent Snippets, Move or Convert CSS, Indent Code, Outdent Code, and Format Source Code, as shown in Figure 32.

**FIGURE 32**
*Coding Toolbar*

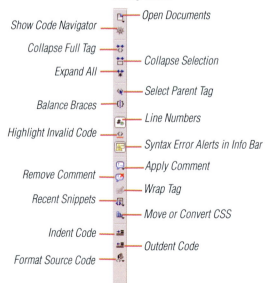

*Using Styles and Style Sheets for Design*

The Coding toolbar is displayed on the left side of the Document window, and is designed to remain stationary. Although you cannot move it, you can hide it.

Remember that you have several View options you can use while viewing your code. These include Word Wrap, Line Numbers, Hidden Characters, Highlight Invalid Code, Syntax Coloring, Auto Indent, Syntax Error Alerts in Info Bar, and Color Icons. You can turn these options on and off by checking or unchecking them on the View options menu (available on the Document toolbar).

### Using Coding Tools to Navigate Code

As your pages get longer and the code more complex, it is helpful to collapse sections of code, similarly to the way you can collapse and expand panels, folders, and styles.

To collapse lines of code, you can click the minus sign (Win) or the triangle (Mac) next to the line number. You can also use the Collapse Full Tag or Collapse Selection buttons on the Coding toolbar. This will allow you to look at two different sections of code that are not adjacent to each other in the code. Applying comments is an easy way to add documentation to your code. Comments are not visible in the browser. The Highlight Invalid Code command is an easy way to spot code containing errors so you can fix it.

### Using Code Hints to Streamline Coding

If you are typing code directly into Code view, one of the nice features Dreamweaver offers is the use of Code hints. **Code hints** are similar to other auto-complete features that you have probably used in other software applications. As you are typing code,

Dreamweaver will recognize the tag name and offer you choices to complete the tag simply by double-clicking a tag choice in the menu, as shown in Figure 33. You can also add your own code hints to the list using JavaScript. The code hints are stored in the file CodeHints.xml.

### Converting Styles

You can also convert one type of style to another. For instance, you can move an embedded style to an external style sheet or an inline style to either an embedded style or a style in an external style sheet. To do this, select the style in Code view, right-click the code, point to CSS Styles, then click Move CSS Rules. You can also move styles in the CSS Styles panel by selecting the style, right-clicking the style, and choosing the action you want from the context menu.

### FIGURE 33
*Using Code Hints*

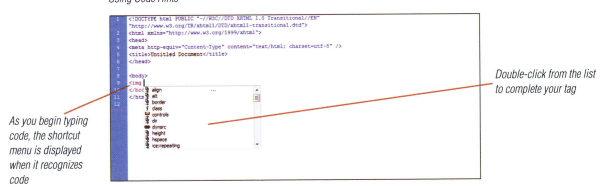

As you begin typing code, the shortcut menu is displayed when it recognizes code

Double-click from the list to complete your tag

## Collapse code

1. Verify that the about_us page is open, then change to Code view.

2. Scroll up the page (if necessary), to display the code that links the external style sheet, su_styles.css, to the page.

   The code will probably be on or close to line 7 in the head section.

3. Select the line of code under the line with the su_styles.css link (It reads <style type = text/css>), then drag down to select all of the code down to the line of code that includes the style for the horizontal rule, as shown in Figure 34.

4. Click the **minus sign** (Win) or **vertical triangle** (Mac) in the last line of selected code to collapse all of the code that is selected.

   You can now see both code fragments—before and after the collapsed code section, as shown in Figure 35. The plus sign (Win) or horizontal triangle (Mac) next to the line of code indicates that there is hidden code. You also see a gap in the line numbers where the hidden code resides.

*You collapsed a block of code in Code view to be able to see two non adjacent sections of the code at the same time.*

### FIGURE 34
*Selecting lines of code on the about_us page to collapse*

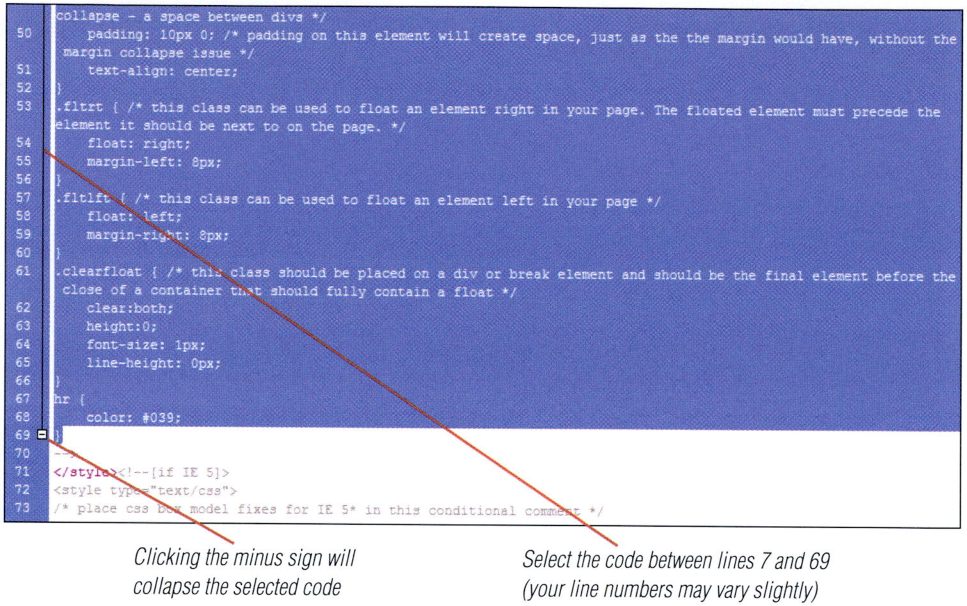

*Clicking the minus sign will collapse the selected code*

*Select the code between lines 7 and 69 (your line numbers may vary slightly)*

### FIGURE 35
*Collapsed code in Code view*

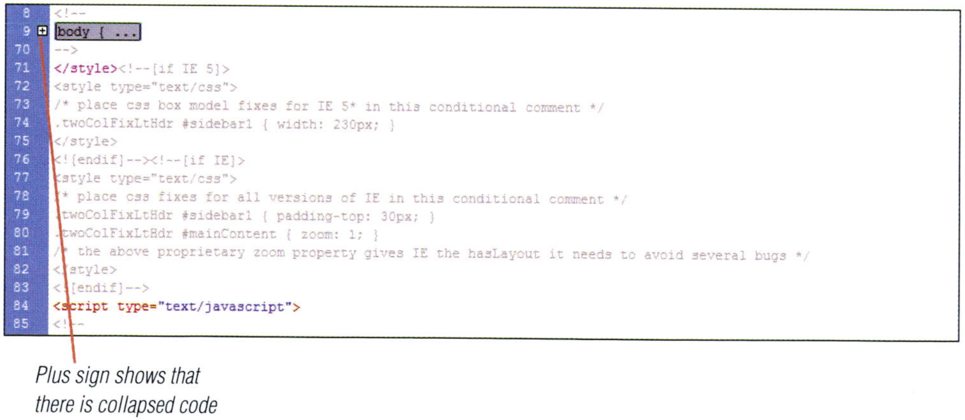

*Plus sign shows that there is collapsed code*

FIGURE 36
*Expanded code for about_us page*

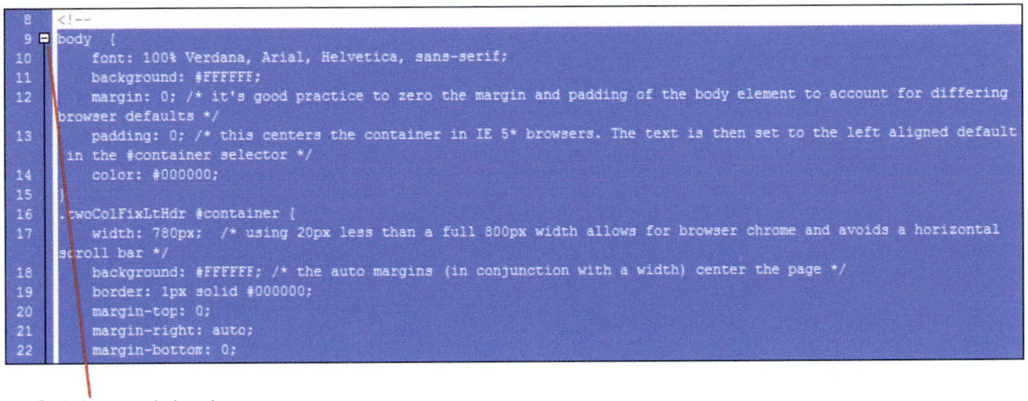

```
 8      <!--
 9  □  body  {
10          font: 100% Verdana, Arial, Helvetica, sans-serif;
11          background: #FFFFFF;
12          margin: 0; /* it's good practice to zero the margin and padding of the body element to account for differing
        browser defaults */
13          padding: 0; /* this centers the container in IE 5* browsers. The text is then set to the left aligned default
        in the #container selector */
14          color: #000000;
15      }
16  .twoColFixLtHdr #container {
17          width: 780px;  /* using 20px less than a full 800px width allows for browser chrome and avoids a horizontal
        scroll bar */
18          background: #FFFFFF; /* the auto margins (in conjunction with a width) center the page */
19          border: 1px solid #000000;
20          margin-top: 0;
21          margin-right: auto;
22          margin-bottom: 0;
```

*Code is expanded again*

## POWER USER SHORTCUTS

| to do this: | use this shortcut: |
|---|---|
| Collapse selection of code | [Ctrl][Shift][C] (Win) or [shift] ⌘ [C] (Mac) |
| Collapse outside selection of code | [Ctrl][Alt][C] (Win) or [option] ⌘ [C] (Mac) |
| Expand selection of code | [Ctrl[Shift][E] (Win) or [shift] ⌘ [E] (Mac) |
| Collapse full tag | [Ctrl][Shift][J] (Win) or [shift] ⌘ [J] (Mac) |
| Collapse outside full tag | [Ctrl][Alt][J] (Win) or [option] ⌘ [J] (Mac) |
| Expand all (code) | [Ctrl][Alt][E] (Win) or [option] ⌘ [E] (Mac) |
| Check links sitewide | [Ctrl][F8] (Win) or ⌘ [F8] (Mac) |
| Indent code | [Ctrl][Shift][>] (Win) or [shift] ⌘ [>] (Mac) |
| Outdent code | [Ctrl][Shift][<] (Win) or [shift] ⌘ [<] (Mac) |
| Balance braces | [Ctrl]['] (Win) or ⌘ ['] (Mac) |
| Go to line (of code) | [Ctrl][G] (Win) or ⌘ [,] (Mac) |
| Show code hints | [Ctrl][Spacebar] (Win) or [control][spacebar] (Mac) |
| Refresh code hints | [Ctrl][.] (Win) or [control][.] (Mac) |

## Expand code

1. Click the **plus sign** (Win) or **horizontal triangle** (Mac) on line 8 to expand the code.

2. Compare your screen to Figure 36, then click in the page to deselect the code.

   All line numbers are visible again.

*You expanded the code to display all lines of the code again.*

## Move an embedded style to an external CSS style sheet

1. Select the **three lines of code** that format the style for the horizontal rule on the about_us page.

   The code will be on or close to lines 67 through 69.

2. Right-click (Win) or control-click (Mac) the **selected code**, point to **CSS Styles**, then click **Move CSS Rules**, as shown in Figure 37.

   TIP  You can also convert a rule in the CSS Styles panel. To do this, right-click the rule name, then click Move CSS Rules.

3. In the Move to External Style Sheet dialog box, verify that su_styles.css appears in the Style Sheet text box, as shown in Figure 38, then click **OK**.

4. Compare your CSS Styles panel with Figure 39 to verify that the style has been moved to the external style sheet file.

   TIP  The name of the trash can icon 🗑 in the CSS Rules panel changes depending on whether you have a rule, a style sheet file, or an embedded style tag selected.

5. Save and close all open files.

*You moved an embedded style for a horizontal rule to an external CSS style sheet.*

**FIGURE 37**

*Moving the embedded hr style to the style sheet file*

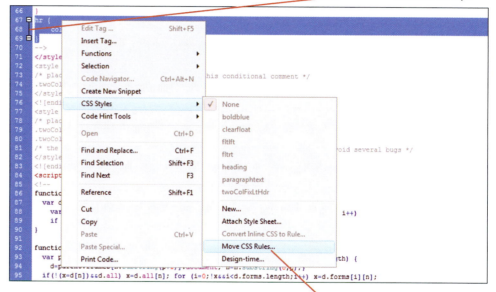

Selected code for horizontal rule style

Move CSS Rules option

**FIGURE 38**

Moving the embedded hr style to the style sheet file

The embedded hr rule will move to the
su_styles file

**FIGURE 39**

Moving the embedded hr style to the style sheet file

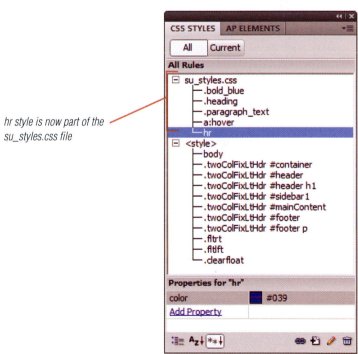

hr style is now part of the
su_styles.css file

### Create and use embedded styles.

1. Remove the blooms & bulbs website and replace your blooms root folder with the blooms folder from the Chapter 7 Data Files folder.
2. Import the blooms & bulbs.ste file and verify that the root folder and assets folder are linked correctly to your files.
3. Open the plants page.
4. Create a new embedded style that will redefine the horizontal rule tag.
5. In the Type category, set the color to #006; In the Block category, set the Text-align to center; and in the Box category, set the Width to 400 px.
6. Insert a horizontal rule right after the first paragraph ending "hanging baskets." (*Hint*: If your horizontal rule is not displayed as centered on the page, view it in the browser.)
7. Insert a horizontal rule right after the second paragraph ending "as beautiful."
8. Insert a horizontal rule right after the third paragraph ending "with cuttings."

### Modify embedded styles.

1. Modify the horizontal rule settings to change the width to 600 px.
2. Save your changes, preview the plants page in your browser, compare your screen to Figure 40, close your browser, and close the page.

### Work with external CSS style sheets.

1. Open the newsletter page.
2. Use the New CSS Rule dialog box to add the **a:link style** to the blooms_styles.css file.

Set the Font-family to Arial, Helvetica, sans-serif; set the Font-size to 14 pixels; set the Font-weight to normal; then set the Color to #039.
3. Save your changes, then make sure that the text links on the page now appear in a different shade of blue.
4. Use the New CSS Rule dialog box to add the a:hover style to the blooms_styles.css file. Set the Font-family to Arial, Helvetica, sans-serif; set the Font-size to 14 pixels; set the Font-weight to bold; then set the Font-color to #06F.
5. Save your work, then preview the newsletter page in your browser and make sure that the links appear according to the settings you specified. (*Hint*: Visited links will remain a purple color.)

6. Close the browser, then edit the headings style to change the Font-weight to bolder.

7. Close the newsletter page, and save the su_styles.css file.

## Work with conflicting styles.

1. Open the index page.

2. Modify the embedded body tag rule to change the Font-family to the Georgia, Times New Roman, Times, serif font.

3. Select the paragraph of text and remove the paragraph_text rule.

4. Reapply the paragraph_text rule and delete the Font-family setting from the body tag.

5. Save the index page.

## Use coding tools to view and edit styles.

1. Open the plants page, then collapse all of the code for the head content.

2. Expand all code.

3. Convert the horizontal rule on the plants page to an external style in the blooms_styles.css file.

4. Save and close all open pages.

**FIGURE 40**

*Completed Skills Review*

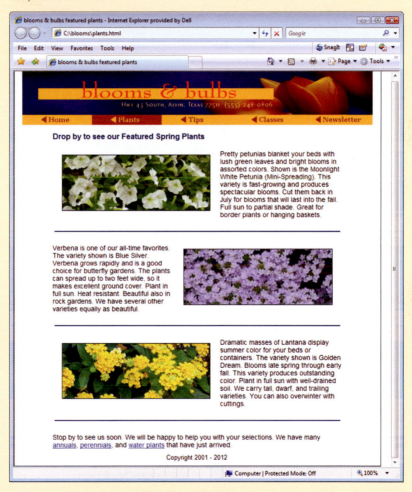

In this Project Builder you will continue your work on the TripSmart website. You have decided to add a few more styles to the style sheet to improve some of the page formatting.

1. Replace your tripsmart folder with the tripsmart folder from where you store your Chapter 7 Data Files.
2. Open the newsletter page, then close the Design Notes dialog box.
3. Create a new embedded class rule named **.bullets** using settings of your choice.
4. Apply the **.bullets** rule to the items listed at the beginning of each bullet, using Figure 41 as a guide.
5. Edit the heading style to change the color to a different color.
6. Add a horizontal rule under the list of items. (*Hint*: Remember to enter two paragraph breaks to end the unordered list. If you have difficulty ending the unordered list, click the Unordered List button.)
7. Create a new rule in the tripsmart_styles.css file that redefines the hr tag as centered and with a color of your choice. Notice how the horizontal rule on the page changes color.

8. Change the horizontal rule width to **500 px**.
9. Convert the bullets style to an external style in the tripsmart_styles.css styles file.
10. Save all files.

**FIGURE 41**
*Sample Project Builder 1*

11. Preview the newsletter page in your browser, then compare your screen to Figure 41.
12. Close your browser, then close all open files.

In this Project Builder, you will continue your work on the Carolyne's Creations website that you started in Project Builder 2 in Chapter 1. You will continue to work on the page formatting to include as much formatting as you can with the use of CSS styles.

1. Replace the Carolyne's Creations website root folder with the new folder from where you store your Chapter 7 Data Files.

2. Open the shop page.

3. Create a new class style in the cc_styles.css file called **prices**.

4. Refer to Figure 42 for ideas, then select the settings of your choice for the prices style that you will then use to format the prices of the two specials on the page.

5. Type the prices on your page and apply the prices style.

6. Create a new class style for this page only, named **special_name**, selecting formatting settings of your choice.

7. Apply the special_name style to the Multifunctional Pot and Cutlery Set text.

8. Convert the special_name style to an external style in the cc_styles.css file.

9. Save your work, then preview the shop page in your browser. See Figure 42 for a possible solution.

10. Close your browser, then close all open files.

**FIGURE 42**
*Completed Project Builder 2*

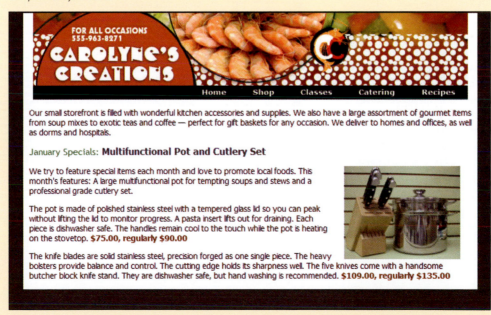

Many of today's leading websites use CSS style sheets to ensure consistent formatting and positioning of text and other elements. For instance, the United States Department of Justice website uses them. Figure 43 shows the Department of Justice home page.

1. Connect to the Internet, then go to the United States Department of Justice website at www.usdoj.gov.
2. Spend some time exploring the many pages of this site.
3. When you finish exploring all of the different pages, return to the home page. Click View on your browser's menu bar, then click Source to view the code for the page.
4. Look in the head content area for code relating to the CSS style sheet used. Note whether any styles are defined for a:link or a:hover and write down the specified formatting for those styles. Write down any other code you see that relates to styles.
5. Close the Source window, then look at the home page. Make a list of all the different text elements that you see on the page that you think should have CSS styles applied to them.

6. Print the home page of this site, along with the source code that contains CSS styles.

**FIGURE 43**
*Design Project*

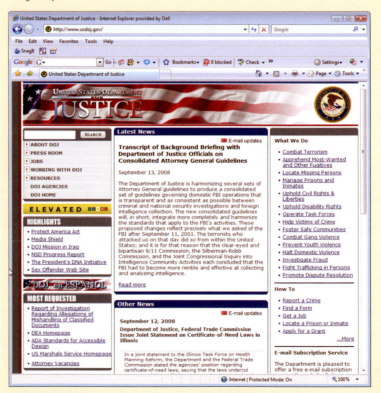

*United States Department of Justice website – www.usdoj.gov*

In this assignment, you will continue to work on the website that you created in Chapters 1 through 6.

You will continue refining your site by using CSS style sheets and embedded styles to format the text in your site consistently.

1.  Write a plan in which you define styles for all of the text elements in your site. Your plan should include how you will use an external style sheet as well as embedded styles. You can use either the external style sheet you created in Chapter 3 or create a new one. Your plan should include at least one custom style, one style that redefines an HTML tag, and one style that uses a selector.

2.  Attach the completed style sheet to all individual pages in the site.

3.  Create and apply the embedded styles you identified in your plan.

4.  Create and apply the styles that will be added to the external style sheet.

5.  Review the pages and make sure that all text elements appear as they should and look appropriate. Use the checklist in Figure 44 to make sure you have completed everything according to the assignment.

6.  Make any necessary changes.

7.  Save your work, then close all open pages.

**FIGURE 44**
*Portfolio Project checklist*

> **Website Checklist**
> 1.  Do all text elements in the site have a style applied to them?
> 2.  Does your site have at least one embedded style?
> 3.  Is the external style sheet attached to each page in the site?
> 4.  Did you define and apply at least one custom style and one style that redefines an HTML tag?
> 5.  Are you happy with the overall appearance of each page?

# 8

# COLLECTING DATA
## WITH FORMS

1. Plan and create a form

2. Edit and format a form

3. Work with form objects

4. Test and process a form

chapter 8 COLLECTING DATA
WITH FORMS

## Introduction

Many websites have pages designed to collect information from viewers. You've likely seen such pages when ordering books online from Amazon.com or purchasing airline tickets from an airline website. Adding a form to a web page provides interactivity between your viewers and your business. To collect information from viewers, you add forms for them to fill out and send to a web server to be processed. Forms on a web page are no different from other forms you use in everyday life. Your checks are simple forms that ask for information: the date, the amount of the check, the name of the check's recipient, and your signature. A form on a web page consists of **form objects** such as text boxes or radio buttons into which viewers type information or from which they make selections.

In this chapter, you will add a form to a page that provides a way for interested viewers to ask for more information about The Striped Umbrella resort. It will also give them the opportunity to comment on the website and make helpful suggestions.

Feedback is a vital part of a website and must be made easy for a viewer to submit.

## Using Forms to Collect Information

Forms are just one of the many different tools that web developers use to collect information from viewers. A simple form can consist of one form object and a button that submits information to a web server, for example, a search text box that you fill out, and a button that you click to start the search. More complex forms can collect contact information, or allow students to take exams online and receive grades instantly. You can use forms to insert information into databases, or to find a specific record in a database. The range of uses for forms is limited only by your imagination.

All forms need to be connected to an application server that will process the information that the form collects. This application can store the form data in a database, or simply send it to you in an email message. You need to specify how you want the information used, stored, and processed.

# Tools You'll Use

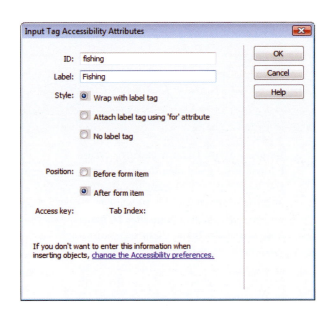

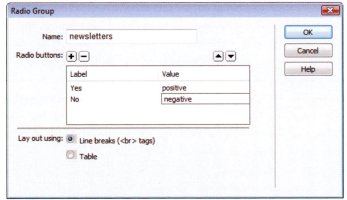

# PLAN AND
## CREATE A FORM

### Planning a Form

Before you use Dreamweaver to create a form, it's a good idea to write down the information you want to collect and the order in which you want to collect it. It's also a good idea to make a sketch of the form. Planning your form content at the beginning saves you from spending time organizing the information when you create the form in Dreamweaver. The Striped Umbrella website will contain a form for viewers to request more information, sign up for an electronic newsletter, and submit their comments about the website. Figure 1 shows a sketch of the form that you will create in this chapter.

When planning your form content, you should organize the information in a logical order that will make sense to viewers. For instance, no one will expect to fill in their address before their name, simply because it isn't typically done that way. Almost all forms, ranging from your birth certificate to your IRS tax forms, request

your name before your address, so you should follow this standard. Placing information in an unusual order will only confuse your viewers.

People on the Internet are notoriously hurried and will often provide only information that is required or that is located on the top half of the form. Therefore, it's a good idea to put the most important information at the top of your form. In fact, this is a good rule to follow for web pages in general. The most important information should be "above the fold" or on the part of the page that is visible before you have to scroll to see the rest.

### Creating Forms

Once you have finished planning your form content, you are ready to create the form in Dreamweaver. To create a form on a web page, you use the Form button in the Forms category on the Insert panel. Clicking the Form button will insert a dashed red outline around the area of the form. To make your form function correctly, you then need to configure the form so that it "talks" to the scripts or email server and processes the information submitted by the viewer. By itself, a form can do nothing. It has to have some type of script or program running behind it that will process the information to be used in a certain way.

There are two methods used to process the information your form collects: server-side scripting and client-side scripting. **Server-side scripting** uses applications that reside on your web server and interact with the information collected in the form. The most common types of server-side applications are **Common Gateway Interface (CGI)** scripts, **Cold Fusion** programs, **Java Server Page (JSP)**, and **Active Server Pages (ASP)** applications. **Client-side scripting** means that the form is processed on the user's computer. The script resides on the web page, rather than on the server. An example of this is a mortgage calculator that allows you to estimate mortgage payments. The data is processed on the user's computer. The most common types of scripts stored on a web page are created with a scripting language called **JavaScript**, or **Jscript**. Server-side applications and scripts collect the information from the form, process the information, and react to the information the form contains.

You can process form information in a variety of ways. The easiest and most common way is to collect the information from the form and email it to the contact person on the website. You can also specify that form data be stored in a database to use at a later date. You can even specify that the application do both: collect the form data in a database, as well as send it in an email message. You can also specify that the form data be processed instead of stored. For instance, you can create a form that totals the various prices and provides a total price to the site viewer on the order page, without recording any subtotals in a database or email message. In this example, only the final total of the order would be stored in the database or sent in an email message.

**FIGURE 1**
*Sketch of the web form you will add to the feedback page*

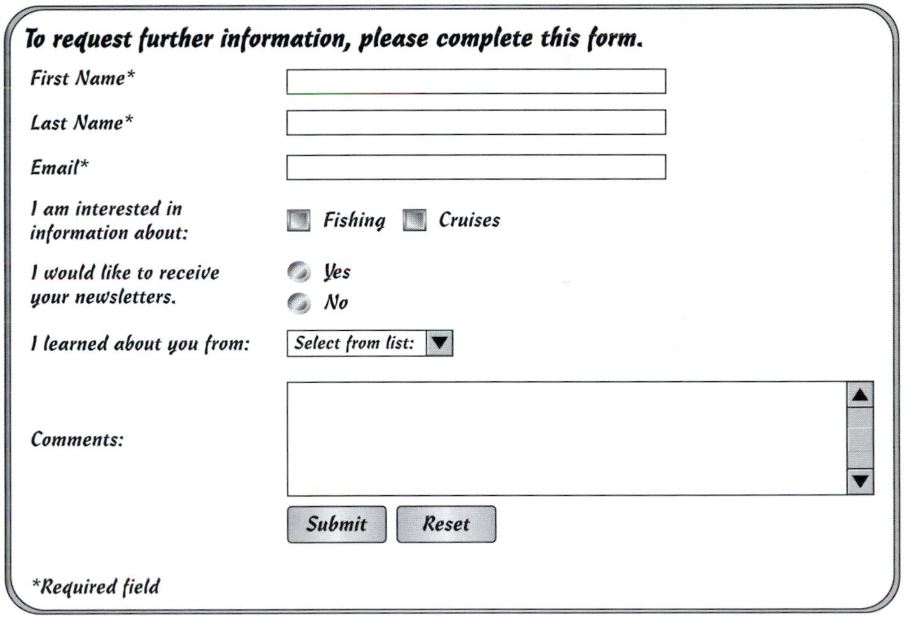

To request further information, please complete this form.

First Name*

Last Name*

Email*

I am interested in information about:   ☐ Fishing   ☐ Cruises

I would like to receive your newsletters.   ◉ Yes   ◉ No

I learned about you from:   Select from list: ▼

Comments:

Submit    Reset

*Required field

You can also create forms that make changes to your web page based on information entered by viewers. For example, you could create a form that asks viewers to select a background color for a web page. In this type of form, the information could be collected and sent to the processor. The processor could then compare the selected background color to the current background color and change the color if it is different from the viewer's selection.

## Setting Form Properties

After you insert a form, use the Property inspector to specify the application that will process the form information and to specify how the information will be sent to the processing application. The **Action** **property** in the Property inspector specifies the application or script that will process the form data. Most of the time the Action property is the name and location of a CGI script, such as /cgi-bin/myscript.cgi; a Cold Fusion page, such as mypage.cfm; or an Active Server Page, such as mypage.asp. Figure 2 shows the properties of a selected form.

**FIGURE 2**

*Form controls in the Property inspector*

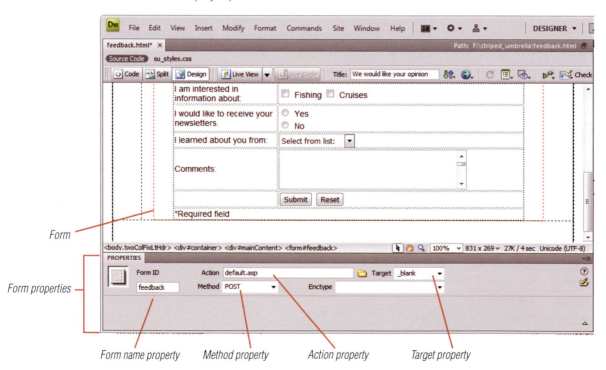

Form

Form properties

Form name property      Method property      Action property      Target property

The **Method property** specifies the **HyperText Transfer Protocol (HTTP)** method used to send the form data to the web server. The **GET method** specifies that ASCII data collected in the form will be sent to the server appended to the URL or file included in the Action property. For instance, if the Action property is set to /cgi-bin/myscript.cgi, then the data will be sent as a string of characters after the address, as follows: /cgi-bin/ myscript.cgi?a+collection+of+data+ collected+by+the+form. Data sent with the GET method is usually limited to 8K or less, depending on the web browser. The **POST method** specifies that the form data be sent to the processing script as a binary or encrypted file, allowing you to send data securely. When you specify the POST method, there is no limit to the amount of information that can be collected in the form, and the information is secure.

The **Form name property** specifies a unique name for the form. The name can be a string of any alphanumeric characters and cannot include spaces. The **Target property** lets you specify the window in which you want the form data to be processed. For instance, the _blank target will open the form in a separate browser window.

## Understanding CGI Scripts

CGI is one of the most popular tools used to collect form data. CGI allows a web browser to work directly with the programs that are running on the server and also makes it possible for a website to change in response to user input. CGI programs can be written in the computer languages Perl or C, depending on the type of server that is hosting your website. When a CGI script collects data from a web form, it passes the data to a program running on a web server, which in turn passes the data back to your web browser, which then makes changes to the website in response to the form data. The resulting data is then stored in a database or sent to an email server, which then sends the information in an email message to a designated recipient. Figure 3 illustrates how a CGI script processes information collected by a form.

**FIGURE 3**

*Illustration of CGI process on a web server*

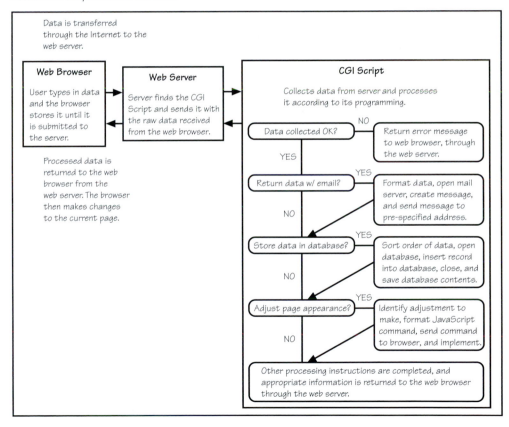

## Insert a form

1. Open the feedback.html page in The Striped Umbrella website.

2. Click inside the twoColFixLtHdr #mainContent container to place the insertion point.

   TIP  The twoColFixLtHdr #mainContent container top border is the second dotted line under the navigation bar. Click right under it to place the insertion point in the correct location.

3. Select the **Forms category** on the Insert panel, then click the **Form button** to insert a new form on the page.

   A dashed red rectangular outline appears on the page, as shown in Figure 4. As you add form objects to the form, the form will expand.

   TIP  You will be able to see the form only if Invisible Elements are turned on. To turn on Invisible Elements, click View on the Application bar (Win) or Menu bar (Mac), point to Visual Aids, then click Invisible Elements.

*You inserted a new form on the feedback page of The Striped Umbrella website.*

### FIGURE 4
*New form inserted on the feedback page*

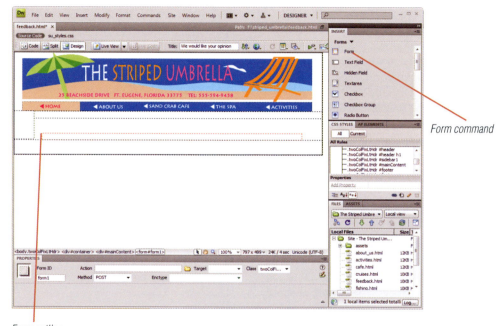

*Form command*

*Form outline*

**FIGURE 5**

*Property inspector showing properties of selected form*

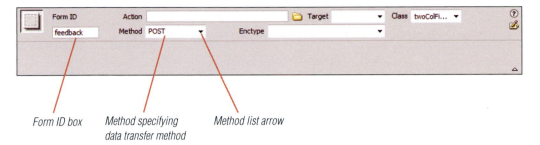

Form ID box    Method specifying    Method list arrow
               data transfer method

1. Click the **Form tag (<form#form1>)** in the tag selector on the status bar to select the form and display the form properties in the Property inspector.

2. Select **form1** in the Form ID box in the Property inspector, then type **feedback**.

3. Click the **Method list arrow** in the Property inspector, then click **POST** (if necessary), as shown in Figure 5.

   TIP  Leave the Action and Target text boxes blank unless you have the information necessary to process the form.

4. Save your work.

*You configured the form on the feedback page.*

### Using CGI scripts

You can use CGI scripts to start and stop external programs or to specify that a page update automatically based on viewer input. You can use CGI scripts to create surveys, site search tools, and games. You can even use CGI to do basic tasks such as record entries to a guest book or count the number of people who have accessed a specific page of your site. CGI also lets you create dynamic web documents "on the fly" so that pages can be generated in response to preferences specified by the viewer. Unless you have a specific application that you want your script applied to, you can probably find a low-priced script by searching on Google. Instructions for creating and modifying CGI scripts are not covered in this book.

# EDIT AND FORMAT A FORM

## What You'll Do

 *In this lesson, you will insert a table to create a basic structure for the form on the feedback page. You will also add and format form labels.*

## Using Tables to Lay Out a Form

Just as you can use CSS or tables to help place page elements on a web page, you can also use CSS or tables to help lay out forms. To make sure that your labels and form objects appear in the exact positions you want on a web page, you can place them on the page using layout options such as div tags, tables, and lists. When you use a table to lay out a form, you can place labels in the first column and place form objects in the second column. In Figure 6, the labels are placed beside the form objects.

## Using Fieldsets to Group Form Objects

If you are creating a long form on a web page, you might want to organize your form elements in sections to make it easier for viewers to fill out the form. You can use fieldsets to group similar form elements together. A **fieldset** is an HTML tag used to group related form elements together. You can have as many fieldsets on a page as you want. To create a fieldset, use the Fieldset button on the Insert panel.

## Adding Labels to Form Objects

When you create a form, you need to include form field labels so that viewers know what information you want them to enter in each field of the form. Because labels play such an important part in identifying the information that the form collects, you need to make sure to use labels that make sense to your viewers. For example, First Name and Last Name are good form field labels, because viewers understand clearly what information they should enter. However, a label such as Top 6 Directory Name might confuse viewers and cause them to leave the field blank or enter incorrect information. If creating a simple and obvious label is not possible, then include a short paragraph that describes the information that should be entered into the form field. Figure 7 shows clearly marked labels for both the form fields and the groups of related information.

You can add labels to a form using one of two methods. You can simply type a label in the appropriate table cell of your form or use the Label button in the Forms category on the Insert panel to link the label to the form object.

---

**FIGURE 6**

*Website that uses tables to lay out a form*

*Federal Bureau of Investigation website – www.fbi.gov*

**FIGURE 7**

*Website that clearly marks groups of related information*

Clearly labeled groups

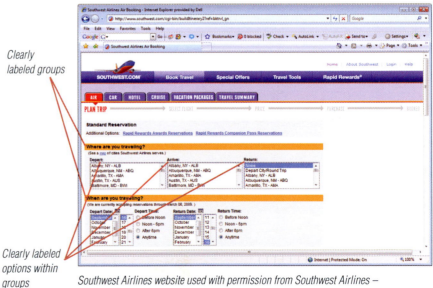

Clearly labeled options within groups

*Southwest Airlines website used with permission from Southwest Airlines – www.southwest.com*

---

## Add a table to a form

1. Click to place the insertion point inside the form outline, as shown in Figure 8.

2. Select the **Common category** on the Insert panel, then click the **Table button**.

3. In the Table dialog box, set the Rows to **10**, Columns to **2**, Table width to **90 percent**, Border thickness to **0**, Cell padding to **2**, and Cell spacing to **1**, then click the **Top header option** in the Header section.

4. Type **Table used for form layout.** in the Summary text box, compare your screen to Figure 9, then click **OK**.

5. With the table selected, click the **Align list arrow** in the Property inspector, click **Center** to center the table in the form, set the bottom-left cell width to **30%**, set the bottom-right cell width to **70%**, as shown in Figure 10, then save your work.

You can set the cell widths by using any of the cells, but if you try to consistently use a specific row to set the cell widths, you can easily find them if you have to change them. It is difficult to correct formatting errors when you have conflicting cell widths set in the same column.

*You added a table to the form on the feedback page. You also set the table alignment and cell widths.*

**FIGURE 8**
*Placing the insertion point inside the form*

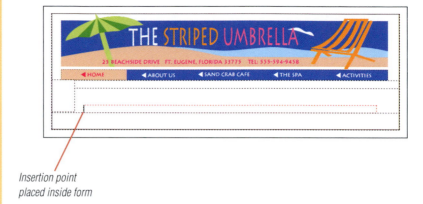

Insertion point
placed inside form

**FIGURE 9**
*Table dialog box*

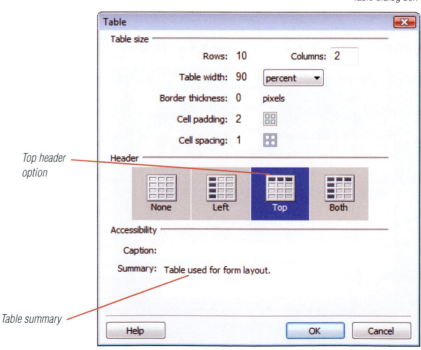

Top header
option

Table summary

*Collecting Data with Forms*

## FIGURE 10

*Setting table and cell properties*

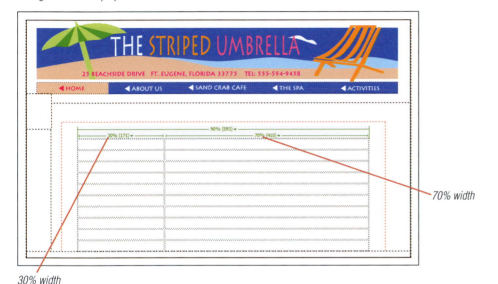

70% width

30% width

## FIGURE 11

*Typing and formatting labels in table cells*

1. Merge the top two cells in the first row of the table, then type **To request further information**, **please complete this form.**, then apply the **paragraph_text** style to the sentence.

   Because you designated a header for this table, the top row text is automatically centered and bolded. The header will be used by screen readers to assist viewers who have visual impairments to identify the table.

2. Click in the first cell in the fifth row, then type **I am interested in information about:**.

3. Press [↓], then type **I would like to receive your newsletters.**

4. Press [↓], type **I learned about you from:**, then press [↓].

5. Format each of the labels you entered with the **paragraph_text** style, deselect the text, then compare your screen to Figure 11.

*You added a header and three form labels to table cells in the form and formatted them with the paragraph_text style.*

## Add form labels using the Label button

1. Click in the cell below the one that contains the text "I learned about you from:".

2. Change to the **Forms** category on the Insert panel, then click the **Label button**.

   The view changes to Code and Design view, as shown in Figure 12. The insertion point is positioned in the Code view pane between the tags <label> and </label>, which were added when you clicked the Label button.

   > TIP You may need to scroll down in the Design pane to see the cell.

   *(continued)*

**FIGURE 12**

*Adding a label to a form using the Label button*

Label button

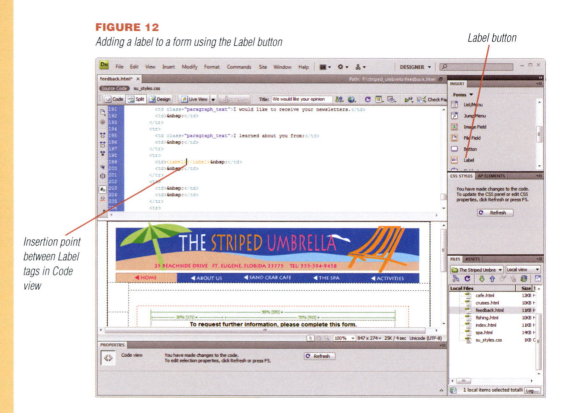

Insertion point between Label tags in Code view

*Collecting Data with Forms*

**FIGURE 13**

*New label added using the Label button*

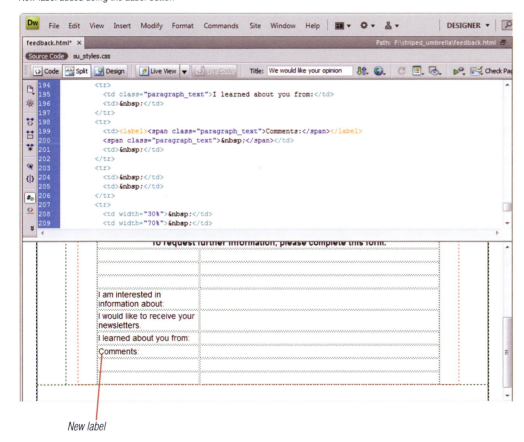

New label

3. Type **Comments:**, then click the **Refresh button** C Refresh in the Property inspector.

   The label appears in the table cell in the Design view pane.

4. Format the new label as **paragraph_text**, then compare your screen to Figure 13.

5. Click the **Show Design view button** Design, then save your work.

*You added a new label to the form on the feedback page using the Label button, then formatted it with the paragraph_text style.*

# WORK WITH
## FORM OBJECTS

## What You'll Do

*In this lesson, you will add form objects to the form on the feedback page.*

### Understanding Form Objects

A form provides a structure in which you can place form objects. Form objects—which are also called **form elements**, **form controls**, or **fields**—are the components of a form such as check boxes, text boxes, and radio buttons that allow viewers to provide information and interact with the website. You can use form objects in any combination to collect the information you require. Figure 14 shows a form that contains a wide range of form objects.

**Text fields** are the most common type of form object and are used for collecting a string of characters, such as a name, address, password, or email address. For some text fields, such as those collecting dollar amounts, you might want to set an initial value of 0. Use the Text Field button on the Insert panel to insert a text field. Text fields can be specified as single line text fields or multi-line text fields.

A **text area field** is a text field that can store several lines of text. You can use text area fields to collect descriptions of problems, answers to long questions, comments, or even a résumé. Use the Textarea button on the Insert panel to insert a text area.

You can use **check boxes** to create a list of options from which a viewer can make multiple selections. For instance, you could add a series of check boxes listing hobbies and ask the viewer to select the ones that interest him/her.

You can use **radio buttons** to provide a list of options from which only one selection can be made. A group of radio buttons is called a **radio group**. Each radio group you create allows only one selection from within that group. You could use radio groups to ask viewers to select their annual salary range, their age group, or the T-shirt color they want to order. You could also use a radio group to answer a yes or no question. To insert a radio group, use the Radio Group button in the Forms category on the Insert panel.

You can insert a **menu** or **list** on a form using the List/Menu button on the Insert panel. You use menus when you want a viewer to select a single option from a list of choices. You use lists when you want a viewer to select one or more options from a list of choices. Menus are often used to provide navigation on a website, while lists are commonly used in order forms to let viewers choose from a list of possibilities. Menus must be opened to see all of the options they contain, whereas lists display some of their options all of the time. When you create a list, you need to specify the number of lines that will be visible on the screen by setting a value for the Height property in the Property inspector.

Using **hidden fields** makes it possible to provide information to the web server and form-processing script without the viewer knowing that the information is being sent. For instance, you could add a hidden field that tells the server who should receive an email message and what the subject of the message should be. You can also use hidden fields to collect information that a viewer does not enter and cannot see on the screen. For instance, you can use a hidden field to send you the viewer's browser type or IP address.

You can insert an **image field** into a form using the Image Field button on the Insert panel. You can use the Image Field button to create buttons that contain custom graphics.

If you want your viewers to upload files to your web server, you can insert a **file field**. You could insert a file field to let your viewers upload sample files to your website or to post photos to your website's photo gallery.

All forms must include a **Submit button,** which a viewer clicks to transfer the form data to the web server. You can also insert a **Reset button,** which lets viewers clear data from a form and reset it to its default values, or a **custom button** to trigger an action that you specify on the page. You can insert a Submit, Reset, or custom button using the Button button on the Insert panel.

## FIGURE 14

*Website displaying several form objects*

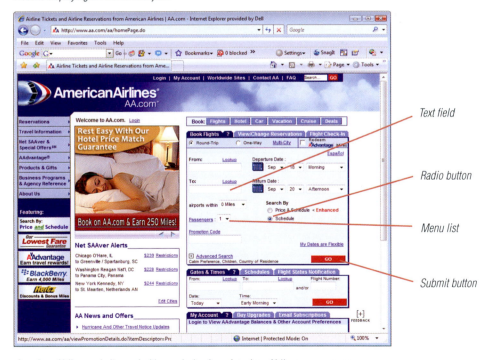

Text field

Radio button

Menu list

Submit button

*American Airlines website used with permission from American Airlines – www.aa.com*

**Jump menus** are navigational menus that let viewers go quickly to different pages in your site or to different sites on the Internet. You can create jump menus quickly and easily by using the Jump Menu button in the Forms category on the Insert panel.

When you insert a form object in a form, you use the Property inspector to specify a unique name for it. You can also use the Property inspector to set other appropriate properties for the object, such as the number of lines or characters you want the object to display.

## Using Dreamweaver Exchange

To obtain form controls designed for creating specific types of forms, such as online tests and surveys, you can visit Adobe Exchange, shown in Figure 15, a central storage location for program extensions, also known as add-ons. You can search the site by using keywords in a standard Search text box. You can also search by categories, highest rated, and newest (www.adobe.com/cfusion/exchange).

**FIGURE 15**
*Using Adobe Exchange*

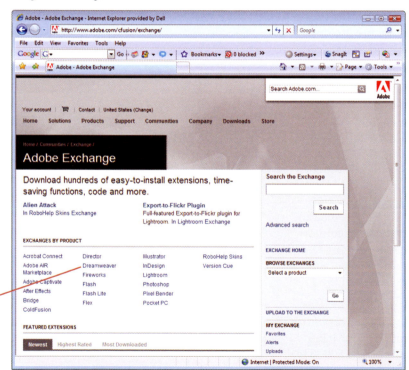

*Click to visit Dreamweaver Exchange*

*Adobe website used with permission from Adobe Systems Incorporated – www.adobe.com*

## FIGURE 16
Input Tag Accessibility Attributes dialog box

ID = first_name

Select No label
tag option

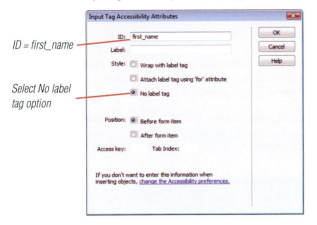

## FIGURE 17
Property inspector showing properties of selected text field

New text field

Text Field
button

ID

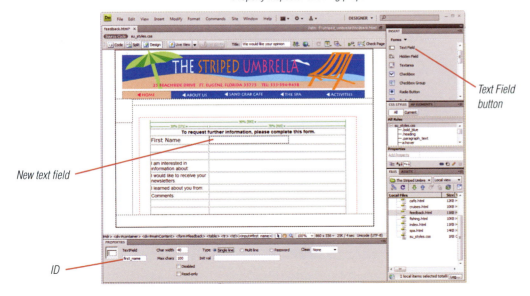

1. Place the insertion point in the first cell under the header, then type **First Name**.

2. Press **[Tab]**, then click the **Text Field button** on the Insert panel.

3. Click the **No label tag option button** in the Style section, type **first_name** in the ID text box, as shown in Figure 16, then click **OK**.

   TIP  You can also type the textfield name in the Text Field name: text box in the Property inspector.

4. Type **40** in the Char width text box in the Property inspector.

   This specifies that 40 characters will be visible inside this text field when displayed in a browser.

5. Type **100** in the Max chars text box in the Property inspector.

   This specifies that a user can type no more than 100 characters in this field.

6. Click the **Single line option button** in the Property inspector (if necessary), then compare your screen to Figure 17.

*(continued)*

7. Repeat Steps 1 through 6 to create another label and single-line text field under the First Name label and text field, using **Last Name** for the label and **last_name** for the text field.

8. Repeat Steps 1 through 6 to create another label and single-line text field under the Last Name label and text field, using **Email** for the label and **email** for the TextField name.

9. Apply the **paragraph_text style** to the three new labels in the first column.

   TIP   Another way to apply styles to the text in a table is to apply the style to a selected cell, rather than selected text in a cell. You can also apply a single style to a table. That way, all text in the table will be formatted with the same style.

10. Save your changes, preview the page in your browser, compare your screen to Figure 18, then close your browser.

   The table heading is left-aligned, rather than centered because the CSS container style specifies a text align setting to left. This overrides the table header alignment setting to center.

   TIP   If you are previewing your page in Internet Explorer and see a yellow background in your text boxes, this is probably caused by the Google toolbar. To remove the yellow background in your browser, Click Settings on the Google toolbar, click Options, click AutoFill Settings, then uncheck the check box "Highlight fields on Web pages that AutoFill can update in yellow." Click OK twice to save the settings.

*You added three single-line text fields to the form and previewed the page in your browser.*

**FIGURE 18**
*Form with single-line text fields added*

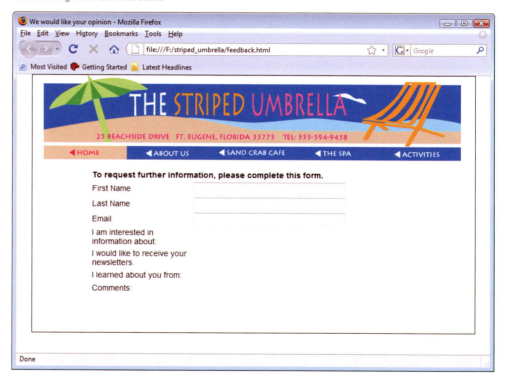

FIGURE 19

Property inspector with properties of selected Textarea button displayed

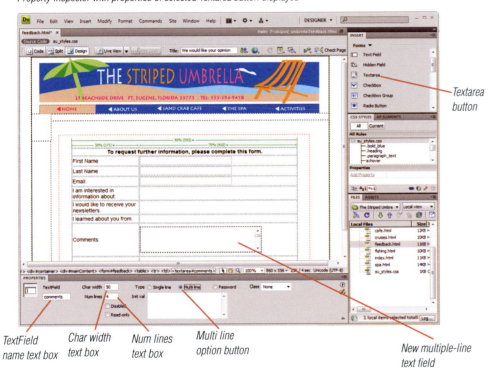

Textarea
button

TextField
name text box

Char width
text box

Num lines
text box

Multi line
option button

New multiple-line
text field

1. Click in the cell to the right of the Comments: label.

2. Click the **Textarea button** on the Insert panel, click the **No label tag option button** on the Input Tag Accessibility Attributes dialog box, type **comments** in the ID text box, then click **OK**.

3. Verify that the **Multi line option button** is selected in the Property inspector.

4. Type **50** in the Char width text box in the Property inspector.

   This specifies that 50 characters will be visible inside this text field when the page is displayed in a browser.

5. Type **4** in the Num lines text box in the Property inspector, as shown in Figure 19.

   This specifies that the text box will display four lines of text.

*You added a multiple-line text field to the form.*

## Insert check boxes

1. Place the insertion point in the empty table cell to the right of "I am interested in information about:".
2. Click the **Checkbox button** on the Insert panel to insert a check box in the form.
3. Type **fishing** in the ID text box, type **Fishing** in the Label text box, click the **Wrap with label tag option button** in the Style section, click the **After form item option button** in the Position section, as shown in Figure 20, then click **OK**.
4. Select the check box on the form.
5. Type **fish** in the Checked value text box in the Property inspector.

   This is the value that will be sent to your script or program when the form is processed.
6. Click the **Unchecked option button** after Initial state in the Property inspector (if necessary), as shown in Figure 21.

   The check box will appear unchecked by default. If the user clicks it, a check mark will appear in the box.

*(continued)*

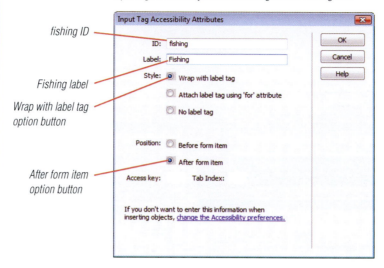

**FIGURE 20**

*Input Tag Accessibility Attributes dialog box for Fishing label*

fishing ID

Fishing label

Wrap with label tag option button

After form item option button

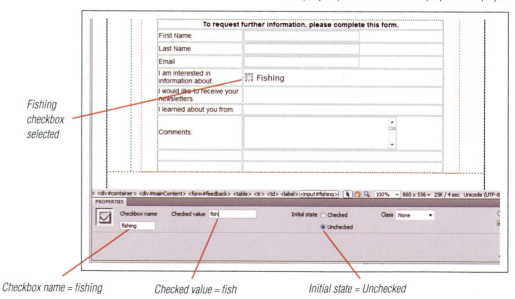

**FIGURE 21**

*Property inspector with check box properties displayed*

Fishing checkbox selected

Checkbox name = fishing

Checked value = fish

Initial state = Unchecked

*Collecting Data with Forms*

**FIGURE 22**

*Feedback page in browser with check boxes added to the form*

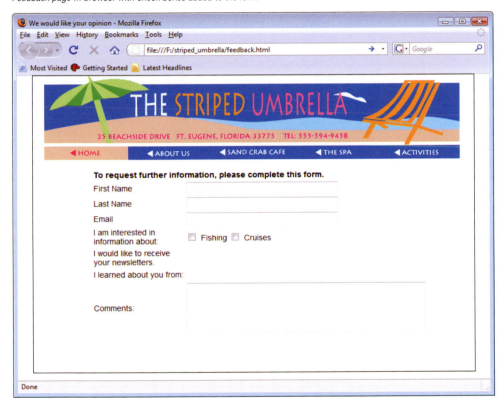

7. Format the Fishing text label with the **paragraph_text** rule.

8. Insert a space after the Fishing label, then repeat Steps 2 through 6 to place a check box to the right of the Fishing text box with the check box name (ID) **cruises**, the label **Cruises**, a Checked value of **cruise**, and the Initial state of **Unchecked**.

9. Format the Cruises label with the **paragraph_text** rule, save your changes, preview the page in your browser, compare your screen to Figure 22, then close your browser.

> TIP  If you are using Firefox as your browser, you might experience difficulty with individual check boxes.

*You added two check boxes to the form that will let viewers request more information about fishing and cruises.*

## Add radio groups to a form

1. Click in the empty table cell to the right of "I would like to receive your newsletters."

2. Click the **Radio Group button** on the Insert panel to open the Radio Group dialog box.

3. Type **newsletters** in the Name text box.

4. Click the **first instance of Radio** in the Label column of the Radio Group dialog box to select it, then type **Yes**.

5. Click the **first instance of Radio** in the Value column to select it, then type **positive**.

   You specified that the first radio button will be named Yes and set positive as the value that will be sent to your script or program when the form is processed.

6. Click the **second instance of Radio** to add another radio button named **No** with a value of **negative**.

7. Click the **Line breaks (<br> tags) option button** (if necessary) to select it.

   TIP   If the Table option button is selected, then the radio buttons will appear in a separate table within the currently selected table.

8. Compare your screen with Figure 23, then click **OK** to close the Radio Group dialog box.

*(continued)*

**FIGURE 23**
*Radio Group dialog box*

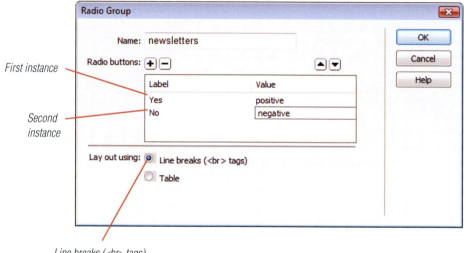

First instance

Second instance

Line breaks (<br> tags) option button

**FIGURE 24**

*Feedback page showing new radio group*

9. Format the radio button labels using the **paragraph_text** rule.

10. Save your work, preview the page in your browser, compare your screen to Figure 24, then close your browser.

> TIP    To create radio buttons that are not part of a radio group, click the Radio Button button on the Insert panel.

*You added a radio group that will let viewers answer whether or not they would like to receive The Striped Umbrella newsletters.*

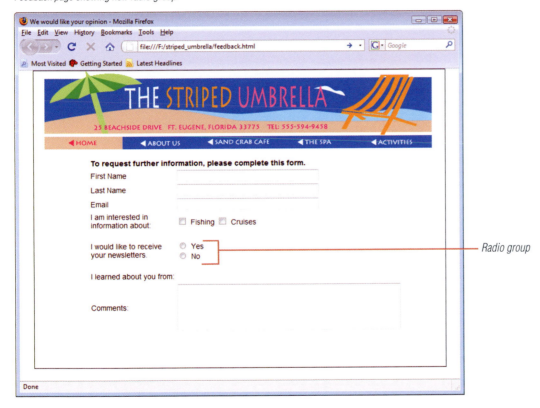

Radio group

## Add a menu

1. Click in the cell to the right of the text "I learned about you from:".

2. Click the **List/Menu button** on the Insert panel, click the **No label tag option button** in the Input Tag Accessibility Attributes dialog box, then click **OK**.

3. Type **reference** in the List/Menu Name text box in the Property inspector.

4. Verify that the **Menu option button** in the Type section is selected in the Property inspector, as shown in Figure 25, then click **List Values** to open the List Values dialog box.

5. Click below the Item Label column heading (if necessary), type **Select from list:**, then press **[Tab]**.

6. Type **none** in the Value column.

   This value will be sent to the processing program when a viewer accidentally skips this menu. If one of the real choices was in the top position, it might return false positives when viewers really did not select it, but just skipped it.

7. Press **[Tab]**, type **From a friend** as a new Item Label, then type **friend** in the Value column.

*(continued)*

**FIGURE 25**
*Property inspector showing properties of selected List/Menu*

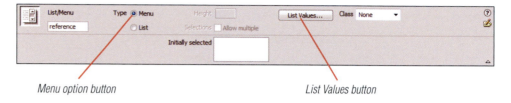

Menu option button          List Values button

## FIGURE 26
*List Values dialog box*

Add button

New item labels

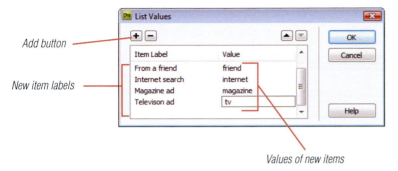

Values of new items

## FIGURE 27
*Feedback page with menu*

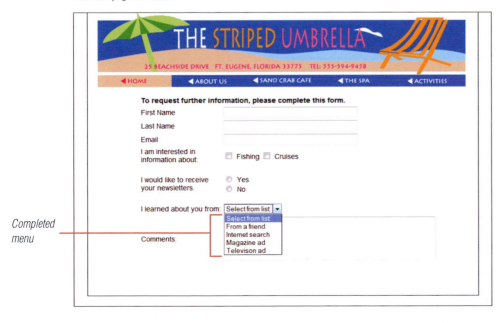

Completed menu

8. Use the **Add button** ⊞ to add the following three Item Labels: **Internet search**, **Magazine ad**, and **Television ad**, setting the Values as **internet**, **magazine**, and **tv**.

   TIP   You can also press [Tab] after entering an entry in the Value column to add a new item label.

9. Compare your screen to Figure 26, then click **OK**.

10. Save your work, preview the page in your browser, click the **list arrow** to view the menu, compare your screen to Figure 27, then close your browser.

*You added a menu to the form on the feedback page.*

## Insert a hidden field

1. Click to the left of the First Name label at the top of the form to place the insertion point.

2. Click the **Hidden Field button** on the Insert panel.

   A Hidden Field icon appears at the insertion point.

   > TIP  If you do not see the Hidden Field icon, click View on the Application bar (Win) or Menu bar (Mac), point to Visual Aids, then click Invisible Elements.

3. Type **required** in the HiddenField text box in the Property inspector, then type **first_name, last_name, email** in the Value text box, as shown in Figure 28.

   Typing first_name, last_name, email in the Value text box specifies that viewers must enter text in the First Name, Last Name, and Email fields before the script can process the form. The text must match the field names in your form exactly.

4. Save your work.

*You added a hidden field to the form that will let viewers know if they neglect to complete the fields for their first name, last name, and email address.*

**FIGURE 28**

*Property inspector showing properties of selected hidden field*

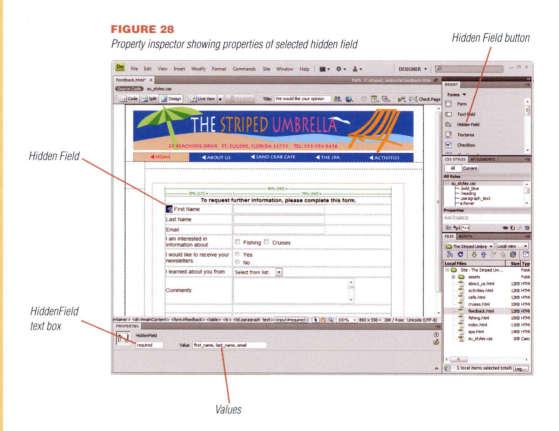

Hidden Field button

Hidden Field

HiddenField text box

Values

## FIGURE 29

New Submit and Reset buttons added to form

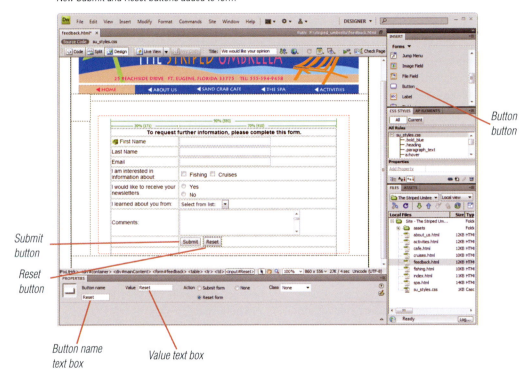

Submit button

Reset button

Button name text box

Value text box

Button button

1. Click in the **second cell** of the second to last row of the table.

2. Click the **Button button** on the Insert panel, type **Submit** in the ID text box, click the **No label tag option button** in the Input Tag Accessiblity Attributes dialog box if necessary, then click **OK**.

3. Verify that the Submit form option button is selected next to Action in the Property inspector.

   When a viewer clicks the Submit button, the information in the form will be sent to the processing script.

4. Verify that "Submit" is the name in the Value text box in the Property inspector.

5. Click to the right of the Submit button on the form, insert a space, then click the **Button button** on the Insert panel, click the **No label tag option button** in the Input Tag Accessibility Attributes dialog box, click **OK**, click the **Reset form option button** in the Property inspector, verify that the Value text box is set to **Reset**, then compare your screen to Figure 29.

   When a viewer clicks the Reset button, the form will remove any information typed by the viewer.

6. Save your work.

*You added a Submit button and a Reset button to the form.*

# TEST AND PROCESS A
## FORM

## What You'll Do

*In this lesson, you will check the spelling on the feedback page and create a link to the feedback page on the about_us page. You will then open the about_us page in your browser, click the feedback link, and then test the form and reset it.*

### Creating User-Friendly Forms

After you create a form, you will want to test it to make sure that it works correctly and is easy to use.

When a form contains several required fields (fields that must be filled out before the form can be processed), it is a good idea to provide visual clues such as a different font color or other notation that label these fields as required fields. Often, you see an asterisk next to a required field with a corresponding note at either the top or the bottom of the form explaining that all fields marked with asterisks are required fields. This will encourage viewers to initially complete these fields rather than attempt to submit the form and then

receive an error message asking them to complete required fields that have been left blank. Using a different font color for the asterisks and notes is an easy way to call attention to them and make them stand out on the page.

As is true with all pages, your forms should have good contrast between the color of the text and the color of the table background. There should be a logical flow for the data fields, so the viewer is not confused about where to go next when completing the form. The Submit and Reset buttons should be at the end of the form. You should always have several people test your form before you publish it.

### Understanding jump menus

If your website contains a large number of pages, you can add a jump menu to make it easier for viewers to navigate the site. Jump menus are menus that let viewers go directly from the current web page to another page in the site with a single click. You can also use jump menus to provide links to other websites. You can create jump menus using the Jump Menu button on the Insert panel to open the Insert Jump Menu dialog box.

FIGURE 30
*Adding visual clues for required fields*

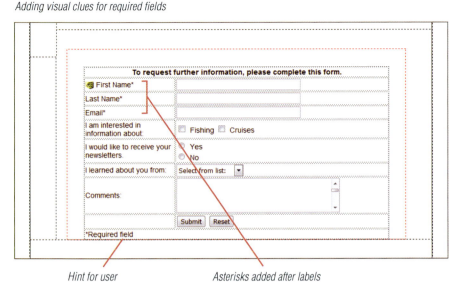

Hint for user          Asterisks added after labels

## Using a testing server and Live View to test dynamic content

When a web page contains content that allows the user to interact with the page by clicking or typing, and then responds to this input in some way, the page is said to contain **dynamic content**. A form is an excellent example of dynamic content, because as the user fills out the form, feedback can be returned, such as the availability of window seats on a particular airplane flight or whether or not certain colors or sizes of clothing items are available for purchase. This exchange of information is made possible through the use of a database, as you learned in Lesson 1. Once a form is developed and a database is tied to it, you should set up a **testing server** to evaluate how the form works and the data is processed. Your local computer or your remote server can serve as a testing server. You set up a testing server by filling out the relevant information in the Testing Server section of the Site Definition dialog box. You can also test your dynamic data in Design view by using Live View. **Live View** is a choice on the View menu that enables you to add, edit, or delete dynamic content or server behaviors. You can use the Switch Design View to Live View button on the document toolbar to change to Live View. The opposite of dynamic content is static content. **Static content** refers to page content that does not change or allow user interaction.

## Create visual clues for required fields

1.  Click **Commands** on the Application bar (Win) or Menu bar (Mac), then click **Check Spelling** to check the spelling on the form.

2.  Correct any spelling errors you find using the Check Spelling dialog box.

3.  Click after the text First Name, then type * (an **asterisk**).

    The asterisk will give viewers a clue that this is a required field.

4.  Repeat Step 3 after the words "Last Name" and "Email."

5.  Merge the two cells in the last row, type **\*Required field** then apply the **paragraph_text** rule to it.

6.  Compare your screen to Figure 30, then save and close the feedback page.

*You checked the spelling on the feedback page, then added asterisks to the required fields on the page. Next, you typed text explaining what the asterisks mean and formatted the text with the paragraph_text rule.*

## Link a file

1. Open the **about_us** page and click to place the insertion point under the two pictures at the bottom of the page, but above the copyright statement.

    TIP  The insertion point may appear partially hidden, but you can continue with the steps.

2. Type **Please give us your feedback so that we may make your next stay the best vacation ever.**

3. Select the text you typed in Step 2, then format it with the **paragraph_text** rule.

4. Select the word "feedback," then use the **Point to File icon** to link the feedback text to the feedback page.

5. Compare your screen with Figure 31, save your work, then preview the page in the browser.

*(continued)*

### FIGURE 31
*Viewing the feedback link*

*Link to feedback page*

## Using Spry Data Sets

One of the ways you can display data in a form is with a Spry data set. A **Spry data set** is a JavaScript object that stores data in rows and columns. You create a Spry data set in Dreamweaver and then write instructions to load the data from another source where the data is stored, such as an XML or HTML file. You can format the data to appear on a web page to your specifications. You create a Spry data set by using the Insert, Spry, Spry Data Set command on the Application bar (Win) or Menu bar (Mac). This command opens the Specify Data Source dialog box, where you then specify the Data Type, Data Set Name, which tags to detect, and the Data File name and location.

**FIGURE 32**

*Testing the feedback page*

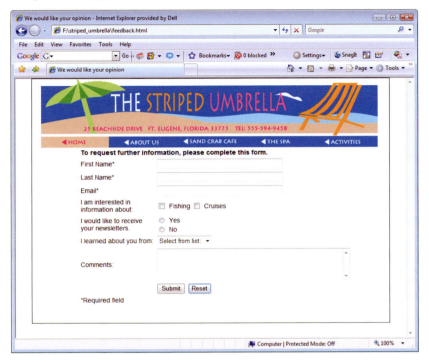

6. Click the **feedback link** to test it.

   The feedback page opens in a new window, as shown in Figure 32.

7. Test the form by filling it out, then clicking the **Reset button.**

   The Reset button will clear the form, but the Submit button will not work because this form has not been set up to send information to a database. Linking to a database is beyond the scope of this book. Refer to the information on pages 8-5 and 8-7 to learn more about CGI scripts.

8. Close the browser and close all open pages.

*You created a link on the about_us page to link to the feedback form, and tested it in your browser.*

## Using Spry Validation Field widgets

A **Spry widget** is a page element that enables user interaction on a web page. Spry widgets are stored within the **Spry framework**, a JavaScript library that provides access to reusable widgets that you can add to your pages. Some of the Spry widgets are fields that can be added to a form. These form fields are called **Spry Validation Field widgets**. These are fields that display valid or invalid states when text is being entered in a form on a web page. This instant feedback provides users the opportunity to correct their form before they try to submit it. Sometimes the widgets provide hints, such as the correct date format to use or the minimum number of characters required in a field. When a user does not enter the data correctly, an error message is returned. To add a Spry Validation Field widget to a form, use the Insert/Spry/Spry Validation (field name) command, or select a button in the Spry category on the Insert panel. Spry widgets use a combination of CSS and JavaScript that work within the HTML code. The CSS code formats the widget and the JavaScript code makes it work.

## Plan and create a form.

1. Open the blooms & bulbs website.
2. Open the tips page.
3. Scroll to the bottom of the page, insert two paragraph breaks to end the ordered list after the last line of text, then insert a form.
4. Set the Method to POST in the Property inspector if necessary.
5. Name the form **submit_tips**.
6. Set the Target to _self.
7. Save your work.

## Edit and format a form.

1. Insert a table within the form that contains **9** rows and **2** columns. Set the Table width to **75%**, set the Border thickness to **0**, the Cell padding to **2**, and the Cell spacing to **1**.
2. Choose the Top row header icon, then include an appropriate table summary that indicates that the table will be used for form layout purposes.
3. Merge the cells in the top row and type **Submit Your Favorite Gardening Tip** in the newly merged cell.
4. Format the text you typed in Step 3 with the bold_blue style.
5. Type **Email** in the first cell in the second row.
6. Type **Category** in the first cell in the third row.
7. Type **Subject** in the first cell in the fourth row.
8. Type **Description** in the first cell in the fifth row.

9. Apply the paragraph_text style to the labels you typed in Steps 5 through 8.
10. Merge both cells in the sixth row of the table, then insert the label **How long have you been gardening?** in the resulting merged cell.
11. Merge both cells in the seventh row of the table, then insert the label **Receive notification when new tips are submitted?** in the resulting merged cell.
12. Apply the paragraph_text rule to the text you typed in Steps 10 and 11, then save your work.

## Work with form objects.

1. Click in the second cell of the second row. Insert a text field with no label tag, naming it **email**. Set the Char width property to **30** and the Max chars property to **150**. (*Hint*: The Image Tag Accessibility Attributes dialog box will not appear if you do not have the accessibility preference set for adding form objects.)
2. Click in the second cell of the fourth row, then insert a text field with no label tag and the name **subject**. Set the Char width to **30** and the Max chars to **150**.
3. Click in the second cell of the fifth row, then insert a textarea with no label tag and the name **description**. Set the Char width to **40** and the Num lines to **5**.
4. Insert a space and a check box with no label tag to the right of the "Receive notification

when new tips are submitted" label. Set the name of the check box to **receivetips**, type **yes** in the Checked value text box, then verify that the initial state is Unchecked.
5. Insert a radio group, using line breaks named **years_gardening** to the right of the text "How long have you been gardening?" that contains the following labels: **1 - 5 years**, **5 - 10 years**, **Over 10 years**. Use the following corresponding values for each label: **1-5**, **5-10**, and **10+**. Apply the paragraph_text style to the labels if necessary.
6. Insert a list/menu named **category** in the empty cell to the right of Category. Set the Type to **List** and the Height to **2**. Use the List Values dialog box to add the following item labels: **Weed control**, **General growth**, and **Pest control**, and set the corresponding values for each to **weeds**, **growth**, and **pests**.
7. Insert a hidden field named **required** in the first cell of the eighth row that has the value **email**.
8. Insert a Submit button named **submit** in the second cell of the eighth row.
9. With your insertion point to the right of the Submit button, insert a Reset button named **reset** with the Reset form action.
10. Save your work.

## Test and process a form.

1. Check the spelling on the form and correct any errors you find.

2. Type * (an asterisk) after the label Email.

3. Merge the cells in the last row, then type **\*Required field** in the last row.

4. Apply the bold_blue rule to the text you typed in Step 3.

5. Insert a horizontal rule that is **630 pixels** wide both before and after the form.

6. Use the Indent button in the Property inspector to indent the form in the CSS container. (*Hint*: To access the indent buttons, select the table, then press the left arrow key.)

7. Save your work.

8. Preview the page in your browser, compare your form to Figure 33, then test the form by filling it out and using the Reset button.

9. Close your browser, then close all open pages.

**FIGURE 33**

*Completed Skills Review*

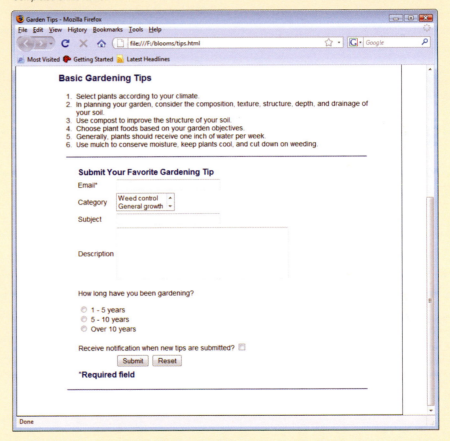

# PROJECT BUILDER 1

In this exercise, you will continue your work on the TripSmart website you created in Chapters 1 through 7. The owner, Thomas Howard, wants you to create a form to collect information from viewers who are interested in receiving more information on one or more of the featured trips.

1. Open the TripSmart website.
2. Open the destinations page.
3. Insert a form named **information** after the last paragraph on the page.
4. Specify the Method as POST, if necessary.
5. Insert a table in the form that contains **11** rows, **2** columns, a Table width of **75%,** a Border thickness of **0**, Cell padding of **1**, Cell spacing of **1**, a top Header, and an appropriate table summary.
6. Merge the cells in the top row, type **Please complete this form for additional information on these tours**., apply the reverse_text rule, then change the cell background color to **#666666.**
7. Beginning in the second row, type the following labels in the cells in the first column: **First Name**, **Last Name**, **Street**, **City**, **State**, **Zip Code**, **Phone**, **Email**, and **I am interested in:**, then apply the paragraph_text rule to all of them.
8. Insert single-line text fields in the eight cells in the second column beginning with row 2 and assign the following names: **first_name**, **last_name**, **street**, **city**, **state**, **zip**, **phone**, and **email**.
9. Set the Char width to **30** and the Max chars to **100** for each of these text fields.
10. In the second cell of the tenth row, insert a check box with the label **The Amazon**, the name **amazon**, and a Checked value of **yes**.

11. Repeat Step 10 to add another check box in the same cell, but under the Amazon check box with the label **Kenya**, the name **kenya**, and a Checked Value of **yes**.

12. Apply the paragraph_text rule to the Amazon and Kenya labels.

13. Set the vertical alignment for each cell except the top cell to Top.

14. Insert a Submit button and a Reset button in the second cell of the eleventh row.

15. Center the table in the form.

16. Insert a horizontal rule that is **550 pixels** wide and centered below the form. (*Hint*: Select the form, press [right arrow], press [Enter], then insert the horizontal rule.)

17. Save your work, preview the page in your browser, test the form, compare your screen to Figure 34, close your browser, then close the destinations page.

**FIGURE 34**

*Completed Project Builder 1*

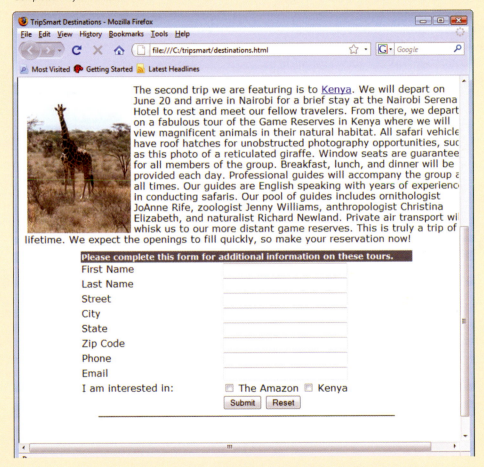

Use Figure 35 as a guide to continue your work on the Carolyne's Catering website you created in Project Builder 2 in Chapters 1 through 7. Chef Carolyne asked you to place a simple form on the catering page that will allow customers to fill in and fax lunch orders.

1. Open the Carolyne's Catering website.

2. Open the catering page.

3. Insert a form called **orders** in the footer block with POST as the method.

4. Insert a table in the form that contains **8** rows, **2** columns, and your choice of table width, border thickness, cell padding, and cell spacing. Use a top header and specify an appropriate table summary and header.

5. Merge the cells in the top row and type **Lunch Order**.

6. In the first column of cells, type the following labels under the table header:

**Please select from the following:**, **Beverage choice:**, **Desired pick-up time:**, **First Name:**, **Last Name:**, **Phone number:**.

7. In the second cell of the second row, insert a radio group named **boxes** with the following labels and values: **Southwest Club Sandwich**, **sandwich**; **Chipotle Chicken Wrap**, **wrap**; **Pecan Chicken Salad**, **salad**.

8. In the second cell in the third row, insert a radio group called **beverages** with the following labels and values: **Raspberry tea**, **tea**; **Berry smoothie**, **smoothie**.

9. In the second cell of the fourth row, insert a single line text field named **time** with a character width and maximum characters of **10**.

10. In the second cell of the fifth, sixth, and seventh rows, insert single-line text fields named **first_name**, **last_name**, and **phone** using character widths of **30** and maximum characters of **100**.

11. Merge the cells in the last row and type **Fax order by 9:00 a.m. to 555-963-5938**.

12. Since they are going to fax the form, there is no need for a submit button. You may add a reset button if you like.

13. Format the text in the form with styles of your choice.

14. Set the cell alignment of each cell to top.

15. Add a horizontal rule above the form.

16. Save your work, preview the page in a browser, test the form, compare your screen to Figure 35, close your browser, then close the catering page.

**FIGURE 35**
*Completed Project Builder 2*

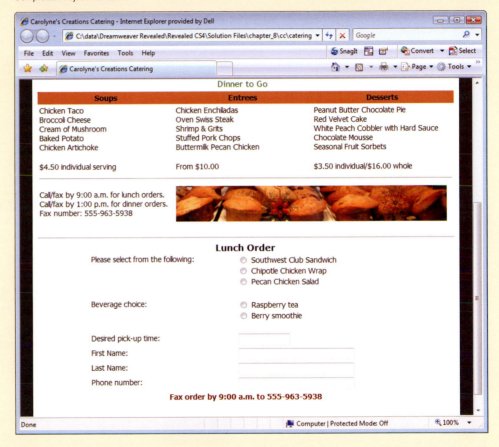

# DESIGN PROJECT

Websites use many form objects to collect donations from viewers. The form shown in Figure 36 is well organized and requests information that most people are comfortable giving over the Internet, such as name, address, and phone number. There are several helpful explanations that guide the viewer in filling out the form correctly to report an environmental violation.

1. Connect to the Internet, then navigate to the U.S. Environmental Protection Agency website, pictured in Figure 36, www.epa.gov. The page in Figure 36 is at www.epa.gov/compliance/complaints/index.html.
2. Does this site use forms to collect information? If so, identify each of the form objects used to create the form.
3. Is the form organized logically? Explain why or why not.
4. What CGI script is being used to process the form? And where is that script located? Remember the name of the processing CGI script is included in the Action attribute of your form tag. (*Hint*: To view the code of a page in a browser, click View on the menu bar of your browser, then click Source or Page Source.)
5. What types of hidden information are being sent to the CGI script?
6. Is this form secure?
7. Could the information in this form be collected with different types of form objects? If so, which form objects would you use?
8. Does the form use tables for page layout?
9. Does the form use labels for its fields? If so, were the labels created using the <label> element or with text labels in table cells?

## FIGURE 36
*Design Project*

*U.S. Environmental Protection Agency website – www.epa.gov*

# PORTFOLIO PROJECT

In this project, you will continue to work on the website that you have been developing since Chapter 1.

You will continue building your site by designing and completing a page that contains a form to collect visitor information as it relates to the topic of your site.

1. Review your storyboard. Choose a page to develop that will use a form to collect information. Choose another page that you already developed on which you will place a jump menu.

2. Plan the content for the new page by making a list of the information that you will collect and the types of form objects you will use to collect that information. Plan to include at least one of every type of form object you learned about in the chapter. Be sure to specify whether you will organize the form into fieldsets and how you will use a table to structure the form.

3. Create the form and its contents.

4. Run a report that checks for broken links in the site. Correct any broken links that appear in the report.

5. Test the form by previewing it in a browser, entering information into it, and resetting it. Check to make sure the information gets to its specified location, whether that is a database or an email address.

6. Preview all the pages in a browser, then test all menus and links. Evaluate the pages for both content and layout.

7. Review the checklist shown in Figure 37. Make any modifications necessary to improve the form, the jump menu, or the page containing the form.

8. Close all open pages.

**FIGURE 37**
*Portfolio Project checklist*

---

**Website Checklist**

1. Do all navigation links work?
2. Do all images appear?
3. Are all colors web-safe?
4. Do all form objects align correctly with their labels?
5. Do any extra items appear on the form that need to be removed?
6. Does the order of form fields make sense?
7. Does the most important information appear at the top of the form?
8. Did you test the pages in at least two different browsers?
9. Do your pages look good in at least two different screen resolutions?

---

# 9

# POSITIONING OBJECTS
## WITH AP DIV TAGS

1. Insert an AP Div

2. Set the position and size of an AP element

3. Add content to an AP element

4. Use the AP Elements panel

## Introduction

You have learned how to control the position of text and graphic elements with precision on your web pages with CSS layout blocks. With **CSS page layout blocks**, you use containers formatted with CSS styles to place content on web pages. These containers can hold images, blocks of text, a Flash movie, or any other page element. The appearance and position of these containers is set through the use of HTML tags known as **div tags**. Using div tags, you can position elements next to each other as well as on top of each other in a stack. In this chapter, you will use another type of div tag called an AP Div tag to place text and graphics on a page. AP stands for Absolutely Positioned. An **AP Div tag** is a div tag with a fixed position on a web page. When you create an AP Div tag, Dreamweaver automatically creates a style for it. The name of the style begins with a pound sign (#) rather than a period. It is an ID type, not a class type.

## Using AP Div Tags

AP Div tags let you control the appearance of elements on your web page. AP Div tags allow you to stack your information in a vertical pile, allowing for just one piece of information to be visible at a time. AP Div tags are treated as their own documents, so you can easily change their contents. You can add behaviors to your div tags with JavaScript. **JavaScript** is a program that is used to add interactivity to web pages. It is a **client-side script**, meaning that the commands from the program are executed on the user's computer. This is the opposite of **server-side scripts**, which are executed on the web server. **Behaviors** are preset pieces of JavaScript code that can be attached to page elements, such as an AP Div tag. A behavior instructs the page element to respond in a specific way when an event occurs, such as when the mouse pointer is positioned over the element. Behaviors are attached to page elements using **ActionScript**, a Flash scripting language developers use to add interactivity to movies, control objects, exchange data, and to create complex animations.

# Tools You'll Use

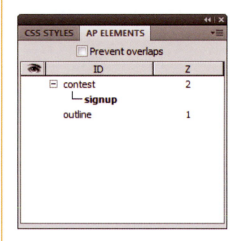

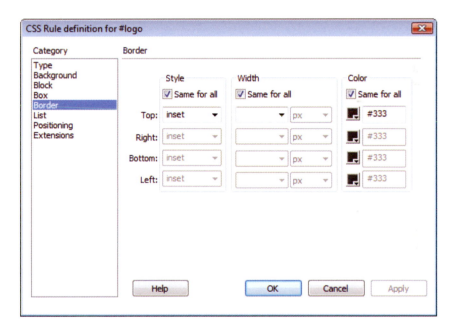

# INSERT
## AN AP DIV

### What You'll Do

*In this lesson, you will draw an AP Div on The Striped Umbrella home page and set its properties using the Property inspector.*

### Understanding AP Elements

AP elements are div tags that are absolutely positioned, or assigned a fixed position on a web page. Using AP Div tags, you can stack AP elements on top of each other and specify that only certain elements be visible at certain times or in specified conditions. AP elements can be used to create special effects on a web page. For instance, you can use AP elements to build a whole image from individual pieces. You can then use them to create a jigsaw puzzle that allows you to slide the pieces into their positions one at a time. You can also use AP elements to create dynamic pages that contain moving parts or objects that become visible or invisible based on a selection made by the website viewer.

Using AP elements to lay out a web page is like working with a stack of transparency sheets that you can stack on top of each other. Figure 1 illustrates how you might use AP elements to stack graphical elements on top of each other to create the single image of a flower.

To insert an AP element, you can use the Draw AP Div button in the Layout Category on the Insert panel and drag to draw a rectangular shape anywhere on your page, as shown in Figure 2. You can also insert an AP element using the Layout Objects, AP Div command on the Insert menu. Specify the exact dimensions, color, and other attributes of a new AP element by changing the settings in the Preferences dialog box for all AP elements, or in the Property inspector for a specific AP element.

### Using HTML Tags to Create AP Elements

Dreamweaver uses the <div> tag to create an AP element. Initially, the default value for the first AP Div tag on a page appears as <div id="apDiv1">. Each additional AP Div tag will be assigned the next number in sequence. You can use either the Property inspector or the AP Elements panel to rename each AP Div tag with a name that is relevant to its content. The styles for AP Div tags reside in the head content as part of the CSS code.

## Understanding AP Elements Content

An AP element is like a separate document within a web page. It can contain the same types of elements that a page can, such as background colors, images, links, tables, and text. You can also set the contents of an AP element to work directly with a specified Dreamweaver behavior to make the page interact with a viewer in a certain way.

## Using Advanced Formatting

You should be careful not to add too much content to an AP element. If it contains more information than it can readily display, you will need to use advanced formatting controls to format the content. You can control the appearance of a selected AP element by making changes to the Clip, Visibility, and Overflow properties in the Property inspector.

The **Clip property** identifies the portion of an AP element's content that is visible when displayed in a web browser. By default, the clipping region matches the outside borders of the AP element, but you can change the amount that is visible by clipping one or all sides. For instance, if you set the L (left) Clip property to 10 pixels, then everything from the eleventh pixel to the right will be displayed in the browser. If you clip off 10 pixels from the right side, you will need to subtract 10 from the total width of the AP element and then type this value in the Clip R text box in the Property inspector. The clip setting can be applied only to AP elements that have an Overflow attribute set to a value other than visible.

The **Vis (visible) property** lets you control whether the selected AP element is visible. You can set the Vis property to default, visible, hidden, or **inherit**, which means that the visibility of the AP element is automatically inherited from its parent AP element or page.

The **Overflow property** specifies how to treat excess content that does not fit inside an AP element. You can make the content visible, hide the content, specify that scroll bars appear, or let the current AP element automatically deal with the extra content in the same manner as its parent AP element or page. However, some browsers do not support the overflow property.

---

**FIGURE 1**

*Using AP elements to create a single image*

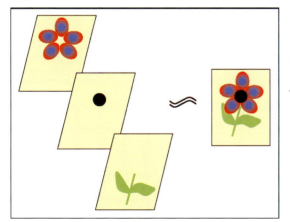

**FIGURE 2**

*Inserting an AP element using the Draw AP Div command*

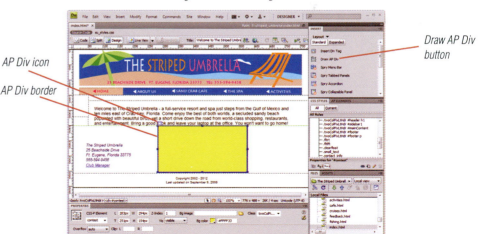

AP Div icon

AP Div border

Draw AP Div button

## Draw an AP Div

1. Open The Striped Umbrella website, open the index page, click **View** on the Application bar (Win) or Menu bar (Mac), point to **Rulers**, then click **Show** to select this option if necessary.

   Rulers appear along the top and left side of the page and will help guide placement of page elements.

2. Place the mouse pointer on the horizontal ruler, then drag down to position a horizontal guide at the **250 pixel mark** on the vertical ruler.

   TIP   Guides help you place page elements or emulate the fold lines in a browser. Fold lines are similar to the top half of a folded newspaper. The most important stories are usually printed at the top of the fold line.

3. Select the **Layout category** on the Insert panel, then click the **Draw AP Div button**.

4. Using Figure 3 as a guide, drag a **rectangle** in the middle of the home page and under the guide that is approximately 300 pixels wide and 150 pixels tall.

   A new AP element appears on the page, but it is not selected. An AP Div icon 🔲 appears above the upper-left corner of the AP element.

   TIP   You can also insert an AP Div by clicking Insert on the Application bar (Win) or Menu bar (Mac), pointing to Layout Objects, and then clicking AP Div.

5. Click the **AP Div icon** 🔲 above the AP element to select it.

   TIP   You can also select an AP Div by clicking one of its borders.

*You drew an AP Div on the home page, then selected it.*

**FIGURE 3**
*New AP element added to the home page*

AP Div icon

Horizontal guide

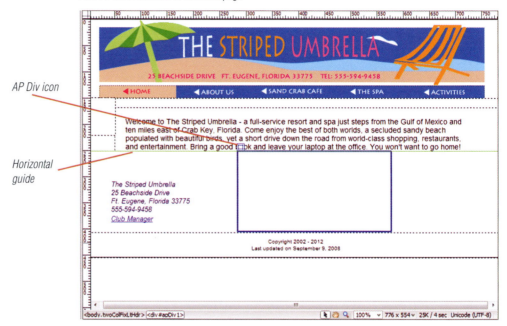

*Positioning Objects with AP Div Tags*

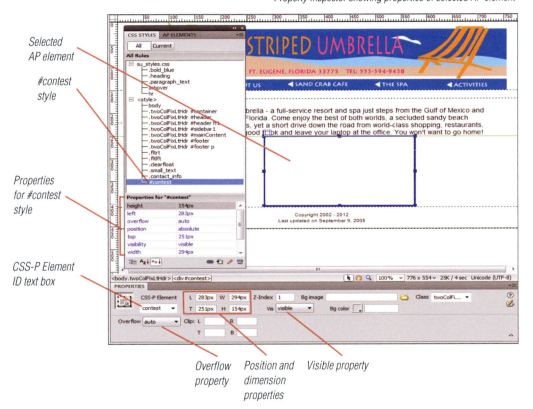

**FIGURE 4**

*Property inspector showing properties of selected AP element*

Selected AP element

#contest style

Properties for #contest style

CSS-P Element ID text box

Overflow property

Position and dimension properties

Visible property

**1.** With the AP Div selected, select **apDiv1** in the CSS-P Element text box in the Property inspector, type **contest**, then press **[Enter]** (Win) or **[return]** (Mac).

> TIP   If the AP element is not selected, click the <div#apDiv1> tag in the Tag selector.

**2.** Verify that <div#contest> is selected in the Tag selector.

**3.** Click the **Overflow list arrow** in the Property inspector, then click **auto**.

**4.** Click the **Vis list arrow**, then click **visible**.

**5.** Compare your screen to Figure 4.

The L, T, W, and H settings in the Property inspector specify the position and size of the AP element. Your settings will probably differ from those shown in the figure because you probably drew your AP Div with slightly different measurements.

**6.** Scroll down to view the new style that has been defined in the CSS Styles panel called #contest.

When you draw an AP Div, Dreamweaver automatically creates a style for it. As you make changes to the element properties, they are displayed in the Properties pane, when the style is selected.

**7.** Save your work.

*You specified a name and other properties for the selected AP element. You viewed the properties in the CSS Styles panel.*

# SET THE POSITION AND SIZE
## OF AN AP ELEMENT

## What You'll Do

*In this lesson, you will use the Property inspector to position and size AP elements on the home page of The Striped Umbrella website.*

### Understanding Absolute Positioning

To use AP elements, you must understand **absolute positioning**. An AP element is positioned absolutely by specifying the distance between the upper-left corner of the AP element and the upper-left corner of the page or parent AP element in which it is contained. Figure 5 illustrates how an AP element keeps its position relative to the top left corner of a page when the page is scrolled. Because Dreamweaver treats AP elements as if they are separate documents contained within a page, they do not interrupt the flow of content on the page or parent AP element in which they are contained. This means that AP elements placed on top of a page can hide the contents on the page.

AP elements have no impact on the location of other AP elements. In other words, if you insert an AP element, the remaining page elements that follow it within the code will continue with the flow of the page, ignoring the presence of the AP element. This means you can create overlapping AP elements. You can create dynamic effects by overlapping AP elements on a web page. You do so by using JavaScript or CGI script to change the attributes associated with each AP element in response to actions by the viewer. For instance, an AP element could move or change its size when a viewer clicks or moves the mouse over a link on the page or in the AP element.

### Setting Positioning Attributes

You can control the placement of AP elements by setting attributes available in the Property inspector. These attributes work together to create an AP element that will hold its position on a page.

The **Left property (L)** in the Property inspector specifies the distance between the left edge of an AP element and the left edge of the page or parent AP element that contains it. The **Top property (T)** in the Property inspector specifies the distance between the top edge of your AP element and the top edge of the page or the AP element that contains it.

The **Width (W)** and **Height (H) properties** specify the dimensions of the AP element, usually in pixels, although the AP element can be specified as a percentage of your screen dimension. For instance, you can specify that your AP element be 250 pixels by 250 pixels, or you can set it to 25% by 25%, which will create an AP element that is roughly 200 by 150 in a web browser on an 800×600 resolution monitor.

Use the **Z-Index property** in the Property inspector to specify the vertical stacking order of AP elements on a page. If you think of the page itself as AP element 0, then any number higher than that will appear on top of the page. For instance, if you have three AP elements with the Z-Index values of 1, 2, and 3, then 1 will appear below 2 and 3, while 3 will always appear above 1 and 2. You can create a dynamic website by adjusting the Z-Index settings on the fly using Dreamweaver's built-in JavaScript behaviors.

**QUICK**TIP
You cannot set Z-Index values below 0.

**FIGURE 5**
*Scrolling a page containing an AP element*

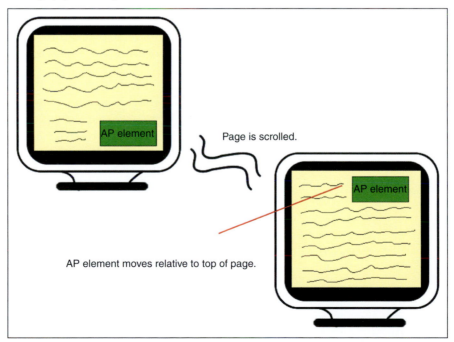

Page is scrolled.

AP element

AP element

AP element moves relative to top of page.

## Set the Left and Top position of an AP Div

1. Click the **AP Div border** to select the AP Div element (if necessary).

2. Type **520px** in the L text box in the CSS-P Element section of the Property inspector, then press **[Tab]** (Win) or **[return]** (Mac).

   The AP Div moves automatically to the position you specified.

3. Type **260px** in the T text box, then press **[Enter]** (Win) or **[return]** (Mac).

4. Save your work, then compare your screen to Figure 6.

   TIP  The AP Div may appear in a different position on your screen, depending on your screen size.

*You adjusted the upper-left corner position of the AP Div.*

## Set AP Div height and width

1. Click the **AP Div border** to select the AP Div (if necessary).

2. Type **200px** in the W text box, then press **[Tab]**.

   The AP Div automatically adjusts its width to the dimension you specified.

3. Type **175px** in the H text box, then press **[Tab]**.

   The AP Div automatically adjusts to the height you specified. Notice that the upper-left corner stays in the same position.

4. Save your work, then compare your screen to Figure 7.

*You adjusted the height and width of the AP Div.*

**FIGURE 6**
*AP element moved down and to the right on the page*

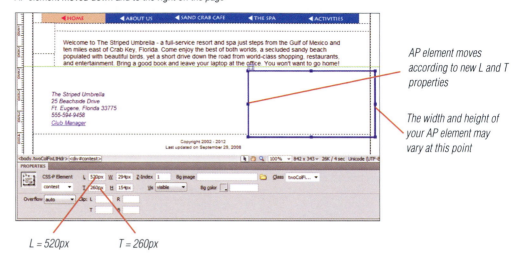

AP element moves according to new L and T properties

The width and height of your AP element may vary at this point

L = 520px     T = 260px

**FIGURE 7**
*AP element with width and height adjusted*

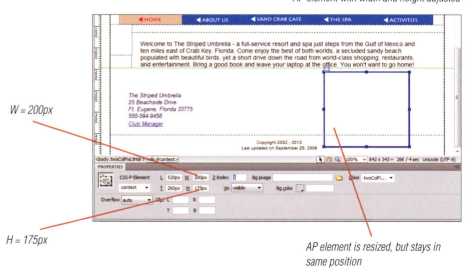

W = 200px

H = 175px

AP element is resized, but stays in same position

**FIGURE 8**

*New background AP element on top of contest AP element*

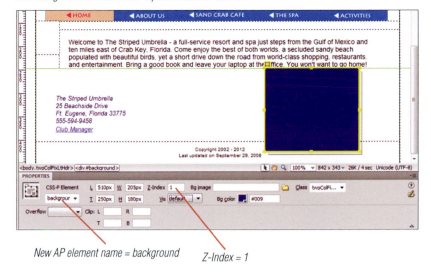

*New AP element name = background*　　*Z-Index = 1*

## Set the Z-Index value for an AP Div

**1.** Draw another AP Div anywhere on the page, select it, then name it **background**.

**2.** Select the **background AP Div** (if necessary), then adjust its size and position by setting the following properties in the Property inspector: L: **510px**, T: **250px**, W: **205px**, and H: **180px**.

The new AP Div is now positioned on top of the contest AP Div, temporarily blocking all but its right and lower borders.

**3.** Click the **Background color button** ▢ next to the Bg color text box, then change the background color of the background AP Div to dark blue, **#009**.

> TIP   You can also select the color number in the text box and type the new color number.

**4.** Change the Z-Index value of the background AP Div to **1** in the Property inspector, as shown in Figure 8.

**5.** Click the **contest AP Div** to select it, by clicking its right or lower border.

**6.** Change the Z-Index value of the contest AP Div to **2** in the Property inspector, then save your work.

The background AP Div is now positioned behind the contest AP Div to act as an outline, as shown in Figure 9. The contest AP Div does not have content yet. You can see the background AP Div above it and to the left.

*You added a new AP Div named background to the home page, and specified its dimensions and position on the page using the Property inspector. You set the background color of the background AP Div, then adjusted the vertical stacking order.*

**FIGURE 9**

*Contest AP element moved on top of background AP element*

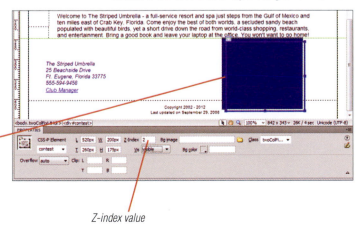

*Contest AP element positioned on top of background AP element with Z-index value changed to 2*

*Z-index value*

# ADD CONTENT
## TO AN AP ELEMENT

## What You'll Do

 *In this lesson, you will add a background color and a background image to an AP element. You will also insert an image and type text on the AP element.*

### Understanding AP Element Content

As you learned in Lesson 1, an AP element is like a separate document within a web page. It contains the same types of elements that a page based on table layout can, such as background colors, images, links, tables, and text. If you just want to include an image as part of the content, but not its background, insert the image just as you would insert one on a page using the Insert panel. Figure 10 shows an AP element with a blue background color and an image with a transparent background inserted at the bottom of the AP element. If you have an image you would like to be able to type over, insert the image as the background of an AP element, as shown in Figure 11.

If you add more content than the preset image size, the AP element will enlarge to display the content on your page in Dreamweaver. However, when you preview the page in the browser, the amount displayed will depend on how you set your Overflow settings.

Like a web page, if you specify both a background color and a background image, the background image will override the background color. As the page is loading, the AP element background color may display until the AP element background image finishes loading.

Also, as with formatting text on a web page, you should use CSS styles to format your text on an AP element. You can also add all other AP element properties such as text indent, padding, margins, and background color using CSS styles.

**FIGURE 10**

*AP element with a background color and an inserted image*

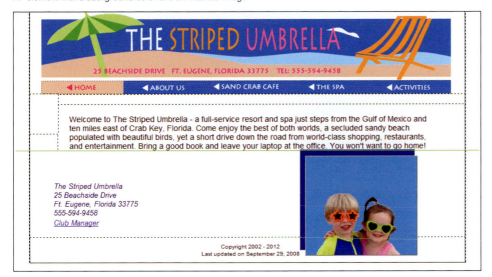

**FIGURE 11**

*AP element with an image inserted as a background image*

## Set a background color

1. With the contest AP Div selected, click the **Bg color text box** in the Property inspector.

2. Type **#FFF**, then press **[Tab]**.

   The AP Div is now filled with white, as shown in Figure 12.

   *You added a background color to the AP Div.*

**FIGURE 12**
*White background color applied to AP element*

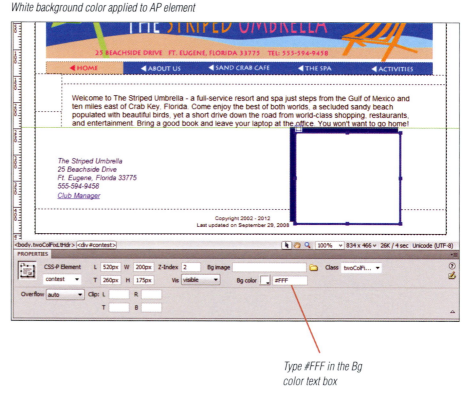

Type #FFF in the Bg
color text box

*Positioning Objects with AP Div Tags*

**FIGURE 13**

*Image added to AP element*

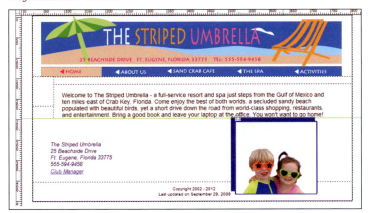

**FIGURE 14**

*AP element displays scroll bar in browser because it has been stretched*

*Scroll bar*

## Add an image to an AP Div

1. Deselect the contest AP Div, then click inside it to set the insertion point.

2. Select the **Common category** on the Insert panel, click the **Images list arrow**, then click **Image**.

3. Navigate to where you store your Data Files, then double-click **contestants.gif**.

4. Type **Two young contestants** in the Alternate text text box in the Image Tag Accessibility Attributes dialog box, then click **OK**.

   TIP  If the Image Tag Accessibility Attributes dialog box does not appear, type Two young contestants in the Alt text box in the Property inspector.

5. Press [←] to place the insertion point before the image, insert three line breaks by pressing **[Shift][Enter]** (Win) or **[Shift][return]** (Mac) three times, then compare your screen to Figure 13.

6. Save your work, preview the page in your Web browser, compare your screen to Figure 14, then close the browser.

   TIP  If your browser window is not resized to the width of the window shown in Figure 14, your AP element will not be positioned as shown.

   In the browser, the AP Div contains a scroll bar. The AP Div had to stretch to fit in the three page breaks and the image. Because the Overflow is set to Auto, the scroll bar automatically appears when there is more content than can fit in the dimensions.

   *You added an image to the AP Div, then added alternate text to it.*

## Set a background image

1. With the contest AP Div tag selected, select **#FFF** in the Bg color text box, press **[Delete]**, select the **contestants.gif** image in the AP div tag, then press **[Delete]** to delete both the background color and image from the AP Div tag.

2. Press **[Backspace]** three times to delete the line breaks.

3. Select the **#contest AP Div**, then click the **Browse for File icon** 📁 next to the Bg image text box in the Property inspector to open the Select Image Source dialog box.

   Using the Bg image text box instead of the Insert panel will insert the image as a background on which we can easily enter text.

4. Navigate to where you store your Data Files, then click **contestants_bak.jpg**.

5. Click **OK** (Win) or **Choose** (Mac), then compare your screen to Figure 15.

6. Refresh the Files panel to verify that contestants_bak.jpg was copied to the assets folder of the website.

*You added a background image to the contest AP Div.*

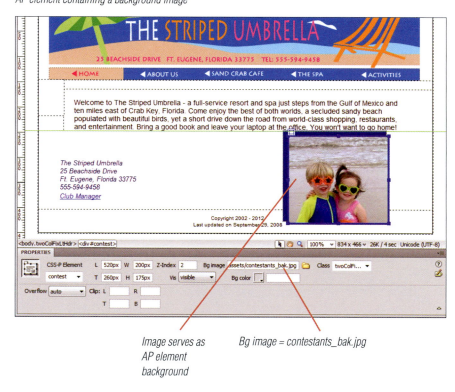

FIGURE 15
*AP element containing a background image*

*Image serves as AP element background*

*Bg image = contestants_bak.jpg*

FIGURE 16
*Editing the #contest style*

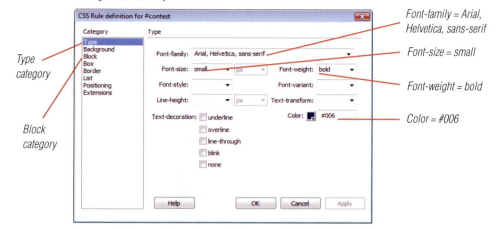

Type category

Block category

Font-family = Arial, Helvetica, sans-serif

Font-size = small

Font-weight = bold

Color = #006

FIGURE 17

*Index page with the formatted AP elements*

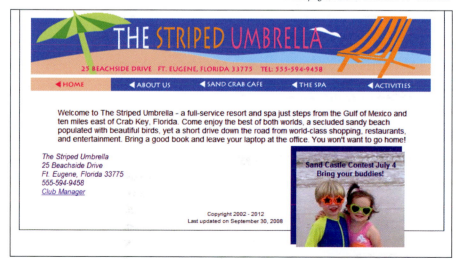

## Add and format text on an AP Div

1. Click inside the contest AP Div to set the insertion point, then enter a line break.

2. Type **Sand Castle Contest July 4**, press **[Shift][Enter]** (Win) or **[Shift][return]** (Mac), then type **Bring your buddies!**.

3. Click the **contest rule** in the CSS Styles panel, then click the **Edit Rule** button.

4. Click the **Type category**, as shown in Figure 16, change Font-family to **Arial, Helvetica, sans-serif**, Font-size to **small**; Font-weight to **bold**, and Color to **#006**.

5. Click the **Block category,** change the Text-align setting to **center**, then click **OK**.

The text changes to reflect the properties you have added to the contest style. It is blue and centered on the AP Div. When you have text on an AP Div, you should format the text using the AP Div tag style in the CSS Styles panel, rather than using the Property inspector, or the Property inspector will create an additional style. It is more efficient to have all rule properties for a div tag in one rule.

6. Save your work, preview the page in your Web browser, compare your screen with Figure 17, then close your browser.

*You added text to the AP Div, and formatted it using the CSS Styles panel.*

# USE THE
## AP ELEMENTS PANEL

 *In this lesson, you will use the AP Elements panel to change the name of an AP element, view and hide an AP element, and work with nested AP elements.*

### Controlling AP Elements

You can use the **AP Elements panel** to control the visibility, name, and Z-Index order of all the AP elements on a web page. You can also use the AP Elements panel to see how an AP element is nested within the page structure and to change the nesting status of an AP element. **Nested AP elements** are those whose HTML code is included within another AP element's code. A nested AP element does not affect the way it appears to the page viewer; it establishes a relationship of how it appears in relation to its parent AP element. To change the nesting status of an AP element, drag it to a new location in the AP Elements panel. Figure 18 shows the AP Elements panel with a nested AP element.

You can open the AP Elements panel using the Window menu. The AP Elements panel is handy when you are trying to select an AP element on the bottom of a stack. Clicking the AP element name selects the AP element on the page. You can access the same information that is available in

the AP Elements panel by selecting the AP element and viewing its settings in the Property inspector.

Using the AP Elements panel is the easiest way to change a series of AP element names, control AP element visibility while testing a site, and control the visible stacking order. The AP Elements panel also keeps track of all the AP elements on a page, making it easy to review the settings for each.

**FIGURE 18**
*AP Elements panel*

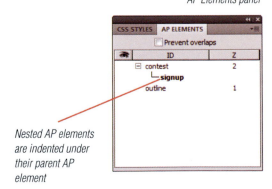

*Nested AP elements are indented under their parent AP element*

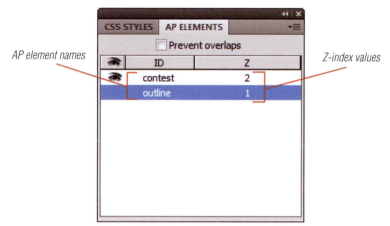

**FIGURE 19**

Using the AP Elements panel to change an AP element name

AP element names

Z-index values

## Change the name of an AP element

1. Click **Window** on the Application bar (Win) or Menu bar (Mac), then click **AP Elements**, or click **AP Elements** in the CSS Styles Tab group.

   The AP Elements panel appears in the CSS Styles Tab group.

2. Click **background** on the AP Elements panel to select the background AP element.

3. Double-click **background** on the AP Elements panel to select its name.

4. Type **outline**, then press **[Enter]** (Win) or **[return]** (Mac), then compare your screen to Figure 19.

   The AP Element is renamed.

5. With the outline AP element selected, press [→] and [↓] on your keyboard each about seven times to reposition the outline AP element so it is centered behind the contest AP element, serving as an outline for the contest AP element.

   TIP   With the outline AP Div tag selected, it appears to be in front of the contest AP Div tag, but it is really behind it. When it is not selected, it appears in its actual position in back of the contest AP Div tag.

*You used the AP Elements panel to change the name of one of the AP elements on the home page, then repositioned the AP element.*

## Control AP element visibility

1. Click the **visibility column** twice for the contest AP element in the AP Elements panel, then compare your screen with Figure 20.

   The Closed eye icon appears, indicating that the contest AP element no longer appears in the document window.

2. Click the **Closed eye icon** 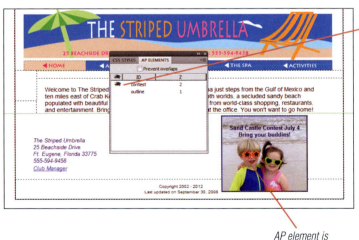 on the contest AP element.

   Clicking the Closed eye icon makes the AP element visible, as shown in Figure 21. The Eye icon appears next to the contest element in the AP Elements panel.

3. Click the **Eye icon** on the contest AP element.

   Clicking the Eye icon makes the AP element inherit the visibility status of its parent objects. In this case, the parent object of the contest AP element is the index page. Because the home page is visible, the contest AP element is visible, too.

*You used the AP Elements panel to change the visibility status of the contest AP element.*

**FIGURE 20**

*Using the AP Elements panel to hide the contest AP element*

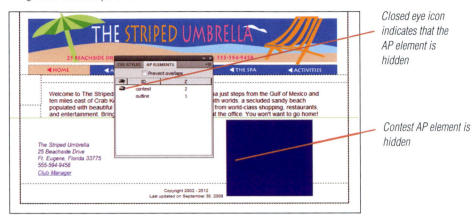

Closed eye icon indicates that the AP element is hidden

Contest AP element is hidden

**FIGURE 21**

*Using the AP Elements panel to make the contest AP element visible*

Eye icon indicates AP element is visible

AP element is visible again

**FIGURE 22**

*Nested AP element shown with parent AP element properties*

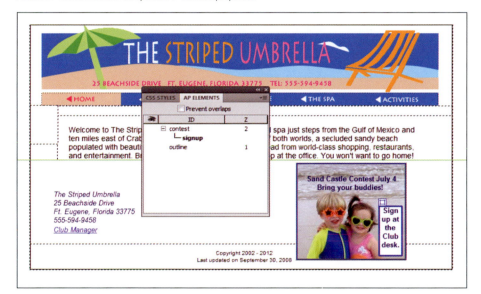

1. Click the **contest AP element** in the AP Elements panel, then click in the contest AP element in the Document window after the word "buddies!" to place the insertion point.

2. Click **Insert** on the Application bar (Win) or Menu bar (Mac), point to **Layout Objects**, then click **AP Div**.

   A new AP element is inserted as a nested AP element of the contest AP element.

3. Use the AP Elements panel to select this new nested **AP element**, then name it **signup**.

4. Type **152px** in the L text box, then type **77px** in the T text box.

5. Type **42px** in the W text box, then type **92px** in the H text box.

   These dimensions specify the position and size of the nested AP element in relation to the upper-left corner of the contest AP element.

6. Set the background color to **#FFF**.

7. Click in the **signup AP element** to place the insertion point, then type **Sign up at the Club desk.**, as shown in Figure 22.

   The text is automatically formatted using the properties for the contest AP element, the parent AP element for the nested AP element.

8. Save your work, preview the page in your browser, close the browser, close all open pages, then exit Dreamweaver.

*You created a nested AP element within the contest AP element.*

**Insert an AP Div.**

1. Open the blooms & bulbs website, then open the index page.
2. Use the Draw AP Div button to draw a tall thin rectangle, about 2 inches tall by 1 inch wide on the bottom half of your page.
3. Name this AP Div **organic**.

**Set the position and size of an AP element.**

1. Select the organic AP Div, then set the Left property to **500 px.**
2. Set the Top property to **230 px.**
3. Set the Width property to **175 px.**
4. Set the Height property to **219 px.**
5. Set the Z-Index property to **1** (if necessary).
6. Create another AP Div anywhere on the page, select it, then name it **background**.

7. Select the background AP Div, then adjust the size with the following settings: Left to **495px**; Top to **225px**; Width to **175px**; and Height to **219px**.
8. Change the color of the background of the background AP Div to a dark blue.
9. Change the Z-Index value of the background AP Div to **1**.
10. Change the Z-Index value of the organic AP Div tag to **2**.
11. Save your work.

**Add content to an AP element.**

1. Select the organic AP Div, remove the background color (if necessary), then insert the background image peaches_small.jpg from where you store your Data Files.
2. Set the organic AP Div tag Vis property to default.

3. Set the organic AP Div tag Overflow property to visible.
4. Place the insertion point in the organic AP Div, then type **Organic Gardening**.
5. Insert a line break, then type **Class begins soon!**.
6. Select the two lines of text, then apply the small_text rule.
7. Save your work.

**Use the AP Elements panel.**

1. Open the AP Elements panel (if necessary).
2. Use the AP Elements panel to change the organic AP Div's name to **organic-class**.
3. Set the Vis property to visible.

4. Save your work.
5. Preview the page in your browser, compare your screen to Figure 23, close your browser, adjust the AP element positions (if necessary), then save and close the index page.

**FIGURE 23**

*Completed Skills Review*

In this exercise, you will continue your work on the TripSmart website. The owner, Thomas Howard, wants you to create a section on the index page that advertises a special price on Packing Cubes.

1. Open the TripSmart website, then open the index page.

2. Draw an AP Div that is approximately 1 inch tall and 3 inches wide in the middle of the page, then name it **special**.

3. Set the background color of the AP Div to transparent by clicking the Default Color button on the color picker toolbar.

4. Insert packing_cube.jpg from where you store your Data Files into the AP Div, adding appropriate alternate text, insert a line break at the beginning of the word Packing, then set the Align option to Left.

5. Set the Left property of the special AP Div tag to **340 px** and the Top property to **360 px**.

6. Set the width to **350 px**, the height to **100 px**, and the Z-Index property to **1** if necessary.

7. Add the following text to the right of the image: **Packing Cubes on sale this week!**, with a line break before the word "this."

8. Format the Packing Cubes on sale this week! text using the heading style.

9. Enter a line break, type **Large: $15.00; Medium: $10.00;** enter a line break, type **Small: $5.00**; then format this text with the item_numbers style.

10. Edit the #special rule in the CSS Styles panel to add a double border around the AP Div with the color **#666666**. (*Hint*: The double border setting can be found in the Border category of the CSS Rule definition dialog box.)

11. Set the Overflow property of the special AP div tagto visible.

12. Save your work, preview the page in your browser, compare your screen to Figure 24, close your browser, make any spacing adjustments necessary for the AP Div size or position, then close the index page.

### FIGURE 24
*Sample Project Builder 1*

Use Figure 25 as a guide to continue your work on the Carolyne's Creations website.

**1.** Open the Carolyne's Creations website, then open the index page.

**2.** Create an AP Div on the page, then place the file cc_logo.jpg from your Data Files folder in the AP Div, adding appropriate alternate text.

**3.** Name the AP Div **logo**.

**4.** Adjust the size and position of the AP Div with settings of your choice.

**5.** Add another AP Div tag that displays the text "Call soon!" and name it call.

**6.** Set the font color for the new AP Div to the color of your choice and then set the Z indexes for each AP Div to correctly display the text over the logo.

**7.** Save your work, preview the page in your browser, close your browser, then close the index page.

**FIGURE 25**
*Completed Project Builder 2*

# DESIGN PROJECT

Sharon Woods has recently been asked to redesign a website for a small business. She has decided to use CSS div tags for her page layout. Because she has never developed a website with these features before, she decides to look at some other websites for ideas and inspiration.

1. Connect to the Internet, then go to www.course.com, as shown in Figure 26.
2. How are div tags used in this site?
3. View the source code for the page and locate the HTML tags that control the CSS page elements.
4. Do you see some div tags with either the dimensions or positions specified?
5. Use the Reference panel in Dreamweaver to look up the code used in this site to place the content on the page.

**FIGURE 26**
*Design Project*

*Course Technology website used with permission from Course Technology, CENGAGE Learning – www.course.com*

# PORTFOLIO PROJECT

For this assignment, you will continue to work on the portfolio project that you have been developing since Chapter 1. There will be no Data Files supplied. You are building this website from chapter to chapter, so you must do each Portfolio Project assignment in each chapter to complete your website.

You will continue building your site by placing at least one AP element on a page.

1. Consult your storyboard to decide which page to develop for this chapter. Draw a sketch of the page to show how you will use an AP element.
2. Open the page and add the appropriate number of AP elements to the page and configure them appropriately, making sure to name them and set the properties for each.
3. Add text, background images, and background colors to the AP elements.

4. Check to ensure that all AP elements are properly stacked using the Z-Index property.
5. Review the checklist in Figure 27 and make any necessary modifications.
6. Save your work, preview the page in your browser, make any necessary modifications to make the page look good, close your browser, then close all open pages.

**FIGURE 27**
*Portfolio Project checklist*

> **Website Checklist**
>
> 1. Are all AP elements properly stacked with Z-Index values assigned correctly?
> 2. Do all pages have titles?
> 3. Do all navigation links work?
> 4. Are all colors in your AP Div tags *web-safe*?
> 5. Do your pages look acceptable in at least the two major browsers?
> 6. Do AP elements hide any information on your pages?
> 7. Do all images in your AP elements appear correctly?

chapter

# 10

## ADDING MEDIA
### OBJECTS

1. Add and modify Flash objects

2. Add rollover images

3. Add behaviors

4. Add Flash video

# 10 ADDING MEDIA
## OBJECTS

### Introduction

You can use Dreamweaver to add media objects created in other programs to the pages of your website. Some of the external media file types include Adobe Fireworks navigation bars, rollover images, and buttons; Flash video, sound, and animation; Flash Paper; Director and Shockwave movies and presentations; Java applets; ActiveX controls; server-side controls; and a variety of plug-ins. A **plug-in** is a computer program that works with a host application such as a web browser to enable certain functions to run. For example, to play a Flash SWF file in a web browser, you will need to install the Flash Player plug-in. To read Adobe PDF files, you need to install the Adobe Reader. Plug-ins allow you to extend the capabilities of the browser to display content, letting you create complex, interactive websites with media effects that can be viewed within the pages themselves. The pages don't have to load an external document player such as Windows Media Player or RealPlayer by RealNetworks. In this chapter, you will use Dreamweaver to add Flash and Fireworks objects to The Striped Umbrella website.

### Understanding Media Objects

The term "media objects" has different meanings, depending on who you are talking to, and the industry in which they work. For our purposes, **media objects** are combinations of visual and audio effects and text to create a fully engaging experience with a website. Although this might be an open-ended definition, it is the experience you are striving for when you add video and audio elements to a web page. Think about the experience of watching a movie. You are engaged not just by the actors, but also by the sounds and special effects you experience. You want to create this same type of experience for your website viewers by adding media elements to your pages.

You can use Dreamweaver to insert a variety of media effects in your web pages, including Flash movies, Flash video, and a series of built-in JavaScript behaviors such as sounds, rollover images, pop-up menus, Go to URLs, and menus. You will learn to identify and use many of these effects in this chapter.

## Tools You'll Use

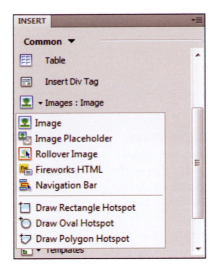

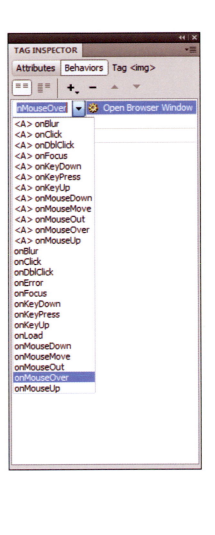

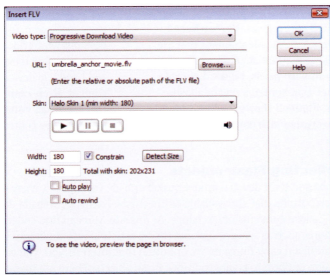

# ADD AND MODIFY
## FLASH OBJECTS

## What You'll Do

*In this lesson, you will insert and modify a Flash movie on the cafe page, and then play the movie both in Dreamweaver and in a browser.*

### Understanding Adobe Flash

Flash is a software program that allows you to create low-bandwidth, high-quality animations and interactive elements that you can place on your web pages. **Low-bandwith** animations are animations that don't require a fast connection to work properly. These animations use a series of vector-based graphics that load quickly and merge with other graphics and sounds to create short movies. **Vector-based graphics** are scalable graphics that are built using mathematical formulas, rather than built with pixels. Figure 1 shows a web page that contains several Flash objects. Figure 2 shows the Flash program used to create Flash objects.

Once you create these short movies, you can place them on your web pages. To view Flash movies, you need the Flash Player, a software program that is included in the latest versions of Internet Explorer, Mozilla Firefox, Safari, and Opera. If you are using an older browser that does not support the version of Flash used to create your movie, you can download the latest Flash player from the Adobe website, located at www.adobe.com. Almost all Internet-enabled desktops worldwide use the Flash player. In addition, other tools, such as cell phones and handheld devices, contain rich Flash content. **Rich content** is a general term that can mean visually stimulating, useful, or interactive content on a web page.

### Collecting Flash objects

Adobe and their devoted product users provide you with a variety of downloadable Flash buttons that are available on the Adobe Exchange website, located at www.adobe.com/cfusion/exchange. At this site, you can find collections of different buttons, such as space and planet theme sets, and just about anything else you might want. If you can't find a movie or button that interests you, you can download a demo version of Flash to create your own Flash objects. There are many other websites that offer downloadable buttons; some of the objects are free and some are for purchase.

## Inserting Flash Buttons and Movies

A **Flash button** is a button made from a small, predefined Flash movie that can be inserted on a web page to provide navigation on your website. Buttons created in Flash can be assigned a variety of behaviors in response to user actions, such as opening a different page in the browser when the mouse pointer is placed over it. Like all Flash objects, Flash buttons have the .swf file extension.

Previous versions of Dreamweaver allowed you to insert customized Flash buttons on your web pages without having Flash installed on your computer. The option to create Flash buttons inside Dreamweaver is not available in Dreamweaver CS4, although you can place buttons created in Flash on your web pages. Flash buttons created directly in older versions of Dreamweaver could not have additional behaviors assigned to them, other than the changes in appearance when a mouse was placed over them.

Using Flash, you can also create Flash movies that include a variety of multimedia elements, such as audio files (both music and voice-overs), animated objects, scripted objects, clickable links, and just about any other animated or clickable object imaginable. Flash movies can be used to add content to your existing website or to create an entire website. To add a Flash movie to a web page, click SWF from the Media menu in the Common category on the Insert panel to open the Select File dialog box, and then choose the Flash movie you want to insert.

**FIGURE 1**
*Website based on Flash*

*NASA website – www.nasa.gov*

**FIGURE 2**
*Adobe Flash CS4 window*

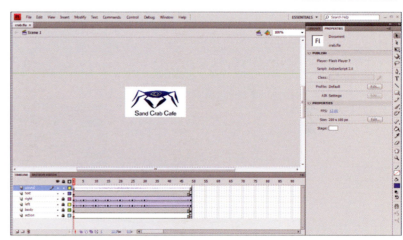

## Insert Flash movies

1. Open the cafe page in The Striped Umbrella website.

2. Select the **cafe logo** in the top-left corner of the page, then press **[Delete]** (Win) or **[delete]** (Mac).

3. Click the **Media button list arrow** on the Common category of the Insert panel, then click **SWF**.

4. Navigate to where you store your Data Files, click **crab.swf**, click **OK** (Win) or **Choose** (Mac), save the movie in the root folder of the website, type **Crab logo animation** in the Title text box in the Object Tag Accessibility Attributes dialog box, then click **OK**. A Flash movie placeholder appears on the page, as shown in Figure 3.

   TIP   If you already have the Flash file in your root folder, you can drag and drop it from the Assets panel or Files panel instead of using the Insert panel or Insert menu.

*You inserted a Flash movie on the cafe page of The Striped Umbrella website.*

FIGURE 3

*Flash movie placeholder on the cafe page*

Properties of selected Flash movie

Flash movie placeholder

*Adding Media Objects*

## FIGURE 4

Flash movie playing in Dreamweaver

Flash movie
playing

Click to stop movie

## FIGURE 5

Flash movie playing in a browser

---

1. With the placeholder selected, click the **Play button** in the Property inspector to view the crab.swf movie, as shown in Figure 4, then click **Stop**.

2. Save your work, then click **OK** to close the Copy Dependent Files dialog box.

   Two supporting files, expressInstall.swf and swfobject_modified.js are copied to a new Scripts folder. These files are necessary for the video to play in the browser correctly.

3. Preview the page in your browser, compare your screen to Figure 5, then close your browser.

   TIP   To play Flash movies in Dreamweaver and in your browser, you must have the Flash Player installed on your computer. If the Flash Player is not installed, you can download it at the Adobe website (www.adobe.com).

4. If the movie did not play in Internet Explorer, click **Tools** on the menu bar, click **Internet Options**, click the **Advanced tab**, then click the **Allow active content to run in files on My Computer check box**.

   TIP   If you are using a different browser or a version of Internet Explorer that is earlier than 6.0, look for a similar setting.

*You played a Flash movie on the cafe page in The Striped Umbrella website in Dreamweaver and in your browser.*

## Modify a Flash file from Dreamweaver

1. If you have Adobe Flash installed on your computer, go to Step 2. If you do not have it installed, skip to Lesson 2 on page 10-10. Remember, if you don't have Flash installed on your computer, you can go to the Adobe Website at *www.adobe.com* to download a trial version.

2. Use Explorer (Win) or Finder (Mac) to copy the file crab.fla from the Data Files folder to the root folder of The Striped Umbrella website.

   To use this source file, you must copy it to your root folder to be able to make changes to it.

3. Close Explorer (Win) or Finder (Mac), then return to Dreamweaver.

4. With the Flash placeholder selected, click **Edit** in the Property inspector.

5. Click **crab.fla** in the striped_umbrella root folder in the Locate FLA File dialog box, as shown in Figure 6, then click **Open**.

   The .swf file is a Flash player file and cannot be edited. The .fla file is the editable Flash file. You must have this source file to edit the movie. After you select the .fla file, the file opens in Flash.

   TIP   If you receive a warning that one or more fonts used for this movie are not available, click Choose Substitute, then choose another font.

**FIGURE 6**

*Selecting the crab.fla file*

The crab.fla file is selected

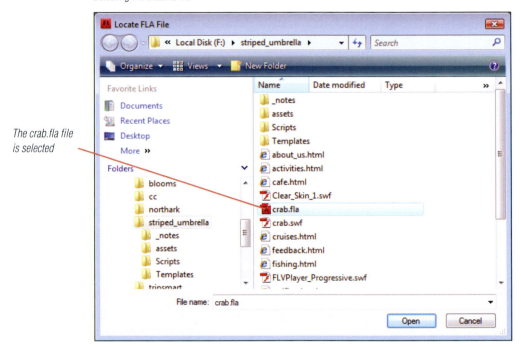

**6.** Click in the **FPS text box** in the Properties panel, change the frame rate from 12 to **24** fps (frames per second), as shown in Figure 7, then click **Done**.

Flash automatically saves both the crab.fla file and the crab.swf file, then closes. (If the crab.fla file opens with an element selected, click in the gray area of the screen to deselect it. If an element is selected, you will not see the FPS text box.)

**7.** Save and preview the page in your browser, then close the browser, close Flash, and close the cafe page.

Notice that the movie plays a little faster now. You changed the frames per second to a larger number, which had the effect of the movie playing faster. The sound, however, plays out after the animation stops. A sound continues playing until it is finished regardless of how long the Flash movie is.

*You used the Edit button in the Property inspector to find and modify the Flash movie in Flash, then returned to Dreamweaver.*

**FIGURE 7**

*Editing the Flash movie and returning to Dreamweaver*

Click Done to save the file and return to Dreamweaver

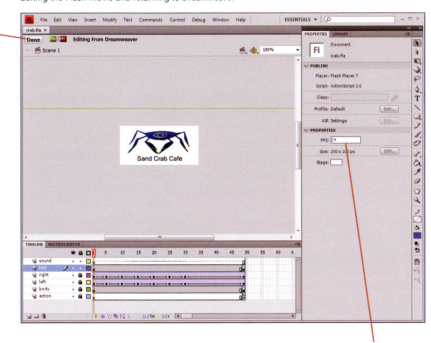

FPS text box

# ADD ROLLOVER IMAGES

## What You'll Do

*In this lesson, you will add two rollover images to the activities page of The Striped Umbrella website.*

## Understanding Rollover Images

A **rollover image** is an image that changes its appearance when the mouse pointer is placed over it in a browser. A rollover image actually consists of two images. The first image is the one that appears when the mouse pointer is not positioned over it, and the second image is the one that appears when the mouse pointer is positioned over it. Rollover images are often used to help create a feeling of action and excitement on a web page. For instance, suppose you are creating a website that promotes a series of dance classes. You could create a rollover image using two images of a dancer in two different poses. When a viewer places the mouse pointer over the image of the dancer in the first pose, the image would change to show the dancer in a different pose, creating a feeling of movement and action.

## Adding Rollover Images

You add rollover images to a web page using the Rollover Image command on the Images menu in the Common category shown in Figure 8. You specify both the original image and the rollover image in the Insert Rollover Image dialog box. The rollover image is the image that is swapped when the mouse rolls over the original image. To prevent one of the images from being resized during the rollover, both images should share the same height and width dimensions. Another way to create a rollover image, button, or navigation bar is to insert it as a Fireworks HTML file. The code for the rollover is inserted in the file when it is created and exported from Fireworks.

The Fireworks HTML command is also on the Images menu, as shown in Figure 8.

Rollover images can also be used to display an image associated with a text link. For instance, suppose you are creating a website for an upcoming election.

You could create a web page that contains a list of candidates for the election and add a rollover image for each candidate's name that would cause a photograph of the candidate to appear when the mouse is placed over his or her name. You can also use this effect to make appropriate images appear when you point to different menu options. For instance, Figure 9 shows the North Arkansas College website, which uses rollover images to highlight each menu option on its home page. When a rollover image is inserted onto a page, Dreamweaver automatically adds two behaviors; a Swap Image behavior and a Swap Image Restore behavior. A **Swap Image behavior** is JavaScript code that directs the browser to display a different image when the mouse is rolled over an image on the page. A **Swap Image Restore** behavior restores the swapped image back to the original image.

**FIGURE 8**

*Images menu on the Insert panel*

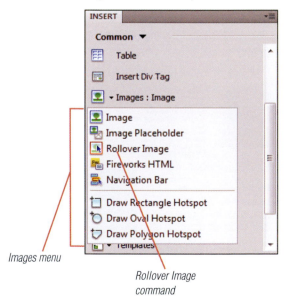

Images menu

Rollover Image command

**FIGURE 9**

*North Arkansas College website with rollover images*

Rollover images change when mouse is positioned over different menu item

North Arkansas College website used with permission from North Arkansas College — www.northark.edu

## Add a rollover image

1. Open the activities page of The Striped Umbrella website. (Click **OK** to close the Design Notes dialog box.)

2. Scroll down to find the image of the two dolphins, then delete it.

3. Click the **Images list arrow** in the Common group on the Insert panel, then click **Rollover Image**.

4. Type **dolphins** in the Image name text box.

5. Click **Browse** next to the Original image text box, browse to where you store your Data Files, then double-click **one_dolphin.jpg**.

6. Click **Browse** next to the Rollover image text box, then double-click the **two_dolphins.jpg** file from where you store your Data Files for the Rollover image text box.

7. Type **Dolphins riding the surf** in the Alternate text text box, compare your screen to Figure 10, then click **OK**.

8. With the image selected, set the Alignment to **Right**, add a 1-pixel border to the image, add a 10-pixel Horizontal space on the sides of the image, save your work, preview the page in your browser, then compare your screen to Figure 11.

   When you point to the image, the one dolphin image is "swapped" with the two-dolphin image.

   *(continued)*

### FIGURE 10
*Browsing to find the source files for the rollover image*

### FIGURE 11
*Viewing the rollover image in the browser*

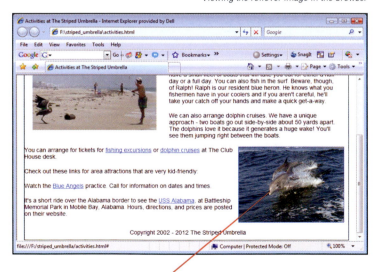

*Image is swapped when the mouse pointer rolls over it*

10. Switch to Code view, then locate the code for the swap image behavior, as shown in Figure 12.

The code directs the browser to display the image with one dolphin "onmouseout"— when the mouse is not over the image. It directs the browser to display the image with two dolphins "onmouseover"—when the mouse is over the image.

> TIP If your code is selected in Code view, that means the image is selected in Design view.

11. Return to Design view.

*You replaced an image with a rollover image on the activities page of The Striped Umbrella website.*

**FIGURE 12**

*Swap behavior code for rollover image*

```
162    <div id="sidebar1"><p><img src="assets/heron_waiting_small.jpg" width="300" height="160" alt=
       "Ralph waiting for breakfast" /></p>
163      <!-- end #sidebar1 -->
164    </div>
165    <div id="mainContent">
166      <p>
167        <!-- end #mainContent -->
168          <span class="paragraph_text"><br />
169            We have many activities for you to choose from, both on site and within the area. Many of
       our visitors enjoy local fishing trips. We have a small fleet of boats that will take you out for
       either a half-day or a full day. You can also fish in the surf. Beware, though, of Ralph! Ralph is
       our resident blue heron. He knows what you fishermen have in your coolers and if you aren't
       careful, he'll take your catch off your hands and make a quick get-a-way.</span></p>
170        <p><span class="paragraph_text">We can also arrange dolphin cruises. We have a unique approach
       - two boats go out side-by-side about 50 yards apart. The dolphins love it because it generates a
       huge wake! You'll see them jumping right between the boats. </span></p>
171    </div>
172      <!-- This clearing element should immediately follow the #mainContent div in order to force
       the #container div to contain all child floats -->
173      <p class="paragraph_text"><a href="#" onmouseout="MM_swapImgRestore()" onmouseover=
       "MM_swapImage('dolphins','','assets/two_dolphins.jpg',1)"><img src="assets/one_dolphin.jpg" alt=
       "Dolphins riding the surf" name="dolphins" width="252" height="180" hspace="10" border="1" align=
       "right" id="dolphins" /></a></p>
174      <p class="paragraph_text">You can arrange for tickets for <a href="fishing.html">fishing
       excursions</a> or <a href="cruises.html">dolphin cruises</a> at The Club House desk.</p>
175      <p class="paragraph_text">Check out these links for area attractions that are very
       kid-friendly: </p>
```

Code for rollover image

# ADD
## BEHAVIORS

## What You'll Do

*In this lesson, you will add an action that plays a sound effect to the activities page of The Striped Umbrella website. You will then change the event for that action.*

### Adding Interactive Elements

You can make your web pages come alive by adding interactive elements such as sounds to them. For instance, if you are creating a page about your favorite animals, you could attach the sound of a dog barking to a photograph of a dog so that the barking sound would play when the viewer clicks the photograph. You can add sound and other multimedia actions to elements by attaching behaviors to them. **Behaviors** are sets of instructions that you can attach to page elements that tell the page element to respond in a specific way when an event occurs, such as when the mouse pointer is positioned over the element. When you attach a behavior to an element, JavaScript code for the behavior is automatically generated and inserted into the code for your page.

### Using the Behaviors Panel

You can use the Behaviors panel located in the Tag panel group to insert a variety of JavaScript-based behaviors on a page. For instance, using the Behaviors panel, you can automate tasks, respond to visitor selections and mouse movements with pop-up menus, add sounds, create games, go to a different URL, or add automatic dynamic effects to a web page. To insert a behavior, click the Add behavior button on the Behaviors panel to open the Actions menu, as shown in Figure 13, then click a behavior from the menu.

### Inserting Sound Effects

Sound effects can add a new dimension to any website. You can use sounds to enhance the effect of positioning the mouse on a rollover image, clicking a link, or even loading or closing a page. By adding sounds, you can make your pages cheep, chirp, click, or squawk.

To apply a sound effect, select the link or object to which you want the sound effect added, and then select the Play Sound behavior located on the

~Deprecated submenu of the Actions menu on the Behaviors panel. Sound effects should be used sparingly, and only if they add to the overall good design for the page. Sound effects that loop, or repeat continuously, may be annoying to viewers.

## Understanding Actions and Events

Actions are triggered by events. For instance, if you want your viewer to hear a sound when an image is clicked, you would attach the Play Sound action using the onClick event to trigger the action. Other examples of events are onMouseOver and onLoad. The onMouseOver event will trigger an action when the mouse is placed over an object. The onLoad event will trigger an action when the page is first loaded in the browser window.

## Using the Spry Framework

Some of the behaviors that can be added to web pages use a JavaScript library called the **Spry framework for AJAX**.

**Asynchronous JavaScript and XML (AJAX)** is a method for developing interactive web pages that respond quickly to user input, such as clicking a map. In the library, you will find **spry widgets**, which are pre-built components for adding interaction to pages; and **spry effects**, which are screen effects such as fading and enlarging page elements. When a spry effect is added to a page element, a SpryAssets folder is automatically added to the root folder with the supporting files inside the folder.

**FIGURE 13**

*Behaviors panel with the Actions menu displayed*

Add behavior button

Actions menu

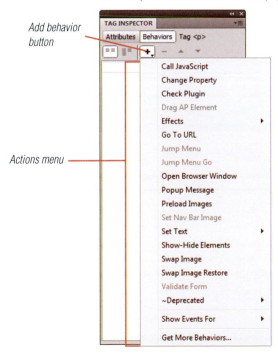

## Add a behavior

1. Open the file **dw10_1.html** from the location where you store your Data Files, then save it in the root folder as **wildlife_message.html**. Do not update links. Close the dw10_1.html page.

2. Select the **fishing image** on the activities page, click **Window** on the Application bar (Win) or Menu bar (Mac), then click **Behaviors** to open the Behaviors panel.

3. Click the **Add behavior button** 🔲 on the Behaviors panel toolbar to open the Actions menu, as shown in Figure 14, then click **Open Browser Window** to open the Open Browser Window dialog box.

4. Click **Browse** next to the URL to display text box to open the Select File dialog box, navigate to the root folder, then double-click **wildlife_message.html**.

5. Type **300** in the Window width text box, type **300** in the Window height text box, type **message** in the Window name text box, compare your screen to Figure 15, then click **OK**.

6. Save your work, preview the page in your browser, test the Open Browser Window effect by clicking the fishing image, as shown in Figure 16, then close both browser windows.

   (*Hint*: The pop-up window will not work if "Block pop-up windows" is enabled in your browser. Click the Options button to choose to temporarily allow pop-ups.

*You added an Open Browser Window effect to an image on the activities page of The Striped Umbrella website.*

**FIGURE 14**

*Adding the Open Browser Window behavior to the fishing image*

Select fishing image

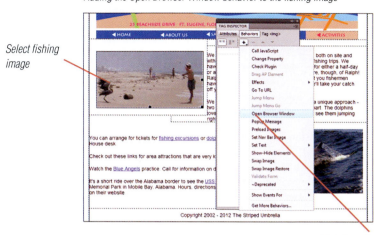

Click Open Browser Window

**FIGURE 15**

*Setting Open Browser Window options*

**FIGURE 16**

*Viewing the wildlife message in a browser*

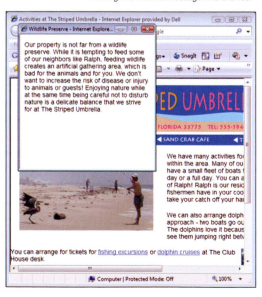

## FIGURE 17
*Viewing the edited window size for the behavior*

## FIGURE 18
*Viewing the edited behavior*

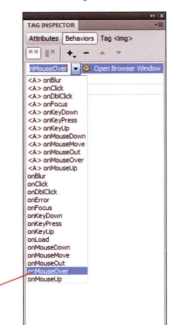

onMouseOver
action

---

### Comparing the Behaviors and the Server Behaviors panels

In addition to the Behaviors panel, there is a Server Behaviors panel. Although the names are similar, the functions are not. The Behaviors panel is used to add JavaScript behaviors to page elements. The Server Behaviors panel is used to add server behaviors, such as creating a login page or a page that is password protected. Building search pages to enable viewers to search a website for specific content is another server behavior that you can add with the Server Behaviors panel. After you have created a server behavior and enabled Dreamweaver to display live data, you can add, edit, or delete the server behavior while you are in Design view, but viewing the page in Live view. The Server Behaviors panel is in the Dynamic Content Tab group with the Databases, Bindings, and Components panels.

---

1. Right-click (Win) or [control]-click (Mac) the **right column** of the Open Browser Window action in the Behaviors panel, then click **Edit Behavior.**

   The Open Browser Window dialog box opens.

2. Change the window height to **200**, save your changes, preview the page in your browser, then click the **fishing image**.

   The browser window with the wildlife message is shorter in height, as shown in Figure 17.

3. Close the browser windows.

4. Click the **left column** of the Open Browser Window action in the Behaviors panel to display the events list arrow, click the **arrow**, then click **onMouseOver**, as shown in Figure 18.

   This will change the event that triggers the action from clicking the image to simply placing the mouse over the image.

5. Save your work, open the page in the browser, then move the mouse over the fishing image.

   Now, simply placing the mouse over the image triggers the Open Browser Window event. *(Hint:* If you see a yellow starburst icon over the fishing image, press the control key and click to view the image.)

6. Close the browser windows, close the Behaviors panel, then close the wildlife_ message page. Leave the activities page open.

*You edited the behavior in the Behaviors panel.*

---

# ADD FLASH VIDEO

## What You'll Do

 In this lesson, you will insert a Flash video on the activities page.

### Inserting Flash Video

Another option you have to present rich media content on your web pages is to insert video files. Although you can use several different formats for video, one of the most popular formats is the Flash video file. **Flash video files** are files that include both video and audio and have an .flv file extension. Like the Flash .swf file, the Flash video file is played through the Flash Player. Since most viewers have the Flash Player installed on their computers, it is a nice format to use without fear of losing viewers. You have two choices for delivering your Flash movie on your site: using a progressive video download or a streaming video download. A **progressive video download** will download the video to the viewer's computer, then allow the video to play before it has completely downloaded. It will finish the download as the video plays, but the viewer will not notice that this is taking place. A **streaming video download** is very similar to a progressive download, except streaming video downloads use buffers to gather the content as it is downloading to ensure a smoother playback. Flash video is not the only video format that can be viewed on a web page. You can also link or embed **AVI (Audio Visual Interleave)**, the Microsoft standard for digital video, or **MPEG (Motion Picture Experts Group)** files.

Figure 19 is a page on the Federal Aviation Administration website that presents educational videos about a variety of topics to those visiting their website. This is an effective way to present content. The user can start and stop the video using controls on the screen. Audio controls are also provided to mute the sound. The user can toggle a closed caption button to display the script. Video used sparingly can be effective and add a lot of interest to the page.

**FIGURE 19**

*Viewing a Flash video in a browser*

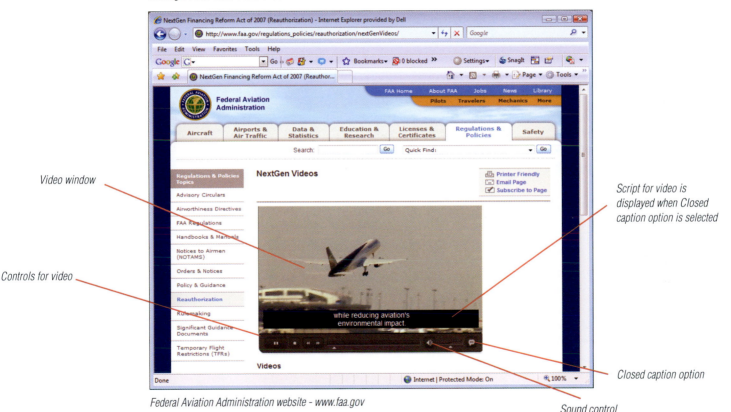

Video window

Script for video is displayed when Closed caption option is selected

Controls for video

Closed caption option

*Federal Aviation Administration website - www.faa.gov*

Sound control

## Add Flash video

1. Using Windows Explorer (Win) or Finder (Mac), copy the file **umbrella_anchor_ movie.flv** from where you store your Data Files, paste it into your Striped Umbrella root folder, then close Windows Explorer (Win) or Finder (Mac).

2. Click to place the insertion point under the last paragraph.

3. Click the **Media list arrow** on the Insert panel, then click **FLV**.

4. Verify that the Video type list menu shows Progressive Download Video as the type for the video.

5. Click the **Browse button** next to the URL text box, browse to your root folder, then double-click **umbrella_anchor_movie.flv**.

6. Choose the **Halo Skin 1 (min width: 180) option** in the Skin menu (if necessary).

7. Type **180** in the Width text box, **180** in the Height text box, verify that the Constrain check box is checked, compare your screen to Figure 20, then click **OK**.

   A placeholder for the movie appears on the page. You will only be able to view the video in the browser.

8. Place the insertion point to the right of the video placeholder image, press **[Shift] [Enter]** (Win) or **[Shift] [return]** (Mac), then type **See us about your complimentary Umbrella Anchor!**

   *(continued)*

**FIGURE 20**
*The Insert FLV settings for the umbrella anchor movie*

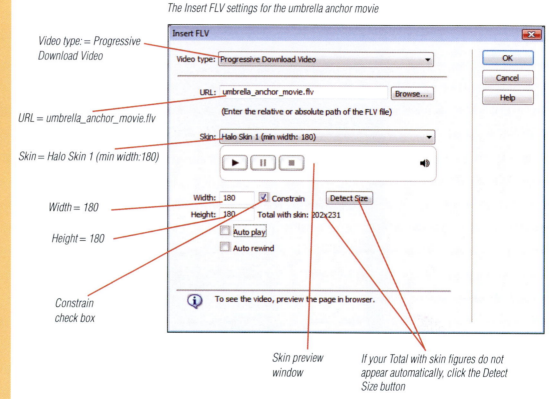

Video type: = Progressive Download Video

URL = umbrella_anchor_movie.flv

Skin = Halo Skin 1 (min width:180)

Width = 180

Height = 180

Constrain check box

Skin preview window

If your Total with skin figures do not appear automatically, click the Detect Size button

FIGURE 21

*Viewing the video in the browser*

*Play button on skin*

FIGURE 22

*Supporting video files added to the website*

FLVPlayer_Progressive.swf

Halo_Skin_1.swf

umbrella_anchor_movie.flv

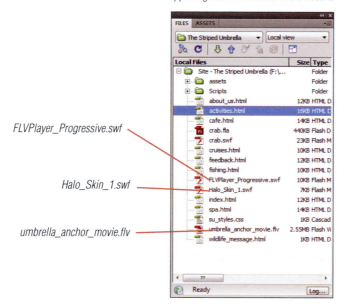

9. Apply the **paragraph_text rule** to the sentence, select the video placeholder, click the left arrow to place the insertion point to the left of the placeholder, then click the **Text Indent button** 📄 seven times to indent both the video placeholder and the sentence.

10. Save your work, preview the page in the browser, then compare your screen to Figure 21.

    The skin is the bar at the bottom of the video with the control buttons. You click the Play button ▶ to play the movie and the Stop button ■ to stop the movie.

11. Play the movie, then close the browser window.

12. Notice the two files, in addition to the umbrella_anchor_movie.flv file, that have been added to the Files panel: Halo_Skin_1.swf and FLVPlayer_Progressive.swf, as shown in Figure 22.

    These two files provide the instructions for the skin to display and function and for the movie to start playing in the browser before it is completely downloaded

13. Close all open pages.

*You inserted a Flash video on the page, then viewed the additional files added to the website as supporting files by Dreamweaver.*

*Lesson 4  Add Flash Video*

## Add and modify Flash objects.

1. Open the blooms & bulbs website, then open the classes page.
2. Insert the garden_quote.swf Flash movie located where you store your Data Files directly below the last paragraph, then type **Garden quote** in the Object Tag Accessibility Attributes dialog box.
3. Play the garden_quote.swf movie in Dreamweaver, save your work, click OK to close the Dependent Files dialog box, preview the page in your browser, compare your screen to Figure 23, then close your browser.
4. Close the classes page.

## Add rollover images.

1. Open the tips page, then delete the Garden Tips graphic at the top of the page.
2. Verify that your insertion point is still where you just deleted the garden tips graphic.

3. Insert a rollover image from where you store your Data Files by clicking Insert on the Application bar (Win) or Menu bar (Mac), pointing to Image Objects, then clicking Rollover Image. Type **rollover** as the name, insert garden_tips.jpg as the original image, garden_tips2.jpg from where you store your Data Files, as the rollover image, type **Garden tips with flower** as the alternate text, then click OK.

4. Save your work, preview the page in the browser to test the rollover, then close the tips page.

## Add behaviors.

1. Open the water_plants page.
2. Select the water plants image, then use the Behaviors panel to add the Appear/Fade effect that will fade from **100% to 50%**, then select the Toggle Effect check box.

**FIGURE 23**

*Completed Skills Review 1*

3. Edit the behavior to use the **onMouseOver** action, then save your work. (*Hint*: Dreamweaver will add a new SpryAssets folder in the site with the SpryEffects.js supporting file.)

4. Preview the page in the browser. (*Hint*: Place the mouse over the image to test the behavior.)

5. Close the browser, then close the water_plants page.

**Add Flash video.**

1. Open the plants page, click right after the last sentence on the page, then insert a paragraph break.

2. Insert the hanging_baskets.flv file from the Chapter 10 Data Files folder using the following settings: Video Type: Progressive Download Video, URL: hanging_baskets.flv, Skin: Clear Skin1 (min width: 140), Width: **150**, Height: **150**. (*Hint*: Remember to copy the file to your root folder first.)

3. Insert a line break after the video placeholder, type **Join us Saturday for a class on baskets.** with a line break after the word "for", then apply the bold_blue rule to the sentence.

4. Create a new class rule named **.video** and set Text-align to center.

5. Click to place the insertion point to the left of the video placeholder and apply the video rule.

6. Save your work, preview the page and play the movie in the browser, then compare your screen to Figure 24.

7. Close the browser, then close all open pages.

**FIGURE 24**

*Completed Skills Review*

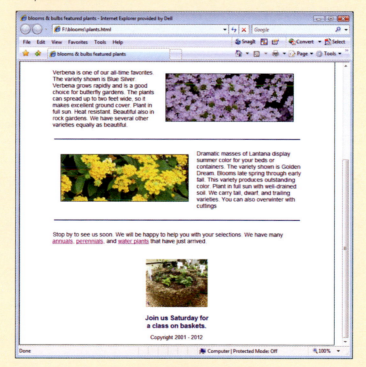

In this exercise, you will continue your work on the TripSmart website. The owner of TripSmart would like you to work on the amazon page. He gives you a Flash file that shows the route of the ship that will take visitors down the Amazon river.

1. Open the TripSmart website, then open the amazon page.

2. Place the insertion point at the end of the second paragraph, then insert a paragraph break.

3. Insert the **amazon_map.swf** file from the Chapter 10 Data Files folder, then add the text **Amazon map animation** in the Object Tag Accessibly Attributes dialog box.

4. Click to the left of the placeholder, insert one text indent to indent the movie, then save the file. Click Yes to close the Dependent Files dialog box.

5. Preview the amazon page in the browser. (You will probably have to scroll down to see the animation play since it is at the bottom of the page. Click Refresh to play it again.)

6. Close the browser, then close the amazon page.

7. Open the file dw10_2.html from where you store your Data Files, then save it in the TripSmart root folder as **amazon_trip.html**. Do not update links.

8. Attach the **tripsmart_styles.css** file to the page, then apply the **bullets** style to the text.

9. Close the dw10_2.html page, then save and close the amazon_trip.html page.

10. Open the amazon page, then attach a behavior to the water lily image that will open a new browser window when the mouse rolls over it that displays the amazon_trip.html file. Use **300** for the window width and **100** for the window height. Name the window **soldout**.

11. Save your work, then preview the page in the browser to test the behavior, as shown in Figure 25.

12. Close the browser, then close all open pages.

**FIGURE 25**
*Sample Project Builder 1*

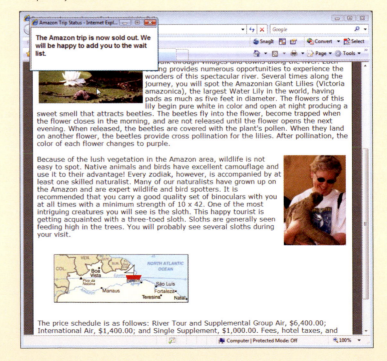

Use Figures 26 and 27 as a guide to continue your work on Carolyne's Creations. You have decided to add a video demonstrating how to sugar flowers for decoration.

1. Open the Carolyne's Creations website.
2. Open the index page.
3. Select the logo on the right side of the page, then attach a behavior and an action of your choice to it.
4. Save and close the index page, then open the adults page.

5. Place the insertion point under the last paragraph, but above the bottom yellow border of the CSS block, insert a new paragraph, then insert the Flash video **sugared_flowers.flv** from your Chapter 10 Data Files folder using settings of your choice for the video. (*Hint*: In Figure 27, a style was used to center the video on the page.)

6. Refer to the text in Figure 27 to add short descriptive text under the video, then format the text with the **special_name** rule.
7. Make any other adjustments you wish, save your page, then preview the page in the browser.
8. Close the browser, then close all open pages.

**FIGURE 27**
*Completed Project Builder 2*

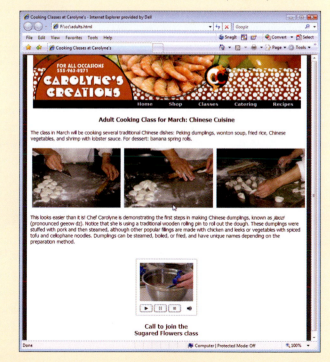

**FIGURE 26**
*Completed Project Builder 2*

# DESIGN PROJECT

Angie Wolf is an astronomer. She would like to design a website about planets, like the example shown in Figure 28. She would like her website to incorporate Flash elements, rollovers, and video and would like to use Dreamweaver to build the site.

1. Connect to the Internet and go to www.nasa.gov.
2. Which elements in the site are Flash objects?
3. Which objects in the site are made with rollover images?
4. How has adding the Flash effects improved the appearance of this site?
5. Go through the site and locate some Flash video.
6. Create a sketch of Angie's site that contains at least five pages. Indicate in your sketch what media elements you would insert in the site, including where you would add Flash objects, rollover images, and video.

**FIGURE 28**
*Design Project*

NASA website – www.nasa.gov

# PORTFOLIO PROJECT

In this assignment, you will continue to work on the group website that you started in Chapter 1. There will be no Data Files supplied. You are building this site from chapter to chapter, so you must do each Portfolio Project assignment in each chapter to complete your site.

You will continue building your site by designing and completing a page that contains rich media content or by adding media content to existing pages. After completing your site, be sure to run appropriate reports to test the site.

1. Evaluate your storyboard, then choose a page, or series of pages, to develop in which you will include Flash objects as well as other media content, such as rollover images, video, and behaviors.

2. Plan the content for your new page so that the layout works well with both the new and old pages in your site. Sketch a plan for the media content you wish to add, showing which media elements you will use and where you will place them.

3. Create or find the media you identified in your sketch, choosing appropriate formatting.

4. Add the rollover images to the page.

5. Add a video, if possible, to the page.

6. Run a report on your new page(s) to ensure that all links work correctly.

7. Preview the new page (or pages) in your browser and test all links. Evaluate your pages for content and layout. Use the checklist in Figure 29 to make sure your website is complete.

8. Make any modifications that are necessary to improve the page.

**FIGURE 29**
*Portfolio Project checklist*

---

**Website Checklist**

1. Do you pages flow well together?
2. Do all Flash movies play properly in your browser?
3. Do all links work?
4. Do all sounds play correctly?
5. Are there any missing images or links on the pages?
6. Do all pages have a title?
7. Do all rollover images display properly?

---

# CREATING AND
## USING TEMPLATES

1. Create templates with editable regions

2. Use templates to create pages

3. Use templates to update a site

4. Use advanced template options

# 11

# CREATING AND
## USING TEMPLATES

## Introduction

When you create a website, it's important to make sure that each page has a unified look so that viewers know they are in your site no matter what page they are viewing. For instance, you should make sure that common elements such as the navigation bar and company banner appear in the same place on every page and that every page has the same background color. You have been using styles to provide continuity in your sites in previous chapters. Another way to make sure that every page in your site has a consistent appearance is through the use of templates. A **template** is a special kind of page that contains both **locked regions**, which are areas on the page that cannot be modified by users of the template, as well as other types of regions that users can change or edit. For instance, an **optional region** is an area in the template that users can choose to show or hide, and an **editable region** is an area where users can add or change content.

Using templates not only ensures a consistent appearance throughout a website, but also saves considerable development time. Templates are especially helpful if different people will be creating pages in your site. In this chapter, you will create a template from an existing page in The Striped Umbrella website and define editable regions in it.

## Understanding How to Use Templates

The ideal process for using templates is for one person (the template author) to create a template that has locked regions containing the design elements common to every page in the site, as well as regions where content can be added or changed. Once the template is fully developed, other team members can use it to create each page of the site, adding appropriate content to the editable regions of each page. If the template author makes changes to the template, all pages to which the template is attached can be automatically updated to reflect those changes.

# Tools You'll Use

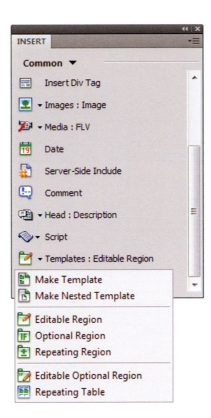

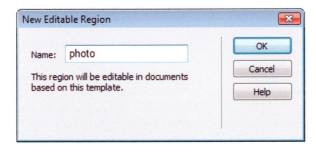

# CREATE TEMPLATES WITH EDITABLE REGIONS

## What You'll Do

 *In this lesson, you will create a template based on the cruises page of The Striped Umbrella website. You will then define editable regions in the template, edit one of the CSS container rules, and add two links to the cruises and fishing pages. Finally, you will delete the template page title.*

## Creating a Template from an Existing Page

If you have already created and designed a page that you think looks great, and you want to use the layout and design for other pages in your site, you can save the page as a template using the Save as Template command. Templates are saved with a .dwt extension and are stored in the Templates folder in the root folder of your website. If your site does not have a Templates folder, one will automatically be created for you the first time you save a template. To view a list of templates in your site, open the Templates folder in the Files panel. To preview a template before opening it, open the Assets panel, click the Templates button on the Assets panel toolbar, and then click a template in the list. The template appears in the preview window above the templates list, as shown in Figure 1.

## Defining Editable Regions

By default, when you save a template, all content on the page will be locked, which means that no one else will be able to add content or modify any part of the template to create new pages. If your template is going to be used effectively, you need to have at least one editable region in it so that other users can add content. You can specify a name for the region using the New Editable Region dialog box. Editable regions are outlined in blue on the template page, and the names of the editable regions appear in blue shaded boxes, as shown in Figure 2.

## Defining Optional Regions

In addition to editable regions, you can also add optional regions to a template. An optional region is an area in a template that users can choose to either show or hide. For instance, you could place an image in an optional region, so that users of the template can decide whether or not to show it on the page they are creating. An optional region's visibility is controlled by the conditional statement **if**. You can specify a page element as an optional region using the New Optional Region dialog box. You can name the region and specify whether to show or hide it by default. The Editable and Optional Region dialog boxes are both accessed by clicking the Templates list arrow in the Common category of the Insert panel.

## Defining Editable Optional Regions

If you want to give users the ability to show or hide a page element, as well as make modifications to it, then you can define the element as an **editable optional region**. For instance, you might want to make an advertisement an editable optional region so that users of the template could change its text and specify whether to show or hide it. Using the New Optional Region dialog box, you can name the region and specify whether to show or hide it by default.

FIGURE 1

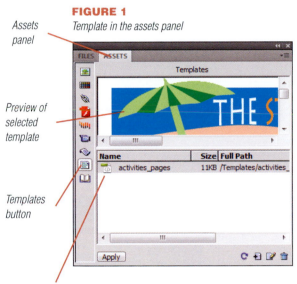

**FIGURE 1**

*Template in the assets panel*

Assets panel

Preview of selected template

Templates button

List of templates available in this site

**FIGURE 2**

*Template with locked and editable regions*

Editable region labels

This is the Dolphin Racer at dock. We leave daily at 4:00 p.m. and 6:30 p.m. for 1 1/2 hour cruises. There are snacks and restrooms available on board. We welcome children of all ages. Our ship is a U.S. Coast Guard approved vessel and our captain is a former member of the Coast Guard. Call The Club desk for reservations.

Blue outlines of editable regions

## Create a template from an existing page

1. Open Dreamweaver, then open the cruises page.

2. Click **File** on the Application bar (Win) or menu bar (Mac), then click **Save as Template** to open the Save As Template dialog box.

3. Verify that The Striped Umbrella is displayed in the Site text box, type **activities_pages** in the Save as text box, compare your screen to Figure 3, click **Save**, update the links, then click the **Refresh button** on the Files panel toolbar.

   The Templates folder, which contains the activities_pages template, appears in the Files panel.

4. Click the **plus sign** next to the Templates folder to display the activities_pages.dwt file.

5. Display the Assets panel, click the **Templates button** to view the list of templates in the site, then compare your Assets panel to Figure 4. Click the **Refresh button** if you don't see the template listed.

   > TIP To create a template from scratch, click File on the Application bar (Win) or Menu bar (Mac), click New to open the New Document dialog box, click Blank Template, click the type of template you want to create in the Template Type list, choose a layout from the Layout list, then click Create.

*You created a template from the cruises page of The Striped Umbrella website.*

**FIGURE 3**
*Save As Template dialog box*

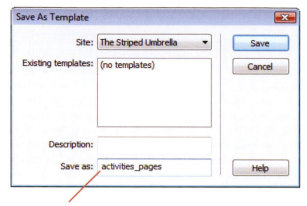

Save as text box

**FIGURE 4**
*Assets panel showing saved template in the Striped Umbrella website*

Preview of activities_pages template

Templates button

activities_pages template

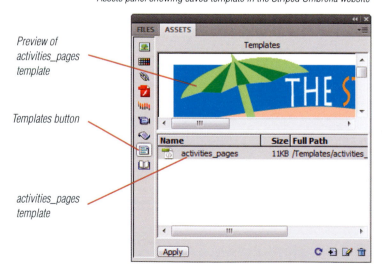

*Creating and Using Templates*

## FIGURE 5

New Editable Region dialog box

Name of new
Editable Region

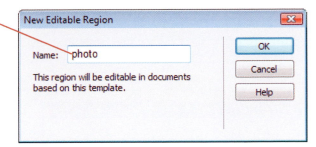

## FIGURE 6

activities_pages template with two editable regions added

Templates
list arrow

Editable
region labels

Selected Editable
Region is marked
by blue outline

1. Click to place the insertion point in the CSS block with the boat graphic, then click the **<div#sidebar1> tag** in the tag selector to select all of the content in that cell.

2. Click the **Common category** on the Insert panel, if necessary.

3. Click the **Templates list arrow** in the Common category, then click **Editable Region** to open the New Editable Region dialog box.

   TIP  You can also press [Ctrl][Alt][V] (Win) or ⌘[option][V] (Mac) to open the New Editable Region dialog box.

4. Type **photo** in the Name text box, as shown in Figure 5, click **OK**, then press [→] to deselect the graphic.

   A blue shaded box containing "photo" appears above the picture of the boat.

   TIP  You must have Invisible Elements turned on to see the blue shaded box.

5. Click to place the insertion point in the CSS block with the description text in it, to the right of the photo, select the **<div#mainContent> tag**, repeat Steps 3 and 4 to create an editable region named **description**, click in the description region, then compare your screen to Figure 6.

   TIP  To remove an editable region from a template, select the editable region in the document window, click Modify on the Application bar (Win) or Menu bar (Mac), point to Templates, then click Remove Template Markup.

*You created two editable regions in the activities_pages template.*

## Modify a template

1. Click to place the insertion point inside the paragraph, then select the **<div#mainContent> tag** on the tag selector.

   The mainContent div tag is selected on the page in Design View.

2. Click the **.twoColFixLtHdr #mainContent rule** in the CSS Styles panel, then click the **Edit Rule button** 🖉 to open the CSS Rule definition for .twoColFixLtHdr #mainContent dialog box.

3. Type **40** in the Right Margin text box, click the list arrow next to the Right margin unit of measure text box, then click **px**, as shown in Figure 7.

4. Replace 230 in the Left Margin text box with **250**.

5. Click **OK** to close the CSS Rule definition for the .twoColFixLtHdr #mainContent dialog box.

   Changing to these settings brings the paragraph more in line with the right edge of the banner and slightly away from the boats image.

   *(continued)*

### FIGURE 7
*Editing the activities_page template*

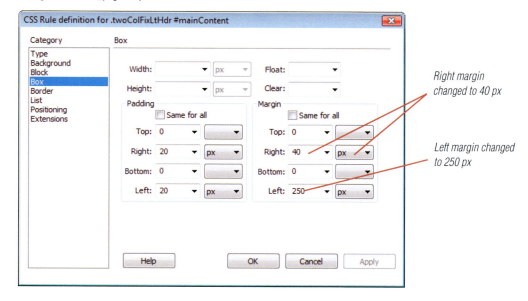

Right margin changed to 40 px

Left margin changed to 250 px

---

## Using InContext Editing

Another way to allow users to modify web pages is through InContext Editing (ICE). **InContext Editing** is an online hosted service that users can log into and be allowed to make changes to designated editable regions on a page while viewing it in a browser. This requires little knowledge of HTML or Dreamweaver. The commands to create editable regions are found in the InContext Editing category on the Insert panel. For more information, search either the Adobe Help files or the Adobe website at www.adobe.com.

## FIGURE 8

*Links added to the activities_pages template*

*Two links added to the template*

6. Delete the copyright statement at the bottom of the page, then type **Cruises**.

   Since this area of the page is not designated as an Editable Area, users will not be able to change the content on pages based on this template unless they open the template itself.

7. Press the **Spacebar,** insert a **Split Vertical bar** (the shift of the backslash key), press the **Spacebar**, type **Fishing**, then apply the **heading style** to the two words.

8. Link the **Cruises text** to cruises.html, then link the **Fishing text** to fishing.html.

   Don't be concerned with the leading periods before the link in the Src text box. They simply indicate that the template file is in a different folder from the CSS file.

9. Delete the page title from the Title text box on the Document toolbar, click **File** on the Application bar (Win) or Menu bar (Mac), click **Save**, then compare your screen to Figure 8.

10. Close the activities_pages template.

*You edited the div tag rule, then added links to the cruises and fishing pages. Last, you deleted the page title from the template.*

# USE TEMPLATES
## TO CREATE PAGES

## What You'll Do

*In this lesson, you will use the activities_pages template to create a new page in The Striped Umbrella website. You will add content to the editable regions, then apply the template to two existing pages in the website.*

### Creating Pages with Templates

There are many advantages to using a template to create a page. First, it saves a lot of time, because part of the content and format of your page is already set. Second, it ensures that the page you create matches the look and format of other pages in the site. You can create a page based on a template using many different methods. One way is to click File on the Application bar (Win) or Menu bar (Mac), click New to open the New Document dialog box, click Page from Template, select the template you want to use, and then click Create. Templates can be used only in the website that contains them.

### QUICKTIP

You can also create a new page based on a template by right-clicking (Win) or [control]-clicking (Mac) a template in the Assets panel, and then clicking New from Template.

### Modifying Editable Regions

When you create a new page that is based on a template, certain areas of the new page will be locked. You can tell which areas are locked by the appearance of the mouse pointer. When positioned over a locked region, the mouse pointer will appear in the shape of a circle with a line cutting through it, as shown in Figure 9. Editable regions are outlined in blue and marked with a blue, shaded label.

Editing, deleting, or adding content in editable regions of a template-based page works just like it does on any other page. Simply select the element you want to modify and make your changes, or click in the editable region and insert the new content.

## Creating Links in Template-Based Pages

When you add a link to a page that is based on a template, it is important to use document-relative links; otherwise, they will not work. The path to a link actually goes from the template file (not from the template-based page) to the linked page. To ensure that all of your links are document-relative, select the page element to which you want to add a link, and then drag the Point to File icon from the Property inspector to the page you want to link to in the Files panel, as shown in Figure 10.

**FIGURE 9**

*Working with a template-based page*

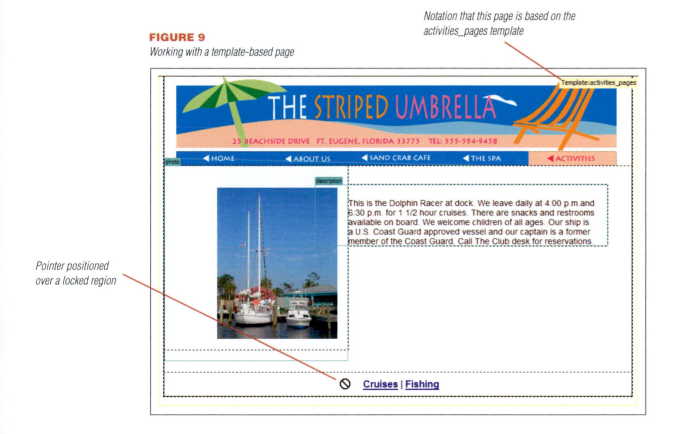

Notation that this page is based on the activities_pages template

Pointer positioned over a locked region

## Attaching a Template to an Existing Page

Sometimes you might need to apply a template to a page that you have already created. For example, suppose you create a page for your department in your company's website, and then your manager tells you that it must be based on the template created by the marketing department. Before you attach a template to an existing page, you should delete any elements from your page that also appear in the template. For instance, if both your page and the template have a company logo, you should delete the logo on your page. If you don't delete it, the logo will appear twice. Once you delete all the duplicate content on your page, attach the template by opening your page, selecting the template in the Assets panel, and clicking the Apply button in the Assets panel. When you do this, the Inconsistent Region Names dialog box opens, allowing you to specify in which regions of the template to place the document head and body content from your page.

QUICKTIP

You can also attach a template to an open page by dragging the template from the Assets panel to the Document window.

### FIGURE 10
Using the Point to File icon to specify a document-relative link

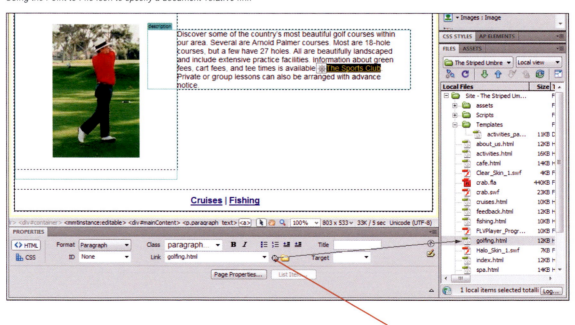

Point to File icon

FIGURE 11
*New Document dialog box*

*Page from Template option*

*Click to create new page based on activities_pages template*

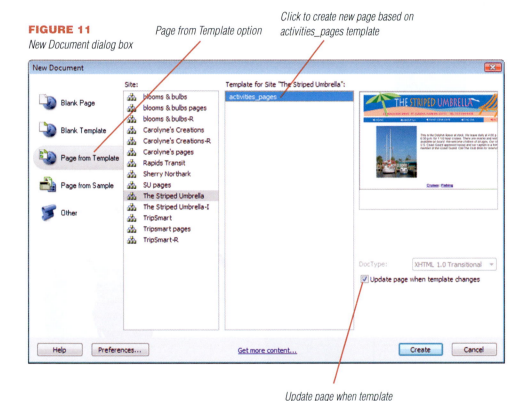

*Update page when template changes checkbox*

## Create a new page based on a template

1. Click **File** on the Application bar (Win) or Menu bar (Mac), click **New** to open the New Document dialog box, then click **Page from Template**.

2. Click **"The Striped Umbrella"** in the Site list box (if necessary), click **activities_pages** in the Template for Site "The Striped Umbrella" list box (if necessary), verify that the **Update page when template changes check box** is selected, compare your screen to Figure 11, then click **Create**.

   A new untitled page opens with the activities_pages template applied to it.

3. Click **File** on the Application bar (Win) or Menu bar (Mac), click **Save As** to open the Save As dialog box, type **golfing.html** in the File name text box, then click **Save**.

   TIP  Another way to create a new page based on a template is to open a new untitled page, click the Templates list arrow on the Insert panel, click Make Template to open the Save As Template dialog box, select a template in the Existing templates text box, then click Save.

*You created a new page in The Striped Umbrella website that has the activities_pages template applied to it. You then saved this page as golfing.html.*

## Modify editable regions in a template

1. Type **Area Golf Courses** in the Title text box.

2. Select the **boats image**, delete it, then insert **golfer.jpg** from where you store your Data Files in the photo editable region, adding **Golfer swinging a club** as the alternate text.

3. Place the insertion point in the description editable region, select and delete the existing text, then use the File, Import, Word Document command to import **golf.doc** (Win).

   | TIP If you are using a Macintosh, you'll need to copy and paste the text into Dreamweaver.

4. Use the Clean Up Word HTML command, click **OK** to close the dialog box that opens, select all of the new text, then apply the **paragraph_text rule** to it.

5. Deselect the text, then compare your screen to Figure 12.

*You deleted content from the editable region of a new golf page based on the activities_pages template. You then replaced the image in the photo editable region and imported text to replace the text in the description editable region.*

## Add links

1. Select the text "The Sports Club" in the paragraph, then link the file **about_us.html** to the selected text, as shown in Figure 13.

2. Place one line break in front of the first word in the paragraph if necessary to add more space between the navigation bar and the paragraph.

3. Save and close the golfing.html page.

*You linked a file to the selected text.*

**FIGURE 12**
*Golfing page with revised content in editable regions*

**FIGURE 13**
*Linking to the about_us.html page*

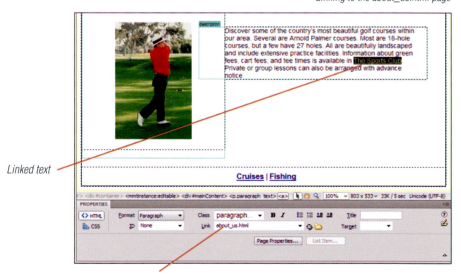

Linked text

Link to about_us.html page

**FIGURE 14**

*New fishing page based on a template*

1. Open the fishing page.
2. Copy the paragraph of text on the right side of the page, then close the fishing page.
3. Create a new page based on the activities_pages template, then save the page as **fishing.html**, overwriting the original fishing.html page.
4. Replace the paragraph in the template with the paragraph you copied from the fishing page.
5. Delete the boat image and replace it with the **heron_small.jpg** image by dragging it from the assets folder into the photo editable region, adding **Ralph and his "catch"** for the alternate text.
6. Title the page **Fishing at The Striped Umbrella**, save the file, compare your screen with Figure 14, then close the page.
7. Repeat Step 3 to create a new cruises page based on the activities_pages template. You will not have to replace any of the content because this is the page that was used for the template.
8. Enter **The Dolphin Racer** as the page title, then save and close the file, overwriting the original cruises.html page.

*You created a new HTML page based on a template and replaced text and images in the page. You then made an existing page into a template-based page.*

# USE TEMPLATES TO
## UPDATE A SITE

## What You'll Do

*In this lesson, you will make a change to the activities_pages template, then update the site so that all pages based on the template reflect the change.*

### Making Changes to a Template

If you create a successful site that draws large numbers of faithful viewers, your site will probably enjoy a long life. However, like everything else, websites need to change with the times. Your company might decide to make new products or offer new services. After a relatively short time, a website can look dated, even with no changes in the company. When changes occur in your company, on a large or small scale, you will need to make changes to your site's appearance and functionality. If your pages are based on a template or group of templates, you will have a much easier time making those changes.

You use the same skills to make changes to a template as you would when creating a template. Start by opening the template from the Files panel or Assets panel, then add, delete, or edit content as you would

### Finding downloadable templates

It is not necessary to create all of your templates from scratch or from existing pages. You can also use templates from outside sources, such as the Internet. A wide range of templates is available for web page components, such as intros and logos, as well as entire websites. These can include sites for businesses, charities, events, and many other venues. Some websites offer free templates for downloading and some offer them for sale. Go to your favorite search engine and type website templates in the Search text box. For example, www.yahootemplates.com offers many types of templates, both free and for sale.

*Creating and Using Templates*

on any non-template-based page. You can turn locked regions into editable regions using the New Editable Region command. To change an editable region back into a locked region, select the region, click Modify on the Application bar (Win) or Menu bar (Mac), point to Templates, and then click Remove Template Markup.

## Updating All Pages Based on a Template

One of the greatest benefits of working with templates is that any change you make to a template can be made automatically to all nested templates and pages that are based on the template. When you save a template that you have modified, the Update

Template Files dialog box opens, asking if you want to update all the files in your site that are based on that template, as shown in Figure 15. When you click Update, the Update Pages dialog box opens and provides a summary of all the files that were updated.

**FIGURE 15**
*Update Template Files dialog box*

*Files based on activities_pages template*

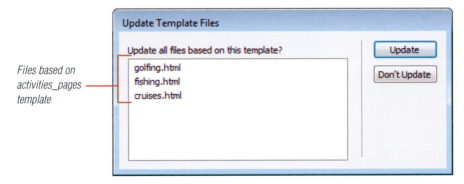

## Make changes to a template

1. Open the activities_pages template from the Templates folder. (You may have to click the plus sign to expand the Templates folder first.)

2. Click to place the insertion point after the second link, add a space, type a split **vertical bar**, then add another space.

3. Create a third link using the word **Golfing**, link it to the golfing page, apply the **heading rule** if necessary, then compare your screen to Figure 16.

4. Open the fishing page.

   The new link does not appear because you have not yet saved the template and updated the site.

5. Close the fishing page.

*You opened the activities_pages template and added a new link.*

**FIGURE 16**
*activities_pages template with new link added*

New link added
to template

*Creating and Using Templates*

**FIGURE 17**

*Update Template Files dialog box*

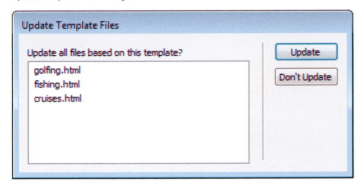

**FIGURE 18**

*Fishing page with template changes incorporated*

*New link to golfing page displays on fishing page*

## Update all template-based pages in a site

1. Return to the activities_pages template (if necessary), click **File** on the Application bar (Win) or Menu bar (Mac), then click **Save All**.

   The Update Template Files dialog box opens, as shown in Figure 17.

2. Click **Update** to open the Update Pages dialog box, then click **Close** after it has finishing updating the pages. (This may take several seconds.)

3. Open the fishing page, then compare your screen to Figure 18.

   The fishing page, the cruises page, and the golfing page in the website now show the new link.

4. Close the fishing page and the activities_ pages template.

5. Open the activities page, close the Design Notes dialog box, click to place the insertion point at the end of the paragraph with the links to the cruises and fishing pages, press the spacebar, then type **We can also arrange tee times for you at area golf courses.**

   This new sentence will provide text for a link to the golfing page.

6. Link the text **tee times** to golfing.html, then save and close the activities page.

*You saved the activities_pages template and used the Update Template Files dialog box and the Update Pages dialog box to specify that all pages in the site based on the template be updated to reflect the template modifications. You also added text to the activities page that was used to provide a link to the golfing page.*

# USE ADVANCED TEMPLATE
## OPTIONS

## What You'll Do

 *In this lesson, you will learn about advanced template settings that can be used for more complex templates.*

### Setting Parameters for Optional Regions

If your template will be used by many people, it might be a good idea to include several optional regions in it so that template users can pick and choose from a wide range of content elements. For example, on a retail site, you might have an optional region for each department to advertise a sale promotion. You would display the optional region for the department you want to feature during the time that department is having its sale. When the sale is over, you would hide that optional region. You might also want to set parameters for optional regions, specifying that they are displayed or hidden based on specific conditions. For instance, let's say you have two optional regions named shoe_sale_text and shoe_images. You could set the shoe_images optional region parameter to shoe_sale_text so that the shoe_images optional region would appear only when the shoe_sale_text optional region is showing, and would be hidden only when the shoe_sale_text optional region is hidden. Use the Advanced settings in the New Optional Region dialog box to set the parameters of an optional region. You can also write a conditional expression based on JavaScript. For instance, you could write the expression *red == false* to specify that a blue optional region appear only when a red optional region is hidden.

### Nesting Templates

If you are working on a complex website that has many different pages used by different people or departments, you might need to create **nested templates**, which are templates that are based on another template. Nested templates are helpful when you want to define a page or parts of a page in greater detail. An advantage of using nested templates is that any changes made to the original template can be automatically updated in the nested template.

To create a nested template, create a new page based on the original template, then use the Save as Template command to save the page as a nested template. You can then make changes to the nested template by adding or deleting content and defining new editable regions. Note that editable regions in the original template are passed on as editable regions to the nested template. However, if you add a new editable or optional region to an editable region that was passed on from the original template, the original editable region changes to a locked region in the nested template.

## Creating Editable Attributes

There might be times when you want users of your template to be able to change certain attributes of an element in a locked region. For instance, perhaps you want to give users the ability to change the cell background color of the top row in a repeating table, or change the source file for an image in a locked area of the template. You can use the Editable Tag Attributes dialog box, shown in Figure 19, to specify that certain attributes of locked regions be editable. To do this, choose an attribute of a selected element, specify to make it editable, assign

it a label, and specify its type and its default setting. For instance, in Figure 19, a table was first selected in a template. Then, the Editable Tag Attributes dialog box was opened by clicking Modify on the Application bar (Win) or Menu bar (Mac), pointing to Templates, and then clicking Make Attribute Editable. From that dialog box, you can choose the attribute and settings that you want to make editable. When you define editable attributes of elements in locked regions, template users can make changes to the element's attributes using the Template Properties dialog box.

FIGURE 19

*Editable Tag Attributes dialog box*

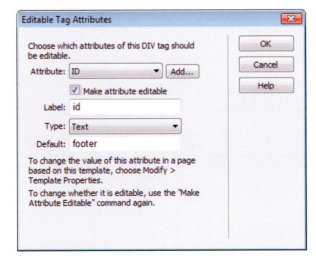

**Create templates with editable regions.**

1. Open the blooms & bulbs website, then open the plants page.

2. Save the plants page as a template called **plant_categories** and update the links.

3. Delete the heading, text paragraphs, horizontal rules, video, and images in the mainContent container. You should have only the banner, navigation bar, and copyright statement left on the page. (Delete any existing line spaces, but be careful not to delete the mainContent CSS block itself.)

4. Delete the copyright statement at the bottom of the page, then type **Annuals - Perennials - Water Plants.** (make sure there is a space before and after each dash).

5. Link the Annuals text to the annuals.html page, the Perennials text to the perennials.html page, and the Water Plants text to the water_plants.html page.

6. Insert an editable region named **type** in the mainContent CSS block.

7. Save and close the plant_categories template.

**Use templates to create pages.**

1. Create a new page from the plant_categories template, then save it as **annuals.html**, overwriting the existing file.

2. Replace the placeholder text in the type editable area with the fuchsia.jpg file from the website assets folder and type **Fuchsia** as the alternate text.

3. Use a word processing program to open the file annuals.doc from where you store your Data Files, then copy and paste the text from the file to the right of the image. (The text will appear below the image until you set the image alignment.)

4. Set the image alignment to left, then add H Space of 10.

5. Apply the bold_blue rule to the Annuals heading and the paragraph_text rule to the paragraph text, then save and close the page.

6. Repeat Steps 1 through 5 to create a new page based on the plant_categories template, then save it as **perennials**, using the iris.jpg file and the perennials.doc text.

7. Repeat Steps 1 through 5 to create a new water_plants page based on the plant_categories template, using the water_hyacinth.jpg file and the water_plants.doc text.

8. Select the water_hyacinth image, then use the Property inspector to change the height of the image to around 200 pixels. (This will slightly lengthen it so the text beside it will not wrap under it in the browser. Adjust the number of pixels as necessary.)

9. Close the Word files and the word processing program.

## Use templates to update a site.

1. Open the plant_categories template, click to place the insertion point in front of the three links in the footer block, then insert a horizontal rule that is 400 pixels wide and center-aligned.

2. Select the three links, then apply the bold_blue rule to them.

3. In the CSS Styles panel, delete the a:link rule to prevent a conflict with the bold_blue rule.

4. Save the template and the style sheet file, then update all files in the site that are based on the template.

5. Preview the annuals.html, perennials.html, and water_plants.html pages in your browser, compare your annuals page to Figure 20, close the browser, then close all open pages.
   (*Hint*: The links will appear with the a:link embedded style before they are clicked. After they are clicked, they become visited links and the bold_blue style is applied.)

**FIGURE 20**
*Completed Skills Review*

In this Project Builder, you will use a template to enhance the TripSmart website. Use Figure 21 as a guide as you work with the template.

1. Open the TripSmart website.
2. Open the catalog page, save it as a template named **catalog_pages**, update the links, delete the catalog.html page, then click **Yes** to close the dialog box warning you that you have links to the file you are deleting.
3. Open the services page, select the text link "on-line catalog," remove the link to the catalog page because it has been deleted, then save and close the page.
4. Switch back to the template, then select the text "Protection from UV rays" and use it to create an editable region named **description1**.
5. Select the text "Cool, light-weight, versatile" and use it to create an editable region named **description2**.
6. Select the text "Pockets for everything" and use it to create an editable region named **description3**.
7. Select the hat and use it to create an editable region named **image1**.

8. Repeat Step 7 to make editable regions called **image2** from the pants image and **image3** from the vest image.
9. Create editable regions called **name1**, **name2**, and **name3** using the text Safari Hat, Kenya Convertible Pants, and Photographer's Vest.
10. Select each item number and create editable regions called **item_number1**, **item_number2**, and **item_number3**.
11. Select each price and make editable regions named **price1**, **price2**, and **price3**.
12. Save and close the template.
13. Create a new page based on the catalog_pages template and save it as **clothing.html**. Because all the information in the editable regions is intact from the template, you do not need to alter it.
14. Close the clothing.html page.
15. Create a new page based on the catalog_pages template and save it as **accessories.html**.
16. Use Figure 21 as a guide to replace the images in the editable regions with the images packing_cube_large.jpg, head-

phones.jpg, and passport_holder.jpg from where you store your Data Files, then add appropriate alternate text.
17. Refer to Figure 21 and the following text to replace the text in the rest of the editable regions:

| description1 | **Makes packing a snap** |
| description2 | **Block out annoying noises** |
| description3 | **Organize your documents** |
| name1 | **Packing Cube** |
| name2 | **Headphones** |
| name3 | **Passport Holder** |
| item_number1 | **74983** |
| item_number2 | **29857** |
| item_number3 | **87432** |
| price1 | **$20, $15, $10** |
| price2 | **$40.00** |
| price3 | **$22.50** |

18. Save and close the accessories page.
19. Open the catalog_pages template and replace the Catalog navigation bar link with two links: **Clothing** and **Accessories**.

20. Link the Clothing text to the clothing.html file and link the Accessories text to the accessories.html file.
21. Save the template and update the pages based on the template.
22. Open each page in the website, delete the Catalog link, and replace it with the two new links. (*Hint*: You can copy the new links and paste them in place on each page as long as you do not copy them from the template page. Because the template is in the Templates folder, the links are slightly different.)
23. Save all pages and preview them in the browser, testing each link.

**FIGURE 21**
*Sample Project Builder 1*

In this Project Builder, you will continue your work on the Carolyne's Creations website. Carolyne would like to make sure that the pages in the site have a consistent appearance. She has asked you to create a template based on the recipes page to use for adding new recipes on the website.

1. Open the Carolyne's Creations website, then create a new template from the recipes page named **recipes** and update the links.
2. Select the paragraph beginning "This is one" and create an editable region from it named **description**.
3. Select the photo, text including the recipe name and list of ingredients, and create an editable region named **photo_name_ingredients**.
4. Select the directions heading and text paragraph and create an editable region named **directions**.
5. Select the last sentence on the page and create an editable region named **notes**.
6. Add a paragraph return right below the navigation bar and type **Featured Recipes: Cranberry Ice - Rolls**, then insert a horizontal rule below the text.
7. Apply a style to the text you added in Step 6.
8. Compare your screen to Figure 22, then save and close the template.
9. Create a new file based on the recipes template and name it **recipes.html**, overwriting the original recipes.html file.
10. Close the new recipes page.
11. Create another new page based on the recipes template, and name it **rolls.html**.
12. Using the rolls.doc Data File, replace the editable regions text in the rolls.html file with the rolls text from the Word file.
13. Replace the cranberry_ice.jpg image with the rolls.jpg image, then type **Rolls** as the alternate text, adding V Space of 10 and H Space of 20 if necessary.
14. Apply styles to all text, preview the page in the browser, compare your screen to Figure 23, then save your work.
15. Close the browser, then open the recipes template and link the text under the navigation bar as follows: Cranberry Ice to recipes.html, and Rolls to rolls.html.
16. Save and close the template, updating the pages based on the template.
17. Save all files, preview the pages in the browser, testing all links, then close the browser and make any spacing adjustments as needed.
18. Close and save all open files.

**FIGURE 22**

*Completed Project Builder 2*

**FIGURE 23**

*Completed Project Builder 2*

# DESIGN PROJECT

There are many sources available to you with templates that can be downloaded to use to build web pages. Many of them are available for nominal fees. One such site is Yahoo!. The website pictured in Figure 24 was built from a template downloaded from the Yahoo! website.

1. Connect to the Internet, then go to www.yahootemplates.com

2. Spend some time exploring the templates on this site by previewing several of them.

3. Think of an idea for a new site that you would like to create. The site can be for a club, organization, event, or any topic or person that interests you. Draw an outline and a sketch of the site, including the content that will be on each page.

4. After you have completed your sketch, look through the Yahoo! templates available, then choose an appropriate template for your site.

5. Explain why you chose this particular template.

6. Seach for other sites on the Internet that offer templates for downloading.

7. List three sites that you found and the prices listed for downloading each template.

**FIGURE 24**
*Design Project*

*Grace Swanson website used with permission from Grace Swanson – www.graceswanson.com*

In this assignment, you will continue to work on the website that you created in earlier chapters.

You will continue to enhance your site by using templates. You will first create a template from one of your existing pages and define editable regions in it. You will then apply the template to a page and add content to the editable regions.

1. Consult your storyboard and decide which page you would like to save as a template. You will use the template to create at least one other page in your site.

2. Create a sketch of the template page you will create. Mark the page elements that will be in locked regions. Identify and mark at least one area that will be an editable region.

3. Create a new template, then define the editable regions in the template.

4. Make any necessary formatting adjustments to make sure it looks attractive, and then save the template. Create a new page based on the template, using the same name as the page on which the template is based, so that the earlier version of the page is overwritten.

5. Apply the template to another existing page in the site, making sure to delete all repeating elements contained in the template.

6. Review the template(s) and the template-based pages, and decide if you need to make improvements. Use the checklist in Figure 25 to make sure you completed everything according to the assignment.

7. Make any necessary changes.

8. Save your work, then close all open pages.

**FIGURE 25**

*Portfolio Project checklist*

Website Checklist
1. Does your template include at least one editable region?
2. Are all links on templates-based pages document-relative?
3. Do all editable regions have appropriate names?
4. Do all links work correctly?
5. Do all pages look good using at least two different browsers?

chapter

# 12

# WORKING WITH LIBRARY
## ITEMS AND SNIPPETS

1. Create and modify library items

2. Add library items to pages

3. Add and modify snippets

# 12 WORKING WITH LIBRARY
## ITEMS AND SNIPPETS

### Introduction

When creating a website, chances are good that you will want certain graphics or text blocks to appear in more than one place in the site. For instance, you might want the company tag line in several different places, or a footer containing links to the main pages of the site at the bottom of every page. Library items and snippets can help you work with these repeating elements more efficiently.

### Understanding Library Items

If you want an element to appear repeatedly, then it's a good idea to save it as a library item. A **library item** is content that can contain text or graphics and is saved in a separate file in the Library folder of your website. The advantage of using library items is that when you make a change to

the library item and then update the site, all instances of that item throughout the website will be updated to reflect the change.

### Understanding Snippets

Another way to use the same content repeatedly throughout a site is to insert code snippets. **Code snippets** are reusable pieces of code that can be inserted on a page. Dreamweaver provides a variety of ready-made code snippets you can use to create footers, drop-down menus, headers, and other page elements. Code snippets are stored in the Snippets panel and can be used on any open page in any website.

In this chapter, you will work with library items and code snippets to enhance The Striped Umbrella website.

# Tools You'll Use

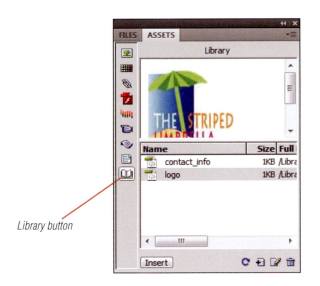

Library button

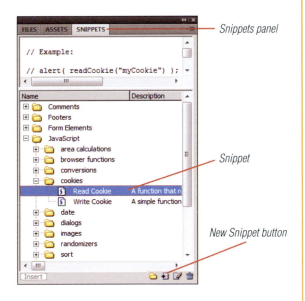

Snippets panel

Snippet

New Snippet button

Open Library item button

12-3

# CREATE AND MODIFY
## LIBRARY ITEMS

## What You'll Do

*In this lesson, you will create a text-based library item. You will also create a library item that contains an image in the activities_pages template. You will then edit both library items and update the site to reflect those edits.*

### Understanding the Benefits of Library Items

Using library items for repetitive elements—especially those that need to be updated frequently—can save you considerable time. For instance, suppose you want to feature an employee of the month photograph on every page in your site. You could create a library item named employee_photo and add it to every page. Then, when you need to update the site to show a new employee photo, you could simply replace the photo contained in the library item, and the photo would be updated throughout the site. Library items can contain a wide range of content, including text, images, tables, Flash files, and sounds.

### Viewing and Creating Library Items

To view library items, show the Assets panel, then click the Library button. The library items appear in a list, and a preview of the selected library item appears above the list, as shown in Figure 1. To save text or an image as a library item, select the item in the Document window, and then drag it to the Library on the Assets panel. You can also click Modify on the Application bar (Win) or Menu bar (Mac), point to Library, and then click Add Object to Library. The item that you added will appear in the preview window on the Assets panel and in the library item list with the temporary name Untitled assigned to it. Type a new name, and then press [Enter] (Win) or [return] (Mac) to give the library item a meaningful name. Library items on a web page appear in shaded yellow in the Document window, but not in the browser. When you click a library item in the Document window, the entire item is selected and the Property inspector changes to display three buttons that you can use to work with the library item, as shown in Figure 2.

**QUICK**TIP

You can also view a list of available library items by expanding the Library folder in the Files panel.

## Modifying Library Items

You cannot edit library items on the web pages in which they appear. To make changes to a library item, you have to open it. To open a library item, select the item in the Document window, and then click Open in the Property inspector. The library item will appear in the Document window, where you can make edits or add content to it. When you are satisfied with your edits, save the library item using the Save command on the File menu. When you do this, the Update Library Items dialog box will appear, asking if you want to update all instances of the library item throughout the site.

**FIGURE 2**
*Web page containing library item*

**FIGURE 1**
*Library items in Assets panel*

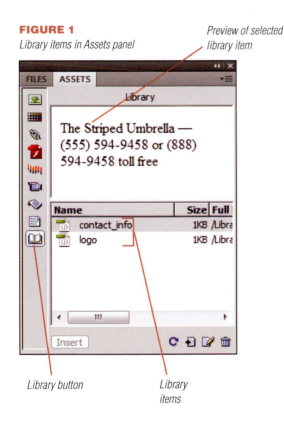

*Preview of selected library item*

*Library button*

*Library items*

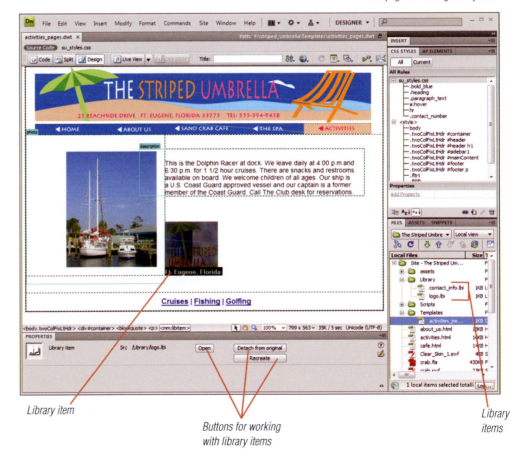

*Library item*

*Buttons for working with library items*

*Library items*

## Create a text-based library item

1. Open The Striped Umbrella website, then open the index page.

2. Create a new class rule in the su_styles.css file called **contact_number** with the following settings: Font-family = **Arial**, **Helvetica**, **sans-serif**, Font-size = **small**, Font-weight = **bold**, color = **#000099**, Text-align = **center**.

3. Move the copyright and last updated statements under the contact information, as shown in Figure 3, then type **The Striped Umbrella 1-555-594-9458** in their previous position in the footer.

4. Apply the **contact_number style** to the text you typed in Step 3.

5. Click to place the insertion point before the telephone number, change to the Text category on the Insert panel, click the **Characters list arrow**, click the **Em Dash button**, then add a space after the Em dash, as shown in Figure 3. (You want a space both before and after the Em dash.)

    TIP You can also insert an Em dash by clicking Insert on the Application bar (Win) or Menu bar (Mac), pointing to HTML, pointing to Special Characters, and clicking Em-Dash.

    *(continued)*

### FIGURE 3
*Inserting an Em dash*

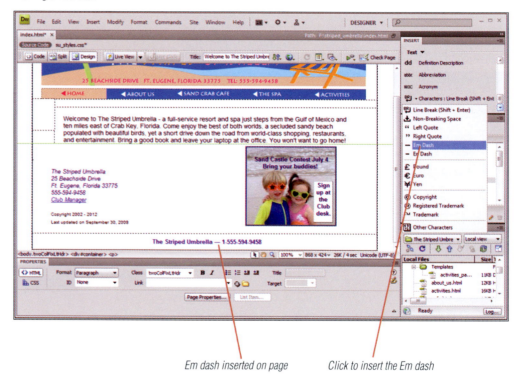

Em dash inserted on page     Click to insert the Em dash

**FIGURE 4**

Assets panel showing new contact_info library item

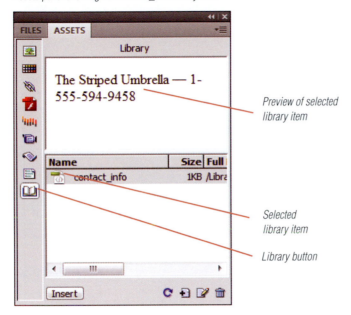

Preview of selected
library item

Selected
library item

Library button

**FIGURE 5**

Viewing the new contact_info library item in Code view

```
259     re. Eugene, Florida 33775<br />
260           555-594-9458<br />
261           <a href="mailto:manager@stripedumbrella.com">Club Manager</a></span></p>
262           <p><span class="paragraph_text"><span class="small_text">Copyright 2002 - 2012 <br />
263   Last updated on
264   <!-- #BeginDate format:Am1 -->
265           September 30, 2008
266           <!-- #EndDate -->
267           </span></span><br class="clearfloat" />
268           </p>
269     </blockquote>
270     <div id="footer">
271        <p class="contact_number"><!-- #BeginLibraryItem "/Library/contact_info.lbi" -->The Striped Umbrella
       &#8212; 1-555-594-9458<!-- #EndLibraryItem --></p>
272     <!-- end #footer --></div>
273   <!-- end #container --></div>
274   </body>
275   </html>
276
```

Code for library item          Library item file extension

6. Display the Assets panel, then click the **Library button**.

7. Select the line of text with the telephone number, then drag it to the Assets panel.

8. Click **OK** to close the dialog box warning you that the library item is not displayed with the style information (if necessary).

   The text that you dragged is now an unnamed library item on the Assets panel.

9. Type **contact_info** in the Name text box to replace "Untitled," press **[Enter]** (Win) or **[return]** (Mac) to name the library item, deselect the library item on the page, refresh the Assets panel if necessary, then compare your Assets panel to Figure 4.

   If you look closely, you will see that the contact information now has a very lightly shaded yellow background on the page behind the text, indicating it is a library item.

   > TIP If you don't see the shading, make sure that Invisible Elements is checked on your View, Visual Aids submenu.

10. Switch to Code view to view the library item, as shown in Figure 5, then switch back to Design view.

    The library item file has the file extension .lbi. The yellow shading is easier to see in Code view.

11. Save all files and close the index.html page.

*You created a text-based library item from text on the index page.*

## Create an image-based library item

1. Click the **Templates button** 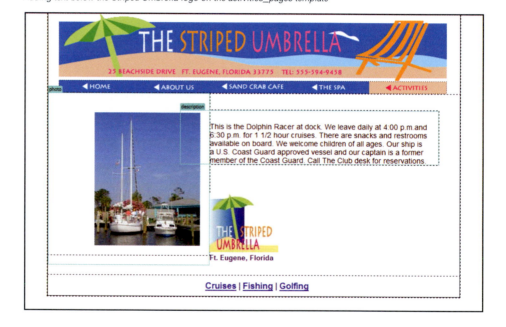 on the Assets panel, then double-click the **activities_pages template** to open it.

2. Click the **Library button** on the Assets panel to display the library item.

3. Place the insertion point in the uneditable region to the right of the boats image and below the text, then insert the **su_logo.jpg** from where you store your Data Files, adding **The Striped Umbrella logo** as the alternate text.

4. Click to the right of the logo, press **[Shift] [Enter]** (Win) or **[Shift][return]** (Mac) to insert a line break, type **Ft. Eugene, Florida**, apply the **bold_blue rule** to the text, then deselect the text, as shown in Figure 6.

   TIP You may need to adjust your spacing before or after the logo and text to match the figure exactly.

5. Select the logo and address, drag the selection to the Library on the Assets panel, then click **OK** to close the dialog box warning you that the style was not copied (if necessary).

   The image and text are stored as one library item and appear in the preview window at the top of the Assets panel. A new untitled library item appears selected in the library item list. (Refresh the Assets panel if it does not appear.)

   *(continued)*

**FIGURE 6**
*Adding text below the Striped Umbrella logo on the activities_pages template*

FIGURE 7
*logo library item added to Assets panel*

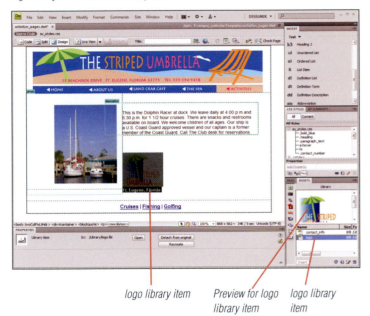

logo library item     Preview for logo    logo library
              library item       item

**FIGURE 8**

*Update Pages dialog box with Library items and Templates check boxes checked*

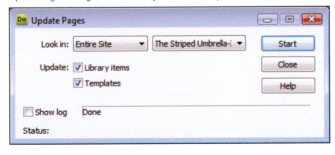

6. Type **logo** to replace "Untitled," press **[Enter]** (Win) or **[return]** (Mac) to name the library item on the Assets panel, then compare your screen to Figure 7.

7. Save your changes, then click **Update** in the Update Template Files dialog box to open the Update Pages dialog box.

8. Click the **Look in list arrow**, click **Entire Site**, check the **Library items** and **Templates** checkboxes, as shown in Figure 8, then click **Start**.

   Dreamweaver updates your files based on the changes made to the library item.

9. Click **Close**, open the golfing and cruises pages to view the library item on the pages. (If the text under the logo on the golfing page is next to the left margin rather than under the logo, click to the right of the golfer image, then enter one paragraph break to force it back under the logo.)

10. Save and close the golfing page, view the library item on the cruises page, then close the cruises page.

*You created a library item named logo that contains an image and text in the activities_pages template. You then saved the template and updated all pages in the site that are based on the template.*

## Edit an image-based library item

1. Click the **logo library item** image at the bottom of the activities_pages template.

2. Click **Open** in the Property inspector, as shown in Figure 9, to open the logo library item.

    The image and text appear in the Document window. The page tab displays the filename logo.lbi. The file extension .lbi denotes a library file.

    TIP You can also open a library item by double-clicking it on the Assets panel.

3. Click the **image** in the Document window, then click the **Crop button** in the Property inspector.

4. Click **OK** to the message warning "The action you are about to perform will permanently alter the selected image."

    An outline surrounds the image, as shown in Figure 10. The outline is used to crop the image.

    *(continued)*

FIGURE 9
*Opening a library item*

Click the Open button to open a library item

FIGURE 10
*Preparing to crop the logo*

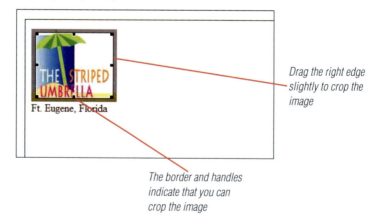

Drag the right edge slightly to crop the image

The border and handles indicate that you can crop the image

**FIGURE 11**

*Viewing the cropped logo*

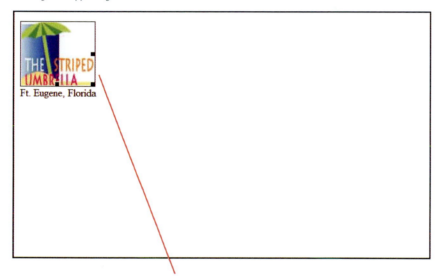

*Edge of image is more in line with text*

5. Drag the right edge toward the center of the image to crop the right edge of the graphic, lining it up with the line of text underneath it.

6. When you are satisfied with the crop, double-click the logo to execute the crop, then compare your screen to Figure 11.

> TIP You can also press [Enter](Win) or [return](Mac) to execute a crop.

*You opened the logo library item, then cropped the image.*

## Update library items

1. Click **File** on the Application bar (Win) or Menu bar (Mac), then click **Save** to open the Update Library Items dialog box.

   The dialog box asks if you want to update the library item on the pages shown.

2. Click **Update** to open the Update Pages dialog box.

3. Click the **Look in list arrow**, click **Entire Site**, check the **Library items** and **Templates** check boxes, then click **Start**.

   Dreamweaver updates the cruises, fishing, golfing, and activities_template files based on the changes you made to the library item.

4. Click **Close**, then close the logo.lbi file.

   The activities_pages template page reflects the change you made to the logo library item.

5. Compare your screen to Figure 12.

6. Save and close the activities_pages template, updating the pages in the site again.

*You saved the logo library item and updated all pages in the site to incorporate the changes you made.*

FIGURE 12

activities_page template showing the updated logo library item

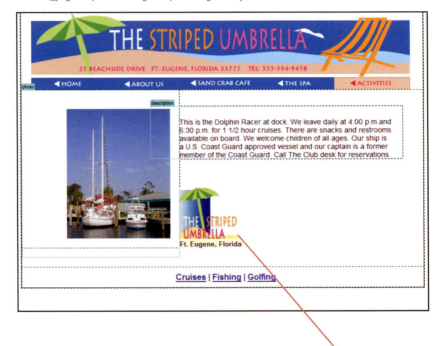

Logo is slightly cropped

**FIGURE 13**

*contact_info library item after editing*

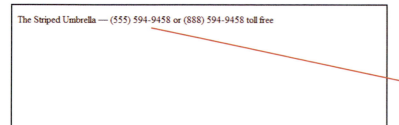

The Striped Umbrella — (555) 594-9458 or (888) 594-9458 toll free

*Phone number edited and toll free number added*

**FIGURE 14**

*Page reflects edits made to contact_info library item.*

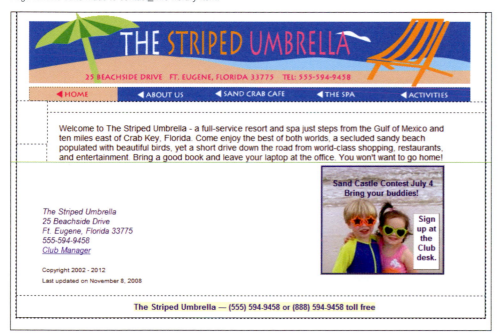

# ADD LIBRARY ITEMS
## TO PAGES

## What You'll Do

 *In this lesson, you will add the text-based library item you created to the about_us, activities, cafe, feedback, and spa pages. You will detach the library item on the index page and edit it. You will then delete one of the library items and restore the deleted item using the Recreate command.*

### Adding Library Items to a Page

Once you create a library item, it's easy to add it to any page in a website. All you do is drag the library item from the Assets panel to the desired location on the page. When you insert a library item, the actual content and a reference to the library item are copied into the code. The inserted library item is shaded in yellow in the Document window and will be automatically updated to reflect any changes you make to the library item.

#### QUICKTIP
You can also insert a library item on a page by selecting the item on the Assets panel, then clicking Insert.

There may be times when you don't want content to be updated when you update the library item. For instance, suppose you want one of your pages to include photos of all past employees of the month. You would insert content from the current library item, but you do not want the photo to change when the library item is updated to reflect next month's employee photo. To achieve this, you would insert the content of a library item on a page, then click the Detach from Original button in the Property inspector. The content from the library item will be inserted on the page, but it will not be linked to the library item.

### Making Library Items Editable on a Page

There may be times when you would like to make changes to a particular instance of a library item on one page, without making those changes to other instances of the library item in the site. You can make a library item editable on a page by breaking its link to the library item. To do this, select the library item, and then click Detach from original in the Property inspector. Once you have detached the library item, you can edit the content like you would any other element on the page. Keep in mind, though, that this edited content will not be updated when you make changes to the library item.

## Deleting and Recreating Library Items

If you know that you will never need to use a library item again, you might want to delete it. To delete a library item, select it on the Assets panel, and then click the Delete button. Deleting a library item removes it from only the Library folder; it does not change the contents of the pages that con-

tain that library item. All instances of the deleted library item will still appear in shaded yellow in the site unless you detach them from the original. Be aware that you cannot use the Undo command to restore a library item. However, you can restore a library item by selecting any instance of the item in the site and clicking Recreate in the Property inspector. You can also recreate a

library item after you have exited and started Dreamweaver again, provided a deleted library item still has an instance remaining on a page. After you recreate a library item, it reappears on the Assets panel and you can make changes to it and update all pages in the site again. Figure 15 shows the Property inspector with Library item settings.

**FIGURE 15**

*Property inspector with Library item settings*

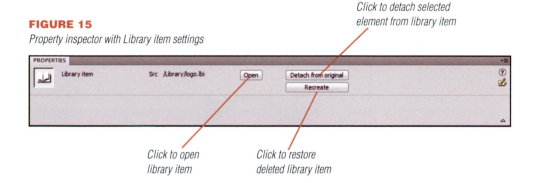

*Click to detach selected element from library item*

*Click to open library item*

*Click to restore deleted library item*

## Add a library item to a page

1. Open the about_us page.

2. Delete the copyright statement at the bottom of the page.

3. Open the Assets panel (if necessary), drag the **contact_info library item** from the Assets panel to the location from where you deleted the copyright statement, then click to deselect the library item.

   The contact_info heading now appears where you placed it. Notice that it is shaded in yellow, indicating it is a library item.

4. Click to the right of the library item on the page, then use the Property inspector to apply the **bold_blue rule**.

5. Deselect the text, then compare your screen to Figure 16.

*(continued)*

FIGURE 16

*about_us page with library item added*

Registration hours:
8:00 a.m. until 6:00 p.m.

The main swimming pool is directly behind The Club House. A lifeguard is on duty from 8:00 a.m. until 9:00 p.m. The pool area includes a wading pool, a lap pool, and a large pool with a diving board. Showers are located in several areas for your use before and after swimming. We also provide poolside service from the cafe for snacks and lunch.

If you would like to play tennis, we have a very nice sports club. Call to reserve court times. Our clay courts are generally busy, so it's not a bad idea to schedule your games as soon as you arrive. We also have a very extensive pro shop where you can find anything you need to play. We can even restring your racket if the need arises. After you arrive, you will want to take a stroll down the boardwalk to the beach. The entrance to the boardwalk is just past the pool area. The boardwalk provides a safe route to the beach for both our guests and the native vegetation. The sea oats and other flora are tender. Please do not step on them or pick them.

Please give us your feedback so that we may make your next stay the best vacation ever.

The Striped Umbrella — (555) 594-9458 or (888) 594-9458 toll free

Library item

**FIGURE 17**
*activities page with library item added*

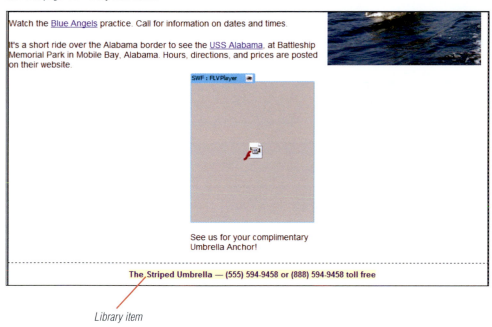

Watch the Blue Angels practice. Call for information on dates and times.

It's a short ride over the Alabama border to see the USS Alabama, at Battleship Memorial Park in Mobile Bay, Alabama. Hours, directions, and prices are posted on their website.

SWF : FLV Player

See us for your complimentary Umbrella Anchor!

The Striped Umbrella — (555) 594-9458 or (888) 594-9458 toll free

Library item

6. Save and close the about_us page.

7. Repeat Steps 2 through 5 to add the **contact_info** library item to the activities page, as shown in Figure 17, then continue with the activities_pages template and the cafe, feedback, and spa pages.

If the page has a copyright statement, delete it before you add the library item. Remember to apply the bold_blue rule to each library item after you add it to a page.

8. Save and preview all of the edited pages in the browser, then close the browser.

9. Close all open pages.

*You added the contact_info library item to the about_us, activities, cafe, feedback, and spa pages.*

## Creating library items

Although you can create library items with images, text, or a combination of the two, you can use only items that contain body elements. For instance, when editing a library item, the CSS Styles panel will be unavailable because style sheet code is embedded in the head section, rather than just the body section. Likewise, the Page Properties dialog box will be unavailable because library items cannot include a body tag attribute such as text color. You can apply a rule after you have placed the library item on the page.

## Make a library item editable on a page

1. Open the index page, then click the **contact_info library item** in the page footer.

   The Property inspector displays three buttons relating to library items.

2. Click **Detach from original** in the Property inspector.

   A dialog box opens, warning you that the item will no longer be automatically updated when the original library item changes.

3. Click **OK**.

   Notice that the contact information no longer appears in shaded yellow, indicating it is no longer a library item.

4. Type **in Florida** after the first telephone number, then compare your screen to Figure 18.

   The contact information is edited on the page.

5. Save and close the index page.

*You detached the contact information from the contact_info library item to make the text editable on the index page. You then added two words to the contact information.*

**FIGURE 18**

*Editing a library on a page*

"in Florida"
added to text

**FIGURE 19**

*Assets panel after deleting the logo library item*

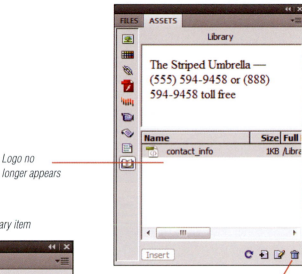

Logo no
longer appears

**FIGURE 20**

*Assests panel after recreating the logo library item*

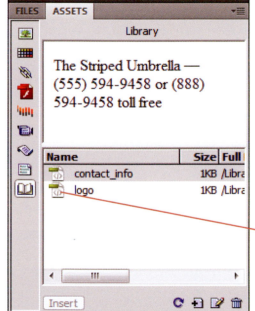

Recreated logo
library item

Delete button

## Delete a library item

1. Select the **logo library item** on the Assets panel.

2. Click the **Delete button** 🗑 on the Assets panel.

    A dialog box opens, asking if you are sure you want to delete the library item.

3. Click **Yes**, then compare your screen to Figure 19.

    The logo library item no longer appears on the Assets panel. Mac users may need to select the contact_info library item to see the change.

*You deleted the logo library item on the Assets panel.*

## Recreate a library item

1. Open the activities_pages template.

    The logo still appears in shaded yellow, indicating it is still a library item, even though you deleted the library item to which it is attached.

2. Click the **logo** to select it.

3. Click **Recreate** in the Property inspector, then compare your screen to Figure 20.

    The logo library item is added to the Assets panel.

    If you do not see the logo library item, refresh the Assets panel.

4. Close the activities_pages template.

*You recreated the logo library item that you deleted in the previous set of steps.*

# ADD AND MODIFY
## SNIPPETS

## What You'll Do

*In this lesson, you will add a predefined snippet from the Snippets panel to create a new footer for the index page. You will then replace the placeholder text and links in the snippet with appropriate text and links. Finally, you will save the modified snippet as a new snippet and add it to other pages.*

## Using the Snippets Panel

Creating a website is a huge task, so it's nice to know that you can save time by using ready-made code snippets to create various elements in your site. The Snippets panel, located in the Files panel group, contains a large collection of reusable code snippets organized in folders and named by element type. The Snippets panel contains two panes, as shown in Figure 21. The lower pane contains folders that can be expanded to view the snippets. The upper pane displays a preview of the selected snippet. Use the buttons at the bottom of the Snippets panel to insert a snippet, create a new folder in the Snippets panel, create a new snippet, edit a snippet, or remove a snippet.

## Inserting and Modifying Snippets

Adding a snippet to a page is an easy task; simply drag the snippet from the Snippets panel to the desired location on the page. Once you position a snippet, you will need to replace the placeholder text, links, and images with appropriate content.

### QUICKTIP

You can also add a snippet to a page by selecting the snippet in the Snippets panel, then clicking the Insert button on the Snippets panel.

## Creating New Snippets

Once you've modified a snippet so that it contains text and graphics appropriate for your site, you might want to save it with a new name. Doing this will save time when using this snippet on other pages. To save a modified snippet as a new snippet, select the snippet content in the Document window, and then click the New Snippet button in the Snippets panel to open the Snippet dialog box. Use this dialog box to name the snippet and give it a description. Because the Snippet dialog box displays the snippet code, you can make edits to the code here if you wish. Any new snippets you create will appear in the Snippets panel.

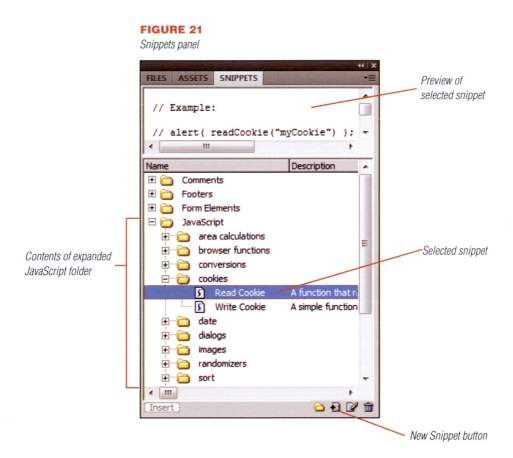

**FIGURE 21**
*Snippets panel*

*Preview of selected snippet*

*Contents of expanded JavaScript folder*

*Selected snippet*

*New Snippet button*

## Add a predefined snippet to a page

1. Open the index page.

2. Scroll to the bottom of the page, click to the right of the contact telephone numbers, then add a paragraph break.

3. Click **Window** on the Application bar (Win) or Menu bar (Mac), then click **Snippets** to open the Snippets panel.

4. Click the **plus sign (+)** (Win) or the **triangle** (Mac) next to the Footers folder in the Snippets panel to display the contents of the Footers folder.

5. Drag **Basic: Text Block** in the Footer folder to the bottom of the index page, under the contact telephone numbers, as shown in Figure 22.

   This text will serve as placeholder text until you replace it with the appropriate links for The Striped Umbrella website.

   TIP Having a navigation bar with plain text links on each main page of a website ensures maximum accessibility for users.

6. Save your changes.

*You added a predefined navigation bar from the Snippets panel.*

**FIGURE 22**

*Index page after inserting snippet*

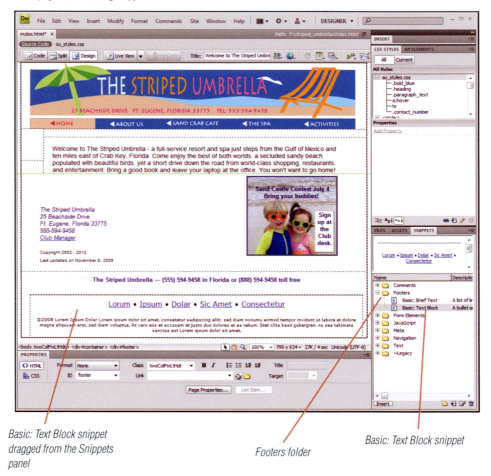

Basic: Text Block snippet dragged from the Snippets panel

Footers folder

Basic: Text Block snippet

**FIGURE 23**

Index page after editing snippet placeholder text

Welcome to The Striped Umbrella - a full-service resort and spa just steps from the Gulf of Mexico and ten miles east of Crab Key, Florida. Come enjoy the best of both worlds, a secluded sandy beach populated with beautiful birds, yet a short drive down the road from world-class shopping, restaurants, and entertainment. Bring a good book and leave your laptop at the office. You won't want to go home!

*The Striped Umbrella*
*25 Beachside Drive*
*Ft. Eugene, Florida 33775*
*555-594-9458*
*Club Manager*

Last updated on November 8, 2008

**The Striped Umbrella — (555) 594-9458 in Florida or (888) 594-9458 toll free**

Lorum • Ipsum • Dolar • Sic Amet • Consectetur

Copyright 2002 - 2012

*Move the copyright statement from this location*

*Placeholder text is replaced with current copyright statement*

## Modify snippet text

1. Select the placeholder paragraph under the placeholder links, then press **[Delete]**.

   You will use the current copyright statement rather than the placeholder text.

2. Cut the current copyright statement (which is under the Club Manager e-mail link) and paste it under the Snippet placeholder links, as shown in Figure 23.

3. If you have extra space left between the e-mail link and the last updated statement, click in front of the last updated statement, then press **[Backspace]**.

4. Save your work, then compare your screen to Figure 23.

*You edited the placeholder text contained in the navigation snippet on the index page.*

## Modify snippet links

1. Select the **Lorum placeholder link**, then type **Home**.

2. Replace the Ipsum placeholder link with **About Us**, replace the Dolor placeholder link with **Sand Crab Cafe**, replace the Sic Amet placeholder link with **The Spa**, then replace the Consectetur placeholder link with **Activities**.

3. Select all of the text in the snippet (including the copyright statement) and apply the **contact_number** rule.

4. Display the Files panel, select the **Home link text** in the footer at the bottom of the home page, then use the Point to File icon ⊕ in the Property inspector to set the Link property to the index page, as shown in Figure 24.

5. Use the Point to File icon ⊕ to set the Link property for the About Us, Sand Crab Cafe, The Spa, and Activities links.

6. Save your changes.

7. Preview the index page in your browser, test all the new navigation links, then close your browser.

8. If your AP element is on top of the contact footer, insert one or two paragraph breaks before the contact footer, then save and preview the page again.

*You changed the names of the placeholder links and used the Point to File icon to create links to the five main pages in The Striped Umbrella website.*

**FIGURE 24**

*Using the Point to File icon to create document-relative links in the new links*

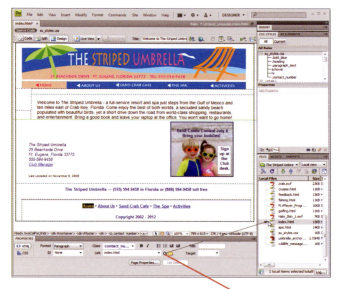

*Point to File icon*

### Hosting a website

You have learned how to publish your site using an Internet service provider. You may decide, however, that you would prefer to host your own site. First, you would need to set up a web server by installing software on a computer, such as Apache or IIS (the Microsoft Internet Information Services). Both are free to use. Apache will run on Windows and Linux. IIS will run on a Windows Server operating system, such as Windows 2003 server. Next, you would need to register the domain name that will be used to access the site. You can register and purchase a permanent domain name at www.networksolutions.com. You would also need the appropriate software to provide security for your site to protect hackers from infiltrating your system. There are many books available to help you install and set up a web server. A search on the Internet will provide a wealth of information. Begin with the Adobe website. Go to www.adobe.com and type "web server" in the search text box to view helpful information about web servers. The NetworkSolutions website is another good resource for information about servers and hosting sites.

FIGURE 25

Selecting the code for the snippet

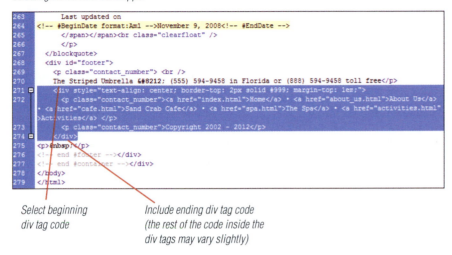

```
263        Last updated on
264 <!-- #BeginDate format:Am1 -->November 9, 2008<!-- #EndDate -->
265        </span></span><br class="clearfloat" />
266        </p>
267  </blockquote>
268  <div id="footer">
269  <p class="contact_number"> <br />
270  The Striped Umbrella &#8212; (555) 594-9458 in Florida or (888) 594-9458 toll free</p>
271    <div style="text-align: center; border-top: 2px solid #999; margin-top: 1em;">
272    <p class="contact_number"><a href="index.html">Home</a> • <a href="about_us.html">About Us</a>
• <a href="cafe.html">Sand Crab Cafe</a> • <a href="spa.html">The Spa</a> • <a href="activities.html"
>Activities</a> </p>
273        <p class="contact_number">Copyright 2002 - 2012</p>
274    </div>
275 <p> </p>
276 <!-- end #footer --></div>
277 <!-- end #container --></div>
278 </body>
279 </html>
```

Select beginning
div tag code

Include ending div tag code
(the rest of the code inside the
div tags may vary slightly)

**FIGURE 26**

Snippet dialog box

Name text box

| | |
|---|---|
| Snippet | |
| Name: | su_footer |
| Description: | This is a text-based navigation bar and copyright statement. |

OK
Cancel
Help

Description text
box

Snippet type: ● Wrap selection     ○ Insert block

Insert before:
```
<div style="text-align: center; border-top: 2px solid #999; m
    <p class="contact_number"><a href="index.html">Home<
    <p class="contact_number">Copyright 2002 - 2012</p>
</div>
```

Code starts
with <div

Insert after:

Preview type: ● Design     ○ Code

1. Select the **navigation footer** on the index page in Code view, as shown in Figure 25, being sure to select the entire div tag code so both lines of text and their formatting are selected.

2. Select the Footers folder in the Snippets panel, then click the **New Snippet button** to open the Snippet dialog box.

3. Type **su_footer** in the Name text box.

4. Type **This is a text-based navigation bar and copyright statement**. In the Description text box, compare your screen to Figure 26, then click **OK**.

   The new snippet is added to the Snippets panel.

5. Open the about_us page, change to Design view, place the insertion point to the right of the telephone contact information, press **[Enter]** (Win) or **[return]** (Mac), then drag the **su_footer** from the Snippets panel to the page.

   You can also double-click a snippet to insert it on a page.

6. Repeat Step 5 to insert the **su_footer snippet** on all pages in the website, including the activities_pages template.

7. Save and preview all open pages in the browser, close the browser, make any necessary spacing adjustments, then close all open pages.

8. Run reports for Untitled Documents, Missing Alt Text, Broken Links, Orphaned Files, and non-Websafe Colors; then correct any errors.

9. Publish your completed site, then exit Dreamweaver.

*You copied the text-based navigation bar from the index page and saved it as a snippet called su_footer. You then copied it to the rest of the main pages.*

### Create and modify library items.

1. Open the blooms & bulbs website, then open the index page.
2. Create a new class rule in the blooms_styles.css file called telephone with the following settings: Font-family: Verdana, Geneva, sans-serif; Font-size: 14 pixels; Font-weight: bold; Font-style: normal; Color: #003; Text-align: **center**.
3. Insert a new paragraph above the copyright statement, type **blooms & bulbs 555-248-0806**, then apply the telephone rule to the text. (*Hint*: You may need to enter several paragraph or line breaks to be able to see the text below the AP element.)
4. Select the text you typed in Step 3, drag it to the Assets panel with the Library category displayed to create a new library item, then name it **telephone**.
5. Select only the copyright and last updated statements, then create a new library item named **copyright_update**.
6. Edit the telephone library item to add parentheses around the area code and remove the hyphen, then save the library item, update all pages with the library item, then close the library item.
7. Open the newsletter page, insert **blooms_logo.jpg** from where you store your Data Files right after the e-mail link near the bottom of the page, then type **blooms & bulbs logo** as the alternate text.
8. Right-align the logo, then drag it to the Assets panel to create a new library item, then name it **logo**.
9. Save and close the newsletter page and blooms_styles.css file.

### Add library items to pages.

1. Open the classes page, then delete the copyright statement.
2. Insert the telephone library item where you just deleted the copyright statement, click to the right of the library item, then apply the telephone rule to it.
3. Enter a paragraph break, then insert the copyright_update library item under the telephone library item.
4. Switch to the index page, then move the .small_text rule to the blooms_styles.css style sheet.
5. Edit the small_text rule by adding the Text-align = center property.
6. Switch back to the classes page, click in front of the copyright_update library item, then apply the small_text rule to the copyright_update library item.
7. Repeat Steps 1, 2, and 3 to add the telephone and copyright_update library items to the newsletter, plants, tips, and plant_categories pages, then apply the telephone style and the small_text styles to the library items on each page. (Delete any existing copyright statements and update the template files after you add the library items to the template page.)
8. Save all pages.
9. Delete the telephone library item from the Assets panel.
10. Switch to the index page, select the telephone library item on the page, then re-create it.
11. Insert a horizontal rule immediately before the telephone library item on the plants and newsletter pages. (*Hint*: The tips, classes, and index pages already have a horizontal rule at the bottom of the page. The horizontal rules will automatically be formatted with the .hr rule in the blooms_styles.css file.)
12. Save your work and preview all pages in the browser, then adjust the spacing to prevent overlaps.

### Add and modify snippets.

1. Scroll to the bottom of the index page and insert a paragraph break after the copyright_update library item.
2. Insert the **Basic: TextBlock snippet** in the new line, then delete the horizontal rule to prevent having two rules on the page. (*Hint*: You may need to use the Insert button on the Snippets panel.)

3. Replace the placeholder links in the footer with text to link to the home, plants, tips, classes, and newsletter pages.

4. Create a link for each link in the navigation bar to the appropriate page.

5. Delete the paragraph under the links in the snippet.

6. Create a new snippet from the footer you just inserted. Name the snippet **blooms_nav_footer**, give it an appropriate description, then apply the telephone rule to the footer.

7. Insert the new footer at the bottom of the classes, newsletter, plants, and tips pages.

8. Insert the footer at the bottom of the plant_categories.dwt page (you may need to use the Insert button instead of dragging), then update all pages based on the template.

9. Delete the a:hover rule from the CSS Styles panel so your navigation footer will be displayed as plain text links.

10. Save all pages, then preview each page in the browser to test the links in the footer to make sure they work, as shown in Figure 27.

11. Close the browser, then close all open pages.

12. Run reports for Untitled Documents, Missing Alt Text, Broken Links, Orphaned Files, and non-Websafe Colors; then correct any errors that you find.

13. Publish your completed site, then exit Dreamweaver.

**FIGURE 27**
*Completed Skills Review*

In this Project Builder, you will continue your work on the TripSmart website. You have been given the TripSmart logo to use in the website and decide to create a library item from the logo combined with the copyright statement.

1. Open the TripSmart website, then open the index page.
2. Place the insertion point after the last updated statement, then enter a paragraph break.
3. Insert the file tripsmart_logo.jpg from where you store your Data Files onto the page, adding **TripSmart logo** for the alternate text.
4. Drag the copyright statement to the right of the logo, then apply the item_numbers rule.
5. Select both the logo and copyright statement, then use them to create a new library item named **logo**.
6. Save the file, preview the page in the browser, make any necessary spacing adjustments to improve the page appearance, then compare your screen to Figure 28.
7. Close the browser.
8. Open the services page, then insert a paragraph break after the last line on the page.
9. Drag the logo library item onto the page, then apply the item_numbers rule.
10. Repeat Steps 8 and 9 to add the logo library item to the rest of the pages in the website. (*Hint*: To add the logo library item to the accessories and clothing pages, add it to the catalog_pages.dwt file, replacing the existing copyright statement.)
11. Save the file, then preview the page in the browser.
12. Close the browser, then make any necessary adjustments to improve the page appearance.
13. Close all files, run reports for Untitled Documents, Missing Alt Text, Broken Links, Orphaned Files, and non-Websafe Colors, then correct any errors that you find.
14. Publish your completed site, then exit Dreamweaver.

**FIGURE 28**

*Sample Project Builder 1*

In this Project Builder, you will continue your work on the Carolyne's Creations website. Chef Carolyne has asked you to add some plain text links at the bottom of each page to provide viewers with more accessible links that do not depend on the image map at the top of each page.

1. Open the Carolyne's Creations website.
2. Open the index page.
3. Insert one or two line breaks after the last updated statement.
4. Insert the Pipe as Separator snippet. (*Hint*: This snippet is located in the Snippets panel. Open the ~Legacy folder, then the Navigation folder, and finally the Horizontal folder.)
5. Delete the two cells with the last text placeholder and pipe, then replace each remaining placeholder with links to the main pages, using Figure 29 as a guide.
6. Apply the paragraph_text rule to the navigation bar, set the table width to 55%, then center it.
7. Click the table tag in the tag selector to select the table with the navigation links, then save it as a new snippet named cc_nav_bar.
8. Insert a horizontal rule that is 80% wide and centered above the navigation bar.
9. Save your work, then preview the page in the browser.
10. Close the browser, then insert the horizontal line and navigation bar snippet at the bottom of the adults, children, classes, catering, recipes template, and shop pages.
11. Make any adjustments to the pages to improve the appearance, save your work, then preview each page in the browser.
12. Close the browser, then close all open pages.
13. Run reports for Untitled Documents, Missing Alt Text, Broken Links, Orphaned Files, and non-Websafe Colors; then correct any errors.
14. Publish your completed site, then exit Dreamweaver.

**FIGURE 29**
*Completed Project Builder 2*

# DESIGN PROJECT

Library items and snippets are commonly used in websites to ensure that repetitive information is updated quickly and accurately.

1. Connect to the Internet, then go to *www.usa.gov* as shown in Figure 30.
2. Spend some time exploring the pages of this site to become familiar with its elements. Do you see many repeating elements?
3. If you were developing this site, which images or text would you convert into library items? Print two pages from this website and write a list of some of the text and visual elements from these pages that you would make into library items.
4. Write a list of all the elements shown on the printed pages that you think should be made into library items.

**FIGURE 30**

*Figure 30 Design Project*

*USA.gov website - www.usa.gov29*

In this project, you will continue to work on the website that you created in Chapter 1.

You will continue to enhance your website by using library items and snippets.

1. Consult your storyboard and decide which text and graphic elements in the site should be converted into library items. Write a list of these items.
2. Discuss what content to include in a footer that you will add to each page of the site using a snippet.
3. Convert all the text elements you identified in your list into library items.
4. Insert the library items that you created in Step 3 in appropriate places in the website.
5. Convert all the graphic elements you identified in Step 1 into library items.
6. Insert the graphic library items that you created in Step 5 in appropriate places in the website.
7. Edit two of the library items that you created, then save and update all instances of the library item in the site.
8. Add a footer to the website using one of the snippets in the Footers folder of the Snippets panel. Replace all placeholder links with appropriate links to each major page in the site and replace placeholder text with text that is suitable for your site.
9. Create a new snippet from the footer that was created in Step 8. Insert this snippet on the other pages of the site.
10. Save your work, preview all pages in a browser, then test all the links. Use the checklist in Figure 31 to make sure your website is complete.
11. Make any necessary changes, then save and close all open pages.
12. Run reports for Untitled Documents, Missing Alt Text, Broken Links, Orphaned Files, and non-Websafe Colors; then correct any errors that you find.
13. Publish your completed site, then exit Dreamweaver.

**FIGURE 31**
*Portfolio Project checklist*

> **Website Checklist**
> 1. Have you converted all repeating text elements into library items?
> 2. Have you converted all repeating graphic elements, such as logos, into library items?
> 3. Did you save and update the library items after making edits to them?
> 4. Do all links work?
> 5. Did you add the footer to all pages in the website?

## Dreamweaver CS4
ACE Exam Objectives

| Topic Area | Objectives | Chapter Number | Page Number |
|---|---|---|---|
| **1.0 Understanding Web technologies** | 1.1 List and describe the infrastructure required to implement and deploy websites. | Chapter 1<br>Chapter 6<br>Chapter 8<br>Chapter 12 | 1-24, 6-2,<br>8-5, 8-6,<br>8-7, 8-31,<br>12-24 |
| | 1.2 Given a scenario, explain the requirements for supporting video, PDF documents, and SWF. | Chapter 2<br>Chapter 10 | 2-2, 10-2,<br>10-4 |
| | 1.3 Explain how to mitigate page weight. | Chapter 2<br>Chapter 8 | 2-2, 2-32,<br>8-4 |
| | 1.4 Given a scenario, describe the infrastructure required to support application servers. (Scenarios include: ColdFusion, ASP, JSP) | Chapter 8 | 8-5, 8-7,<br>8-9 |
| | 1.5 List and describe the difference between client-side and server-side scripting. | Chapter 4<br>Chapter 5<br>Chapter 8 | 4-16, 5-6,<br>8-5, 8-9 |
| | 1.6 Describe techniques for making pages accessible. | Chapter 2<br>Chapter 3<br>Chapter 4<br>Chapter 5 | 2-5, 3-33,<br>3-39, 4-24,<br>5-28 |
| **2.0 Managing sites** | 2.1 Given a scenario, create a site. (Scenarios include: using the Site menu bar and Files panel) | Chapter 1 | 1-28, 1-32,<br>1-33 |
| | 2.2 Locate files associated with a Dreamweaver site. | Chapter 3<br>Chapter 6 | 3-35, 3-38,<br>6-11, 6-12,<br>6-13 |
| | 2.3 Manage files associated with a Dreamweaver site. (Including: moving, deleting, renaming, copying, associating) | Chapter 3<br>Chapter 6 | 3-34, 3-35,<br>3-38, 6-30<br>through 6-33 |

**CERTIFICATION GRID**

| Topic Area | Objective | Chapter Number | Page Number |
|---|---|---|---|
| **3.0 Remote connectivity** | 3.1 List and describe the methods available for connecting to a remote server. (Methods include: ftp, sftp, WebDAV, and network file share) | Chapter 1<br>Chapter 6 | 1-21, 1-25, 6-14, 6-15, 6-16, 6-17 through 6-20 |
| | 3.2 Synchronize files. (Methods include: Using the Files panel, Site menu, cloaking) | Chapter 6 | 6-16, 6-21, 6-26 through 6-29 |
| | 3.3 Use get, put, check-in, and check-out to transfer files. | Chapter 6 | 6-15, 6-20, 6-22 through 6-25 |
| | 3.4 Configure local, testing, and remote servers. | Chapter 1<br>Chapter 8 | 1-21, 1-25, 8-31 |
| **4.0 Working in Design view** | 4.1 Describe options available for positioning objects. (Options include: AP DIV, CSS, and tables) | Chapter 1<br>Chapter 5<br>Chapter 9 | 1-4, Chapter 5, Chapter 9 |
| | 4.2 Design a page by using a tracing image. | Chapter 5 | 5-5 |
| | 4.3 Given a visual aid, explain the purpose of and/or when that visual aid would be useful. (Visual aids include: Layers, tables, CSS, invisible elements) | Chapter 4<br>Chapter 5 | 4-10, 4-12, 5-5, 5-14, 5-18, 5-19, 5-30, 5-37 |
| | 4.4 Work with the Properties panel and Tag bar. | Chapter 3<br>Chapter 4<br>Chapter 8 | 3-6 through 3-9, 4-5 through 4-8, 4-14, 4-15, 4-22, 4-24, 4-26, 8-19, 8-20, 8-21, 8-22, 8-23, 8-26, 8-28, 8-29 |
| | 4.5 Explain the benefits of using Live View and Live Data. | Chapter 1<br>Chapter 8<br>Chapter 10 | 1-10, 8-31, 10-19 |

| Topic Area | Objective | Chapter Number | Page Number |
|---|---|---|---|
| **5.0 Working in Code view** | 5.1 Configure preferences for Code view. | Chapter 7 | 7-27 |
| | 5.2 Manage code by using Code view. (Options include: Collapsing, word wrap, highlighting invalid code, and formatting) | Chapter 7 | 7-27 through 7-29 |
| | 5.3 Explain how to get information about tags. (Options include: Properties Inspector and Tag Editor) | Chapter 2 | 2-8, 2-27 |
| | 5.4 Find and replace code in Code view. (Options include: entire site and current page) | Chapter 6 | 6-7 |
| | 5.5 Explain how to select blocks of code in Code view. | Chapter 7 | 7-23 |
| **6.0 Working with templates** | 6.1 Create editable areas in templates. | Chapter 11 | 11-4 through 11-9 |
| | 6.2 Apply a template to a page. | Chapter 2 Chapter 11 | 2-6, 11-10 through 11-15 |
| | 6.3 Create and use template variables. | Chapter 11 | 11-20 |
| | 6.4 Create and use editable attributes. | Chapter 11 | 11-21 |
| | 6.5 Explain the process of and issues associated with distributing template changes to pages. | Chapter 11 | 11-16 through 11-19 |
| | 6.6 Create and use library items. | Chapter 12 | Chapter 12 |
| **7.0 Working with assets** | 7.1 Manage assets by using the Assets panel. | Chapter 1 Chapter 2 Chapter 3 Chapter 4 Chapter 6 Chapter 11 | 1-11, 2-23, 3-25, 3-35, 4-9, 4-29, 6-4, 6-7, 11-4, 11-5, 11-6 |
| | 7.2 Given a media type, insert and deploy that media type into a page. (Media types include: SWF, FLV, Flash Paper, images) | Chapter 3 Chapter 10 | 3-22 through 3-39, 10-2, 10-4 through 10-9, 10-18 through 10-21 |

CERTIFICATION GRID

| Topic Area | Objective | Chapter Number | Page Number |
|---|---|---|---|
| **8.0 Designing pages with CSS** | 8.1  Create and work with AP elements. | Chapter 9 | Chapter 9 |
| | 8.2  Create styles for typography and positioning by using the CSS and properties panels. | Chapter 3 Chapter 7 | 3-10 through 3-21, Chapter 7 |
| | 8.3  Describe the Box model. | Chapter 5 | 5-5 |
| | 8.4  Create and attach style sheets to pages. | Chapter 3 Chapter 7 | 3-10 through 3-21, 7-2, 7-4, 7-5, 7-10, 7-11, 7-18, 7-19 |
| | 8.5  Explain the behavior of inheritance with respect to styles and style sheets. | Chapter 7 | 7-24, 7-25 |
| **9.0 Testing Web pages and sites** | 9.1  Validate that pages and sites conform to accessibility standards. | Chapter 6 | 6-9 |
| | 9.2  Describe the HTML reports that are available for testing. | Chapter 6 | 6-4, 6-8, 6-9 |
| | 9.3  Identify and fix broken links. | Chapter 2 Chapter 4 Chapter 6 | 2-18, 4-2, 4-6, 4-28, 4-29, 6-6 |
| **10.0 Application development** | 10.1  Create forms and use data sets by using Spry. | Chapter 8 | 8-11 through 8-29, 8-32, 8-33 |
| | 10.2  Describe the functionality provided by the Behaviors panel. | Chapter 10 | 10-14 through 10-17 |
| | 10.3  Describe the role of an application server. | Chapter 8 | 8-2, 8-5 though 8-7 |

## Read the following information carefully.

### Find out from your instructor the location where you will store your files.

- To complete many of the chapters in this book, you need to use the Data Files provided on the CD at the back of this book.

- Your instructor will tell you whether you will be working from the CD or copying the files to a drive on your computer or on a server. Your instructor will also tell you where you will store the files you create and modify.

- All the Data Files are organized in folders named after the chapter in which they are used. For instance, all Chapter 1 Data Files are stored in the chapter_1 folder. You should leave all the Data Files in these folders; do not move any Data File out of the folder in which it is originally stored.

### Copy and organize your Data Files.

- Copy the folders that contain the Data Files to a USB storage device, network folder, hard drive, or other storage device if you will not be working from the CD.

- As you build each website, the exercises in this book will guide you to copy the Data Files you need from the appropriate Data Files folder to the folder where you are storing the website. Your Data Files should always remain intact because you are copying (and not moving) them to the website.

- Because you will be building a website from one chapter to the next, sometimes you will need to use a Data File that is already contained in the website you are working on.

### Find and keep track of your Data Files and completed files.

- Use the **Data File Supplied** column to make sure you have the files you need before starting the chapter or exercise indicated in the **Chapter** column.

- Sometimes the file listed in the **Data File Supplied** column is one that you created or used in a previous chapter, and that is already part of the website you are working on. For instance, if the file tripsmart/amazon_trip.html is listed in the **Data File Supplied** column, this means that you need to use the amazon_trip.html file in the tripsmart site that you already created.

- Use the **Student Creates File** column to find out the filename you use when saving your new file for the exercise.

## Files used in this book

### Adobe Dreamweaver CS4

| Chapter | Data File Supplied | Student Creates File | Used In |
|---|---|---|---|
| 1 | dw1_1.html<br>about_us.swf<br>accommodations.swf<br>activities.swf<br>cafe.swf<br>index.swf<br>shop.swf<br>spa.swf<br>assets/pool.jpg<br>assets/su_background.jpg<br>assets/su_banner.gif | | Lesson 2 |
| | dw1_2.html<br>assets/su_banner.gif | about_us.html<br>activities.html<br>cafe.html<br>cruises.html<br>fishing.html<br>index.html<br>spa.html | Lesson 4 |
| | dw1_3.html<br>dw1_4.html<br><br>assets/blooms_banner.jpg<br>assets/blooms_logo.jpg | annuals.html<br>classes.html<br>index.html<br>newsletter.html<br>perennials.html<br>plants.html<br>tips.html<br>water_plants.html | Skills Review |
| | dw1_5.html<br>assets/tripsmart_banner.jpg | amazon.html<br>catalog.html<br>destinations.html<br>kenya.html<br>newsletter.html<br>services.html | Project Builder 1 |
| | dw1_6.html<br>assets/cc_banner.jpg | adults.html<br>catering.html<br>children.html<br>classes.html<br>recipes.html<br>shop.html | Project Builder 2 |

| Chapter | Data File Supplied | Student Creates File | Used In |
|---|---|---|---|
| | none | | Design Project |
| | none | | Portfolio Project |
| 2 | dw2_1.html<br>spa.doc<br>assets/su_banner.gif<br>assets/the_spa.jpg | | Lesson 2 |
| | dw2_2.html<br>gardening_tips.doc<br>assets/blooms_banner.jpg<br>assets/garden_tips.jpg | | Skills Review |
| | none | | Project Builder 1 |
| | none | | Project Builder 2 |
| | none | | Design Project |
| | none | | Portfolio Project |
| 3 | questions.doc | | Lesson 1 |
| | | su_styles.css | Lesson 2 |
| | dw3_1.html<br>assets/boardwalk.jpg<br>assets/club_house.jpg<br>assets/pool.jpg<br>assets/sago_palm.jpg<br>assets/sports_club.jpg<br>assets/su_banner.gif | | Lesson 4 |
| | assets/stripes_back.gif<br>assets/umbrella_back.gif | | Lesson 6 |
| | dw3_2.html<br>assets/blooms_banner.jpg<br>assets/daisies.jpg<br>assets/lantana.jpg<br>assets/petunias.jpg<br>assets/verbena.jpg | blooms_styles.css | Skills Review |
| | dw3_3.html<br>dw3_4.html<br>assets/lion.jpg<br>assets/tripsmart_banner.jpg<br>assets/zebra_mothers.jpg | tripsmart_styles.css | Project Builder 1 |

| Chapter | Data File Supplied | Student Creates File | Used In |
|---|---|---|---|
| | dw3_5.html<br>dw3_6.html<br>assets/cc_banner.jpg<br>assets/cranberry_ice.jpg<br>assets/pot_knives.jpg | cc_styles.css | Project Builder 2 |
| | none | | Design Project |
| | none | | Portfolio Project |
| 4 | dw4_1.html<br>assets/heron_waiting_small.jpg<br>assets/su_banner.gif<br>assets/two_dolphins_small.jpg | | Lesson 1 |
| | assets/about_us_down.gif<br>assets/about_us_up.gif<br>assets/activities_down.gif<br>assets/activities_up.gif<br>assets/cafe_down.gif<br>assets/cafe_up.gif<br>assets/home_down.gif<br>assets/home_up.gif<br>assets/spa_down.gif<br>assets/spa_up.gif | | Lesson 3 |
| | dw4_2.html<br>dw4_3.html<br>assets/boats.jpg<br>assets/heron_small.jpg | | Lesson 5 |
| | dw4_4.html<br>dw4_5.html<br>dw4_6.html<br>dw4_7.html<br>assets/b_classes_down.jpg<br>assets/b_classes_up.jpg<br>assets/b_home_down.jpg<br>assets/b_home_up.jpg<br>assets/b_newsletter_down.jpg<br>assets/b_newsletter_up.jpg<br>assets/b_plants_down.jpg<br>assets/b_plants_up.jpg | | Skills Review |

| Chapter | Data File Supplied | Student Creates File | Used In |
|---|---|---|---|
| | assets/b_tips_down.jpg<br>assets/b_tips_up.jpg<br>assets/blooms_banner.jpg<br>assets/fuchsia.jpg<br>assets/iris.jpg<br>assets/water_hyacinth.jpg | | |
| | dw4_8.html<br>dw4_9.html<br>dw4_10.html<br>assets/giraffe.jpg<br>assets/parrot.jpg<br>assets/sloth.jpg<br>assets/tripsmart_banner.jpg<br>assets/water_lily.jpg | | Project Builder 1 |
| | dw4_11.html<br>dw4_12.html<br>dw4_13.html<br>assets/cc_banner.jpg<br>assets/cc_banner_with_text.jpg<br>assets/children_cooking.jpg<br>assets/cookies_oven.jpg<br>assets/dumplings1.jpg<br>assets/dumplings2.jpg<br>assets/dumplings3.jpg<br>assets/fish.jpg | | Project Builder 2 |
| | none | | Design Project |
| | none | | Portfolio Project |
| 5 | cafe.doc<br>assets/cafe_logo.gif<br>assets/cafe_photo.jpg | | Lesson 2 |
| | assets/cheesecake.jpg | | Lesson 6 |
| | gardeners.doc<br>assets/flower_bed.jpg<br>assets/gardening_gloves.gif | | Skills Review |

| Chapter | Data File Supplied | Student Creates File | Used In |
|---------|--------------------|--------------------|---------|
| | assets/hat.jpg<br>assets/pants.jpg<br>assets/vest.jpg | | Project Builder 1 |
| | menu items.doc<br>assets/muffins.jpg | | Project Builder 2 |
| | none | | Design Project |
| | none | | Portfolio Project |
| 6 | | The Striped Umbrella.ste | Lesson 5 |
| | | blooms & bulbs.ste | Skills Review |
| | | TripSmart.ste | Project Builder 1 |
| | | Carolyne's Creations.ste | Project Builder 2 |
| | none | | Design Project |
| | none | | Portfolio Project |
| 7 | The Striped Umbrella.ste<br>striped_umbrella folder containing these files:<br>about_us.html<br>activities.html<br>cafe.html<br>cruises.html<br>feedback.html<br>fishing.html<br>index.html<br>spa.html<br>su_styles.css<br>_notes/activities.html.mno<br>_notes/dwsync.xml<br>assets/about_us_down.gif<br>assets/about_us_up.gif<br>assets/activities_down.gif<br>assets/activities_up.gif<br>assets/boardwalk.jpg<br>assets/boats.jpg<br>assets/cafe_down.gif<br>assets/cafe_logo.gif<br>assets/cafe_photo.jpg<br>assets/cafe_up.gif<br>assets/cheesecake.jpg<br>assets/club_house.jpg | | Lesson 1 |

| Chapter | Data File Supplied | Student Creates File | Used In |
|---------|-------------------|---------------------|---------|
|         | assets/heron_small.jpg |  |  |
|         | assets/heron_waiting_small.jpg |  |  |
|         | assets/home_down.gif |  |  |
|         | assets/home_up.gif |  |  |
|         | assets/pool.jpg |  |  |
|         | assets/spa_down.gif |  |  |
|         | assets/spa_up.gif |  |  |
|         | assets/sports_club.jpg |  |  |
|         | assets/su_banner.gif |  |  |
|         | assets/the_spa.jpg |  |  |
|         | assets/two_dolphins_small.jpg |  |  |
|         | blooms & bulbs.ste |  | Skills Review |
|         | blooms folder |  |  |
|         | containing these files: |  |  |
|         | annuals.html |  |  |
|         | blooms_styles.css |  |  |
|         | classes.html |  |  |
|         | index.html |  |  |
|         | newsletter.html |  |  |
|         | perennials.html |  |  |
|         | plants.html |  |  |
|         | tips.html |  |  |
|         | water_plants.html |  |  |
|         | _notes/classes.html.mno |  |  |
|         | _notes/dwsync.xml |  |  |
|         | assets/b_classes_down.jpg |  |  |
|         | assets/b_classes_up.jpg |  |  |
|         | assets/b_home_down.jpg |  |  |
|         | assets/b_home_up.jpg |  |  |
|         | assets/b_newsletter_down.jpg |  |  |
|         | assets/b_newsletter_up.jpg |  |  |
|         | assets/b_plants_down.jpg |  |  |
|         | assets/b_plants_up.jpg |  |  |
|         | assets/b_tips_down.jpg |  |  |
|         | assets/b_tips_up.jpg |  |  |
|         | assets/blooms_banner.jpg |  |  |
|         | assets/flower_bed.jpg |  |  |
|         | assets/fuchsia.jpg |  |  |
|         | assets/garden_tips.jpg |  |  |
|         | assets/gardening_gloves.gif |  |  |

| Chapter | Data File Supplied | Student Creates File | Used In |
|---|---|---|---|
| | assets/iris.jpg<br>assets/lantana.jpg<br>assets/petunias.jpg<br>assets/verbena.jpg<br>assets/water_hyacinth.jpg<br>assets/_notes/dwsync.xml | | |
| | tripsmart folder containing<br>these files:<br>amazon.html<br>catalog.html<br>destinations.html<br>index.html<br>kenya.html<br>newsletter.html<br>services.html<br>tripsmart_styles.css<br>_notes/dwsync.xml<br>_notes/newsletter.html.mno<br>assets/giraffe.jpg<br>assets/hat.jpg<br>assets/lion.jpg<br>assets/pants.jpg<br>assets/parrot.jpg<br>assets/sloth.jpg<br>assets/tripsmart_banner.jpg<br>assets/vest.jpg<br>assets/water_lily.jpg<br>assets/zebra_mothers.jpg<br>assets/_notes/dwsync.xml | | Project Builder 1 |
| | cc folder containing<br>these files:<br>adults.html<br>catering.html<br>cc_styles.css<br>children.html<br>classes.html<br>index.html<br>recipes.html<br>shop.html | | Project Builder 2 |

| Chapter | Data File Supplied | Student Creates File | Used In |
|---|---|---|---|
| | _notes/dwsync.xml<br>assets/cc_banner_with_text.jpg<br>assets/children_cooking.jpg<br>assets/cookies_oven.jpg<br>assets/cranberry_ice.jpg<br>assets/dumplings1.jpg<br>assets/dumplinsg2.jpg<br>assets/dumplings3.jpg<br>assets/fish.jpg<br>assets/muffins.jpg<br>assets/pot_knives.jpg<br>assets/_notes/dwsync.xml | | |
| | none | | Design Project |
| | none | | Portfolio Project |
| 8 | No files provided | | |
| 9 | contestants.gif<br>contestants_bak.jpg | | Lesson 3 |
| | peaches_small.jpg | | Skills Review |
| | packing_cube.jpg | | Project Builder 1 |
| | cc_logo.jpg | | Project Builder 2 |
| | none | | Design Project |
| | none | | Portfolio Project |
| 10 | AC_RunActiveContent.js crab.fla<br>crab.swf | | Lesson 1 |
| | assets/one_dolphin.jpg<br>assets/two_dolphins.jpg | | Lesson 2 |
| | dw10_1.html | | Lesson 3 |
| | umbrella_anchor_movie.flv | | Lesson 4 |
| | garden_quote.swf<br>hanging_baskets.flv<br>assets/garden_tips.jpg<br>assets/garden_tips2.jpg | | Skills Review |
| | amazon_map.swf<br>dw10_2.html | | Project Builder 1 |
| | sugared_flowers.flv | | Project Builder 2 |
| | none | | Design Project |
| | none | | Portfolio Project |

| Chapter | Data File Supplied | Student Creates File | Used In |
|---|---|---|---|
| 11 | | Templates/activities_pages.dwt | Lesson 1 |
| | golf.doc<br>assets/golfer.jpg | golf.html | Lesson 2 |
| | annuals.doc<br>perennials.doc<br>water_plants.doc | annuals.html<br>water_plants.html<br>Templates/plant_categories.dwt | Skills Review |
| | assets/headphones.jpg<br>assets/packing_cube_large.jpg<br>assets/passport_holder.jpg | accessories.html<br>clothing.html<br>Templates/catalog_pages.dwt | Project Builder 1 |
| | rolls.doc<br>assets/rolls.jpg | rolls.html<br>Templates/recipes.dwt | Project Builder 2 |
| | none | | Design Project |
| | none | | Portfolio Project |
| 12 | assets/su_logo.jpg | | Lesson 1 |
| | assets/blooms_logo.jpg | | Skills Review |
| | assets/tripsmart_logo.jpg | | Project Builder 1 |
| | none | | Project Builder 2 |
| | none | | Design Project |
| | none | | Portfolio Project |

**Absolute path**
A path containing an external link that references a link on a web page outside the current website, and includes the protocol "http" and the URL, or address, of the web page.

**Absolute positioning**
The positioning of an AP element according to the distance between the AP element's upper-left corner and the upper-left corner of the page or AP element in which it is contained.

**Action**
A response to an event trigger that causes a change, such as text changing color.

**ActionScript**
A Flash scripting language developers use to add interactivity to movies, control objects, exchange data, and to create complex animations.

**Action property**
Property that specifies the application or script that will process form data.

**Active Server Page (ASP)**
A server-side application for processing forms.

**Adobe Community Help**
A collection of materials such as tutorials, published articles, or blogs, that is part of the Adobe Help content.

**Adobe CSS Advisor**
A part of the Adobe website that offers solutions for resolving issues with your pages.

**Adobe Flash**
A program that is used to create animations and video content for the web.

**Adobe Flash Player**
A program that must be installed on a computer to view Flash movies.

**Aligning an image**
Positioning an image on a web page in relation to other elements on the page.

**All Rules pane**
The top half of the CSS Styles panel.

**Alternate text**
Descriptive text that can be set to appear in place of an image while the image is downloading or when a user places the mouse pointer over the image.

**AP div tag**
A div tag that is assigned a fixed position on a page (absolute position).

**AP element**
The resulting container that an AP div tag creates on a page.

**AP elements panel**
Panel in the CSS panel group that is used to control the visibility, name, and Z-Index stacking order of AP elements on a web page.

**Apache web server**
A public domain, open source web server that is available using several different operating systems including UNIX and windows.

**Application bar**
The toolbar located above the Document window which includes menu names (Windows only), a Workspace switcher, and other application commands.

**ASP**
The acronym for Active Server Pages. ASP is a server-side application tool.

**Assets**
Files that are not web pages, such as images, audio files, and video clips.

**Assets folder**
A subfolder in a website in which you store most of the files that are not web pages, such as images, audio files, and video clips.

**Assets panel**
A panel that contains nine categories of assets, such as images, used in a website. Clicking a category button will display a list of those assets.

**Asynchronous JavaScript and XML (AJAX)**
A method for developing interactive web pages that respond quickly to user input.

**AVI**
Audio Visual Interleave. The Microsoft standard for digital video.

## B

**Background color**
A color that fills an entire web page, frame, table, cell, or document.

**Background image**
A graphic file used in place of a background color.

**Banner**
Graphic that generally appears across the top of a web page that can incorporate the company's logo, contact information, and navigation buttons.

**Behavior**
A preset piece of JavaScript code that can be attached to page elements. A behavior tells the page element to respond in a specific way when an event occurs, such as when the mouse pointer is positioned over the element.

**BMP**
Bitmapped file. A file format used for images that is based on pixels.

**Body**
The part of a web page that is seen when the page is viewed in a browser window.

**Border**
An outline that surrounds a cell, table, or frame.

**Bread crumbs trail**
A list of links that provides a path from the initial page opened in a website to the page being viewed.

**Broken links**
Links that cannot find the intended destination file for the link.

**Browser**
Software used to display web pages, such as Microsoft Internet Explorer or Mozilla Firefox.

**Bullet**
A small raised dot or similar icon.

**Bulleted list**
The name that is sometimes given to unordered lists using bullets.

## C

**Cascading Style Sheet (CSS)**
A file used to assign sets of common formatting characteristics to page elements such as text, objects, and tables.

**CAST**
Acronym for the Center for Applied Special Technology.

**Cell padding**
The distance between the cell content and cell walls in a table.

**Cell spacing**
The distance between cells in a table.

**Cell walls**
The edges surrounding a cell.

**Cells**
Small boxes within a table that are used to hold text or graphics. Cells are arranged horizontally in rows and vertically in columns.

**Check box**
Form object that can be used on a web page to let viewers choose from a range of possible options.

**Checked out files**
Files that are being used by other team members.

**Child page**
A page at a lower level in a web hierarchy that links to a parent page.

**Class style**
*See* custom style.

**Client-side scripting**
A method used to process information a form collects by using the user's computer.

**Clip property**
Property that determines the portion of a layer's content that will be visible when displayed in a web browser.

**Cloaked file**
File that is marked to be excluded from certain processes, such as being transferred to the remote site.

**Code and Design view**
A view that is a combination of Code view and Design view.

**Code hints**
A feature that recognizes sections of code that are being typed and offers choices to complete the tag.

**Code Inspector**
A window that works just like Code view except that it is a floating window.

**Code snippet**
*See* snippet.

**Code view**
A view that shows the underlying HTML code for the page. Use this view to read or edit the code.

**Coding toolbar**
A toolbar that contains buttons that are used when working directly in the code.

**ColdFusion**
Development tool that can be used to build data-driven web applications.

**Columns**
Table cells arranged vertically.

**Comments**
Notes of explanation that are inserted into the code and are not visible in the browser window.

**Common Gateway Interface (CGI)**
Server-side application used for processing data in a form.

**Compound type**
A type of CSS rule that is used to format a selection.

**Copyright**
A legal protection for the particular and tangible expression of an idea.

**CSS page layout**
A method of positioning objects on web pages through the use of containers formatted with CSS styles.

**CSS page layout block**
A section of a web page defined and formatted using a Cascading Style Sheet.

**Custom button**
In a form, a button that triggers action that you specify on the page.

**Custom style**
A style that can contain a combination of formatting attributes that can be applied to a block of text or other page elements. Custom style names begin with a period (.). Also known as a class style.

**Debug**
To find and correct coding errors.

**Declaration**
The property and value of a style in a Cascading Style Sheet.

**Default base font**
The font that is applied by default to any text that does not have a font assigned.

**Default font color**
The color the browser uses to display text if no other color is assigned.

**Default link color**
The color the browser uses to display links if no other color is assigned. The default link color is blue.

**Definition lists**
Lists composed of terms with indented descriptions or definitions.

**Delimited files**
Database or spreadsheet files that have been saved as text files with delimiters.

**Delimiter**
A comma, tab, colon, semicolon, or similar character that separates tabular data.

**Dependent file**
File that another file needs to be complete, such as an image or navigation bar element.

**Derivative work**
An adaptation of another work, such as a movie version of a book.

**Description**
A short summary of website content that resides in the head section.

**Design notes**
Separate files in a website that contain additional information about a file.

**Design view**
The view that shows the page as it would appear in a browser and is primarily used when designing and creating a web page.

**Diagonal symmetry**
A design principle in which page elements are balanced along the invisible diagonal line of the page.

**Div tag**
An HTML tag that is used to format and position web page elements.

**Dock**
A collection of panels or panel groups.

**Document**
For this book, an HTML page created in Dreamweaver.

**Document toolbar**
A toolbar that contains buttons and drop-down menus you can use to change the current work mode, preview web pages, debug web pages, choose visual aids, and view file-management options.

**Document-relative path**
A path referenced in relation to the web page that is currently displayed.

**Document window**
The large white area in the Dreamweaver workspace where you create and edit web pages.

**Domain name**
An IP address expressed in letters instead of numbers, usually reflecting the name of the business represented by the website.

**Down image state**
The state of a page element when the element has been clicked.

**Download**
Transfer a file or files from a remote server to a computer.

**Download time**
The time it takes to transfer a file to another computer.

**Dreamweaver workspace**
*See* workspace.

**DSL**
Digital Subscriber Line. A type of high-speed Internet connection.

**Dual Screen layout**
A layout that allows you to use two monitors while working in Dreamweaver.

**Dynamic content**
Content on a web page that allows the user to interact with the page by clicking or

typing, and then responds to the input in some way.

**Editable optional region**
An area in a template where users can add or change content, and that users can also choose to show or hide.

**Editable region**
An area in a template where users of the template can add or change content.

**Element**
A graphic link that is part of a navigation bar and can have one of four possible appearances.

**Embedded CSS style sheet**
Styles that are part of an HTML page and that reside in the head content.

**Enable cache**
A setting to direct the computer system to use space on the hard drive as temporary memory or cache while you are working in Dreamweaver.

**Event trigger**
An event, such as a mouse click on an object, that causes a behavior to start.

**Export data**
To save data by using a special file format so that you can open it in another application.

**External CSS style sheet**
Collection of rules stored in a separate file that control the formatting of content on a web page. External CSS style sheets have a .css file extension.

**External links**
Links that connect to web pages in other websites or to e-mail addresses.

**Fair use**
A concept that allows consumers to copy all or part of a copyrighted work in support of their First Amendment rights.

**Favorites**
Assets that are used repeatedly in a website and are included in their own category in the Assets panel.

**Field**
*See* form object.

**Fieldset**
HTML tag used to group related form elements together.

**File field**
Form object that allows viewers to upload files to a web server.

**Files panel**
The panel you use to manage your website files.

**Flash button object**
Button made from a small, predefined Flash movie that can be inserted on a web page to provide navigation in a website.

**Flash Paper**
A program built into Microsoft Word and PowerPoint that allows you to easily convert a Word or PowerPoint file into a Flash .swf file that a browser can open and read.

**Flash player**
A free program included with many browsers that allows you to view content created with Adobe Flash.

**Flash text**
A vector-based graphic file that contains text.

**Flash video files**
Flash files that include both video and audio and have an .flv file extension.

**Focus group**
A marketing tool where a group of people are asked for feedback about a product.

**Font combination**
A set of three fonts that specifies which fonts a browser should use to display the text on a web page.

**Form control**
*See* form object.

**Form element**
*See* form object.

**Form object**
An object on a web page, such as a text box, radio button, or check box, that collects information from viewers. Also referred to as **form element**, **form control**, or **field**.

**FormName property**
Property that specifies a unique name for a form.

**FTP**
File Transfer Protocol. The process of uploading and downloading files to and from a remote site.

**Get**
Transferring files from a remote location.

**GET method**
Method property that specifies that ASCII data collected in a form will be sent to the server appended to the URL or file included in the Action property.

**GIF**
Graphics interchange format. Type of file format used for images placed on web pages that can support both transparency and animation.

**Graphics**
Pictures or design elements that add visual interest to a page.

**Grids**
Horizontal and vertical lines that fill the page and are used to place page elements.

**Guides**
Horizontal or vertical lines that you can drag onto the page from the rulers to use to align page elements.

**Head content**
The part of a web page that is not viewed in the browser window. It includes meta tags, which are HTML codes that include information about the page, such as keywords and descriptions.

**Headings**
Six different styles that can be applied to text: Heading 1 (the largest size) through Heading 6 (the smallest size).

**Height property**
Property that specifies the height of an AP element either in pixels or as a percentage of the screen's height.

**Hex triplet**
*See* hexidecimal RGB value.

**Hexadecimal RGB value**
A value that represents the amount of red, green, and blue in a color and is based on the Base 16 number system. Also called a hex triplet.

**Hidden field**
Form object that makes it possible to provide information to the web server and form-processing script without the viewer knowing that the information is being sent.

**History panel**
A panel that lists the steps that have been performed in Dreamweaver while editing and formatting a document.

**Home page**
Usually the first web page that appears when viewers visit a website.

**Horizontal symmetry**
A design principle in which page elements are balanced across the page.

**Hotspot**
An area on a graphic, that, when clicked, links to a different location on the page or to another web page.

**HTML**
Hypertext Markup Language. A language web developers use to create web pages.

**HTML style**
A style used to redefine an HTML tag.

**HTTP**
HyperText Transfer Protocol. A protocol used by web servers to display web pages.

**Hyperlink**
Graphic or text element on a web page that users click to display another location on the page, another web page on the same website, or a web page on a different website. Hyperlinks are also known as links.

**HyperText Transfer Protocol**
*See* HTTP.

**Id type**
A type of CSS rule that is used to redefine an HTML tag.

**Image**
*See* graphics.

**Image field**
Form object used to insert an image in a form.

**Image map**
A graphic that has been divided into sections, each of which contains a link.

**Import data**
To bring data created in another software program into an application.

**Inherit**
An AP element value of the Vis (visible) property that sets the visibility of the AP element to be the same as its parent AP element or page.

**Inline CSS rule**
A CSS rule whose code is contained within the body section of the HTML code on a web page.

**Insert panel**
Eight categories of buttons for creating and inserting objects displayed as a drop-down menu.

**Intangible assets**
Assets that are referred to as intellectual property.

**Intellectual property**
A product resulting from human creativity such as a movie or a song.

**Interactivity**
Allows visitors to your website to affect its content.

**Internal links**
Links to web pages within the same website.

**Internal style**
*See* embedded CSS style sheet.

**IP address**
An assigned series of numbers, separated by periods, that designates an address on the Internet.

**ISP**
Internet Service Provider. A service to which you subscribe to be able to connect your computer to the Internet.

**J**

**Java Server Page (JSP)**
A server-side application for processing forms.

**JavaScript**
A web-scripting language that interacts with HTML code to create interactive content. Also referred to as Jscript.

**JPEG file**
Joint photographic experts group. Type of file format used for images that appear on web pages, typically used for photographs.

**Jump menu**
Navigational menu that lets viewers go quickly to different pages in a site or to different sites on the Internet.

**H**

**Keywords**
Words that relate to the content of a website and reside in the head content.

**L**

**LAN**
A local area network.

**Left property**
Property that specifies the distance between the left edge of an AP element and the left edge of the page or AP element that contains it.

**Library item**
Content that can contain text or graphics and is saved in a separate file in the Library folder of a website.

**Licensing agreement**
The permission given by a copyright holder that conveys the right to use the copyright holder's work.

**Link**
*See* hyperlink.

**List**
Element on a web page from which viewers can make a choice from several options. Lists are often used in order forms.

**List form object**
A form object that lets users choose one or more options from a list of choices.

**Live View**
A choice on the View menu that enables you to add, edit, or delete dynamic content or server behaviors.

**Local site**
The location of your local root folder where your website files are stored while being developed.

**Locked region**
An area on a template that cannot be changed by users of the template.

**Low bandwidth animations**
Animations that don't require a fast connection to work properly.

**M**

**mailto: link**
A common point of contact that viewers with questions or problems can use to contact someone for a response.

**Media-dependent style sheet**
A tool for identifying the device being used to view a web page and formatting the page accordingly.

**Media objects**
Combinations of visual and audio effects and text to create a fully engaging experience with a website.

**Menu**
Element on a web page from which viewers can make choices. Menus are often used for navigation in a website.

**Menu bar (Mac)**
A bar located above the document window that includes names of menus, each of which contain Dreamweaver commands.

**Menu form object**
A form object, commonly used for navigation on a website, that lets viewers select a single option from a list of choices.

**Menu list**
Lists that are very similar to unordered lists.

**Merge cells**
To combine multiple cells in a table into one cell.

**Meta tags**
HTML codes that include information about the page, such as keywords and descriptions, and reside in the head content.

**Metadata**
Information about a file, such as keywords, descriptions, and copyright information.

**Method property**
Property that specifies the HyperText Transfer Protocol (HTTP) method used to send form data to a web server.

**MPEG**
Motion Picture Experts Group. A digital video format.

**Multiple Document Interface**
A Dreamweaver interface choice in which all document windows and panels are positioned within one large application window.

**N**

**Named anchor**
A specific location on a web page that has a unique name.

**Navigation bar**
Bar that contains multiple links, usually organized in rows or columns, that link to the major pages in a website.

**Navigation structure**
The way viewers navigate from page to page in a website.

**Nested AP element**
AP element whose HTML code is included within another AP element's code.

**Nested table**
A table within a table.

**Nested template**
A template that is based on another template.

**Non-web-safe colors**
Colors that might not be displayed uniformly across computer platforms.

**Numbered lists**
Lists of items that are presented in a specific order and are preceded by numbers or letters in sequence. Also called ordered lists.

**O**

**Objects**
The individual elements in a document, such as text or images.

**Opacity**
A graphic's degree of transparency.

**Optional region**
Region in a template that template users can choose either to show or hide.

**Ordered list**
List of items that need to be placed in a specific order, where each item is preceded by a number or letter. Also called numbered lists.

**Orphaned files**
Files that are not linked to any pages in a website.

**Over image state**
The state of a page element when the mouse pointer is positioned over it.

**Over While Down image state**
The state of a page element when the mouse pointer is clicked and held over it.

**Overflow property**
Property that specifies how to handle excess content that does not fit inside an AP element.

**Panel**
A window that contains related commands or displays information on a particular topic.

**Panel groups**
Sets of related panels that are grouped together. Also known as Tab groups.

**Paragraph style**
HTML style that is applied to an entire paragraph.

**Parent page**
A page at a higher level in a web hierarchy that links to other pages on a lower level, called child pages.

**Path**
The location of a file in relation to other folders in the website.

**PICS**
The acronym for Platform for Internet Content Selection. This is a rating system for web pages.

**Plug-in**
A computer program that works with a host application such as a web browser to enable certain functions to run.

**PNG**
Portable network graphics. A type of file format for graphics.

**Point of contact**
A place on a web page that provides viewers a means of contacting a company representative.

**Pop-up menu**
A menu that appears when you move the pointer over a trigger image in a browser.

**Pop-up message**
Message that opens in a browser to either clarify or provide information, or alert viewers of an action that is being taken.

**Position property**
Property used to define an AP element's position on a page.

**POST method**
Method property that specifies that form data be sent to the processing script as a binary or encrypted file, so that data will be sent securely.

**Progressive video download**
A download type that will download a video to the viewer's computer, and then allow the video to play before it has completely downloaded.

**Properties pane**
The bottom half of the CSS Styles panel that lists the rule properties.

**Property inspector**
A panel located at the bottom of the Dreamweaver window that lets you view and change the properties of a selected object.

**Public domain**
Work that is no longer protected by copyright. Anyone can use it for any purpose.

**Publish a website**
To make a website available for viewing on the Internet or on an intranet.

**Put**
Transfer files to a remote location.

**Radial symmetry**
A design principle in which page elements are balanced from the center of the page outward, like the petals of a flower.

**Radio button**
Form object that can be used to provide a choice between two options.

**Radio group**
A group of radio buttons from which viewers can make only one selection.

**RDS**
Remote Development Services, used with web servers using ColdFusion for transferring files.

**Reference panel**
A panel used to find answers to coding questions, covering topics such as HTML, JavaScript, and Accessibility.

**Refresh Local File List Automatically option**
A setting that directs Dreamweaver to automatically reflect changes made in your file listings.

**Regular expressions**
Combinations of characters, such as a phrase that begins or ends with a particular word or tag.

**Related files**
Files that are linked to a document and are necessary for the document to display and function correctly.

**Related Files toolbar**
A toolbar located below an open document's filename tab that displays the names of any related files.

**Relative path**
A path containing a link to another page within the same website.

**Remote server**
A web server that hosts websites and is not directly connected to the computer hosting the local site.

**Remote site**
A website that has been published to a remote server.

**Repeating region**
An area in a template whose format is repeated over and over again. Used for presenting information that repeats, such as product listings in a catalog.

**Repeating table**
A table in a template that has a predefined structure, making it very easy for template users to add content to it.

**Required field**
A field on a form that must be completed before the form can be processed.

**Reset button**
A button that, when clicked, will clear data from a form and reset it to its default values.

**Resolution**
The number of pixels per inch in an image; also refers to an image's clarity and fineness of detail.

**Rich content**
Attractive and engaging images, interactive elements, video, or animations. Also called rich media content.

**Rollover**
A special effect that changes the appearance of an object when the mouse rolls over it.

**Rollover color**
The color in which text will appear when the rollover is taking place.

**Rollover image**
An image on a web page that changes its appearance when the mouse pointer is positioned over it.

**Root folder (local root folder)**
A folder used to store all web pages or HTML files for the site. The root folder is given a name to describe the site, such as the company name.

**Root relative path**
A path referenced from a website's root folder.

**Rows**
Table cells arranged horizontally.

**Rule of Thirds**
The rule of thirds is a design principle that entails dividing a page into nine squares and then placing the page elements of most interest on the intersections of the grid lines.

**Rules**
Sets of formatting attributes in a Cascading Style Sheet.

**Rules pane**
The location in the CSS Styles panel that displays the location of the currently selected rule in the open document.

**Sans-serif fonts**
Block-style characters used frequently for headings and subheadings.

**Screen reader**
A device used by the visually impaired to convert written text on a computer monitor to spoken words.

**Selector**
The name or the tag to which the style declarations have been assigned.

**Serif fonts**
Ornate fonts with small extra strokes at the beginning and end of characters. Used frequently for paragraph text in printed materials.

**Server-side application**
An application that resides on a web server and interacts with the information collected in a form.

**Server-side scripting**
A method used to process information a form collects that uses applications that reside on the web server.

**Show Code and Design views**
A combination of Code view and Design view. The best view for correcting errors.

**Site definition**
Information about the site, including the URL, preferences, and password information.

**Site usability test**
A process of using and evaluating a website for ease of use.

**Slider**
The small icon on the left side of the History panel that you can drag to undo or redo an action.

**Snippet**
A reusable piece of code that can be inserted on a page to create footers, headers, drop-down menus, and other items.

**Split cells**
To divide cells into multiple cells.

**Spry Data Set**
A JavaScript object that stores data in rows and columns.

**Spry effects**
Screen effects such as fading and enlarging page elements.

**Spry framework for AJAX**
Asynchronous JavaScript and XML (AJAX). A method for developing interactive web pages that respond quickly to user input, such as a map.

**Spry validation field widgets**
Fields that display valid or invalid states when text is being entered in a form on a web page.

**Spry widgets**
Prebuilt components for adding interaction to pages.

**Standard mode**
A mode that is used to insert a table using the Insert Table button or command.

**Standard toolbar**
A toolbar that contains buttons you can use to execute frequently used commands that are also available on the File and Edit menus.

**States**
The four appearances a button can assume in response to a mouse action. These include: Up, Over, Down, and Over While Down.

**Static content**
Content on a website that does not change or allow user interaction.

**Status bar**
A bar located below the document window that displays HTML tags being used at the insertion point location as well as other information, such as estimated download time for the current page and window size.

**Step**
Each task performed in the History panel.

**Storyboard**
A small sketch that represents every page in a website.

**Streaming video download**
Similar to a progressive download, except streaming video downloads use buffers to

gather the content as it is downloading to ensure a smoother playback.

**Style**
Preset attribute, such as size, color, and texture, that you can apply to objects and text. Styles are also called rules.

**Style Rendering toolbar**
A toolbar with options for rendering a web page on different media types, such as a handheld device.

**Submit button**
A button which when clicked, will send the data from a form on a web page to a web server to be processed.

**Swap image behavior**
A behavior similar to a rollover effect.

**Swap Image Restore**
A behavior that restores a swapped image back to the original image.

**Synchronize files**
To synchronize files is to compare the dates of the files in a remote and local site and then transfer only the files that have changed.

**Tab groups**
Sets of related panels that are grouped together. Also known as panel groups.

**Table**
Grid of rows and columns that can either be used to hold tabular data on a web page or can be used as a basic design tool for page layout.

**Table header**
Text placed at the top or sides of a table on a web page that is read by screen readers.

**Tabular data**
Data that is arranged in columns and rows and separated by a delimiter.

**Tag selector**
A location on the status bar that displays HTML tags for the various page elements, including tables and cells.

**Tag type**
A type of CSS rule used to redefine an HTML tag.

**Tags**
HTML codes that define the formatting of page elements. They are usually, but not always, written in pairs with beginning and ending tags that surround the affected content in the code.

**Target**
The location on a web page that the browser will display in full view when an internal link is clicked, or the frame that will open when a link is clicked.

**Target property**
Property that specifies the window in which you want form data to be processed.

**Template**
A template contains the basic layout for pages in websites and contains both locked regions, which are areas on the template page that cannot be modified by users of the template, as well as other types of regions that users can change or edit.

**Terms of use**
The rules that a copyright owner uses to establish use of his work.

**Testing server**
A server used to test a website to evaluate the way that features such as a form work.

**Text area field**
A text field in a form that can store several lines of text.

**Text field**
Form object used for collecting a string of characters such as a name, address, or password.

**TIFF**
Tagged image file format.

**Tiled image**
A small graphic that repeats across and down a web page, appearing as individual squares or rectangles.

**Top property**
Property that specifies the distance between the top edge of an AP element and the top edge of the page or AP element that contains it.

**Tracing image**
An image that is placed in the background of a document as a guide to create page elements on top of it, similar to the way tracing paper is used.

**Trademark**
Protects an image, word, slogan, symbol, or design used to identify goods or services.

**Tree structure**
A diagram that visually represents the way the pages in a website are linked to each other.

**Unordered lists**
Lists of items that do not need to be placed in a specific order and are usually preceded by bullets.

**Unvisited links**
Links that have not been clicked by the viewer.

**Up image state**
The state of a page element when the mouse pointer is not on the element.

**Upload**
Transfer files to a remote server.

**URL**
Uniform resource locator. An address that determines a route on the Internet or to a web page.

**Vector-based graphics**
Graphics that are based on mathematical formulas.

**Vertical symmetry**
A design principle in which page elements are balanced down a page.

**View**
A particular way of displaying page content. Dreamweaver has three views: Design view, Code view, and Show Code and Design views.

**Visible property**
Property that lets you control whether the selected layer is visible or hidden.

**Visited links**
Links that have been previously clicked or visited. The default color for visited links is purple.

**VSS**
Microsoft Visual SafeSource, used with the Windows operating system for transferring files.

**Web browser**
A program, such as Microsoft Internet Explorer or Mozilla Firefox, that lets you display HTML-developed web pages.

**Web design software**
Software for creating interactive web pages containing text, images, hyperlinks, animation, sounds, and video.

**Web-safe colors**
Colors that are common to both Macintosh, UNIX, and Windows platforms.

**Web server**
A computer dedicated to hosting websites that is connected to the Internet and configured with software to handle requests from browsers.

**WebDav**
Web-based Distributed Authoring and Versioning, used with the WebDav protocol for transferring files.

**Website**
A group of related web pages that are linked together and share a common interface and design.

**White space**
An area on a web page that is not filled with text or graphics.

**Width property**
Property that specifies the width of an AP element either in pixels or as a percentage of the screen's width.

**Workspace**
The area in the Dreamweaver program window where you work with documents, movies, tools, and panels.

**Workspace switcher**
A drop-down menu located in the top right corner on the Application bar that allows you to change the workspace layout.

**WYSIWYG**
An acronym for What You See is What You Get, meaning that your web page should look the same in the browser as it does in the web editor.

**XHTML**
The acronym for eXtensible HyperText Markup Language, the most current standard for developing web pages.

**XML**
A language used to create the structure of blocks of information, similar to HTML.

**XSL**
Similar to CSS; the XSL stylesheet information formats containers created with XML.

**XSLT**
Extensible Stylesheet Language Transformations.

**Z-Index property**
Property that specifies the vertical stacking order of AP elements on a page. A Z-Index value of 1 indicates that an AP element's position is at the bottom of the stack. A Z-Index position of 3 indicates that the AP element is positioned on top of two other AP elements.

tracing images, 5–5
trademarks, 6–34
transferring files
Dreamweaver connection options,
6–16
to and from remote sites, 6–15,
6–16, 6–20

uncloaking folders, 6–28
"under construction" pages, 2–30
unfinished pages, 2–30
Universal Resource Locators. *See*
URLs (Universal Resource Locators)
unordered lists
creating, 3–4, 3–6
formatting, 3–7
untitled documents, checking for, 6–8
unvisited links, 2–5
updating
library items, 12–12
sites, templates, 11–16—11–19
web pages, website links,
4–30—4–31
uploading files
excluding selected files,
6–26—6–29
to remote sites, 6–15, 6–20
URLs (Universal Resource Locators),
4–4
typing, 4–6
usability testing, websites, 6–19

validating
accessibility standards, 6–9
markup, 6–5

Validation panel, 6–5
vector-based graphics, 10–5
Version Cue, asset management, 6–11
vertical space, images, 3–29, 3–30
view(s), 1–7, 1–10—1–11
changing, 1–10—1–11
viewing
CSS layout blocks,
5–5, 5–14
download time, 3–22
imported sites, 6–33
library items, 12–4, 12–5
links in Assets panel, 4–9
remote sites, 6–14—6–15, 6–19
Vis (visible) property, AP element
content, 9–5
visibility of AP elements, 9–20
visited links, 2–5
Visual Aids, 5–37
visual cues, required fields in
forms, 8–31
Visual Safe Source (VSS), 6–16
VSS (Visual Safe Source), 6–16

web browsers, 1–2
cross-browser rendering
issues, 5–13
playing Flash movies, 10–7
testing web pages, 2–31, 2–33
web pages
adding to websites, 1–27
attaching external style sheets,
7–18—7–19
links to, 2–21
opening, 1–12, 1–14
related files, 1–14

viewing basic elements,
1–12—1–13, 1–14—1–15
web servers, 1–21, 6–14. *See also*
remote sites
setting up access, 1–25, 6–18
WebDav, 6–16
web-safe color palette, 2–4
website(s), 1–2
importing, 7–6—7–9
website links, 4–28—4–31
managing, 4–28, 4–29
updating pages, 4–30—4–31
website maintenance, 6–4—6–13
Assets panel, 6–4
checking for missing alternate
text, 6–9
checking for orphaned files, 6–6
checking for untitled
documents, 6–8
checking links, 6–4, 6–6
Design Notes, 6–10—6–13
site reports, 6–4—6–5
testing pages, 6–5
validating accessibility
standards, 6–9
validating markup, 6–5
verifying that colors are
web-safe, 6–7
white space, 2–2
Width property (W), AP elements,
9–9, 9–10
window size, selecting, 2–33
Windows
adding folders to websites, 1–28
adding pages to websites, 1–32
importing Microsoft Office
documents, 2–15

## Dreamweaver Chapter Opener Art Credits

| Chapter | Art credit for opening pages |
| --- | --- |
| Chapter 1 | © David Newham/Alamy |
| Chapter 2 | © Josephine Marsden/Alamy |
| Chapter 3 | © Radius Images/Alamy |
| Chapter 4 | © Christopher Scott/Alamy |
| Chapter 5 | © Radius Images/Alamy |
| Chapter 6 | © Darryl Leniuk/Lifesize/Getty Images |
| Chapter 7 | © Dimitri Vervitsiotis/Digital Vision/Getty Images |
| Chapter 8 | © Veer |
| Chapter 9 | © Barbara Peacock/Photodisc/Getty Images |
| Chapter 10 | © Stuart Westmorland/Digital Vision/Getty Images |
| Chapter 11 | © Nick Norman/National Geographic Image Collection/Getty Images |
| Chapter 12 | © Georgette Douwma/Photodisc/Getty Images |
| Data Files/Glossary/Index | © Veer |